Hollywoo
Melodramatic In

MW00581657

ALSO BY GEOFF MAYER

Encyclopedia of American Film Serials
(McFarland, 2017)

Hollywood's Melodramatic Imagination

*Film Noir, the Western
and Other Genres
from the 1920s to the 1950s*

GEOFF MAYER

McFarland & Company, Inc., Publishers
Jefferson, North Carolina

LIBRARY OF CONGRESS CATALOGUING-IN-PUBLICATION DATA

Names: Mayer, Geoff, author.
Title: Hollywood's melodramatic imagination : film noir, the western
and other genres from the 1920s to the 1950s / Geoff Mayer.
Description: Jefferson : McFarland & Company, Inc., Publishers, 2022 |
Includes bibliographical references and index.
Identifiers: LCCN 2021052749 | ISBN 9781476674773 (paperback : acid free paper) ∞
ISBN 9781476643076 (ebook)
Subjects: LCSH: Melodrama in motion pictures. | Film genres—United States. |
Motion pictures—United States—History—20th century. | BISAC: PERFORMING ARTS /
Film / Genres / Westerns
Classification: LCC PN1995.9.M45 M39 2022 | DDC 791.43/655—dc23/eng/20211124
LC record available at https://lccn.loc.gov/2021052749

BRITISH LIBRARY CATALOGUING DATA ARE AVAILABLE

ISBN (print) 978-1-4766-7477-3
ISBN (ebook) 978-1-4766-4307-6

© 2022 Geoff Mayer. All rights reserved

*No part of this book may be reproduced or transmitted in any form
or by any means, electronic or mechanical, including photocopying
or recording, or by any information storage and retrieval system,
without permission in writing from the publisher.*

Front cover: (top) Wallace Ford and Jean Harlow in poster art
from the 1932 film *The Beast in the City*;
(bottom) Lois Wilson and Walter Huston in poster art
for the 1932 film *Law and Order* (author's collection)

Printed in the United States of America

*McFarland & Company, Inc., Publishers
Box 611, Jefferson, North Carolina 28640
www.mcfarlandpub.com*

Table of Contents

Acknowledgments

I wish to thank my wife Lesley for the hours spent proofreading the manuscript and attempting, not always successfully, to remove my use of commas while also trying to shorten my long and convoluted sentences. Any mistakes are, of course, mine. I would also like to thank friends and colleagues including Professor Tony Jarvis, Dr. Dean Brandum, Dr. Liz Dance, Dr. Kevin Brianton, Ross Schnioff-sky and Warren Davey who were always willing to listen to my thoughts and ideas while not necessarily agreeing with them. Also, my regular "football luncheon group," Professor David Tacey, John Benson and Rolando Caputo who cleverly steered the conversation away from film history to more important issues—notably Australian Rules Football. Finally, my thanks and love to my daughters Lisa, Kylie and Rebecca and granddaughters Alicia, Lily, Harper and Olivia.

I wish also to thank Matthew Sorrento from Rutgers University and co-editor of *Film International* which published a portion of my work on Sax Rohmer and "Yellow Peril Fiction" which appears in chapter one of the book.

Preface

Not everything in the Hollywood cinema prior to 1960 was melodrama. Yet it is the foundation of the American cinema. It is not a singular genre; it is more expansive as it functions as a "genre-generating machine" responsible for a wide range of Hollywood genres. Above all else it dramatizes a world with (ethical) meaning as opposed to, for example, the nihilistic universe portrayed in Dashiell Hammett's Flitcraft parable in *The Maltese Falcon*. The Introduction, Chapters One and Two focus on the characteristics of the most popular form of melodrama, sensational melodrama. This type of melodrama offers the visceral pleasures of spectacle, confrontation, high emotion and performance embedded in a bipolar clash between good and evil. This book stresses, however, that while the function of melodrama is to identify the existence of a moral universe, the social and political terms of this universe are not decided by melodrama. They are culturally determined. This is shown through a wide range of examples, from the "populist" westerns of the 1930s, to William Randolph Hearst's 1917 propaganda serial *Patria* and the "Yellow Peril" fiction of Sax Rohmer as well as President Roosevelt's response to the Japanese attack on Pearl Harbor on December 7, 1941.

Chapters Two and Three examine different types of melodrama produced in Hollywood in the 1930s for different audiences. The series western appealed to rural, small town and provincial audiences. These films, exemplars of sensational melodrama, were different aesthetically and thematically from the small number of A budgeted westerns produced by the major studios. On the other hand, the "sophisticated melodramas of passion" favored by the major studios for their first run theaters in large urban centers were often anathema to rural and small-town audiences. Chapter Three focuses on this type of melodrama and examples are drawn from W. Somerset Maugham's short stories "The Letter" and "Miss Thompson" (retitled "Rain"). Particularly important is the comparison between the 1929 film version of *The Letter* starring Jeanne Eagels and the 1940 version starring Bette Davis, the same story with different outcomes, largely as a result of different institutional and social factors. Unlike the morally "subversive" 1929 version, the conservatism of the 1940 film was primarily determined by Hollywood censor Joseph Breen's systemic application of the principle of compensating moral values.

Chapter Four focuses on the "problematic" world of "film noir," a world that is often presented as traumatized protagonists struggling to survive in an arbitrary universe. This chapter traces the shift from the gentleman detective formula to the

1

hard-boiled variation, James M. Cain's extravagant melodramas of violence and passion and the importance of the gothic tradition in the 1940s crime/suspense film. Despite claims that film noir subverted the moral and formal basis of the Hollywood system, this chapter includes a wide range of examples to demonstrate that while there were notable shifts in the crime/suspense film in the 1940s, most Hollywood films, especially A budgeted films from the major studios, retreated to the ethical world of melodrama. Particular attention is directed to the ramifications of John Huston's decision not to film the final scene in his script for *The Maltese Falcon* along with Billy Wilder's elimination of the gas chamber sequence from *Double Indemnity*. On the other hand, *Out of the Past* and *Criss Cross* represent rare examples of studio films that challenged the world of melodrama. This deviation from Hollywood's determining dramatic mode was even more pronounced in a number of low budget films such as *Detour* and *Decoy* where the financial risks were minimal. The book concludes with a comparison between two seemingly similar films starring Robert Mitchum: *Where Danger Lives* and *Angel Face*. This follows an earlier comparison between two films directed back to back by Joseph Lewis in the mid–1940s: *My Name Is Julia Ross* and *So Dark the Night*. Only one film in each example is a melodrama.

Introduction: Populist Fables

> Arguably, the type of film that comes closest of all to "classical"[1] melodrama, with its clear-cut heroes, villains, and heroines, its comic sidekicks and comic relief, its moments of action, spectacle, and conflict, its thrills, its performing animals, its hair-breadth escapes, its chases, its jokes, and its songs is, in fact the singing western.—Steve Neale[2]

> If emotional and moral registers are sounded, if a work invites us to feel sympathy for the virtues of beset victims, if the narrative trajectory is ultimately concerned with a retrieval and staging of virtue through adversity and suffering, then the operative mode is melodrama.—Linda Williams[3]

This book is about melodrama, a much-despised mode, often poorly understood, and the foundation of the American cinema. Melodrama is not a genre, an aberrant aesthetic form, or a mode that can be relegated to "somewhere in the distant past." It is not tied to any specific moral system or culture. While it generates a wide range of genres, it does not determine the specific attributes of each genre. It does not, for example, determine what constitutes "good" and "evil." Nor does it determine the character types, the settings, the iconography or the conventions of a genre. What it does is structure the drama around the clash between "good" and "evil" and provide a sense of "poetic justice." The specific values embedded in notions of good and evil are determined by the culture and they shift from nation to nation, from region to region and from period to period. Above all else, melodrama reassures us that the world has meaning, that it is not an arbitrary universe dependent on fate alone.

This book owes much to Peter Brooks and his 1976 study of melodrama, *The Melodramatic Imagination: Balzac, Henry James, Melodrama, and the Mode of Excess*.[4] I endorse Linda Williams and her claim that Brooks's book is "the most important single work contributing to the rehabilitation of the term *melodrama* as a cultural form."[5] Brooks, however, does not mention one film in his 1976 study.[6] What it does do is present a clear presentation of melodrama as the preeminent dramatic mode, its formal attributes, its cultural function and how it deviates from other modes. To provide a counterpoint to melodrama, he cites writers such as Maupassant, Beckett and Robbe-Grillet for their "radically ironic and anti-metaphorical stance"[7] while paying particular attention to the fiction of Gustave Flaubert, notably his 1869 novel *L'Éducation sentimentale*. Brooks argues that those who "stand in the Flaubertian tradition accept as the unfixed, unstable standpoint of their writing the very 'decentering' of modern consciousness, its lack of a central plenitude."[8] Melodrama, on the other hand, insists that the "surface reality" of a melodrama constantly points to something else and that something else involves ethical forces and imperatives that are articulated in "large and bold characters."[9] While the outcome of a melodrama can often present the triumph of virtue and the eradication of evil, this is not mandatory. What is mandatory in melodrama is its ability to reassure us of the existence of a moral world, a world of meaning.[10]

The antithesis of melodrama in this book, as discussed in Chapter Four, is the Flitcraft parable in Dashiell's Hammett's 1930 novel *The Maltese Falcon*. Crime novelist Robert B. Parker, in his Introduction to the 1989 reprinting of Hammett's novella *Woman in the Dark*, highlighted the importance of this parable to Hammett's fiction when he wrote that it "seems like a time killer, idle talk while waiting. But of course it is not. It is Spade's motive spring. And it is this vision of an impeccably random universe which informs nearly all of Hammett's work."[11] And it is a vision of the universe that the Hollywood studios in the 1940s were very reluctant, except for a relatively small number of films, to replicate.

In melodrama the personal is embedded in the social. Yet the specifics of the social, the moral values, are not determined by melodrama. They are decided by the culture. The raison d'être of melodrama is to establish an ethical universe and the most common form of melodrama, sensational melodrama, accomplishes this by generating excitement through techniques such as emotional pathos and/or the visceral appeal of spectacle. But, as Christine Gledhill points out, the convergence between spectacle and the "interesting" depends for the "dramatic frisson of conflict on something being at stake."[12] Hence, excitement and suspense "depend on our involvement at some level—of sensation, of empathy—in the contest between malevolent power and those struggling for survival or for justice."[13] The cultural values underpinning melodrama emerge out of this conjuncture. In other words, while sensational melodrama is structured as a fundamental bipolar clash between moral absolutes, the specific moral, political and religious terms of this clash are not part of the aesthetic. They are rooted in the culture.

Chapter One opens with a brief history of perceptions of "melodrama." The focus shifts to the most popular, the most elemental form of melodrama, sensational melodrama. To highlight the pervasiveness of sensational melodrama a broad range of examples is provided. They include two films directed back to back by Joseph Lewis in the mid–1940s, *My Name Is Julia Ross* and *So Dark the Night*; the "serial queens" that dominated the American cinema from 1912 to the early 1920s; William Randolph Hearst's 1917 propaganda serial *Patria*; Sax Rohmer's creation Fu Manchu and the 1930s Hollywood adaptations of his stories; President Roosevelt's melodramatic response to the Japanese attack on Pearl Harbor and the cultural and filmic significance of "December 7," the sign of virtue. The chapter concludes by demonstrating how melodrama adapted and mutated according to changing military fortunes during the Second World War as expressed in the combat film between 1942 and 1945.

In Chapter Two the 1930s western provides a case study of the ability of melodrama to adjust to regional differences with a different formal presentation that embraced social, cultural and economic anxieties arising out of the Depression. This involves a comparison between the series western and the A budget western. Series westerns, with their emphasis on performance (songs, comedy and romance) and spectacle (stunts, fights and hard riding), were popular in rural, small town and provincial areas. But they were of little interest to "sophisticated" audiences who attended the palatial picture palaces in large urban centers. As the major studios were financially dependent on the large, first-run urban theaters, and less dependent on rural and regional audiences, the production of A budgeted westerns was sporadic throughout the 1930s with fewer than fifty westerns released between 1930 and 1939. At first this gap was, primarily, filled by independent producers and later in the decade by Republic Studio. There were more than one thousand B and series westerns released between 1930 and 1939. The formal and ideological differences between these two types of western melodramas are significant.

Chapter Three considers a different type of melodrama, one favored by audiences who attended the first run urban picture palaces in the 1930s. In this type, variously known as "modified" melodrama, "drawing room" melodrama, and "melodramas of passion," the focus is on pathos and "feminine" emotion and less on action and spectacle. Examples are drawn from Hollywood adaptions of stories by W. Somerset Maugham. They include the 1929 and 1940 versions of *The Letter* and the 1928, 1931, 1946 and 1953 versions of Maugham's 1921 short story "Miss Thompson."

The final chapter examines a complex form of melodrama that involved a profound shift in perceptions of virtue, victims and perpetrators. The chapter challenges the view that film noir was universally characterized by alienated protagonists trapped in a meaningless universe. While acknowledging the prevalence of downbeat endings, most of the films designated "noir" represented a shift in melodrama, not a rejection of it. This chapter will include a wide range of examples to illustrate this shift to a more psychologically inflected mode where the gothic was more influential than the hard-boiled detective tradition. Drawing upon shooting scripts and literary sources, the chapter will show how key decisions taken in films such as *The Maltese Falcon* and *Double Indemnity* ultimately pulled back from any suggestion of a world devoid of ethical meaning. On the other hand, a few films, including *Out of the Past, The Seventh Victim* and *Angel Face,* represented a clear challenge to the basics tenets of melodrama and embraced a different mode, tragedy. In these films virtue is drained of its moral significance, resulting in a sense of "nothingness."

The Significance of the "Sensation Scene" in Melodrama

The recognition of virtue and evil is integral to melodrama. In sensational melodrama (also known as "blood and thunder" melodrama), it is enveloped in performance (music, dancing and comedy) and spectacle (action). Often in sensational melodrama a key scene, the "sensation scene," clarified the moral terms of the drama.

The clear demarcation between good and evil in sensational melodrama. Evil Dick Curtis battling the white hatted hero Charles Starrett in *Two Gun Law* (1937). Curtis and Starrett would regularly confront each other in Starrett's long running western series (1936 to 1952) for Columbia.

Under Western Stars (1938)

Late in 1937 Gene Autry was in dispute with Herbert Yates, the president of Republic Studios, over a pay increase. Autry wanted $15,000 a film; Yates wanted to keep Autry at his current rate of $5,000 a film. After completing *The Old Barn Dance* on December 9, Autry announced he would not report to the studio for his next film, *Washington Cowboy*. When he failed to appear for the first day of filming, Yates suspended him and said the film would go ahead with a new cowboy star. Yates, anticipating Autry's action, had already begun the process of finding a replacement, at least in the short term as the studio believed Autry would eventually return. The man selected by producer Sol Siegel to replace Autry in *Washington Cowboy*, at $75 a week, was a young man from Cincinnati, Ohio, named Leonard Slye. Autry's departure paved the way for Slye, who was working under the name Dick Weston, to star in his first film with his new name, Roy Rogers. The title of the film was changed to *Under Western Stars*.

Under Western Stars is discussed in more detail in Chapter Two. There is, however, one moment in the film that illustrates the significance of the "big sensation scene"[14] in melodrama. It is an emotional high point where virtue is able to articulate its true (ethical) status. The plot of *Under Western Stars* involves a young cowboy, Roy Rogers, from the southwest rural community of Sage County. He is elected to Congress on the platform of obtaining federal assistance to the ranchers in his area. The ranchers are suffering from dust bowl conditions due to the exorbitant water rates charged by a monolithic corporation, the Great Western Power and Water Company. Rogers wants Congress to enact a water bill to provide financial relief to his constituents and assume control of the supply of water to the county. However, John D. Fairbanks (Guy Usher), the head of the water company, uses his political influence to block Rogers from seeking an audience with the influential Congressman Edward H. Marlowe (Tom Chatterton). Rogers is assisted by Fairbanks's daughter, Eleanor (Carol Hughes), who suggests he invite Marlowe and his wife, along with other politicians, to a western party at a Washington country club. Rogers, after calling a square dance for the politicians, takes the stage at the function and shows newsreel images, without dialogue, of devastation caused by the climate and the monopoly control of water by the Great Western Power and Water Company. While speaking to the newsreel images, a soft tune plays quietly in the background until Rogers breaks into song. There is no motivation for the song, other than generically as this film is a singing western. It has little to do with narrative logic and more to do with spectacle and performance.

The song, the moving Johnny Marvin/Gene Autry composition "Dust," which was nominated for an Academy Award, reiterates and invests the messages of the newsreel images with melodramatic pathos. It is, as Peter Stanfield points out, "an extraordinary song, easily equal to any written by the great dust bowl balladeer Woody Guthrie."[15] The theme of the song is paradise turned into hell through appalling weather conditions and over a "slow marching rhythm the song tells of the coming of the dust bowl."[16] The song records the endless dust, the dust in your eyes, the dust that continually blocks out the sun. The only possible solution offered by Rogers comes when he appeals directly to God to intervene and relieve the suffering of the drought-stricken cattlemen.

Images of fertile farming areas and healthy cattle are replaced by scenes of barren land and cattle suffering as the song, in a moment of intended irony,[17] breaks into a few lines from "Home on the Range."[18] During the song the film cuts from the images of desolation and dust to Marlowe and the other politicians in the audience. Their body language indicates that they are moved and at the conclusion of the song a politician goes over to Marlowe and says we had better start enacting that water bill. The song, the high point of the sensation scene, has the effect of transforming cynical Washington politicians into supporters for Rogers's cause. Their admiration for virtue is without equivocation or qualification and the scene performs the same function as Peter Brooks outlines in Guilbert de Pixerécourt's 1819 melodrama *La Fille de l'exilé* (*The Exile's Daughter*): "The spectacular excitement, the hyperbolic situation, and the grandiose phraseology that this situation elicits are in full evidence; and virtue, triumphant, sets off a moment of conversion that brings barbarian tribesmen to their knees. This may be easily identified as the stuff of melodrama."[19]

In *Under Western Stars* scenes of "realism," actual drought condition in the newsreel images, are assimilated into the melodramatic discourse of song and high emotion. In this sense, as Linda Williams points out, melodrama "is the form by which timely social problems and controversies can be addressed."[20] Realism, as a separate mode, is easily assimilated into its discourse. A familiar technique in melodrama is to create blockages to desire and the function of the narrative is to frustrate the audience until the blockage, or blockages, are removed. Rogers's rendition of *Dust* performs that function, at least temporarily until a new blockage is created. It reminds the audience that something is at stake. And that something was underpinned by a populist value system. The values espoused in *Under Western Stars* were the same as the ones dramatized by Frank Capra in *Mr. Smith Goes to Washington* which was released eighteen months after the Republic film.

Tom Keene in *Scarlet River* (1933), one of twelve series westerns Keene made between 1931 and 1933. Cinematographer Nicholas Musuraca, musical director Max Steiner and David O. Selznick (uncredited) worked on the series.

The Admiration of Virtue: Come On Danger! *(1932)*

The sensation scene in melodrama is a moment of high drama. It involves confrontation and peripety, a sudden surprise. It often represents a pause in the narrative as the drama "freezes" to clarify its ethical terms. In nineteenth-century theatrical melodrama the sensation scene involved a "different register of signification,"[21] sometimes bypassing dialogue altogether. To illustrate its significance in the melodramatic

(From left) Child star Billy Butts, who retired from acting when he was seventeen years old, Tom Keene and legendary stuntman and actor Yakima Canutt in *Scarlet River* (1933).

discourse I have selected a moment from a low budget RKO western titled *Come On Danger!*[22] I could have chosen a similar scene from literally thousands of Hollywood melodramas. In the film the hero, Larry Madden (Tom Keene), is a young, irresponsible Texas Ranger assigned to investigate the murder of a wealthy rancher, Sam Dunning. The chief suspect for the killing is Joan Stanton (Julie Haydon), the leader of a group of vigilantes, dispossessed ranchers fighting Dunning and his partner Frank Sanderson (Robert Ellis). The evidence against Stanton consists of a note pinned to Dunning's body claiming his murder was the result of an "Eye for an Eye, signed Joan Stanton." Larry's superior officer, Inspector Clay (Roy Stewart), is not convinced that Larry is mature enough to undertake the investigation and he appoints Larry's older brother Jim (William Scott) to replace him. However, after Larry finds his brother's body strapped to his horse with the note: "This is a warning of what will happen to any meddler that comes into Pecos Valley, Joan Stanton," he demands that he be allowed to go after Stanton.

Larry manages to insinuate himself into Joan Stanton's vigilante group after he saves her from Sanderson's men. During their escape he is wounded and Joan takes him to her mountain hideout. Here Larry's romantic feelings for the young woman develop, despite his belief that she killed his brother. This is a major obstacle in this melodrama along with Joan's determination to regain her property from

Sanderson. The film's sensation scene brings together these narrative strands while articulating the ethical basis of the drama. Hence, this scene is filmed differently than other scenes which utilize the customary two-shot method employed by low budget films to cover scenes as quickly as possible. In the sensation scene, on the other hand, there are a series of expressive images to emphasize the importance of this scene in the overall narrative. For example, cinematographer Nicholas Musuraca's lighting highlights Joan's innocence by capturing the bright gleam of her blonde hair. This is accompanied by a series of dramatic edits and compositions, including the superimposition of an image of Larry's dead brother at a pivotal moment in the sequence. The scene begins when Larry reminds Joan that she has a price on her head:

> JOAN: Yes! Thanks to Sanderson. His lies have branded me with every crime that has ever occurred here. Everything!
> LARRY: But you took Sanderson's money.
> JOAN: I had the right to take it from a man who stole our cattle, burned our homes, killed my father.
> LARRY: But that does not give you the right to be mixed up in rustling, thieving, murder.
> [a close-up of Joan during Larry's accusations highlights her torment]
> JOAN: Murder? Not murder, Larry. You can't believe that.
> [a close-up of Larry's face shows that he is beginning to have doubts as to her guilt]
> LARRY: Well, there was Dunning. And that Ranger [Larry's brother] I heard about in Sanger.
> JOAN: More of Sanderson's lies. Larry, you must believe me.
> LARRY: Why didn't you go to the authorities and tell them your story?
> JOAN: Because Sanderson had branded me in advance. What chance did I have?
> LARRY: You could have tried.
> [cut to a close-up of Joan's pained expression]
> JOAN: How could I hope to convince them when even you don't believe me.

The scene climaxes with Larry moving towards Joan to comfort and kiss her. The film, however, inserts and superimposes a flashback image showing Larry holding his dead brother. As a consequence he pauses his movement towards Joan. This moment of high drama approximates the function of the tableau in nineteenth-century theatrical melodrama which invites the audience to consider the ethical ramifications of the drama while highlighting the obstacle still confronting virtue.

Eventually, the obstacles to virtue are removed. However, before this takes place there is a scene not found in other versions of this story. Disturbed by Joan's plea, Larry rides into a forested area in an attempt to sort out his feelings. In this pastoral setting, framed against the towering trees, Larry, in a short soliloquy, says that "if she's telling the truth we are following a blind trail." The film ends with Larry overhearing Sanderson admit he murdered Larry's brother, followed by a shootout between the warring parties. This results in the villain's capitulation and the public recognition of Joan's true ethical status. The epilogue shows Larry and Joan preparing to return to their mountain hideout, their "space of innocence."[23]

RKO remade *Come On Danger!* six years later with a different screenwriter (Oliver Drake) for their George O'Brien western series. Although the title was changed to *The Renegade Ranger*, the plot was similar despite some name changes and additional characters to accommodate the casting of George O'Brien as the older Ranger, Captain Jack Steele, and Tim Holt as his hot-headed younger colleague Larry Corwin. The sensation scene is set-up in a similar manner although in the 1938 version the barrier between the hero and heroine is not his desire to avenge his brother but his determination that the law must be upheld and Judith Alvarez (Rita Hayworth) brought to justice. By 1938 there had been a shift in the series western, as discussed in Chapter Two. There was a greater interest in the theme of dislocation and dispossession following the economic ramifications of the Depression. In *The Renegade Range* the villain, Ben Sanderson (William Royle), is the local tax collector who cheats the heroine, Judith Alvarez (Rita Hayworth), out of her land. In a scene not found in the 1932, Steele expresses his sympathy to the ranchers dispossessed by Sanderson. He tells his superior officer, Major Jameson (Guy Usher), that he can understand Judith's anger:

RKO's 1938 film *The Renegade Ranger,* a remake of *Come On Danger!* In the 1938 film the Tom Keene role from the 1932 film was played by George O'Brien and the leader of the vigilantes, Judith Alvarez, was played by Rita Hayworth with Tim Holt as a disenchanted Texas Ranger who joins Alverez's outlaw band.

STEELE: Yes, and she probably had plenty of reason for blaming him [Sanderson] too, Major. Ever since the Civil War crooked politicians have been gradually dispossessing people along the border of their land grants and selling them for a song to the same grafting citizens.

JAMESON: I know, I know. But no one can take the law into their own hands. Judith Alvarez is the leader of a band of border renegades and she must be brought to justice immediately.

An additional scene, not found in the 1932 version, reiterates this theme in a confrontation between the tax collector (Sanderson) and Carson (Frank M. Thomas), a local rancher struggling to hold on to his property due to exorbitant taxes. The scene ends with the villain telling the rancher that if he cannot pay his taxes he (Sanderson) will be forced to collect them the best way he can. Angered, Carson tells Sanderson that if the law cannot help him, he will support the vigilante methods of Judith Alvarez. Carson is then arrested by the crooked sheriff (Neal Hart) who works for Sanderson. Steele watches this confrontation in the bar. While sympathetic to Carson, and unimpressed by Sanderson, he still retains his belief that Sanderson's greed does not justify or excuse Judith Alvarez's vigilante methods. However, he is beginning to comprehend her predicament and tells fellow Ranger Happy (Ray Whitley) that the "law makes us do a lot of unpleasant things sometimes."

The plot follows the earlier film. After Steele is wounded rescuing Judith from Sanderson's men, she takes him back to her hideout to tend his wounds. For the sensation scene there is, however, a significant change in Judith's costume. Her largely "masculine" clothes, consisting of leather and dark colors, are replaced by a bright, "feminine" dress as she tries to convince Steele:

> JUDITH: I'm only trying to get what rightfully belongs to me.
> STEELE: I know exactly how you feel. But killing Sam Dunning was the worst possible thing you could have done.
> JUDITH: Dunning got what he deserved. Sanderson probably murdered him leaving the note to make sure the crime was blamed on me.

Jack, unsure of Judith's innocence, reiterates his reservations to ex-Ranger Larry Corwin, who has joined Judith's band of renegades.

> STEELE: Judith [has] placed herself outside the law.
> CORWIN: Sanderson controls the law.

The remainder of the film follows the earlier film. In a similar scene to the 1932 film Judith is vindicated when Steele overhears Sanderson's confession that he ordered Dunning's murder. Although Steele and Judith are captured, they overcome Sanderson and his men when her vigilantes ride to their rescue. Following the public recognition of Judith's innocence, the film ends with a musical celebration.

Populism

Melodrama is a mode, as Christine Gledhill points out, that addresses basic questions such as how to live, who is justified, who is innocent, where evil resides and what motivates it.[24] Each culture and each historical period will answer these questions differently. In 1930s Hollywood they were often addressed within the context of a broad value system that is often described as populist or populism. This system valued small, independent landowners, small merchants while opposing large corporations, large landowners, intrusive governments, especially tax agents, banks and urban trade unions. The dark side of this system involved its tendency to resort to violent vigilantism when it was unable to legally restore property and achieve "justice." Although they have much in common, it is useful to distinguish between the Populist Political Party formed in 1891 and populism as a broad philosophical system. Both had their roots in Thomas Jefferson's ideal of an agrarian democracy. Broadly, there are two major phases of populism. Agrarian populism in the eighteenth century, dominated by Jefferson's notion of the yeoman farmer, and its reconfiguration in the nineteenth and twentieth centuries as "small town populism."[25] While there were changes over time, certain basic tenets remained constant. Particularly important was the belief that the universe and all of its inhabitants are governed by natural law, as defined by the French philosopher Comte de Volney: "Natural law is the regular and constant order of facts by which God rules the universe; the order which his wisdom presents to the sense and reason of men, to serve them as an equal and common rule of conduct, and to guide them without distinction of race or sect, towards perfection and happiness."[26]

The doctrine of natural rights, and its faith in each individual, underpinned Jefferson's belief in man's right to freedom from arbitrary political

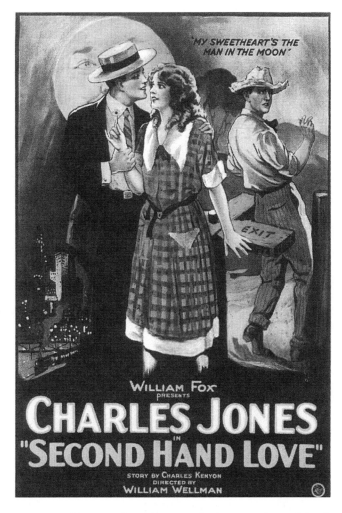

American film populism showing the (innocent) rural/(evil) city dichotomy. Charles Jones, later Buck Jones, as the rural lad facing opposition from Charles Coleman and his big city appeal in the courtship of Ruth Dwyer in the William Wellman melodrama *Second Hand Love* (1923).

authority. The best way to secure natural rights was to leave people as free as possible, for God will restore a just equilibrium. This conception of the ideal society was based on Jefferson's dictum that the "government is best which governs least."[27] His ideal social unit was the small agrarian community similar to the one he lived in at Monticello. The resilience of this concept of an agrarian democracy can be traced, according to Richard Hofstadter, to the fact that the American tradition of democracy was formed on the farm and in small villages, and its central ideas were embodied in rural sentiments and rural metaphors, such as "grass roots democracy."[28] The antithesis to this belief system was, according to Jefferson, found in industrial communities in large cities which were considered the breeding ground for corrupt "money power." This was often linked, in the minds of the populists, with corrupt political influence. Utopia for them was always in the rural past before industrialization became a major influence. As a political and social philosophy, populism celebrated individualism against the encroaching forces of "Organization" (big business and "corporate money"), centralized government and political machines. Overall, its basic fear was "bigness."[29]

Populism in the Hollywood cinema peaked in the 1930s, notably in films directed by Frank Capra, Leo McCarey and John Ford.[30] Jeffrey Richards in his study of the cinema of populism points out that like all movements populism has its mythology and a key myth involved the man of the people rising upwards to be the leader of people in a time of need. Richards cites Jefferson and Andrew Jackson as examples but the most significant of all, "the man who personified the ideals and aspirations of America and whose legend stands at the heart of populism, is Abraham Lincoln."[31] Described as "the greatest character since Christ,"[32] who is the "ultimate prototype,"[33] Lincoln was "tailor-made to fit this image. The classic Good Man, the sort of leader the populists envisaged for the nation."[34] Physically, writes Richards, "he represents the archetype: tall, lean, dignified, with humility, honesty and integrity etched into every line of his rugged frontiersman face."[35] He was, like Christ, the classic savior hero. In the western, this culturally archetype was replicated in the mythic (screen) persona of Wyatt Earp.

Hollywood and Populism: The "Earp" Template

Scott Simmon writes that "something about Wyatt Earp and the O.K. Corral has made the story the single most extreme example of a Western-history phenomenon."[36] The Earp story was never filmed in the silent period.[37] Hollywood's interest in Earp followed the publication of three very different and historically inaccurate books between 1927 and 1931: Walter Noble Burn's romanticized history *Tombstone: An Iliad of the Southwest* (1927); Billy Breckenridge's *Helldorado* (1928), a trenchant attack on Earp; and Stuart Lake's highly romanticized celebration of the Earps in *Frontier Marshal* (1931). Lake's "biography" fashioned Earp into a savior hero, providing a narrative template for many westerns.

Between the first screen version of this event, *Law and Order* (1932), and the most famous screen version, John Ford's *My Darling Clementine* in 1946, there were, at least, eight other films that retold this story: *Frontier Marshal* (1934), *The Arizonian* (1935), *Law for Tombstone* (1937), *In Early Arizona* (1938), *Frontier Marshal* (1939), *The Marshal of Mesa City* (1939), *Law and Order* (1940) and *Tombstone, the Town Too Tough to Die* (1942).[38] Each version, except the first (*Law and Order*), followed the same narrative formula. A hero reluctantly takes on the position of town marshal and with the assistance of his brothers and Doc Holliday eliminates the lawless elements. He then leaves the town.

Will Wright in his book *Six Guns and Society: A Structural Study of the Western,* divides the genre into four plot types. The most important being the classical plot which dominated the genre between the start of his survey, 1930, and the mid–1950s. The classical plot, Wright argues, "is the prototype of all Westerns ... the story of the lone stranger who rides into a troubled town and cleans it up, winning the respect of the townsfolk and the love of the schoolmarm."[39] The determining factor in Wright's study is the relationship between the hero and society. He argues that in the "forty-year period from 1930 and 1970 'there were four significantly different forms of this relationship which seemed to change with time, particularly after the war [the Second World War].'" While the characterizations of the key protagonists, the heroes, the villains and society, were essentially the same within any one plot structure, there were significant differences across structures, across different historical periods.[40] In the period from 1930 to the mid–1950s, the classical period, the story of the reluctant hero who is recruited to save his community dominates the western according to Wright.[41] The classical plot, Wright argues, involves the integration of hero into a community that requires his special skills to protect it. This describes every film version of the Earp story between 1932 and 1946, except the first version, *Law and Order*.

Wyatt Earp and the Gunfight at the O.K. Corral

Wyatt Berry Stapp Earp was born in Monmouth, Illinois, on March 19, 1848, the fourth son of Nicholas Porter Earp. For some years he worked a variety of jobs, including stagecoach messenger and professional gambler. In Lamar, Missouri, Wyatt was appointed constable after replacing his father in the position. Although Wyatt's reputation in Lamar was tainted by allegations of embezzlement, he was appointed to law officer positions in Ellsworth, Kansas, Wichita, where he was appointed Marshal, and later in Dodge City. In Dodge City he met John Henry "Doc" Holliday after Holliday saved his life during a saloon fight. Holliday was a former dentist who preferred the life of a gambler to dentistry.

Wyatt Earp, with his second wife Mattie and his brothers James, Virgil, Morgan and Warren, moved to Tombstone in 1879 in the hope of acquiring wealth and social standing in the local community. Virgil was appointed town Marshal while Wyatt, on occasion, assisted him as his deputy. Wyatt also worked as a deputy sheriff for Pima County and as a faro dealer after buying a share in the Oriental Saloon. Wyatt, keen to be elected sheriff, tried to solve a series of stagecoach robberies by persuading rancher/outlaw Joseph Isaac "Ike" Clanton to identify the culprits. Clanton was ready to make the deal but before he could act the men responsible for the robberies were killed. After Wyatt let it be known that Ike gave him the information, Clanton turned on the Earps. On the night of October 25, 1881, after a series of drunken threats against the Earps, Clanton was arrested and jailed for carrying a firearm. He was also fined $25. The next morning Tom McLaury objected to Clanton's arrest and Wyatt hit him over the head with his gun during an argument. Tom's brother Frank, along with Billy Clanton, continued to harass and threaten the Earps until Virgil, Morgan, Wyatt, and Holliday decided to confront the cowboys. On their way to the fight, Virgil passed a shotgun to Holliday who placed it under his trench coat.

As the Earps moved along Fremont Street towards the O.K. Corral, Cochise County Sheriff John Behan persuaded them to give him a chance to disarm the cowboys. When this failed the Earps and Holliday continued along Fremont Street past the rear entrance to the O.K. Corral. The shooting lasted a bare 30 seconds. Doc

Holliday killed Tom McLaury, hitting him in the chest with a shotgun blast. Morgan Earp was wounded after being hit in the shoulder by Billy Clanton. Billy was killed by Wyatt. Frank McLaury shot Virgil in the calf and also wounded Holliday before both Holliday and Morgan killed him. Holliday's bullet hit him in the chest while Morgan's bullet hit him in the head. Ike Clanton ran away after pleading with Wyatt not to kill him. Wyatt responded to Ike's plea with the famous line: "The fightin's commenced. Either get to fighting or get away."[42] William Claiborne and Wesley Fuller also ran away after the firing began.

Although Virgil and Morgan were wounded in the fight, and Doc Holliday was superficially grazed along his lower back, Wyatt emerged unscathed. Sheriff Behan tried to arrest Wyatt Earp and Doc Holliday but Wyatt refused to accept the arrest, telling Behan he would answer to what he had done. Wyatt and Holliday were eventually arrested after Ike Clanton filed murder charges against them. After conflicting versions of the event, the pre-trial ended on December 1, 1881, with Judge Spicer ruling that there was insufficient evidence to convict Wyatt Earp or Doc Holliday.

Hollywood's versions of the "Earp story" between 1932 and 1946 demonstrate the protean qualities of melodrama, its ability to transform through different periods by selecting different "realities" in accordance with the prevailing value systems. The appeal of this story is easy to understand. A savior hero who protects a weak and threatened community. To intensify audience involvement the narrative employs familiar devices such as suspense, spectacle, thrills and romance. But these narrative devices are not unique to melodrama. What is unique is the depiction of a world predicated on an "irreducible manichaeism."[43] It is this manichaeistic structure that assimilates the prevailing social values that determine the qualities embodied by the hero, heroine and the villain. Thus the mechanics of melodrama operate on two levels. The "vertical level,"[44] the clash of "pure psychic signs,"[45] the hero, heroine and villain, and the "horizontal"[46] where these social archetypes are deployed within a regular pattern of emotional highs and lows. In this manner melodrama, to the annoyance of some critics, eliminates the middle condition[47] to focus on the external clash between whole characters and, in the process, avoid any sustained focus on divided characters who are torn between competing, and viable, moral positions. Thus polarization in melodrama serves not only a dramatic function but also an ideological one. It is the way in which the underlying social and cultural values of the drama are clearly identified.[48] It is these values which determine the terms upon which the story is resolved. For example, in each version of the Earp story filmed between 1932 and 1946 the determining value system was populism. Except the first (1932) version.

Law and Order *(1932)*

The film was based on W.R. Burnett's 1930 novel *Saint Johnson*, a fictionalized account of the Earps during their period in Tombstone. Burnett, ever fearful of a lawsuit from Earp's widow, made a number of name changes. Wyatt becomes Wayt

Johnson, Doc Holliday is Brant White, Virgil Earp is Luther Johnson and the gunman Deadwood is based on Morgan Earp. James Earp is Jim Johnson and the Clantons are the Northrups. However, you may wonder why Burnett bothered with these name changes as his Note at the start of the novel acknowledges that his story was, in actuality, based on the conflict between the Earps and the Clantons in the "southeast corner of Arizona"[49]:

> It may interest the readers to learn that the "Alkali" of the story is drawn in part from the old Arizona frontier town, Tombstone....
> Two of the principal characters, Wayt Johnson and Brant White, are drawn in part from two of the Old West's most famous men: Wyatt Earp, Dodge City and Tombstone peace officer, and Doc Holliday, gambler, gunfighter and wit.
> The story itself is based on the event leading up to and arising out of the Earp-Clanton feud.

The novel begins with Luther as town marshal of Alkali and Wayt the Federal deputy marshal, by appointment. Wayt desperately wants to be the next sheriff of San Miguel County. Known as "Mr. Law and Order Johnson,"[50] he is also determined to eradicate the lawless elements such as Poe Northrup and his family along with Frame Tod. In the process Wayt needs to remove the current sheriff, Fin Elder, a close friend of the Northrups. Wayt is supported by his brothers Luther and Jim, the gambler Brant White and the gunman Deadwood. Wayt also has a share in the Golden Girl Saloon with co-partner Ed Deal. Despite Luther's warning that the town "ain't ready for law and order nohow, and you're getting yourself in trouble trying to give it to 'em,"[51] Wayt orders his friends to control their shooting, a warning that Brant White has trouble accepting when he tells Wayt that "law and order don't go in this here city if the object is to arrest a cattleman, no sir! Shoot it out with 'em, Wayt, and there's an end on it."[52] Wayt rejects Brant's advice and tells him: "'Boys,' he said, 'you act like yearlings. Trust me, that's all I'm asking you. I'm aiming to take over this town 'fore long. And I'm telling you, she's ready for law and order and she's going to get it.'"[53]

With the support of the city council Wayt imposes a city ordinance prohibiting the carrying of firearms. This upsets Poe Northrup and the other cattlemen, especially Frame Tod who describes Wayt as "Mr. Rectitudinous Johnson"[54] and accuses him of only being out for himself and the Johnsons. Frame tells Wayt that he missed "his calling.... He should've been a gospel-expounder. Look at him there! Ain't he a proper man with his nice black suit fit for a corpse. Yes sir."[55]

When the cowboys threaten to ignore the ordinance against the carrying of firearms, and shoot at Deadwood, Brant tells Wayt that "them boys need killing. Why can't you let us loose some, Wayt, and give us a little elbow room."[56] Wayt, however, refuses to let the Northrup-Tod bunch provoke him and he asks Brant and Deadwood to let "me play my own game.... You know I can't be standing for no two-gun work and Luther and me wearing badges."[57] Nevertheless, there is a limit to his patience and when, at 3:00 a.m., a dozen cowboys associated with the Northrups ride up Main Street "whooping and shooting"[58] and cursing the Johnsons, Wayt opens the second-floor window of his hotel room and fires two shots at the horses, killing one horse and throwing its rider onto the wooden sidewalk. This action results in an anti–Johnson editorial from the local paper, the *Alkali Herald*, claiming that "Alkali

[is] suffering under misrule of peace officers … cowboy's horse, a valuable animal, callously shot down on Main Street…. Dodge City methods of two-gun enforcement deplorable … citizens actually endangered by reckless peace officers."[59]

Wayt and his group have, up to this point, the support of Judge Williams and the local citizens. This changes following the attempted robbery of the Holmesburg stage[60] and the murder of the driver and one of the passengers. The robbery exposes Wayt's weakness, his brother Jimmy who was involved in the holdup. After Jimmy runs away Wayt locates him and takes him to Elderville where he fabricates an alibi for him. Distressed, Wayt tells Jimmy that "as a deputy marshal I'm in as deep as you are, so shut your mouth."[61] Forced to form a posse Wayt tells Brant, Luther and Deadwood that "I aint looking for these road agents and I ain't aiming to find 'em…. If we should happen to run into these fellers, kill 'em and no palavering. I don't want nary one of 'em alive."[62]

When they come across two members of the holdup gang, one already dead, the other is murdered by Brant. This action, temporarily, restores Wayt's status in the community and local businessman Marcus Wingett toasts Wayt as "the next sheriff of San Miguel County."[63] However, things begin to fall apart when rumors circulate regarding Jimmy's involvement in the robbery. Wayt, searching for a way out, ponders the possibility that, as Federal deputy marshal, he might be able to "find some excuse and stage a killing that might solve his problem."[64] It is clear in Burnett's novel that Wayt is not a savior figure. He is willing to kill to protect his brother and his own interests. He is a complex, morally problematic character. He has, according to Burnett, "a rigid sense of order, [and] the extravagance and lawlessness of the frontier offended him; and born with a somewhat exaggerated sense of his own worth and importance, the swaggering insolence of the badmen, the two-gun men, infuriated him."[65] His reputation before coming to Akali was poor. In Dodge City he was known to be "as dangerous as any of the lawless element."

After Wayt is presented with an affidavit claiming that Jimmy participated in the Holmesburge stage robbery, support for him within the community falls away, especially after Wingett tells him that "some of the faithful is [sic] getting worried."[66] Although he denies Jimmy's involvement in the robbery, the pressure on the Johnsons escalates until Wayt realizes that he will never be sheriff and his pent-up violence erupts and he tells Brant and his brothers that "for the last year or so I have been doing my best to make Alkali a fit place to live and I don't say I'm done but there's a few fellas in this town that are aching to be settled and I'm not fixing to disappoint them"[67]:

> Brant and Wayt's brothers knew what this meant. Wayt's enemies had pushed him too far. He would never stop now until things were settled to suit him. Smith and Deadwood, who had known Wayt only during his Alkali days, had no idea to what lengths he would go. They had never seen him, as Luther, Jim and Brant had, go into a saloon, where there were at least a dozen men who had threatened to kill him, and cut loose indiscriminately with two six-shooters.[68]

After Wayt's name is removed from the ballot for sheriff, he tells Brant and his brothers that he is "fed up. I done my best for the citizens of this community, but they're aiming to be bossed by cattle thieves and tin horn politicians. That's their business. But when it comes to send us threatening letters and bullets and banging away at Luther with a shot-gun, that's ours! Now I ain't aiming to break the peace but I hereby declare that not one inch of lip will I take from ary citizen, tin horn or such."[69] As he heads towards the North End Corral to confront Poe Northrup, Frame and Joe Tod and El Guero, Wayt tells Luther that "I'm done with law and order."[70]

Wingett attempts to dissuade Wayt and his men from proceeding to the North End Corral and tells Wayt that "you're aiming to kill 'em, Wayt Johnson … and it ain't got nothing to do with law and order nohow. It's your finish in this community."[71] Wayt disregards Wingett's advice and in the ensuing fight Poe Northrup and Frame Tod are killed, Joe Tod, Luther, Deadwood and Brant are injured while Wayt escapes unscathed. During the fight Walt Northrup runs to Wayt who tells him: "Fight or git."[72] Walt "gits." El Guero, a Northrup supporter, rides away before the start of the gunfight.

Unlike other versions of the gunfight at the O.K. Corral, Burnett depicts the fight as the final break between Earp and the citizens of Alkali. When the *Alkali Herald* declares that the Johnsons should be sent to the Yuma penitentiary,[73] Wayt realizes that he is "through in Alkali."[74] Even though Wayt, Deadwood, Luther and Brant are exonerated by Judge Williams, community attitude continues to harden against them. Wayt is removed from office and censured by the Federal marshal for his part in the killings. After Jimmy is murdered by El Guero Wayt finally breaks down: "He wanted to go out into the street with a shot-gun and kill. He wanted to see men fall before him, because of Jim."[75] Now totally estranged from his community ("He was a stranger to Alkali"),[76] Wayt realizes that "all his carefully laid plans had come to nothing, and he didn't care."[77] He sells the Golden Girl Saloon and Luther withdraws his candidacy for town marshal. Brant and Wayt kill El Guero and then leave Akali with Luther and Deadwood. With all of Wayt's dreams shattered, Deadwood tells Brant that Wayt "don't seem to give a damn for nothing nohow."[78] The novel ends as they ride away with Fin Elder still in control of the town: "Wayt said nothing. The four of them rode along in silence. At the edge of town they turned south and hit the trail for War Bonnet."[79]

Burnett's novel is not a melodrama. It is almost impossible to discern any perception of virtue in the novel and there is no presentation of poetic justice. Wayt is no savior and the narrative traces his alienation from his community, not his integration. While Burnett's novel was almost impossible to film in 1932, John Huston cleverly adapted the story and reached a similar point by the end of the film. He transforms the Earp prototype (renamed Frame Johnson) by eliminating his corrupt tendencies and accentuating his self-righteousness and morally rigid, evangelical qualities. These attributes in the film are not directed towards self-interest but into an anti-gun treatise via Frame's obsession to eliminate the six-shooter from Tombstone, and elsewhere. In this manner Huston's adaptation refuses to endorse the prevailing populism of the 1930s and by the end of the film Frame is a broken man, estranged from his community with nothing to show for it except the death of his brother Luther and friends Ed Brandt and Deadwood.

In the film Wayt Johnson becomes Frame "Saint" Johnson (Walter Huston), Brant White is Ed Brandt (Harry Carey), Jimmy is omitted and the gunman

Deadwood (Raymond Hatton) remains along with Frame's brother Luther (Russell Hopton) although he is no longer town marshal of Alkali. Frame Tod, a villain in the novel, is omitted and the villains are Poe Northrup (Ralph Ince) and his brothers Walt (Harry Woods) and Kurt (Richard Alexander). The crooked sheriff Fin Elder (Alphonse Ethier) is retained along with the head of the local council, Judge Williams (Russell Simpson).

After leaving an unnamed western town at the start of the film, where the audience learns that Frame is the man who cleaned up Kansas and killed thirty-five men, one man for each year of his life, Frame, Luther, Brandt and Deadwood camp under a signpost pointing to Alkali in one direction and Tombstone in another. Around the campfire the men sing *"My Pretty Quadroon,"* a traditional Civil War song involving a slave grieving for his lost love. During the evening Frame tells the group that it was not the "Injuns" that caused trouble in the West, it was the six-gun. He pulls out his six-shooter and tells them: "They made a mistake when they passed that out. Even made the skunks brave."

Undecided which way to go, peaceful Alkali or the wild township of Tombstone, Brandt cuts cards with Frame and when Brandt wins, with "aces and eights," he chooses Tombstone. "Aces and eights," the notorious "dead man's hand," foreshadows the tone of the film. Deadwood reinforces this fatalistic omen by telling them that the "life we're following we're going to get a bellyful of lead for breakfast sooner or later." The four men arrive in Tombstone at night to a montage of gambling, dancing girls, street fires, corruption and the sense of a community out of control. It is election night for the position of sheriff and the Northrups, who are endorsing the corrupt Fin Elder, terrorize and murder anyone who doesn't vote for him. This includes buying the votes of a wagonload of Indians, controlled by a white man, heading for the voting booth after selling each vote for a dollar.[80]

When Judge Williams is alerted by Ed Deal (Dewey Robinson), a bartender in the Golden Girl, as to Frame's reputation, the judge offers Frame the position of deputy marshal. Unlike the novel, where Wayt is already deputy marshal and desperately seeks the sheriff's office, Frame has to be convinced by Williams and the town council. After he accepts, he asks Brandt, Luther and Deadwood to help him and they immediately come into conflict with the Northrups. When Luther reminds Frame that Tombstone doesn't want law and order, Frame replies: "Well, somebody has got to do it. Someday the six-guns will be out away and it will be a fit country to live. But until then I'll do my share."

The film, unlike other versions of the Earp story, rejects the notion of a weak community in need of a savior hero. Although he stops the lynching of Johnny Kinsman (Andy Devine), he proceeds to carry out the lawful execution of the young man. After he bans the carrying of firearms in the town, his relationship with the community deteriorates. The town also resents his appointment of Luther, Brandt and Deadwood as his deputies as Judge Williams warns Frame that it "looks like you are trying to take over" Tombstone.

After Luther kills Kurt Northrup in the Golden Girl Saloon, Frame insists that his deputies must also give up their guns. This proves a fatal mistake as Brandt, without his shotgun, is ambushed and killed by the Northrups. Brandt's murder, along with the growing hostility from the town, pushes Frame over the edge and the distraught lawman abandons his plans to bring law and order to Tombstone. He warns the locals "there is a reckoning to be done before I quit, as God is my judge." This "flawed Old Testament" moralist[81] vows to get even with them "to the last drop of my blood." Luther, on the other hand, is more fatalistic and tells the group "here's where we get our belly full of lead for breakfast." At dawn at the O.K. Corral, which is also referred to as "the O.K. Barn," Frame, Luther and Deadwood confront Poe, Walt Northrup and their gang. Everybody dies, except Frame, and the shootout concludes when Frame shoots Poe in the back as he attempts to escape.

The final minutes in the film, one of the bleakest in the genre, see Frame tell his dying brother that "it was my fault, Lute." With his head bowed over his horse, Frame leaves Tombstone after throwing his badge to Judge Williams ("well, you've wanted law and order and you've got it"). A high angle image of his departure, devoid of music, is accompanied by the plaintive sound of church bells. It shows Frame riding past the townspeople and away from Tombstone. The break between the hero and the community is complete.

In a schematic, linear perception of the genre, as in Wright's study, *Law and Order* should appear twenty years later as it has more in common with *High Noon* which was released in 1952.[82] The narrative movement in both films is one of estrangement between the hero and his community. Genres, however, do not always move in a neat manner. As Christine Gledhill points out, they are "cyclical, coming around again in corkscrew fashion, never quite in the same place."[83] Instead of a structuralist approach which removes any consideration of the film's dramatic mode, melodrama, it is more productive to consider *Law and Order* within the context of other melodramas produced in the same period (1930–1932). Scott Simmon, for example, points to the cross-generic associations between the western and other genres during this period.[84] He argues that *Law and Order,* along with King Vidor's *Billy the Kid* (1930), "fused the gangster ethic to William S. Hart's Old Testament gunfighter morality"[85] as it contained not only the "expressionist emotional bite of a hard-boiled gangster film,"[86] but also the "darkness of the horror cycle."[87] He cites the George O'Brien western *Mystery Ranch* (1932), which is discussed below, as further evidence that it is the "dark forces within European expressionism that these lawmen must fight. Walter Huston's character [in *Law and Order*] does not merely evict darkness from Tombstone but recognizes it within himself, which contributes to his defeat as he rides from town, head bowed."[88]

The Beast of the City (1932)

Simmons, correctly, argues that *Law and Order* "has other meanings arising from cross-formulations with other genres."[89] While he cites *Little Caesar* (1931), largely because W.R. Burnett also wrote the novel on which *Little Caesar* was based, there is an even stronger parallel between *Law and Order* and MGM's *The Beast of the City.* Both films were released within two weeks of each other in February 1932 and *The Beast of the City* was scripted by W.R. Burnett, with assistance from John L. Mahin who worked on the dialogue and continuity. Ben Hecht also contributed to the screenplay without a credit. The working title for the film was *City Sentinels* and it developed, according to the *Hollywood Reporter*,[90] from a meeting between Louis B. Mayer, the head of production at MGM, and President Hoover with the stated aim of producing a film that would restore respect for the police. Their aim for the film is articulated in the prologue:

> Instead of the glorification of cowardly gangsters, we need the glorification of policemen who do their duty and give their lives in public protection. If the police had the vigilant, universal backing of public opinion in their communities, if they had the implacable support of the prosecuting authorities and the courts—I am convinced that our police would stamp out the excessive crime—which has disgraced some of our great cities. President Herbert Hoover.

The meeting between Mayer and Hoover followed complaints from civic and other groups about the celebration of the gangster in Hollywood films such as *The Doorway to Hell* (1930), *Little Caesar* and *Public Enemy* (1931). In April 1931 the controlling industry body, The Motion Picture Producers and Distributors Association (MPPDA), effectively curtailed the gangster cycle by establishing guidelines for "the proper treatment of crime" in films. This made it very difficult for the studios to continue with the classic gangster film.[91] *The Beast of the City* emerged as a result of a desire to celebrate the police, not the gangster. Yet something did not go to plan and the film presents a picture of a corrupt society where vigilantism becomes the only viable option.

The hero in *The Beast of the City*, police captain Jim Fitzpatrick (Walter Huston), shares many of the same characteristics as Frame Johnson in *Law and Order*. He wants to re-establish law and order in his city and his aim is to put gangster Sam Belmonte (Jean Hersholt), a thinly veiled portrait of Al Capone, behind bars. However, a corrupt judicial system frustrates Fitzpatrick's desires. Soon after the film begins, after the court allows Belmonte to escape justice once again, Fitzpatrick is demoted to a quiet suburban precinct in Glendale. After attracting positive publicity following the capture of a couple of bank robbers, the mayor (Elmer Ballard), seeking favorable publicity in an election year, replaces the Chief of Police Burton (Emmett Corrigan) with Fitzpatrick. Fitzpatrick, delighted to be in charge, spells out his approach in a speech to his officers:

> We're going to start with a clean slate, see? I don't know a thing about any of you. Good, bad, efficient or inefficient.... Every man keeps his job he's got now until he proves to me he's worth a better one or he has no right on the force at all. I'm not fighting you and you're not fighting me. We're going to fight together. Now this town has become about as rotten as an open grave. Only some of you have got so used to it you don't hold your noses anymore. Well, we're going to clean it up, understand? We're going to knock over every speakeasy, hook [brothel] shop, wheel joint and gin mill from South Canal to North Haven. We're going to keep pulling in every monkey until they get so tired of it they'll all want to lie in the tanks or leave town.... If I don't get results there's going to be a shake-up like the inside of a cement mixer. I'll get results if I have to put a patrolman at the head of the vice squad and precinct captains back to teaching rookie drill.

Although Fitzpatrick enjoys early success in closing down some of Belmonte's speakeasies, he is betrayed by his younger brother Ed (Wallace Ford) who is seduced by Daisy Stevens (Jean Harlow), Belmonte's former "stenographer." She "recruits" Ed

(From left) Jean Hersholt, Montgomery Tully, Jean Harlow and Walter Huston in *The Beast of the City* (1932).

after a night of drinking and sex.[92] Desperate to fund Daisy's expensive lifestyle, Ed accepts money from Belmonte for information that allows his illegal shipments to move through the city without police detection. Jim, in an attempt to reinvigorate Ed's languishing career, assigns him to look after the transportation of a large sum of money. The younger brother, however, betrays his mentor and tells Daisy about the shipment. She passes this information to Pietro Cholo (J. Carrol Naish), Belmonte's chief henchman. Unaware that two police detectives, Tom (Warner Richmond) and Mac (Sandy Roth), are keeping watch on the assignment, Ed allows Cholo's men, the Gorman brothers, to knock him down and steal the money. However, in the ensuing chase, Mac and a young child are killed by the robbers. When one of the robbers incriminates Ed, Jim disowns his brother. Jim's depression intensifies when the court fails to convict Ed and the Gorman brothers of two counts of murder.

Ed, desperate to redeem himself in the eyes of his brother, accepts Jim's suggestion to goad Belmonte into a gunfight while he is celebrating the court's verdict in his night-club. Jim, sickened by a corrupt judicial system, abandons the possibility of legal action and becomes a vigilante. After Cholo shoots Ed, the nightclub erupts in gunfire as Jim's colleagues (disillusioned police officers) and mobsters trade shots at each other. During the prolonged gunfight, similar to the ending in *Law and Order*, Jim, Ed, Belmont, Daisy and the gangsters perish. The film's closing image

Police chief Walter Huston is not impressed with his younger brother (Wallace Ford) and his relationship with Jean Harlow in *The Beast of the City* (1932).

shows the mortally wounded Jim reaching for his brother's (dead) hand on the floor of the nightclub.

A novel, *The Beast of the City,* was published by Grosset and Dunlap to coincide with the release of the film in 1932. It was written by former newspaper reporter, editor and playwright, Jack Lait. The front page of Lait's novel points out that it was "adapted from the original motion picture story of W.R. Burnett."[93] It includes a number of production stills from the film. In other words, it is what is known today as a "movie tie-in." A comparison between the book and the film is revealing. The film differs from Burnett's script, with substantial changes most likely made by Ben Hecht. The script/novel is a sentimental, heroic presentation of the police in general and Fitzpatrick in particular. In the novel's ending, for example, instead of the film's bleak final image showing Fitzpatrick and Ed dead on the floor of the nightclub, it depicts a last-minute rescue by Fitzpatrick where he saves Daisy and his son. Fitzpatrick in the novel, unlike the film, is not a vigilante, but a savior hero. The setting for his heroic deed is Belmonte's hunting lodge fifty miles out of the city and the gangster has kidnapped Daisy, a reformed character in the script/novel, and Fitzpatrick's son Mickey (Mickey Rooney). After Ed dies trying to rescue them, and just as Guiseppe Belmonte is about to shoot Daisy, "a big man bristled in, a revolver in his hand. ... Fightin' Jim Fitzpatrick's gun took the final toll of the Belmonte gang, leveling a surprised

Guiseppe where he stood. 'That's one rap you won't beat,' he breathed. And Fightin' Jim made his way through the chaos of broken furniture and crumpled bodies, to the body of Ed, the last of his own flesh and blood."[94]

After Jim recovers his son Mickey, the novel ends on a sentimental note as Jim tells Mickey:

> "Come here—while I pin my star on a man who died as a copper wants to die— his duty, Mickey, was his honor."
> And Fightin' Jim pinned the chief's sparkling star over Ed's heart.[95]

This was the film Louis B. Mayer and President Hoover expected—a sensational melodrama involving pathos and last-minute rescues as it celebrates its populist hero. Instead, they received a film that replicated the downbeat tone of *Law and Order*. In the western Frame Johnson is alien-

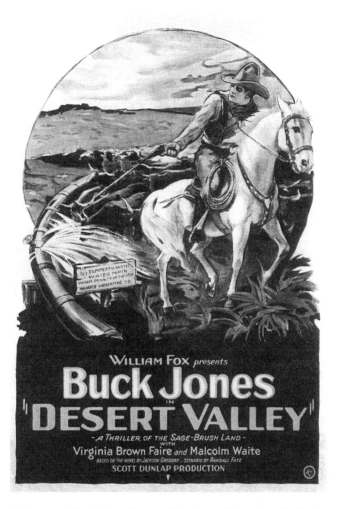

WILLIAM FOX *presents*
Buck Jones
IN
"DESERT VALLEY"
- *A Thriller of the Sage-Brush Land* -
WITH
Virginia Brown Faire *and* Malcolm Waite
BASED ON THE NOVEL BY JACKSON GREGORY .. SCENARIO BY RANDALL FAYE
SCOTT DUNLAP PRODUCTION

A stranger (Buck Jones) saves thirsty cattle by shooting holes in a pipeline owned by a rancher hoarding water in *Desert Valley*, a 1926 melodrama produced by Fox.

ated from his community. Distraught and devastated, he is psychologically "dead" as he throws his marshal's badge away in contempt. Similarly, Jim Fitzpatrick at the close of *The Beast of the City* is literally dead. Both men abandon their attempts to establish law and order. Both are abandoned by society. *The Beast of the City* was not a B picture and it starred Walter Huston, Jean Harlow and Jean Hersholt. Yet it so shocked Louis B. Mayer that despite having commissioned the film at Hoover's request, he relegated it to the lower half of the company's double features and refused to promote it.[96]

Law and Order (1940):
Singing, Comedy, Action and a Populist Hero

Eight years after the release of *Law and Order* in 1932 Universal decided to adapt W.R. Burnett's novel as part of their series of Johnny Mack Brown westerns. In 1940, as in earlier years, Brown starred in eight westerns, with running times of just under one hour, each year for the studio. If the 1940 film is reduced to a broad story outline and compared with the 1932 film they would appear to be very similar. A former lawman (Frame Johnson in 1932, Bill Ralston in 1940) comes to a western town (Tombstone in 1932, Rhyolite in 1940) under the control of a corrupt Sheriff, Fin Elder, and a brutal family of cattlemen (the Northrups in 1932, the Daggetts in 1940). With the assistance of a gambler (Brandt in 1932 and Brant in 1940), and a drifter (Deadwood), the hero cleans up the town and kills the villains. Along the way he stares down a mob wanting to lynch a young man (Johnny Kinsman in 1932 and Jimmy Dixon in 1940), bans the wearing of guns in town and reluctantly takes on the role of marshal when the villains murder a political rival during the election for the position of sheriff. He is supported, at least initially in the 1932 film, by Judge Williams and the town council. He renews his friendship with Ed Deal, a bartender in 1932 and saloon owner in 1940, and rides away at the end in both films.

This comparison is misleading. Both films are melodramas but different types of melodrama. The 1940 film is a representative example of sensational melodrama. It is a reassuring film with a stark bipolar structure involving a strong hero who eliminates those elements threatening a vulnerable community. The film's narrative movement, unlike the 1932 film, is one of integration. The storyline is relaxed and highly predictable and the film, designed to comfort, not confront, its target audience of rural and small-town people. The film's predictable storyline is reinforced by the casting, most notably Johnny Mack Brown who was a familiar actor to this audience. After a brief stint as a leading man at MGM in the late 1920s and early 1930s, he began starring in series westerns in 1935 and continued making six to eight low budget westerns each year for the next seventeen years. In 1940 he starred in eight westerns for Universal. In each he played, with name changes, the same affable but tough western stereotype. This sense of familiarity was bolstered by the supporting actors. Fuzzy Knight, the comic relief, was the sidekick in each of Brown's eight westerns in 1940. Also, in five of these films Nell O'Day co-starred as his leading lady. The rest of the cast comprised many actors who specialized in series westerns, including Harry Cording, Ethan Laidlaw, Ted Adams and Earle Hodgins as the villains along with Robert Fisk as slightly shady Ed Deal. Veteran low budget screenwriters Sherman Lowe and Victor McLeod did not have to spend much time on exposition as audience expectations were firmly established early in the film, if not before the start of the film. The emphasis in the series western, as will be discussed in Chapter Two, was on performance, on gunfight, fistfights, horse riding stunts, broad comedy, songs, a little romance, an action-based climax and retribution. No psychological realism, no convoluted plots or morally flawed heroes and no bleak endings.

The 1940 film opens with action during the film's credits. Bill Ralston (Johnny Mack Brown) and Deadwood (Fuzzy Knight) are traveling to Rhyolite by stagecoach. This provides the pretext for a comedy sequence from Deadwood which is immediately followed by an action sequence as gambler Brant (James Craig) boards the moving stage from his horse, hotly pursued by the Kurt Daggett (Ethan Laidlaw) and his gang. Ralston saves Brant and the stage arrives in Rhyolite as Jimmy Dodd, as Jimmy Dixon, and the heroine Sally Dixon, played by singer, dancer and expert horsewoman Nell O'Day, sing a lively duet, "Oklahoma's Oke with Me." This becomes the pattern for the rest of the film. Action, songs, comedy and a little romance. The action includes the requisite fist fight between the hero and chief villain Poe Daggett (Harry Cording) as well as a horse race to showcase Nell O'Day's equestrian skills.

Unlike the grim climax to the 1932 film, which strips away any sense of romance and heroism in its grim shootout, the 1940 film heightens the visceral aspect with Ralston and Deadwood involved in a prolonged chase across the prairie (the Iverson Ranch in Chatsworth) after Brant is shot in the back by Poe Daggett. This provides the motivation for spectacle as the film's camera truck captures the riders at full tilt as they perform a series of stunts. The action is interspersed by comedy in the form of Deadwood's trick pistol. The film's epilogue, always upbeat in a series western,[97] ends with a laugh as Deadwood reprises his slot machine routine with a black cat—only this time when the machine pays out it takes the form of a litter of black kittens, not coins.

Melodrama and the Gothic: Mystery Ranch *(1932)*

> Gothic horror is the flip side of melodramatic pathos. In the American context the end of the Calvinist moral and religious certainty about the power of God and the sinning nature of the human soul gave rise to a modern fascination with, on the one hand, the spectacle of the good person who suffers and, on the other hand, the evil person who creates suffering.[98]

Throughout the book melodrama and the gothic are presented as similar manifestations of the same aesthetic mode. Both share the same dramatic structure, what Brooks describes as "the logic of the excluded middle (the very logic of melodrama)"[99] as both are predicated on a world of moral extremes. Each begins with depictions of "frightening new worlds in which the traditional patterns of moral order no longer provide the necessary social glue."[100] Both demonstrate the existence of ethical forces. Where they diverge is the sense of optimism found in melodrama. However, as Brooks acknowledges, melodrama shares many characteristics with the gothic. Both are preoccupied with nightmare states, a sense of claustration, failed escapes, innocence violated and both dramatize the inability of virtue to express its moral legitimacy for the bulk of the narrative. Each also emphasizes that evil is a real and irreducible force in the world.[101] But, and this is important, the basic function of melodrama is to demonstrate, to validate, the existence of a moral universe, a universe that has ethical meaning and is not an arbitrary void.

The close association between these two early romantic forms began more than two centuries ago. In eighteenth-century theatrical drama, as Christine Gledhill points out, the "displacement of rank as dramatic source of moral authority reoriented the focus of tragedy from the idea of fate and heroic endurance toward 'poetic justice,' a new ideal consonant with Protestant morality, based in private, individual conscience, demanding that virtue be rewarded and misdeeds punished."[102] This shift appealed to middle-class notions of respectability,[103] and resulted in a new dramatic mode, sentimental drama, the forerunner of melodrama. From the eighteenth century onwards London's patent theaters staged new forms of sentimental drama that

Fox's production of the 1927 gothic film *The Wizard*. The film's plot involved a demented man who creates a gorilla to kill the jurors whose verdict sentenced his son to death. The film starred Edmund Lowe. The image shows Norman Trevor as Judge Webster and his daughter Ann played by Leila Hyams.

"sought to restore a moral economy suited to mercantile enterprise, turning on individual energy, capital accumulation, social responsibility, and familial stability. These goals merged social, personal and moral conflict in a way that would eventually support melodrama."[104]

Accompanying the development of sentimental melodrama was the gothic. The gothic formed part of a European resurgence in the arts in the eighteenth century that focused on the morbid, the supernatural, a fascination with death, sexual and psychological violation and female entrapment. A key literary work in this tradition was Anne Radcliffe's *The Mysteries of Udolpho* (1794) with its tale of a persecuted heroine imprisoned in an old castle by her aunt's husband. Christine Gledhill argues that this tradition began with Horace Walpole's *The Castle of Otranto* (1764) which utilized the trappings of medieval demonology while opening up a psycho-sexual domain. The gothic challenged the moral tenets of sentimental melodrama while merging spectacle with the domestic. Both the gothic and melodrama shared almost parallel developments. Matthew Gregory Lewis's gothic tale *The Castle Spectre* was staged at Covent Garden in December 1797 and five years later the first play to be advertised as a "melo-drama," Thomas Holcroft's adaptation of Pixérécourt's *Coelina*, titled *A Tale of Mystery*, was also staged at Covent Garden.[105]

Thereafter, melodrama and the Gothic "nourished" one another.[106] One offered reassurance of an ethical world, the other "retributive, purgative terror."[107] In the Hollywood cinema the demarcation between melodrama and the gothic is not always clear as frequently they co-exist within the same film. Hollywood revived the gothic horror film in 1931 to great success at the box office with films such as *The Bat Whispers* (1930), *The Cat Creeps* (1930), *The Gorilla* (1930), *The Unholy Three* (1930), *Doctor X* (1931), *Dr. Jekyll and Mr. Hyde* (1931), *Dracula* (1931) and *Frankenstein* (1931). During this period Universal, the studio most closely associated with the revival of the horror film, released one of genre's darkest, bleakest westerns, *Law and Order*. At the same time there was a relatively short-lived cycle of "gothic westerns" where the darkness of the horror cycle spread to the western genre.[108] The best example of this is Fox's *Mystery Ranch,* released on July 1, 1932.[109]

Mystery Ranch, unlike its source novel, is a hybrid film that assimilates gothic themes, notably a sense of dread and violation, into a conventional series western narrative underpinned by optimistic populist values. The film illustrates the close association between melodrama and the gothic as both dramatize the inability of virtue to voice its claim to recognition while acknowledging that evil is a powerful presence in the world. The film was based on Stewart Edward White's 1919 novella "The Killer."[110] Fox purchased the rights to White's story towards the end of 1931[111] and Al

Haunted Gold (1932), starring John Wayne, was Warner's contribution to the short-lived "gothic western" cycle of the early 1930s. *Haunted Gold* was a remake of the 1928 Ken Maynard film *The Phantom City*.

Cohn's script made a number of significant changes to the story. To accommodate the casting of George O'Brien, who stars as Bob Sanborn, the age limit of the hero was increased by 10 years (or more) as White's Sanborn describes himself in the novel as a "kid."[112]

A more significant change involves the transformation of the villain's home into a gothic nightmare, courtesy of Joseph August and George Schneiderman's low key cinematography and Joseph Wright's expressive sets. The interiors are consistently photographed by a chiaroscuro lighting pattern with areas of bright light engulfed by darkness. Very few early 1930s westerns, let alone series westerns with limited budgets,[113] employed this style of interior lighting, preferring instead the conventional "invisible" Hollywood style where contrasting shadows are diffused by the use of soft, or indirect, "fill" lights and back lights to distinguish the characters from the background.[114] In *Mystery Ranch* Joseph August and George Schneiderman limit the degree of fill and back lights to create a nightmare world with powerful key lights and large areas of darkness. This sense of dread was intensified by director David Howard's use of low level and off-angle compositions to highlight the cruel, stark features of Charles Middleton, as well as the sinister countenance of Charles Stevens as Tonto, Steele's right-hand man, and Noble Johnson as Mudo, Steele's mute executioner.

The other major change involves the motivation of Henry Hooper in the novella and Henry Steele in the film. While both are mercenary sadists, only the film adds a sexual dimension with Steele's determination to violate the (very) young blonde heroine. Cecilia Parker, as the heroine Jane Emory, was only seventeen years old when production began while Charles Middleton, as Steele, was fifty-eight years old.[115] This casting only accentuates the perversity of the film and intensifies the gothic theme of psychological and sexual violation.

The film's opening is 1930s Hollywood gothic. It shows a solitary rider, a deputy marshal, approaching Steele's adobe ranch in a storm. With the wind lashing the bushes, his movement is suddenly halted by a pair of powerful hands that grab him from behind. A slow fade in to Henry Steele playing the piano is interrupted by his native American assistant, Tonto, who tells him "it is done." The camera pans to the window where the body of the deputy marshal is silhouetted hanging outside in the storm. The chiaroscuro lighting combines with an extreme low angle to highlight Steele's cruel features as he tells Tonto that "someday they will learn. In this valley Henry Steele is the only law." The film cuts to the face of a young blonde woman (Jane Emory), in bright lighting, waiting anxiously to find out if the deputy marshal can save her. Her hopes are dashed when a flash of lightning shows the body of the deputy marshal, illuminated against the compound wall, swaying in the wind.

Throughout the film Steele's "Darwinian" philosophy ("sometimes we must kill in order to live [and] only the fit survive") is contrasted with the hero's (Bob Sanborn) sunny disposition. Unlike the psychologically perverse world of Henry Steele, Sanborn is visually associated with the optimism of the western, the open plains and "masculine" action. He is first seen singing (to himself) as he rides across the Arizona landscape. Along the way he visits a friend in the local town of Paraiso, one of those bizarre western towns, a mix of familiar western iconography (horses, saloons and guns) and contemporary features.[116] The saloon in Paraiso, a prohibition style bar, would not have looked out of place in many Pre-Code urban films of the early 1930s with its African American pianist and blonde "hostesses" accompanying the cowboys at the bar. The bar's main performer, a boisterous platinum blonde named Appetite Mae (Betty Francisco), sings and "entertains" the customers and when a drunken cowboy, Tex (Frank Rice), asks after her, the bartender tells him to "look out in the alley." This is an aberrant setting for a series western with its conservative populist values and it is not one that would have survived Joseph Breen's stringent changes to the Production Code in mid–1934. The effects of Breen's changes on melodrama are discussed in Chapter Three, notably in relation to William Wyler's 1940 production of *The Letter*.

In Paraiso Sanborn meets an old friend, Buck Johnson (Roy Stewart). After telling him he has come to arrest Steele for murder, Johnson warns Sanborn that Steele is insane as he will not countenance any living creature on his property that will not obey his will. Undeterred Sanborn rides to the Sierra Vista Ranch where he sees a young woman, Jane Emory, frantically riding away from Steele's ranch. Unaware that she is trying to escape, he returns her to the compound where Steele is busily whipping one of his Apaches for allowing Jane to escape. Steele invites Sanborn to stay the night and, after dinner, he plays the piano for him in his expensively decorated living room. When Jane appears, Steele introduces her as his "niece." Later, however, Steele signals his real intentions towards the young girl when he plays Felix Mendelssohn's *Wedding March*. Jane, determined to escape, slips Sanborn a note explaining that she is not Steele's niece and that he is holding her prisoner. Later, Sanborn learns that Steele invited her to the ranch on the pretext that he would give her 50 percent of the ranch following the death of her father, Steele's partner. At this point the novella and the film differ as to the villain's motivation in refusing to let her leave the ranch. In White's story it is greed. The film provides a different reason. He intends not to kill her but to violate her. Additional scenes between Jane and Steele in the film, not found in the novella, amplify this point, including his sadistic proclamation to Jane that he intends marrying her against her will. Later, he enters her room at night with the intention of raping her. The lighting, the body language and the compositions reveal his desire for the young woman and only Sanborn's timely arrival prevents the consummation of the act.

Sanborn rescues Jane during his second visit to Sierra Vista after Steele pointedly warns him never to return. Sanborn, the western "knight-errant," is determined to prevent Steele marrying/violating Jane. Unlike the low-key ending to the novella, when Hooper quietly dies from a gunshot wound on the prairie, the film gives Steele an appropriately melodramatic finale. Trapped on the top of a mountain, surrounded by Sanborn, Buck Johnson and his Arizona Rangers, he tells Sanborn, after the Ranger tries to serve a warrant for his arrest: "Young man, if you want to serve that on me, you'll have to do it in hell." Steele proceeds to jump to his death from the clifftop.

Although the trade reviews and newspaper reviews of *Mystery Ranch* were mixed, they highlight the cultural and formal demarcation between the A 1930s western and the series western. *Mystery Ranch* was intended for rural areas, small towns and provincial cities—not the first-run theaters in large urban centers. The

Winter Garden, one of New York's more prestigious theaters, changed the title of the film from *Mystery Ranch* to *The Killer* to hide the fact that it was a fifty-six-minute series western. The change was designed to "fool sophisticated Broadway viewers not inclined to patronize horse operas."[117] Mordaunt Hall, in his June 1930 review of the film for *The New York Times*, headed the review with "George O'Brien as a Gallant Ranger in a Melodrama of Arizona." He noted in his review that outside the theater it was advertised "in big letters" as "The Killer" but onscreen the credits read "Mystery Ranch." This was intended, according to Hall, to suggest that the film was either a "spoof" or a "naïve melodrama of the great Southwest." Either way he did not like the film except for the scenery: "The photography is so good that it seems almost stereoscopic. But that is, alas, all that there is to praise." George O'Brien, he noted was the "stalwart Bob," Cecilia Parker "appears as the carefully dressed Jane" and Charles Middleton "is almost believable at times as Steele."

Hall's patronizing attitude towards the film was reiterated by *Variety* critic Abel Green who also watched the film at the Winter Garden. He dismissed it as nothing special, describing the film as "conventional Western hokum." However, his review also highlighted the dismissive reaction from "the Garden first-nighters [who] turned [the film] into a rollicking affair by hissing the villain and applauding the to-the-rescue Texas Rangers, or anything heroic that George O'Brien did."[118] On the same note, "McCarthy" in the *Motion Picture Herald* warned theater owners and bookers:

> Careful on this one. Don't try to oversell it. Don't try to label it anything stronger than pleasing Western entertainment. Don't exaggerate with the idea of luring a few additional dollars into the box office. If you do, expect complaints from your patrons.
> *Mystery Ranch* undoubtedly was made for neighborhood and small city and town theaters. In those houses where Westerns, particularly George O'Brien pictures, have an appeal it can be built up into an average or better box office picture…. Likewise, the class of your patrons that are not so sophisticated in their picture demands constitute a sales field. Therefore, go after the kids as strongly as you can, and bring in the other class by an appeal that suggests thrills, action, danger, daring heroism, and a typical Western-hero romance.[119]

In the 1930s, A budgeted westerns from the major studios were promoted as anything but westerns, sometimes with vague descriptors such as "outdoor dramas" or "romance."[120] Series and B westerns, like *Mystery Ranch,* were advertised as westerns. This dichotomy provides another example of melodrama's ability to appeal to different audiences. Both the A budgeted studio western and the series western were sensational melodramas. Each catered for a different audience. This was clear in the warning from the *Motion Picture Herald* not to label *Mystery Ranch* as anything else except a western and focus on "neighborhood and small city and town theaters" where audiences were not so "sophisticated" as they enjoyed "thrills, action, danger, daring heroism, and a typical Western-hero romance." This is explored further in Chapter Two.

ONE

The Melodramatic Imagination

Melodrama is the fundamental mode of popular American moving pictures. It is not a specific genre like the western or horror film; it is not a "deviation" of the classical realist narrative; it cannot be located primarily in woman's films, "weepies," or family melodramas—though it includes them. Rather, melodrama is a peculiarly democratic and American form that seeks dramatic revelation of moral and emotional truths through a dialectic of pathos and action. It is the foundation of the classical Hollywood movie.—Linda Williams[1]

What exactly is American film melodrama? A genre, a mode and debased form of cinematic drama or a subversive stylistic cycle exploited by a few directors such as Douglas Sirk, Max Ophuls, Vincente Minelli, Nicholas Ray in the 1950s? Prior to the 1972 publication of Thomas Elsaesser's influential essay "Tales of Sound and Fury: Observations on the Family Melodrama,"[2] there was little academic interest from film scholars in melodrama. What interest there was focused on the early years of the cinema and its antecedents in nineteenth-century theatrical melodrama. John Fell's essay "Dissolves by Gaslight," for example, points to the evolutionary process by which theatrical devices and conventions had direct counterparts in early films. Fell, however, does not provide a detailed analysis of melodrama but merely sketches in a number of general characteristics whereby plays and films were simplified to "trivial ethical dimensions"[3] as melodrama "presented a world of problems and character made fraudulently comprehensible."[4]

Fell's study presumes the existence of melodrama as a recognizable genre that was subsequently subdivided into "identifiable subspecies"[5] such as military, horror, nautical crime and even "evidence for the perils of city life."[6] Interestingly, towards the end of his essay Fell implies that melodrama was more than just a popular, albeit static, theatrical genre but functioned as a conceptual mode that manifested itself throughout many levels of the culture. He cites, for example, a study that argues that Marx's Capital is a "Victorian melodrama."[7]

Before Fell and Elsaesser, it was theatrical and literary scholars such as Michael Booth, Robert Corrigan, Eric Bentley, David Grimsted, Frank Rahill, Robert Heilman and James L. Smith[8] who rehabilitated the study of melodrama. Booth, for example, described English melodrama as

the concentration on externals, the emphasis on situation at the expense of motivation and characterisation, the firm moral distinctions, the unchanging character stereotypes of hero, heroine, villain, comic man, comic woman, and good old man, physical sensation, spectacular

Lincoln J. Carter, the author of *The Arizona Express* (1924), was the author and producer of some of the more spectacular theatrical sensational melodramas such as *Bedford Hope* (1906). This Fox film, described as a "honest melodrama," was a race against time story to save a condemned man unjustly accused of murdering his uncle. Pauline Starke starred as the sister of the condemned man with Harold Goodwin as her assistant and Francis McDonald as the villain.

> effects … marked musical accompaniment, the rewarding of virtue and punishing of vice, the rapid alteration between extremes of violence, pathos, and low comedy.[9]

The eternalization of the drama, the focus on "good" and "evil" in mortal conflict, was seen as integral to melodrama in most of these studies.

American scholar Robert B. Heilman refined the distinction between melodrama and tragedy in two major books: *Tragedy and Melodrama: Versions of Experience*, published in 1968, and *The Iceman, the Arsonist, and the Troubled Agent: Tragedy and Melodrama on the Modern Stage*, published in 1973. Heilman was particularly interested in the way in which a text/dramatist responded to different "versions of reality."[10] He argued that whilst tragedy is characterized by a "polypathic" structure that acknowledges a "sense of ambiguity and contradictoriness in reality,"[11] melodrama has a "monopathic" structure where characters are viewed essentially as "undivided," where "a part is taken for the whole, and it does duty for the whole."[12] The function of melodrama, according to Heilman, was an "ordering the world."[13] Tragedy, on the other hand, was concerned with "ordering the self."[14] This distinction is simple, but useful, in describing the broad appeal of melodrama which offers audiences pleasures that don't require self introspection. Instead they can focus on powerful villains that provoke feelings of righteousness accompanied by a desire for retribution enveloped by the visceral appeal of spectacle and performance along with pathos.

Melodramatic "excess" is an integral part of Peter Brooks's 1976 study *The Melodramatic Imagination: Balzac, Henry James, Melodrama and the Mode of Excess.* While Elsaesser also stressed the excessive nature of the mode, each writer perceives the specific function of the excess differently. Elsaesser, unlike Brooks, was not particularly interested in exploring the formal basis of melodrama, its "simple dualisms of moral contrast."[15] Instead, his essay focused on its subversive potential in the hands of a relatively small number of American directors who employed the principle of "cinematic counterpoint."[16]

"A Mighty Drama of the Great Northwest," *When the Door Opened* (1925), a Fox film, featured Walter McGrail as Clive Grenfal who returns home to find his wife in the arms of Henry Morgan (Robert Cain). Grenfal fires his gun at Morgan and believing he has killed him, flees to the Canadian woods where he meets Teresa de Fontenac (Jacqueline Logan).

In the hands of these directors American melodrama film was able to work either for or against the "surface" content of the film as "stylistic means, i.e., the lower register of punctuation (parallel montage, cross cutting, visual repetition, musical accompaniment) serves to intensify the melodic line of the upper register (the story, the intrigue); … [or] the same techniques are used to construct a different line 'against the current,' which, if developed consistently, can constitute itself as a theme in it own right."[17] These films, he argued, exposed contradictions and inadequacies in mainstream American society in much the same way theatrical productions and novels functioned in the late eighteenth and nineteenth centuries. His essay emphasized the importance of color, set design, music, composition and performance. With directors such as Douglas Sirk, these elements coalesced into a "critique [of] the middle-class ideologies underpinning their narratives."[18] Although this was largely unintended by Elsaesser's essay, melodrama became synonymous with the "family melodrama" and the "woman's film."[19] Elsaesser's essay struck a chord with film scholars at a time when there was a focus on ideology and politics and the work of Bertolt Brecht.

An important corrective to this appeared in Steve Neale's exhaustive research of the Hollywood trade journals published in the period from 1938 to 1960. Neale focused on how the term melodrama was employed in the industry. He demonstrated that as far as the industry was concerned, melodrama was never used in reference to female centered narratives or films that focused on domesticity. In Hollywood during this period the terms "romantic melodrama" or "domestic melodrama" were rarely employed.[20] He points out: "As for popular or classical melodrama, its principal locations in Hollywood, as the trade press clearly recognized, were the adventure film, the thriller, the horror film, the war film, and the western."[21]

While not prepared to jettison the romantic/family orientated film as part of melodrama's corpus, Christine Gledhill and Linda Williams acknowledge that "feminist scholars ... defined melodrama too narrowly as part of women's culture under patriarchy, focusing in particular on the emotional, personal, and psychosexual problems of the Oedipal family."[22] Instead, Gledhill and Williams highlight the importance of Brooks's study and, in particular, his view of melodrama as a flexible aesthetic mode able to travel from stage to screen, from the nineteenth to twentieth and twenty-first centuries and across national cultures.[23] Instead of fixating on its perceived excess, both Gledhill and Williams emphasize melodrama's ability to generate a wide range of genres. Hence, Williams argues, we should be thinking of melodrama's "expansiveness, many facets and pervasiveness."[24]

Both Williams and Gledhill emphasize that the melodrama should be perceived as an aesthetic mode, not a singular genre. A "mode," according to this view, is defined by as a "general form of expressiveness using the drama of light and dark, staging, color, music, speech, intonation and, importantly, plot."[25] This view of melodrama as an expressive mode of aesthetic articulation that shapes the operation of many generic worlds,[26] rescued melodrama from the limitations imposed on it by scholars who extrapolated its supposedly subversive potential from Elsaesser's essay. As Gledhill and Williams point out:

> Through its neglect of interdisciplinary study, born of the need to establish cinema's own unique institutional status, film melodrama appeared to be a new discovery in the 1970s, detached from work already developing in theater studies. Narrowly defining in its Sirkian manifestation as a form of ironic ideological subversion, or as a late addition to the successive mapping of Hollywood's genres in only one generic form, the family melodrama of the late 1940s and 1950s, film studies missed the pervasive cross-generic *modality* of melodrama.[27]

Williams and Gledhill, in effect, restored Brooks's view of melodrama as the quintessential modern form, as a broad response to modernity, that developed from a specific historical juncture and was characterized by a repertoire of dramatic signs, visual aural, within a fictional system. As Williams notes, the ramifications of Brooks's study was not limited to the theater or literature as it is "the most important single work contributing to the rehabilitation of the term melodrama as a cultural form…. This appreciation is still the best grounding for an understanding of its carryover into twentieth-century mass culture."[28]

Brooks locates the development and consolidation of melodrama in French theatrical productions of the late eighteenth and early nineteenth century. The specific impetus was the collapse of the existing social order:

> The origins of melodrama can be accurately located within the context of the French Revolution and its aftermath. This is the epistemological moment which it illustrates and to which it contributes: the moment that symbolically, and really, marks the final liquidation of the traditional Sacred and its representative institutions (Church and Monarch), the shattering of the myth of Christendom, the dissolution of an organic and hierarchical cohesive society, and the invalidation of the literary forms—tragedy, comedy of manners—that depended on such a society. Melodrama does not simply represent a "fall" from tragedy, but a response to the loss of the tragic vision. It comes into being in a world where the traditional imperatives of truth and ethics have been violently thrown into question, yet where the promulgation of truth and ethics, their instauration as a way of life, is of immediate, daily, political concern.[29]

More recently Matthew Buckley challenged Brooks and his argument that the origin of melodrama took place in the French Revolution and its aftermath. He acknowledged that "the first appearance of theatrical melodrama as a nominate dramatic genre of the popular stage—of 'melodrama' in the specific modern sense of the term—occurred on the boulevard stage of Paris in the last years of the 1790s, and that the final development of this nominate genre was shaped and catalyzed by the events and context of the French Revolution and its aftermath."[30] Yet, he maintains, the advent of melodrama was the culmination of a long movement that goes as far back as the Reformation.[31] When melodrama emerged as a named form in Paris, in Guilbert de Pixérécourt's ("the father of melodrama") production of *Coelina*, Buckley agues it was a "cosmopolitan hybrid, composed entirely of parts, techniques, emphases, and aims already developed in earlier, pre–Revolutionary work produced all over Europe."[32]

While I am not disputing Buckley's thesis regarding the origin of melodrama's "revolutionary birth," what is more interesting from the point of view of this book are the formal characteristics of melodrama he lists in his criticism of Brooks and his "origin myth." To this end Buckley cites one of melodrama's key works, *Coelina*:

> Its [*Coelina*] formal character … is not new but conventional in the extreme. By the 1780s, in fact, every one of the ostensibly distinguishing elements of melodrama that this origin myth attributes to the Revolution's cataclysmic effects—from its emphasis on extreme emotion, its mixture of diverse dramatic genres and theatrical modes, and its sentimental and spectacular appeals to its polarized morality and heightened, often monopathic, dream-image version of character—were not merely transnational commonplaces but nearly normative assumptions, both well-established and well-mined by the rising tides of late eighteenth-century sentimental drama and opera, gothic literature and plays, and popular spectacular entertainment of many kinds.[33]

Buckley's description of melodrama's use of "extreme emotion," its monopathic presentation of character, its protean abilities to generate a diverse range of different genres and theatrical modes, with the ability to move from one medium to another, from sentimental drama and opera to gothic literature and popular spectacular entertainment of many kinds across different cultures, provides a useful summary of Brooks's view of melodrama, especially its spectacular "appeals to a polarized morality."

Brooks's thesis is that during the French Revolution a narrative paradigm developed based on a polarized view of a world threatened by the "suborners of morality"[34] who had to be confronted and eliminated. While for the greater part of the play evil dominates, virtue is ultimately triumphant after a relentless struggle. While this is the most common ending, it was not mandatory. More important than the triumph of virtue was presenting the world as morally legible, spelling out its "ethical forces and imperatives in large and bold characters."[35]

An important facet of its dramaturgy is its use of physical and emotional blockages. When these obstacles to desire are removed in the final moments of the drama, when virtue is liberated from those forces that have oppressed it, the effect on the audience is cathartic. Just like the characters in the drama, the audience experiences powerful emotions until, as Brooks points out, virtue is able to extricate itself from the "primal horror" and fulfill its desires.[36]

To the melodramatic imagination the world is subsumed by an underlying Manichaeism and the narrative strives to articulate those operative spiritual values that are both repressed and indicated by the surface of reality. In this context melodrama is both a heightened and polarized mode where its narrative voice is not content to merely describe and record gesture. Instead, it places pressure on this "surface reality" to yield its "true" meaning, "to give up to consciousness its full potentialities as an ethical 'parable.'"[37]

Linda Williams, in her study of racial melodrama *Playing the Race Card. Melodramas of Black and White from Uncle Tom to O.J. Simpson*, draws upon D.W. Griffith's 1920 film *Way Down East* and, to a lesser extent James Cameron's *Titanic* (1997), in an attempt to isolate, or point to, the "melodramatic qualities"[38] of these films. From this she isolates five characteristics "that can be applied to the melodramatic mode as a whole."[39]

(1) *Home: Melodrama begins, and wants to end, in a "space of innocence."*[40]
     This, as Williams acknowledges, emanates from Brooks's differentiation between tragedy and melodrama. Tragedy typically begins at a point of crisis leading to the fall while melodrama, at least in the period from 1800 to 1830, "typically opens with a presentation of virtue and innocence, or perhaps more accurately, virtue *as* innocence."[41] While virtue enjoys "a state of taking pleasure in itself, aided by those who recognize and support it,"[42] this pleasure is short-lived as "there swiftly supervenes a threat to virtue, a situation—and most often a person—to cast its very survival into question, obscure its identity, and elicit the process of its fight for recognition."[43]
     Brooks argues that certain "*topoi* belong to this structure," including the play's opening moments which are located in an enclosed setting, such as a garden, "a space of innocence," which is soon violated by the villain who insinuates himself under the guise of friendship or courtship. While the villain may be temporarily driven out, he will return triumphant as virtue has not yet had the chance to establish its moral identity.[44]

Toward the end of act 1 or in act 11, villainy emerges, leading to the fall, eclipse or even the expulsion of virtue.[45] Thereafter virtue must wander, and struggle, until it can establish its true ethical sign.[46]

(2) *Melodrama focuses on victim-heroes and on recognizing their virtue. Recognition of virtue orchestrates the moral legibility that is key to melodrama's function.*[47]

The function of melodrama is to locate, clarify and make public what Brooks calls the moral occult. The narrative must push toward it, the pressure of the prose must uncover it. However Brooks uses the terms moral occult and moral legibility as interchangeable. Instead, Williams points out that moral occult suggests a "Lacanian notion that melodrama resurrects a lost sacred."[48] Hence, she prefers the term moral legibility. Melodrama exists to recognize virtue. The recognition of virtue is important as it clarifies the moral issues at stake. To achieve this the drama is structured, at least in sensational melodrama, as a stark bipolar confrontation between persecuted innocence and evil. Other forms of melodrama, such as the 1929 film adaption of W. Somerset Maugham's *The Letter* as discussed in Chapter Three, as well as a number of examples of film noir in Chapter Four, are less clear cut. Nevertheless, at its essence melodrama does not just employ virtue as the source of its dramaturgy, it is, as Brooks argues, about virtue made visible and acknowledged. Hence melodrama is the drama of recognition.[49]

Matthew Buckley questions whether melodrama is a drama of morality. He argues that while Pixérécourt's work, for example, can be legitimately perceived as a "drama of morality, … that most of melodrama has laid at least a superficial claim to be moral, and that nearly all melodrama thereafter, insofar as it enlists that Pixérécourtian recipe's morally polarized character structures, shares a basic trajectory of moral crisis and redemption and appeals to a shared popular-collective moral imagination, has been moralistic."[50] This, he contends, emerges from a narrow view of melodrama's early history[51] and that by 1805 "the great wave of cape-and-sword plays, lurid gothic extravaganzas, and exotic/romantic adventure fantasies produced by Pixérécourt's imitators made it all to evident … that melodrama's engagement with morality can … be exploited, rendered ironic, or simply pushed into the background as a slight gesture in more sensational fare."[52] Buckley admits that melodrama has been, and can be, a drama of morality. But, he maintains, this is not fundamentally so. Morality in itself, he argues, does not necessarily distinguish melodrama from other dramatic forms. It can be a drama of sentiment, of sensation, of ethics, of horror as it is the "distillate" of an extreme and physical response.[53]

In his argument Buckley places "moral feeling" at one end of a spectrum and visceral shock at the other,[54] as if they are antithetical to each other. It is not clear, however, what Buckley means by "moral feeling." His initial focus is on Brooks's claim that the French Revolution destroyed the hierarchical framework based on the authority of the church and the king. This came about by the loss of the "traditional Scared." In the resulting vacuum, Brooks argues, melodrama arose to satisfy the need to recover and make clear the presence of ethical forces in the world. Buckley rejects this view and argues against the "myth of melodrama's moral foundation."[55] He goes further and discounts its primacy after the popularity of Pixérécourt's dramas and that by 1820 "morality could—and even did—become mere moralism or simple exploitation of moral feeling."[56] He argues that with melodrama's success as a "mass cultural form … the criterion of morality as a measure of artistic legitimacy declined and largely disappeared from view in critical debate, as in cultural valuation at large. What has replaced it, and what distinguishes melodrama, is rather the criterion of feeling and emotional effect—the demand that we be moved, not instructed."[57]

The importance of spectacle to melodrama, or at least sensational melodrama, is undeniable. Yet it is not an either/or situation. This was addressed in the Introduction but, to reiterate, "melodrama's recalibration of moral feelings … suggesting less discordance than convergence between spectacle and the 'interesting'—depends for the dramatic frisson of conflict on something being at stake. Excitement and suspense depend on our involvement at some level—of sensation, of empathy—in the contest between malevolent power and those struggling for survival or for justice."[58] In other words, spectacle, suspense and thrills, if they are to emotionally involve the audience, require a moral context and this becomes the convergence between spectacle and the 'interesting.'

The role of the victim in melodrama is more than just a narrative device. Their visible suffering is often proof of their virtue as victimization is to orchestrate the moral legibility crucial to the mode.[59] The success of virtue to assert itself is only a "secondary manifestation of the more important *recognition* of virtue in a world in which such recognition is not obvious."[60] As Brooks argues, the central function of melodrama is to assure us again and again that the universe is in fact morally legible, that it possesses an ethical identity and significance.[61] Of the five characteristics listed by Williams, this is the most important and will be discussed throughout the book, particularly with regard to film noir in Chapter Four.

(3) *Melodrama's recognition of virtue involves a dialectic of pathos and action—a give and take of "too late" and "in the nick of time."*[62]

(4) *Melodrama borrows from realism but realism serves the melodrama of pathos and action.*[63]

(5) *Melodrama presents characters who embody primary psychic roles organized in Manichaean conflicts between good and evil.*[64]

Often characters in melodrama do not possess any "interior depth." This is true of sensational melodrama where the dramatic emphasis is on the clash between characters who represent polar opposites placed at the "point of intersection of primal ethical forces."[65] However, this is not the only type of melodrama as will be discussed in Chapters Three and Four.

Melodrama, the "Genre-Generating Machine"

Melodrama is not a genre. It is an overarching dramatic mode that functions, as Christine Gledhill points out, as a genre-generating machine.[66] In Britain in the early nineteenth century melodrama demonstrated its generic hybridity by "drawing together gothic, sentimental, folk, and urban working-class traditions [which] helped consolidate a flexible melodramatic mode capable of generating and shaping a diversity of theatrical subgenres."[67] A myriad of sub-genres flourished in the United Kingdom including oriental, nautical, historical, domestic, romantic, cape-and-sword and temperance melodramas. In the United States a range of subgenres were imported from Europe along with nativist forms such as frontier, backwoods, western, civil war, and antislavery melodramas.[68] Yet, as argued in the Introduction, while melodrama involves a victim and oppressor, it does not determine the specific cultural attributes that constitute what it is to be a "victim" or an "oppressor." As Williams and Gledhill point out:

Constituting an expressive mode of aesthetic articulation that shapes the operation of generic worlds, melodrama does not determine the specificity of locale, character types, décor, or situation that characterizes specific film genres. In a concept we retain from Peter Brooks, the most central function of the mode of melodrama lies in its recognition of the personalized virtues and vices of characters whose actions have consequences for others. The contest between them is not played out according to fixed moral values; rather it enacts a struggle for a felt sense of justice that operates differently within different generic worlds. The point is that although conflict

The Deadly Ray Brought The Eagle Down!

PETE MORRISON AND LIGHTNING in "The Mystery of Lost Ranch"

The Mystery of the Lost Ranch, an 1925 independent production starring Pete Morrison. The film demonstrates melodrama's capacity as a "genre-generating machine" capable of producing a wide range of genres. This film is a mixture of western, science fiction and espionage as cowboy Morrison tries to keep a death ray out of the hands of foreign agents.

between perpetrator and victim is shared across genres, any *body* can fill these positions, and conflict can be played out in innumerable ways.[69]

The Aesthetics of Astonishment

The revelatory moment in melodrama, what Brooks calls the "aesthetics of astonishment,"[70] follows a prolonged period of suffering and struggle against a powerful obstacle. In nineteenth-century theatrical melodrama it usually occurred in the big sensation scene as discussed in the Introduction. For example, Guilbert de Pixerécourt's 1819 play *La Fille de l'exilé* (*The Exile's Daughter*) concerns Elizabeth, a sixteen-year-old Siberian girl, who undertakes a perilous journey from Siberia to Moscow to seek a pardon from the Czar for her exiled father. In Act 11 she shelters with a boatman, Ivan, the man responsible for her father's exile. When an attack from hostile Tartars threatens Ivan's life, Elizabeth rushes from the cabin, takes the cross given to her by her blind mother and holds it above Ivan's head, saying, "Wretches! Bow down before this revered sign, and do not forget that in this vast Empire any being placed under its protection is inviolable."[71] The Tartars, devastated by this holy sign of innocence, drop their weapons. Ivan, confirming Elizabeth's status as virtue, tells the Tartars that she is the devoted daughter of the man he once persecuted and who is traveling a great distance to intercede with the Czar on her father's behalf: "Ah! such generosity overwhelms me! I lack the words to express…. Elizabeth, all I can do is admire you and bow my head before you."[72] After calling on the Tartars to "render to virtue the homage that it merits,"[73] they fall on their knees in a semicircle around Elizabeth in a spectacular homage to virtue. This scene, Brooks argues, represents the core of melodrama's premises and design. Its function is to provide a "remarkable, public, spectacular homage to virtue, a demonstration of its power and effect."[74] Above all else, this "melodramatic moment of astonishment is a moment of ethical evidence and recognition."[75]

The sensation scene often involved a tableau which was performed at the end of a scene to intensify, and reinforce, the scene's moral basis. In the tableau the actors form a deliberate composition on stage and freeze, or hold, that composition for a moment to provide a visual summary of the emotional situation.[76] Sometimes the tableau would imitate a famous painting or, more likely, provide an exaggerated pose intended to heighten the emotional basis of the scene. In the tableau "more than any other single device of dramaturgy, we grasp melodrama's primordial concern to make its signs clear, unambiguous, and impressive."[77]

My Name Is Julia Ross (1945)/So Dark the Night (1946)

My Name Is Julia Ross, as the title indicates, shares the same raison d'être as Pixerécourt's *La Fille de l'exilé.* The film follows virtue's struggle to establish her identity. For much of the drama this is suppressed by evil. *My Name Is Julia Ross* was scripted by Muriel Roy Bolton from Anthony Gilbert's (the pseudonym for Lucy Malleson) novel *The Woman in Red.* Bolton made many changes, including the important one

Director Joseph Lewis's celebrated low budget gothic melodrama *My Name Is Julia Ross* (1945) starring Nina Foch as the innocent young woman striving to escape her sadistic captors played by George Macready and Dame May Whitty.

of deleting Malleson's series character, lawyer Arthur Crook, to focus solely on Julia Ross (Nina Foch). Julia is the epitome of innocence, desperately seeking employment in London after an appendectomy. Three weeks behind in her rent at Mrs. Mackie's (Doris Lloyd) boarding house, she suffers another setback after receiving a wedding invitation involving a young man, Dennis Bruce (Roland Varno), she had hoped to marry. Alone and without money, she reads the classified ads which takes her to the Allison Employment Agency. The manager at the agency, Mrs. Sparkes (Anita Bolster), invites Julia to apply for the job of private secretary to Mrs. Williamson Hughes (Dame May Whitty) and her son Ralph (George Macready) after ascertaining that Julia has no family in England ("I'm absolutely alone"). After interviewing Julia, Mrs. Hughes offers her the position. To indicate that something sinister is happening, they immediately close the Agency after Julia accepts the position.

When she returns to her boarding house, Dennis tells her that he is not getting married and asks Julia to go out with him. However, as she has accepted a live-in position this is impossible and she spends the night at the Hughes's Hendrique Square apartment in London. Here she is drugged, stripped of her clothes and taken to a remote house in Cornwall where her identity is destroyed. Ralph and his mother destroy Julia's clothes and belongings and as her papers are thrown into the fire, the camera picks up a photo of Julia slowly burning.

Working with cinematographer Burnett Guffey, director Joseph Lewis visually imprisons Julia whenever possible, within window frames, door frames crisscrossed by lattice work or vertical bars, steel gates or whatever physical object he can use to show her claustration. This staging is not just decorative as it conveys the central theme involving Julia's entrapment. Her violation is not only psychological but, the film implies, it is also sexual. Within the censorship prohibitions at that time there is sufficient information for the audience to speculate as to what actually took place after Julia was drugged at the Hendrique Square apartment. While Julia is sleeping a hand emerges from the left side of the frame to steal her bag and all of her clothes, the first attempt to erase her identity. During the night Ralph's aberrant sexual predilections emerge. He is shown sitting in the lounge room of the apartment cutting up Julia's underwear with his knife. When Julia wakes she is no longer in London but in remote Cornwall wearing a different nightgown with the letters "M H" (Marion Hughes) woven into the fabric. Soon after a nurse, Alice (Queenie Leonard), enters the room and addresses Julia as "Mrs. Hughes." When Julia becomes agitated the nurse calls for Ralph and his mother who deny Julia's true identity by calling her "Marion." After Julia demands an explanation, Mrs. Hughes explains that she is psychologically unwell. Ralph then grips Julia's arm tightly causing bruising as Mrs. Sparkes arrives and tells Julia that she is the housekeeper, not the manager of an employment agency. Julia now realizes she is a prisoner of this deranged family.

During her first night in Cornwall the camera pans down an illuminated bed at 12:02 a.m. to show her sleeping in a darkened room. Suddenly a hand appears to stop the clock. This movement causes her to wake up and as she peers into the darkness, hands, shown in shadow, move over her lower body to her breasts where they briefly pause before moving upwards to her throat and chin. Julia screams and tries to turn on the lights but they have been disabled. She then throws an ornament at an eye peering at her in the dark. This disturbance brings Mrs. Hughes and Ralph into her room. Julia, terrorized by this intrusion, asks: "Why did you bring me here? What are you planning to do with me? Are you trying to drive me crazy, is that it?" Lewis's low angle composition emphasizes Julia's vulnerability with Ralph and his mother looking down on her. The whole sequence embodies a sense of dread and violation. This feeling is reinforced when Ralph, in an agitated state, is shown cutting a piece of wood with his knife. He only calms down when his mother takes the knife out of his hand and places it in a drawer. The sexual implications of Ralph and his "knife" are obvious and the scene is repeated later in the film when Ralph describes how he murdered his wife. As he becomes increasingly excited, he begins to repeatedly stab the couch until his mother confiscates his knife.

The film's dominant theme, encapsulated in the title, is the recognition of virtue. Like the young heroine in *La Fille de l'exilé*, Julia is innocent, independent, resourceful and determined to regain her own identity. The narrative involves moral absolutes, characters without intrinsic depth. To intensify the bipolar nature of the drama, the film employs a system of moral signs. Just as the cross, the use of prayer, a lightning bolt and a grave marker, "all of which have a high emotional and ethical charge,"[78] are employed in *La Fille de l'exilé*, *My Name Is Julia Ross* utilizes a similar system of signs. This extends to the casting of young Nina Foch as Julia and George Macready as Ralph. Macready was often used by Columbia as psychologically unstable villains with sadistic tendencies (*Gilda*). Director Joseph Lewis's compositions often showing Julia trapped and the setting, a remote old manor with secret panels on a clifftop in Cornwall provides the film's gothic ambience. As Brooks points out with regard to Pixerécourt's play, while these signs have symbolic meaning the audience is not asked to ascertain any sense of moral complexity. As in theatrical melodrama, they appear simple and pure signifiers. What really matters is their interaction and clash. Their simplicity only serves to clarify and heighten the significance of the ethical struggle to the audience.[79]

For the greater part of the film evil reigns triumphant, controlling events while virtue is unable to "effectively articulate the cause of the right."[80] The dramatic blockage, or series of blockages, are intended to frustrate the audience until virtue is able to break through its helplessness, find its name and liberate itself from that which is persecuting it.[81] The more intense the audience feels this frustration, the greater the sense of catharsis when the blockage is removed and virtue is recognized. Julia makes four attempts to escape. In the first, she seizes a moment when the front door is open and runs down the driveway only to be stopped by the gatekeeper (Charles McNaughton), and a large gate. When the gatekeeper is not looking, Julia scribbles a note asking for help on a piece of newspaper and throws it onto the road. Later, when a car pulls up into the driveway, Julia eagerly opens the front door anticipating the arrival of the police. However, her hopes are dashed when the visitors turn out to be the Rev. Jonathan Lewis (Olaf Hytten) with two villagers, Mr. Robinson (Harry Hays Morgan) and Mrs. Robinson (Ottola Nesmith). Julia pleads with them: "Please listen to me. They are holding me here by force. I don't know why. You must call the police." After Mrs. Hughes reassures the visitors that her daughter-in-law is hysterical and suffering from a nervous breakdown, Julia, frustrated by her ability to convince them, screams: "Why doesn't somebody listen to me for once instead of believing her all of the time!"

Julia's second attempt to get away takes place when she secretly hides herself behind the Reverend Lewis as he leaves the property. However, Julia's attempt to open the car door alerts him to her presence and he takes her back to Ralph. Julia, in an attempt to find out why she has been kidnapped, changes her tactics and agrees to take a walk with Ralph through the grounds to a nearby cliff. Pretending that she is beginning to believe that she is Marion, and that she is psychologically disturbed, Julia's entrapment becomes, in effect, the "sensation scene" when the director suddenly changes the composition from a standard two-shot, as Ralph muses about the beauty of the sea, to a tight close-up of the upper portion of Julia's face that reveals only her nose and eyes looking over Ralph's shoulder. Ralph, with his back to the camera, blocks out most of the screen, allowing only a portion of Julia's face to be seen. This effectively heightens Ralph's domination of Julia as her (physical) identity is almost eradicated. The scene ends with Ralph kissing her. Later, he enters her room and physically attacks her and when she slaps him he tries to push her out of the window onto the rocks below. Only the sudden entry of Alice saves her life.

Julia's third attempt to escape involves an exchange of letters. When she insists on a visit to the village, her note to Dennis is discovered by Mrs. Hughes who substitutes a blank piece of paper. However, while traveling in the car with Alice and Ralph, Julia, anticipating that they will find her note, removes it and inserts another note to Dennis which she places in a letter box after arriving in the village. That night, after discovering a secret passage from her bedroom, Julia overhears Mrs. Hughes reassuring Ralph that Julia's murder will look like suicide. To preempt this Julia fakes her own suicide by suggesting that she has ingested poison, hoping that she can convince the local doctor of her sanity. Again, her escape attempt is thwarted as Mrs. Hughes sends her employee, Peters (Leonard Mudie), in place of the doctor. Julia, not realizing that Peters is not a doctor, alerts him to the letter she mailed to Dennis and Peters is sent to Mrs. Mackie's boarding house to retrieve it.

That night, as Julia waits for them to try to kill her, she blockades her door, pries open the bars on her window and screams. When Ralph and his mother rush into the room, hoping that Julia has jumped from the window, they see her nightgown on the rocks below. When the real village doctor, Dr. Keller (Evan Thomas), arrives at dawn, Mrs. Hughes tells him that regrettably Marion has committed suicide. She then sends Ralph ahead to check that Julia is actually dead. As he is about to bludgeon her with a rock, Dennis and a police officer arrive and save Julia in nick of time. Mrs. Hughes is arrested and Ralph is shot by the police trying to escape. Julia explains to Dennis that she feigned suicide and escaped through the secret passage from her room. As Dennis drives Julia back to London, he proposes and she accepts.

While *Variety* in its November 14, 1945, review of the film described it as a "mystery melodrama with a psychological twist" more recent commentators have questioned the film's "happy ending" by arguing that Julia has substituted one form of subjugation for another (marriage), as Marlisa Santos writes:

> The denouement of the film shows Dennis offering Julia another "job"—as his wife, encompassing the duties of "secretary, nurse, companion." The terms of her rescue involve another kind of captivity; though she is awakened, Sleeping Beauty–like with a male kiss, from the nightmare of this kidnapped existence, it is not to her restored independence. The reiteration of the film's title holds true, as Julia can reassert her own identity, but only for a time, as her salvation depends on her "new job" as Dennis's wife. Ironically, she will soon assume a new name and a new identity, although one presumably not at the hands of a violent psychopath.[82]

In assessing the cultural meaning of the epilogue it is important to place the film within its historical context, the final year of the Second World War when many couples were about to marry after years of separation due to the war. Marriage to many women in 1945 did not represent a "new job," "another kind of captivity," or, necessarily a loss of independence. Within the context of melodrama, and the function of the epilogue, Julia's "reward" at the end of the film is set up in the opening scenes in Mrs. Mackie's boarding house which shows her disappointment when she learns that Dennis is preparing to marry another woman. The epilogue is, in other words, motivated by the body of the film and is in keeping with the social norms in the immediate post-war years.

Director Joseph Lewis followed *My Name Is Julia Ross* with another low budget film, *So Dark the Night* (1946). *My Name Is Julia Ross* is a representative example of a sensational melodrama. *So Dark the Night* is not. The story involves a middle-aged man who falls in love with a much younger woman. Henri Cassin (Steven Geray), a celebrated, respected detective at the Paris Sûreté, is sent on vacation to the village of St. Margot by Dr. Manet (Jean Del Vali), the Sûreté's doctor. Arriving in the village, with his chauffeur-driven car, Cassin immediately attracts the attention of a young woman, Nanette Michaud (Micheline Cheireli). Nanette's interest in Cassin is mercenary along with the prospect of extricating herself from the provincial village. Nanette encourages Cassin's interest while simultaneously deflecting the jealousy of her fiancé, Leon Archard (Paul Marion), by telling him that Cassin is "an old man." Unconvinced, Leon tells Nanette "I know the way he looks at you, like a hungry dog begging for a favor, and you love it." She calms her fiancé down by stroking his lips although her distracted gaze suggests she is not going to relinquish Cassin. This is confirmed in a matching scene between Nanette and Cassin. After he proposes to her, a similar movement of her eyes exposes her lack of romantic interest in the middle-aged detective as he kisses her fingers.

Nanette's interest in Cassin is encouraged by her mother, Mama Michaud (Ann Codee), who is delighted by the prospect of a wealthy son-in-law. However, her husband, Pierre (Eugene Borden), is opposed to the union due to Cassin's advanced age. After Nanette agrees to marry Cassin, Pierre tells the detective that a man of his age is not meant for marriage. To emphasize the difference between the sexually potent Leon and the middle-aged detective, director Lewis places an overt phallic symbol, a very large bottle of champagne with a long neck, foregrounded in the center of the frame when Leon confronts Henri at the wedding ceremony in Pierre's inn. Nanette subsequently abandons Cassin and follows Leon from the inn. This importance of sexual potency to her decision is confirmed by Pierre when he says that it is not surprising that Nanette has not contacted her family since the aborted ceremony as "two people in love on their honeymoon don't take time for letter writing."

This only compounds Henri's humiliation. Thereafter, Lewis presents the detective as a divided man, most notably when he is filmed from outside the inn, showing him enclosed within a small window frame divided by a single piece of wood. In another scene identical lamps are shown in the foreground of Henri's desk, while a more explicit image occurs during the discovery of Mama Michaud's body. The detective appears in the back of the frame while steam from a boiling kettle dominates the foreground.

A few days after the failed wedding ceremony Nanette's body is found near the river and, tracing the evidence upstream, Leon's body is discovered on his farm. The local police invite Henri to investigate the murders. Mama Michaud is then found dead in her kitchen. Cassin, frustrated by his inability to find the killer, returns to Paris where an artist draws an image of the murderer based on the known clues. Cassin's friend, and superior, Commissaire Grande (Gregory Gay), jokingly suggests that the drawing looks like Cassin. When his shoe fits the footprint left near Leon's body, Henri realizes that he is the killer. After murdering his police guard, Cassin travels back to St. Margot where he is shot dead by his friend, Commissaire Grande, while attempting to kill Pierre.

The film's startling epilogue, as Myron Meisel points out, involved "framing, objects in the foreground, reprised bells on the sound track, deep focus, mirror images, and ratcheted light are orchestrated to the theme of realization."[83] This display of visual excess shows the detective fatally wounded on the floor of the village inn. As he peers through the window, the film reprises, in a reflection, Henri as he first appeared in the village—without a worry in the world. This tranquil image is suddenly replaced by his image as a disgraced serial killer. His duality is now visually obvious. His murderous side destroys the rational side by smashing its reflection in the glass window. The film concludes with Cassin's declaration: "Henri Cassin is no more. I caught him. I killed him." Glenn Erickson described the film as a "minor masterpiece," a "definite film noir for its dark mood and stress on psychological chaos. *So Dark the Night* is a bold departure from the Hollywood norm."[84] And a bold departure from Hollywood's conventional presentation of melodrama. Instead of virtue confronting evil in the form of two separate people, as shown in *My Name Is Julia Ross, So Dark the Night* assimilates them into one person, Henri Cassin.

Sensational Melodrama

The Silent Film Serial: "The Serial-Queens"

Steve Neale argues that the singing Western is the purest form of classical (sensational) melodrama. However, there is a strong case for the film serial, especially the silent film serial. All film serials were sensational melodramas and while they consisted of a wide range of sub-genres, such as the western, detective, science fiction, gothic, war, propaganda, pirate, circus, jungle, aviation and working-girl melodramas, all involved spectacular action in the form of chases, fights, abductions, entrapments, last minute rescues and retribution. They replicated all of the attributes Brooks ascribed to melodrama. It was a world of moral Manichaeism involving a bipolar clash between good and evil. Or what Ben Singer describes as "narratively stark conflicts between a heroine, or hero-heroine team and a villain and his criminal accomplices."[85]

In his book *Melodrama and Modernity: Early Sensational Cinema and Its Contexts* Singer describes the silent film serial as "early sensational or blood-and-thunder melodrama."[86] His examples are drawn from serials starring serial queens such as Pearl White, Helen Holmes and Ruth Roland. He describes these serials as the "melodrama of spectacular diegetic realism."[87] His interest is in examining late nineteenth-century theatrical melodrama and early twentieth-century film melodrama within the context of the cultural changes brought about by modernity. They took the form of "codified modes of histrionic 'overacting' that further accentuated the quality of excess."[88] This, he argues, activated "various kinds of excess in the spectator's visceral response."[89] Hate and a desire for retribution, for example, were intrinsic to the mode:

> Classical melodrama, particularly on stage, gave the audience the cathartic pleasure of the very purest, unequivocal kind of hatred, repulsion, or disdain for the villain. Melodrama was designed to arouse, and morally validate, a kind of primal bloodlust, in the sense that the villain is so despicable, hated so intensely, that there was no more urgent gratification than to see him extinguished.[90]

Singer's study is useful in establishing the key attributes of sensational melodrama while providing a social context for its emergence at this particular point in history. They dramatized situations of extreme moral injustice that invoked feelings of distress and outrage.[91] But, as E. Deidre Pribram points out, dramas of injustice cannot be solely visceral "because they rely on social norms, expectations, beliefs, and traditions sustained through communally exercised behavior and practices. Recognition of justice and injustice depends on various complex forms of acculteration, a process that combines social notions of morality and emotionality—how we ought to feel about and respond to events, for example—with outrage at acts of injustice. This is to say, our recognition of and reactions to depictions of morality and immorality are locked in narratives of emotion."[92] Such emotions, Pribram argues, are "socially induced or socially charged emotional states"[93] that are not displaced into privatized or personalized concerns.[94]

Singer argues that there was an association

The Flame Fighter (1925), a ten-chapter serial produced by Rayart starring Herbert Rawlinson as a fire fighter who battles a crooked city government.

between the environment of urban modernity and the sudden emergence of sensational amusements.[95] There is no question, he claims, that popular amusements in the 1890s underwent a profound shift towards sensationalism. This involved the intensification of the spectacle in both stage melodrama and vaudeville along with new attraction such as amusement parks, daredevil displays and, eventually, the cinema. All, Singer argues, were designed to provoke a powerful sensory stimulation.[96] This resulted, according to Singer, in significant changes in modes of perception.

This included popular amusements in the late nineteenth century, such as the Coney Island amusement complex which opened in 1895, along with other parks that specialized in "exotic sights, disaster spectacles, running electric illumination and thrilling mechanical rides."[97] Vaudeville, he points out, also emerged as a major source of popular amusement in the 1890s and it was a medium that "encapsulated the new trend toward brief, forceful, and sensually 'busy' attractions, with its eclectic series stunts, slapstick, song-and-dance routines, trained dogs, female wrestlers, and the like."[98]

At the same time there was a shift in theatrical melodrama away from melodramas that "highlighted the pathos and moralizing oratory of innocent victims and their brawny champions"[99] to a more dramatically visceral mode that "emphasized violent action, stunts, exciting spectacles of catastrophe and physical peril based on elaborate mechanical stagecraft."[100] To this end he cites a New York critic who described melodrama in 1903 as a "series of adventures calculated to give anyone except a hardened boy the echoes of delirium tremens."[101]

Singer's thesis is that this late nineteenth-century shift in melodrama was "the product of modernity"[102] and audience support for this change was "derived in part from its [melodrama] capacity to capture the sense of upheaval and vulnerability experienced by the masses in a world of unprecedented cultural discontinuity and social atomization."[103] The functions of the mode were two-fold. To express specific cultural anxieties while also serving an ameliorative function by providing "reassurance of ultimate divine protection and fortifying faith in simple, immutable moral verities."[104] The emphasis was not on characterization, character development or complex plotting—it was on action and spectacle, thrills and narrative pacing. It was thrill upon thrill as Archibald Haddon observed in 1905 when he noted that a "startling change has come over the tone and spirit of melodrama."[105] This perception was reinforced by a 1905 newspaper review of *The Queen of the White Slaves*:

> Those who like sensation piled upon sensation with no let-up from the very beginning until the very end will find [this melodrama] admirably suited to their taste. It is a play of thrilling and sensational incidents, events and climaxes … with little extraneous matter…. Each [scene] ends with a thrilling rescue, or timely foiling of villainy, or some other episode that meets with the entire approval of the audience.[106]

Known as the "10–20–30" melodrama, a name reflecting the prices charged by theaters specializing in this type of melodrama, sensational theatrical productions declined following the rise of the nickelodeon in 1907 and 1908. By 1910 only smaller theaters, with cheaper productions, survived in the large cities such as New York and the number of touring theatrical companies declined from 420 in 1904 to 236 in 1910, 95 in 1915 and 25 in 1918.[107] Melodrama, where it did exist in the theater, transformed itself from expensive spectacular productions to the less costly, drawing room melodramas designed for middle class audiences that, as yet, had not abandoned the theater for the movies.[108]

Melodrama underwent a reasonably seamless shift from one medium, the stage, to another, the cinema. As the prolific theatrical producer Lincoln J. Carter remarked after the movies had ended his career: "The heroine and the hero and all the scenic effects of the melodrama have simply moved over into the films. That's all."[109] While part of the reason for this shift was economic, as most movies cost only five cents compared to 25 to 75 cents for theatrical productions,[110] another major reason was the ability of the cinema to economically, and more efficiently, emulate the action, suspense and sensation scenes that made the stage melodrama so popular. As Ben Singer points out, whatever the stylistic and structural differences between theatrical melo-drama and film melodrama, the latter captured the essence of sensational melodrama by delivering continuous action, violence, spectacle, suspense and a sense of physical peril. At the narrative level film melodramas relied on clear-cut characters, either good or bad, along with a frequent use of coincidence and sudden revelations.[111]

The silent film serial enjoyed great success at the box office in the period from 1914 to the early 1920s. Critics, however, despised the form. This provoked a response from the prolific and highly successful Pathé serial producer and director George Seitz, who directed most of Pearl White's box office successes. In a 1916 article titled "The Serial Speaks" he sarcastically cried out: "I am the serial. I am the black sheep of the picture family and the reviled of critics. I am the soulless one with no moral, no character, no uplift. I am ashamed…. Ah me, if only I could be respectable. If only the hair of the great critic would rise whenever I pass by and if only he would not cry, 'Shame! Child of commerce! Bastard of art!'"[112]

Ellis Oberholtzer, Pennsylvania's chief censor during this period, was a hostile critic of the serial and he described them as consisting of "crime, violence, blood-and-thunder, and always obtruding and outstanding is the idea of sex."[113] Overall, he considered them "dangerous rabble trash."[114] However, in the period from 1914 to 1920 they appealed not just to a working-class audience but a broad audience and, for a time, grossed more at the box-office than feature films. In 1916, after the release of *Pearl and the Army,* its star Pearl White, was voted most popular actress in a poll conducted by the *Motion Picture Magazine.* When a rival studio, Mutual, claimed that its serial queen Helen Hughes was a bigger star, Pearl's studio, Pathé, retaliated by pointing out that four serials starring Pearl White grossed a total of $24,570,000 in ticket sales between 1916 and 1918.[115]

While sensational melodrama was just one genre among many in regular short subjects and feature films, with serials, as Singer points out, it was virtually the *only* genre.[116] Sensational melodrama became the over-arching mode that embraced a large range of sub-genres, such as the detective, western, gothic, railway, espionage and many other types of serials. All are characterized by clearly defined characters, physical conflict, exhilarating action scenes, and last-minute rescues.[117] All adhere to a strict polarization of the drama on moral grounds.

In the United States, where serialized stories attracted an enormous following, there was a long history of magazine and newspaper serials and the relationship between the newspaper/magazine serial and the film serial was closely intertwined from the beginning. Literary models, as Ben Singer argues, "exerted a tremendous influence on the film industry because popular fiction constituted the dominant entertainment medium throughout the decades surrounding the turn of the century."[118] In 1915, for example, when the population in the United States was less than two-fifths the size of today's population, there were at least 57 national magazines and syndicated Sunday newspaper supplements that featured serials and short stories.[119]

The first film serial, *What Happened to Mary,* released on July 26, 1912, emanated from a meeting between Charles Dwyer, the editor of *The Ladies' World*, and the general manager of Thomas Edison's Kinetoscope Company, Horace G. Plympton, in the summer of 1912. Both Dwyer and Plympton were interested in the cross-promotional possibilities of a film/magazine tie-in and *The Ladies' World* exploited the commercial possibilities of the serial by publishing stills from the film. The first chapter, "The Escape from Bondage," begins when a baby girl (Mary) is left in a basket on the doorstep of small-town shopkeeper Billy Peart. Accompanying the baby is $500 and a note promising one thousand more if the shopkeeper looks after the girl and finds a husband for her. Eighteen years later Peart, determined to collect the extra thousand dollars, tries to marry Mary to a friend. However, Mary, learning of Peart's intentions, takes $100 and leaves her small town for the big city. The first episode in the magazine concludes with the questions: "How long would the hundred dollars last? What would she do when it was gone?"

To promote interest in the serial *The Ladies' World* notified readers that something would happen in the next episode to Mary as she walks toward the local railway station. The magazine also offered $100 to the reader who guessed correctly as to the nature of this event and the prize was won by Lucy Proctor of Armstrong, California, when she guessed that when Peart and Wintergreen trapped Mary at the station, a mysterious young man would rescue her in his rig. Mary's subsequent adventures take her to dangerous and exotic locations such as Broadway, Wall Street and London as she tries to avoid the evil machinations of her greedy uncle, Richard Craig and sundry villains.

All episodes in the twelve-chapter serial were self-contained, except episode 9 ("A Way of the Underworld,") which was unresolved, prompting a critic to complain that the serial was not only very "melodramatic," "lurid" but also "incomplete, leaving the action hanging in the air."[120] The absence of a traditional cliffhanger, which was still some years away as a regular feature, was offset by the continuing basis of the story involving the same characters. The commercial success of this serial encouraged the production of *Who Will Marry Mary*, a six-chapter sequel in 1913, followed in December 1913 by an even greater success, *The Adventures of Kathlyn*, a joint production between the Selig Polyscope Company and the *Chicago Tribune*. The *Chicago Tribune*, which was facing increasing competition from other newspapers, paid Selig $12,000 for the rights to publish a literary version of the serial which was then syndicated and published in the *Los Angeles Times*, and other papers, throughout the first half of 1914.

The financial success of *What Happened to Mary* and *The Adventures of Kathlyn* prepared the way for *The Perils of Pauline*, an influential serial that grossed nearly a million dollars following its release in 1914. Its financial, cultural and institutional ramifications were immeasurable and confirmed the commercial possibilities of the film serial. It also intensified the cycle of serial queen melodramas and represented a structural bridge between the narratively complete chapters (in most episodes) in *What Happened to Mary* (1912) to the incomplete chapter endings in *The Adventures of Kathlyn* (1914) and the cliffhanger endings in (some episodes) in *The Perils of Pauline*. It also consolidated the literary tie-in practice that began with *What Happened to Mary*. Above all else, its narrative premise, a young woman who refuses to marry her handsome, wealthy boyfriend until she experiences a year of freedom and liberation from domesticity, was a significant ideological statement in 1914.

The Perils of Pauline was produced by the French studio Pathé and the company, eager to distribute its European and American films in the United States, formed a subsidiary, Cosmopolitan Films, which was renamed the Eclectic Film Company. Following the success of *What Happened to Mary* and *The Adventures of Kathlyn,* Pathé formed a partnership with the newspaper empire magnate William Randolph Hearst to produce *The Perils of Pauline,* starring Pearl White. As a result of this collaboration, prose versions of the serial appeared in the Hearst papers each Sunday followed each fortnight by the film version.

Hearst editor Morrill Goddard selected his brother Charles Goddard, a playwright, to devise a 500-word synopsis. George B. Seitz, a major screenwriter at Pathé, transformed this synopsis into a film script. The simple premise of Goddard's story

Pearl White in her breakthrough role as the young heiress Pauline Marvin who undertakes a year of adventure, danger and domestic freedom in the twenty chapter serial *The Perils of Pauline* which grossed nearly a million dollars after its release in 1914.

begins with the death of a millionaire who leaves 50 percent of his fortune to his ward, Pauline Marvin (Pearl White). Pauline, however, cannot claim the inheritance until she turns 21. If she dies before reaching 21, the inheritance transfers to the millionaire's secretary, Raymond Owen (Paul Panzer). Although the millionaire's son Harry (Crane Wilbur) loves Pauline and wants to marry her, Pauline insists on a year of adventure and freedom.

This set-up sustains the story through 20 chapters. Owen, wanting the inheritance money, encourages Pauline to participate in one dangerous event after another—including car racing, airplane racing, submarine exploration, balloon flights and jockeying a race horse. In most chapters he hires assorted men to abduct, sabotage and try to murder the heiress. Each time Pauline survives due to a combination of luck, her athletic skills and Harry's dogged tenacity to save her. She is kidnapped by Sioux Indians and treated as their long-lost white goddess, imperiled by pirates, threatened by gangsters and attacked by gypsies. She is left to die in caves, burning houses, flooded cellars and, in the final episode, a makeshift pontoon that is the designated target for the guns on a naval destroyer. Each episode exploits Pauline's fascination with speed—racing cars, planes, trains, a hot air balloon and a fast-moving yacht.

The serial attracted a new clientele to the cinema, primarily middle-class patrons motivated by the prose tie-in with the Hearst newspapers. Pathé claimed that 20 million people a week read the serialization of *The Perils of Pauline* and this practice continued when the *Chicago Tribune* negotiated with Universal for the serial *Lucille Love, Girl of Mystery* (1914). *The Perils of Pauline* also marked a profound shift in film marketing. Prior to the film serial, exhibitors and producers were reluctant to spend large amounts of money on advertising as most theaters changed their programs up to five times a week. Serials, with their long play dates consisting of 15 to 20 weekly or fortnightly chapters, made film marketing more attractive. Pathé claimed that they used 52 billboards to promote *The Perils of Pauline* in New York City alone.[121]

The success of *The Perils of Pauline* intensified the cycle of serial queen melodramas. These films featured energetic, athletic heroines who often usurped the film domain, the action melodrama, of male protagonists. While these films functioned as utopian fantasies based on female freedom and empowerment, each serial coupled this desire with scenes showing subjugation and violation.[122] This pattern is clear in *The Perils of Pauline* and while each chapter begins with Pauline eagerly embracing her next adventure, helplessness, due to Owen's machinations, often follows. This results in a cyclical pattern of freedom, entrapment, victimization and, ultimately, liberation. Significantly, however, pathos and domesticity virtually play no part in the serial.

Pearl White continued her phenomenal run of commercially successful serials after *The Perils of Pauline* with the even more successful "Elaine" series: *The Exploits of Elaine* (1914), *The New Exploits of Elaine* (1915) and *The Romance of Elaine* (1915). Renamed *Les Mystéres de New York,* the Elaine series did very well in Europe. She followed with *The Iron Claw* (1916), *Pearl of the Army* (1916), *The Fatal Ring* (1917), *The House of Hate* (1918), *The Lightning Raider* (1919) and *The Black Secret* (1919). After the release of *Pearl of the Army* in 1916, Pearl was voted most popular film actress in a poll conducted by the magazine *Motion Picture.* As late as 1917 serials were often billed as "feature attractions" as they formed the centerpiece of cinemas screening a mixture of short films and "variety" attractions.[123]

The House of Hate, one of Pearl White's most popular serials, is a representative example of sensational melodrama. In terms of the box office *The House of Hate* easily surpassed revenues from feature films of this period, including D.W. Griffith's *The Birth of a Nation* (1915) and *Intolerance: Love's Struggle Throughout the Ages* (1916). A report prepared by Pathé in March 1918, a few weeks after the March 10 national release of the serial, claimed it attracted the most advanced bookings of any Pathé serial up to that time.[124] This included a record number of screens in New York City, including first-run theaters such as the Grand Opera House on Twenty-Third Street and Eighth Avenue in Manhattan. Famed Russian director and film theorist Sergei Mikhailovich Eisenstein also cited *The House of Hate* as an important influence on his career.

Even though not all chapters of *The House of Hate* are available today, it encapsulates key features of the mode while showcasing Pearl White's appeal to the public. Not only does she excel in the action sequences by demonstrating her athleticism (and courage), the serial gives her ample opportunity to demonstrate her acting ability. To gather information about her nemesis, she sheds her virginal innocence and assumes the guise of a "good-time girl." On another occasion, a sub-plot provides an opportunity to play a woman, Jenny Acton, awaiting execution on death row. This facilitates a suspenseful cliffhanger. After Jenny's father arranges the kidnapping of Pearl, who looks like Acton, so as to substitute her for his daughter, the chapter ends with Pearl seemingly executed. However, an inventive take-out explains that Jenny's last-minute change of mind allowed Pearl to escape. It is also reminds us of how important emotion, often generated by action and spectacle, the "synergy between visceral practices of shock, surprise and mayhem,"[125] is in the sensational melodrama. And how unimportant narrative causality, the causal logic of narrative, is. It is the

Pearl White's final film which was filmed in Paris where she was living. The French title was *Terreur* and it was released in the United States as *Perils of Paris* (1924).

protagonist's emotions, not the narrative logic, that drive the serial. This is evident in the perfunctory resolution to the serial. After pointing the finger of guilt at a number of relatives throughout the serial, the plot suddenly introduces a new character, an insane brother, as the Hooded Terror. This is "explained" by a long flashback showing him smuggled him into Waldon Castle to eliminate Pearl so that the villain could take control of the factory.

It would be reasonably safe to conclude that audiences flocked to the silent serial for reasons other than innovative storylines or complex characters. The basic narrative structure did not change. The hero and/or heroine is threatened/opposed by a powerful villain as both are in pursuit of the "weenie," the narrative device described by Pearl White as the essence of the film serial.[126] It is the coveted object in the narrative and it could take many forms—a formula, invention, map, inheritance, mineral mine, oil deposit and so on. All of the essential plot ingredients were introduced in the first chapter, including the "weenie." The heroine was immediately plunged into danger which generally ended in a cliffhanger to close the chapter. This structure, which Singer described as possessing the simplicity and reliability of a "two stroke engine, the back-and-forth movement of virtue and villainy."[127] While retaining the overarching battle between good and evil, serial plots, which had to extend over many weeks, became more and more convoluted. This was largely the result of the frantic need to have sufficient chapters to meet the obligations to exhibitors. This, along with the serial's relatively low budget, created narrative inconsistencies and a heavy reliance on coincidence. This mattered little to an audience who were primarily interested in thrills and spectacle, not narrative continuity.

Melodrama, in the form of the silent serial, provided an aesthetic mode to express profound shifts in social attitudes in the early years of the twentieth century. The audience, as Singer notes, recognized the serial queen as a familiar and conventional melodramatic character from both literature and the theater. Yet the serial queen melodramas were able to embody changing cultural values, notably the cultural construction of womanhood, that accompanied shifts in industrial capitalism and the urban consumer economy. As a consequence, the serial queen's sphere of experience was not constricted to the protective boundaries of domesticity.[128]

Melodrama and Propaganda: William Randolph Hearst and Patria (1917)

Melodrama is not inherently socially progressive. It can be. And it can be reactionary, even Fascist. It is not tied to any specific political system and its goal, poetic justice, is culturally determined. Propaganda, with its need to elicit strong emotional feelings through a bipolar presentation, is ideally suited to melodrama. Steve Neale in his article on "Propaganda"[129] compares two German films produced during the Nazi period, *Der ewige Jude* (1940), an anti–Semitic documentary, and *Jud Süss* (1940), an historical melodrama. Although both films share an anti–Semitic position with regard to race, Neale argues that if these films are considered solely by their textual systems, only the documentary can be considered "propaganda" film. This is because in *Jud Süss* "the anti-semitic component of Nazi ideology is inscribed within the text in a similar manner to the inscription of Populism within Hollywood texts [in the 1930s]."[130] This is due to the fact that "in *Jud Süss,* anti-semitism is inscribed as the specificity of meaning produced within the mechanisms of the classical text."[131] In other words, this film is not a propaganda text as the discourse is "contained" by the textual system. As a "classical realist text," there are "definite procedures for marking closure *as* closure, for demarcating a definite space and distance between the text and the discourses and practices around it."[132] In other words, an audience would read *Jud Süss* differently than *Der ewige Jude* as its message is enveloped within a form designated as "fictional." *Der ewige Jude*, with a different mode of textual address, can be perceived as a propaganda text. For example, it includes a third-person omniscient commentator throughout the film who ends his narration with the final exhortation: "Keep our race pure. Racial purity for ever." This "exhortation aligns the subject as in a position of struggle vis-a-vis certain of the discourses and practices that have been signified within it, and signified in such a way as to mark them as existing outside and beyond it. It is this position that I would maintain as the fundamental mark of a propagandist text."[133]

It is not, however, as simple as this, as Neale acknowledges. Both films serve a propagandist function when considered within the context of their production. The fact that both films were supervised by Nazi filmmakers under instructions from the Propaganda Ministry is important. *Jud Süss* was supervised by Joseph Goebbels[134] and screened to specially selected audiences.[135] *Der ewige Jude* was "produced by the Party and distributed and exhibited within the Party apparatus [and] also shown in public cinemas."[136] The production of both films, along with *Die Rothschilds* (1940), were produced, according to David Stewart Hull, within the context "of the planned 'Final Solution of the Jewish Problem.'"[137] Thus, although the textual properties of *Jud Süss* are not necessarily those of a propaganda text, when considered within the context of their function in a specific historical context it becomes a propagandist text.[138] And melodrama was the mode selected to execute the aims of Goebbels and his Propaganda Ministry.

The same applies to William Randolph Hearst's 1917 bizarre serial, *Patria*. This serial was designed to exploit the fear of the "Yellow Peril," specifically the Japanese, to further Hearst's political interests. It was conceived in the summer of 1916 by Hearst as a propaganda film, or what was described as a "preparedness" film, to shift attention away from Germany and the Central Powers and focus on Japan. This aim was also shared by the German Government. The real threat to the United States, in Hearst's view, was not Germany but an alliance between Japan and Mexico. He also opposed President Wilson's foreign policy, especially any suggestion that America should enter World War I on the side of Britain and its allies. After the war *Patria* was investigated by a Senate Committee on the grounds that it propagated German propaganda in its attempt to discredit Japan.

The genesis of the serial came from a story by crime author, and the creator of *The Lone Wolf* (1914), Louis Joseph Vance. Prior to *Patria*, Vance authored *The Trey O'Hearts* which was released as a serial in 1914 with Cleo Madison in dual roles and George Larkin as the upper-class hero George Law. Vance subsequently wrote a novel-length story which he titled *Patria—The Last of the Fighting Channings*. The story was serialized in the Hearst newspapers and the celebrated ballroom dancer Irene Castle was selected to play wealthy heiress, and super patriot, Patria. Castle accepted a contract from Hearst for 20 weeks at $1500 per week after her husband (and dancing partner) left the United States to enlist as a pilot in the Royal Flying Corps.

Charles Goddard, a Broadway playwright who scripted the serials *The Perils of Pauline* and *The Exploits of Elaine*, and J.B. Clymer transformed Vance's story into a script. Production began in mid–1916 under the direction of Leopold and Theodore Wharton who filmed the first 10 chapters at their Ithaca Studio in New York with location shooting at Fort Lee and Buffalo. However, the relationship between the Whartons and Hearst deteriorated and the final five chapters were filmed in California with Jacques Jaccard as director and Vance overseeing production.

Although only stills remain to detail the events in chapter one, most of chapters two, three, four and ten survive and are now lodged in the New York's Museum of Modern Art. Chapter one begins in Newport where Patria Channing meets Captain Donald Parr (Milton Sills) who is investigating the espionage activities of Baron Huroki (Warner Oland), the chief of Japan's military intelligence, and a Mexican agent, Juan de Lima (George Majeroni). In order to carry out their joint invasion of the United States, Huroki and de Lima require munitions from the Channing factories. Their request, however, is denied.

In Chapter two Patria learns that a patriotic ancestor secreted millions of dollars in gold in a concealed cellar under the family mansion to fund, when needed, a local militia. As Huroki also covets the gold, the chapter focuses on the battle for its possession and this provides one of the best sequences in the serial. After Patria discovers that the gold has been removed from the cellar, she is captured and tied to a chair. To destroy evidence of the theft, one of Huroki's agents lights a fuse to a bundle of dynamite. Left alone, Patria strains against the ropes and manages to free an arm which allows her to retrieve a gun from her pocket. Then, just as the flame is about to ignite the dynamite, Patria fires a single shot severing the burning fuse.

While chapter three continues the battle for the gold, chapter four takes the serial into another direction which provides a pretext to exploit Castle's talent as a dancer. In this chapter she appears in dual roles, Elaine, a dancer in a New York nightclub, and Patria. This provides Huroki with another opportunity to attack the heiress.[139] Chapter 10 is the most revealing episode in terms of Hearst's intentions as Huroki organizes an alliance of Japanese and Mexican forces for an attack on the Channing plant. Hearst's combination of jingoism and paranoia is evident in this sequence which begins with the workers leaving the Channing munitions plant in their normal clothes. These images dissolve to show the same men in their militia uniforms marching through the gates. It also shows Patria waving a giant American flag after inspecting her militia, a theme in accord with Heart's view that capitalism was a positive force through its ability to shape the working class into disciplined fighting units.

Production on the serial continued from July 1916 to April 1917 and in November 1916 Hearst, who invested more than $90,000, was becoming agitated about the costs and demanded financial returns from the serial. He ordered prints of the first three chapters followed by previews and heavy promotion in his media companies. *Patria* went into general release on January 14, 1917, while the remaining five chapters were being filmed in California. External events, however, intervened as the serial became the subject of intense interest from both the Japanese Government and the Woodrow Wilson Administration.

On January 16, 1917, Arthur Zimmermann, the Foreign Secretary of the German Government, sent a coded telegram to Heinrich von Eckardt, the German ambassador in Mexico. The telegram instructed Eckardt to begin negotiations with the Mexican Government for an alliance with Germany if the United States continued its move towards entry into World War I. Mexico was also urged to assist Germany in forming an alliance with Japan. Germany, in turn, would help Mexico regain areas in Texas, New Mexico and Arizona. However, British code breakers intercepted the Zimmermann telegram and it was shown to Edward Bell, secretary of the United States embassy in Great Britain, on February 24, 1917. When news of the telegram reached the media some papers, including the Hearst press, claimed the telegram was a forgery devised by the British Government. However, on March 3 Zimmerman confirmed that the telegram was authentic. This communication, combined with other factors, such as Germany breaking its pledge not to resume unrestricted submarine warfare, resulted in the United States Congress declaring war on Germany and its allies on April 6, 1917.

When President Wilson viewed portions of the serial he was disturbed by its anti–Japanese perspective. He wrote to Pathé on June 4 asking the company to withdraw it from circulation. However, as the content was controlled by Hearst, there was little Pathé could do. As a minor concession in August 1917 shots showing the Japanese and Mexican flags were removed and some of the title cards were changed. Baron Huroki, for example, became Señor Manuel Morales. However, this alteration was purely cosmetic as Huroki frequently wears a kimono and the serial retained sufficient Japanese iconography to indicate the nationality of the villains.[140] Although the Japanese Embassy in Washington objected to the revised version when it was screened in October, there were no further changes and by this time it had completed its run at most of the major theaters in the United States.

Although *Patria* was the last serial that Hearst would involve himself in it proved to be a financial success, despite misgivings from the *New York Telegraph*'s film critic who complained that the serial was "frankly anti–Mexican and anti–Japanese in line with William Randolph Hearst's policies."[141] A fear of the Yellow Peril was a constant theme in Hearst publications. This began in 1907 when he published an article titled "The Yellow Peril is Here." This theme intensified in the early years of the First World War and continued in the post war years and *Time* magazine noted in its September 11, 1933, issue that the "Yellow Peril has for 30 years been a great circulation-getter for the Hearst papers." Yet the fear of the Yellow Peril was not restricted to the United States. It was also pervasive in many European counties, including Great Britain.

Sax Rohmer, Fu Manchu and Sensational Melodrama

Sax Rohmer's creation Fu Manchu appeared at the same time as the first serial. The next section is a short case study of Rohmer's fiction and the Hollywood adaptations of his novels in the 1930s. Why? Two reasons. Rohmer was an extremely skilled practitioner of sensational melodrama and this should be acknowledged. Secondly, his fiction provides a stark example of melodrama's facility in assimilating the prevailing values of a period, values that are not shared by most people today. For the best part of 30 years, until the late 1930s, his novels regularly appeared on best seller lists. Today, his legacy is more problematic, as the editors of a recent collection of essays dedicated to him point out: "he is largely remembered as a disgraceful instance of racism."[142] His reputation and sales began to diminish after the Second World War and by 1972 editor, author and critic Julian Symons concluded:

> The Fu Manchu stories are absolute rubbish, penny dreadfuls in hard covers, interesting chiefly in the way they reflect popular feelings about the "Yellow Peril" which in these books, as a character remarks, is "incarnate in one man." The stories proceed with practically no regard for possibility, and several of the books include scenes in which Smith and his friend Petrie face some kind of torture.[143]

Even Christopher Frayling, in his study of Fu Manchu within the context of the rise of Chinaphobia,[144] is careful to distance himself from Rohmer's references to the "Yellow Peril" and treat his fiction as a kind of (juvenile) guilty pleasure.[145] Similarly, in *Lord of Strange Deaths,* a recent collection of essays on various aspects of Rohmer's fiction, the editors appear to hold his work in low regard while simultaneously expressing a fascination with Rohmer's ability to inject "juice" into his stories with comments such as this: "juice makes up for bad style and general ridiculousness."[146] This response, like many others, was eager to evaluate Rohmer's fiction in an entirely different historical and ideological context than the period when Rohmer was writing his stories. Because Rohmer is an Edwardian author, with Edwardian values, it is easier to discern both melodrama's system of aesthetic articulation and its cultural function. We can more easily perceive what Christine Gledhill describes as the "convergence between spectacle and the 'interesting,'"[147] where the "interesting" is located in the everyday and the spectacle is its mode of aesthetic articulation (sensational melodrama). Rohmer's fiction provides another example of how melodrama's integral concepts involving virtue, evil and justice are not static and are always subject to the culture in which the melodrama is produced. As Linda Williams points out, "perceptions of justice and injustice will always be relative. It might be the injustice of slavery in one melodrama (*Uncle Tom's Cabin*), the injustice committed by former slaves in another (*The Birth of a Nation*)."[148]

The pejorative term the "Yellow Peril," and the literary sub-genre known as "Yellow Peril" fiction, has a long history. Its usage intensified following the reported massacres, sometimes untrue, of Western missionaries during the Boxer Uprising. The term and the fiction, however, predates this event. It is, from the perspective of more than a century later, an irrational, but widespread, ethos that assimilated reports of physical violence, including sexual violence, with deeply held racist views based on ignorant stereotypical projections of Asian cultures, especially the Chinese. These views were grouped together under a rubric based on a fear of the "other," a fear that had little basis in reality. Added to this cultural revulsion, especially in the United States, was an economic dimension involving anxieties concerning the importation of cheap Chinese labor. Added to this were prevailing sexist and racist fears involving miscegenation. These fears coalesced in the United States in legislation such as the 1882 Chinese Exclusion Act which prevented Chinese laborers from entering the United States. This followed years of agitation and racial violence directed at Chinese workers—despite the self-interested lobbying of railway magnates always eager for cheap labor.

The Chinese Exclusion Act was the first ban in the United States directed at a specific nationality and it was extended in 1892 and 1924. Violence extended to naturalized Chinese who had arrived prior to 1882. In 1885, for example, a local labor leader encouraged white workers to attack the Chinese workers in a coal mining community, killing 15 workers and causing extensive damage.[149] These attacks intensified following inflammatory reporting of Chinese "atrocities" committed during the Boxer Uprising of 1898–1901. The Hearst newspapers, which regularly editorialized concerning the supposed dangers of the Yellow Peril in the United States, were influential.

Xenophobia intensified in the United States after the First World War as the country increasingly drifted into a state of isolationism. Anti-immigration laws were accompanied by the notorious 1922 Cable Act that decreed that the marriage of a foreign national to a female American citizen would lead to the revocation of the (American) female's citizenship.[150] The State of Virginia in 1924 went further with their Racial Integrity Act that made it a crime for members of one racial group to marry a member of another racial group. The Act also provided state sanctions for the sterilization of "undesirables," a law that remained on the state's statue books until 1967.[151]

The first "Yellow Emperor" character, a prototype embodied and enhanced in Rohmer's Fu Manchu stories, appeared before the Boxer Rebellion in the February 11, 1892, edition of *The Nugget Weekly* in a science fiction tale titled "Tom Edison Jr's Electric Sea Spider, or, the Wizard of the Submarine World" by Philip Reade. The villain in the story, Kiang Ho, was a Harvard educated Mongolian pirate "educated and trained in American universities [who] terrorized the world's shipping with the Sea Serpent, a submersible vessel."[152] Designed to exploit anti–Chinese feelings in the United States, it perpetuated the notion that "Asiatics" trained in American/Western universities would overthrow the Anglo-Saxon hegemony with their newly gained scientific knowledge, a theme that Rohmer would perpetuate.[153]

Robert Chambers' 1896 story "The Makers of Moons" featured Yue-Laou, a Chinese sorcerer and leader of a secret society while Dr. C.W. Doyle's 1900 novel *The Shadow of Quong Lung* anticipated some of the attributes of Fu Manchu as its villain was a graduate of Yale and Barrister of the Inner Temple as well as a Tong leader who controlled San Francisco's Chinatown.[154] However, the most influential exponent of the "Yellow Emperor" ethos before Rohmer was the "yellow trilogy" by Irish-West Indian novelist Matthew Phipps Shiel. Shiel's 1898 prophetic novel *The Yellow Danger* appeared in eight separate editions between 1898 and 1908.[155] The story featured Dr.

Yen How, a half Japanese and half Chinese villain who rises to power in China and foments war with the West. Yen How, a physician educated at Heidelburg, was based on the Chinese nationalist leader Dr. Sun Yet Sen,[156] a character Rohmer featured, as the "Mandarin Yen-Sun-Yat," in his first two Fu Manchu novels. In Rohmer's stories he is a former member of The Seven, the murderous cosmopolitan group also known as the Si-Fan. Later he becomes a traitor and informer. In Rohmer's *The Return of Dr. Fu-Manchu*,[157] for example, Fu Manchu receives a message that Yen-Sun-Yat has been assassinated in his garden in Nan-Yang.[158] The real life kidnapping of the Chinese leader by Manchu sponsored officials in Portland Place, as Christopher Frayling points out, "clearly made a strong impression on Sax Rohmer."[159] It is also likely that Rohmer was aware of Shiel's *The Yellow Danger* as the novel was based on the fear that the East would unite to remove the colonial powers from their territories. This provided the thematic basis for Rohmer's 1932 novel *The Mask of Fu Manchu*. It also formed the basis for the 1932 MGM film *The Mask of Fu Manchu* and the 1940 Republic serial, *Drums of Fu Manchu*.

It would be a mistake, however, to attribute the genesis of the "Yellow Peril" to either Matthew Shiel or Sax Rohmer. While both were important in its dissemination, its racist ethos formed an intrinsic part of western culture long before they were writing. It appeared more than a decade before the first Fu Manchu novel.[160] Christopher Frayling traces its origin to a reference by Kaiser Wilhelm 11, the grandson of Queen Victoria, in 1895 when he wrote "Russia's historic mission was to help protect Europe from the Yellow Peril."[161] In July 1898 *The Spectator* speculated about a Japanese military caste controlling China and referred to this possibility as "the Yellow Peril."[162] These fears intensified following media coverage of the Boxer Uprising. Coupled with this was the fact, as Rohmer recognized, that the end of the British empire was in sight, a distressing prospect for many people in Great Britain.

This was a period when school textbooks, children's comics and religious magazines presented the Chinese as pagan, cruel and in need of western missionary salvation. A time when, as Christopher Frayling writes, Britain's arrogance and bullying in China was justified on the grounds that China was a "static land of arrogance, warlords, infanticide, bound feet, pigtails and effeminacy, a land where people spat in the streets and ate cats and dogs."[163] Rohmer, in his description of Fu Manchu at the end of chapter two of the first Fu Manchu novel, *The Mystery of Dr. Fu-Manchu*, and repeated towards the end of the novel and in his next Fu Manchu novel, *The Return of Dr. Fu-Manchu,* encapsulates the prevailing western fear of the intelligent and devil-like qualities of this Chinese super-villain:

> Imagine a person, tall, lean and feline, high-shouldered, with a brow like Shakespeare and a face like Satan, a close-shaven skull, and long, magnetic eyes of the true cat-green. Invest him with all the cruel cunning of an entire Eastern race, accumulated in one giant intellect, with all the resources of science past and present, with all the resources, if you will, of a wealthy government—which, however, already has denied all knowledge of his existence. Imagine that awful being, and you have a mental picture of Dr. Fu-Manchu, the yellow peril incarnate in one man.[164]

The chapter is not directly concerned with detailing examples of Rohmer's racism. While it should be noted, which I will do briefly for readers not familiar with his fiction, it does not encompass the totality of this author. In Chapter 10 in *The Mystery of Dr. Fu-Manchu*, titled "Secret China," Dr. Petrie, Rohmer's narrator, writes, following a traumatic visit by Petrie and Nayland Smith to the rural estate of Redmoat in Norfolk: "No white man, I honestly believe, appreciates the unemotional cruelty of the Chinese."[165] In the second Fu Manchu novel, *The Return of Dr. Fu-Manchu*, when, once again, our heroes, Nayland Smith and Petrie, are manacled to a wall and are facing the prospects of torture from Fu Manchu, Petrie notes:

> By this fact alone did he [Smith] reveal his knowledge that he lay at the mercy of this enemy of the white race, of this inhuman being who himself knew no mercy, of this man whose very genius was inspired by the cool, calculated cruelty of his race, of that race which to this day disposes of hundreds, nay! thousands, of its unwanted girl-children by the simple measure of throwing them down a well specially dedicated to the purpose.[166]

Unless one wants to labor this point, it is best to acknowledge its existence, provide a context for such beliefs, and, as Ruth Mayer acknowledges, it does not exhaust the study of his fiction.[167] Instead my focus is on his ability as a skilled practitioner of sensational melodrama. Rohmer's first Fu Manchu story, "The Zayat Kiss," appeared in the British magazine *The Story-Teller* in October 1912. The first episode of the first film serial, *What Happened to Mary,* appeared a few months earlier on July 26, 1912. As Rohmer's stories grew in popularity between 1913 to 1917, so did the film serial. Both forms elicited contempt from the critics who placed no aesthetic value on them. Yet, Judith Walkowitz in her study of late Victorian fiction, noted,

> the appeal of melodrama for working class audiences resided its ability to capture their sense of instability and vulnerability in the unstable market culture of the early nineteenth century, where traditional patterns of deference and paternalism had been eroded. Below the surface order of reality lurked a terrible secret that could erupt unexpectedly with violence and irrationality. The melodramatic narrative acted arbitrarily in its very structure calling into question the operation of law and justice. Melodramatic plots overwhelmingly reinforced the sense of destiny out of control.[168]

Sax Rohmer's[169] first Fu Manchu story was influenced by the fiction of Arthur Conan Doyle, especially "The Speckled Band." "The Zayat Kiss" introduced the Sherlock Holmes/Dr. Watson facsimiles, Burmese Police Commissioner Nayland Smith and medical practitioner and aspiring author Dr. Petrie. The "Andaman-Second," which appeared in *The Story-Teller* in April 1913, and was reworked as chapters 18 to 20 in *The Mystery of Dr. Fu-Manchu*, also had clear echoes to Doyle's "The Adventures of the Bruce-Partington Plans." Chapters 14 to 17 in the second Fu Manchu novel, *The Return of Dr. Fu-Manchu*, which began as "The Coughing Horror" published in *Collier's* on April 3, 1915, was influenced by *The Hounds of the Baskervilles*. However, aside from his penchant for locked room mysteries and exotic forms of murder, the association between Smith and Petrie and Holmes and Watson is not strong. Rohmer's novels are not "who-done-its," as we know who done it (Fu Manchu). They are more concerned with the how and the why (a gigantic Oriental conspiracy). As Christopher Frayling points out:

> Whereas in the Sherlock Holmes stories the threat to the established order comes from homicides or burglaries or attempts at blackmail, in Rohmer's Fu Manchu novels it comes from the Yellow Peril…. Because Smith is so often caught on the back foot, the national sense of

optimism and invulner-
ability which features so
strongly in most Edwardian
adventure and detective stories becomes, as one critic
has put it, 'a grim racial
fatalism'; a sense of standing
on the darkling plain.[170]

Rohmer's fiction was
characterized by his ability to infuse the banal
and the ordinary with the
excitement of grandiose
conflict.[171] There are, literally, hundreds of exam-
ples of his ability to tap
into the everyday world
of his readers and trans-
form it into a paranoid
melodrama. To take one
example, chapter 27 ("The
Pit and the Furnace") of
his 1934 novel *The Trail of
Fu-Manchu*. When Alan
Sterling, who is assist-
ing Sir Dennis Nayland
Smith, is captured by the
Devil Doctor (Fu Manchu)
while attempting to rescue
his lover Fleurette. Sterling is hit over the head
and taken to a large fur-
nace under the Thames
in the Limehouse district
where Fu Manchu's "Bur-

Sir Arthur Conan Doyle's 1902 Sherlock Holmes story *The
Hound of the Baskervilles* influenced chapters 14 to 17 in Sax
Rohmer's second Fu Manchu novel *The Return of Fu Manchu*.
This was first published as "The Coughing Horror" in *Col-
lier's* in 1915.

mans" are feeding human bodies as fuel while he transmutes base metal into gold.
Sterling, appalled, stands on a wooden platform "looking down upon a scene which
reminded him of nothing so much as an illustration of Dante's Inferno."[172] Unaware
of his exact location, he recalls a warning from Smith that Fu Manchu has, over the
years, successfully insinuated himself into every aspect of British suburban life:
"Behind a house which we have passed a hundred times, over a hill which we have
looked at every morning for months together, on the roof of a building in which we
have lived, beneath a pavement upon which we walk daily, there are secret things
which we don't even suspect. Dr. Fu-Manchu has made it his business to seek out
these secret things...."[173]

His ability to constantly situate his characters at what Brooks describes as the "point of intersection of primal ethical forces and to confer on these characters' enactments a charge of meaning referred to the clash of these forces"[174] was crucial to Rohmer's success. His fiction exploits paranoia for all that it is worthwhile reassuring his readers of the existence of a higher cosmic moral force, the existence of a divine Providence, that will, ultimately protect them. Thus, Sterling and Smith survive the furnace through the "intervention of a Higher Power."[175] On another occasion Sterling reminds Smith, after a failed assassination attempt by one of Fu Manchu's "religious assassins"[176]:

> "That knife was meant for me, Sterling," he said, grimly, "and Dr. Fu-Manchu's thugs rarely miss."
> "It was an act of Providence—the protection of heaven!"[177]

In his first three Fu Manchu novels, and the sixth novel, *The Trail of Fu-Manchu*, published in 1934, Rohmer returned again and again to this paranoid depiction of everyday Britain. In his stories, the quiet commons was disrupted by the "blazing modernity" of a nearby major metropolis (London) with its electric cars. As Frayling points out, Rohmer's stories with their "sense of fragmentation and dislocation, of things falling apart,"[178] was his way of responding "to the alienating experience of trying to navigate the modern metropolis."[179] However, instead of responding to this fragmentation and dislocation with formal and linguistic innovations, as did many Modernists and poets writing at the same time as Rohmer, his response was to "racialize the problem."[180]

There are many parallels between Rohmer's fiction and the early film serial. Spectacle, action, suspense and thrills dominated both forms. For example, in Rohmer's serialized short story, "The Silver Buddha," first published in *Collier's* on May 15, 1915, and expanded to chapters 18 to 20 in Rohmer's second Fu Manchu novel, *The Return of Dr. Fu-Manchu*, the story begins with Dr. Petrie searching for his Arab lover, and Fu Manchu's slave, Káramanèh in an antique shop on Museum Street in London. However, after he comes face to face with Fu Manchu, Petrie is rendered unconscious by a blow to his head. He wakes up with his wrists handcuffed in Dr. Fu Manchu's laboratory where the Devil Doctor plans to ship Petrie, while under the influence of a new drug, to his facilities in Kiang-su in China to help him establish a New World Force. After Fu Manchu leaves, Káramanèh quietly slips into the room and, once again, rescues Petrie. She sets him free and takes him into another room where he can see Museum Street, and freedom, from the window. She also shows him a wooden crossbar attached to a cord looped over the telegraph poles that will carry him from his first-floor prison across the street to another apartment on the ground floor. She explains that the "length of rope is just sufficient to enable you to swing through the open window opposite, and there is a mattress inside to drop upon."[181] However, as he draws her towards him ("My very soul seemed to thrill at the contact of her lithe body..."),[182] he looks out of the window into the "upturned face of Fu-Manchu"[183] on the street below: "Wearing a heavy fur-collared coat, and with his yellow malignant countenance grotesquely horrible beneath the shade of a large tweed motor cap, he stood motionless, looking up at me. That he had seen me, I could not doubt; but had he seen my companion?"[184]

It turns out that Fu Manchu did not notice Káramanèh with Petrie and to protect her from Fu Manchu's fury he handcuffs her wrists and tears a strip from her dress, places the "fabric over the girl's mouth and tied it behind, experiencing a pang half pleasurable and half fearful as I found my hands in contact with the foamy luxuriance of her hair."[185] While this takes place Fu Manchu is racing from the street to his laboratory to stop Petrie's escape. In the reader's mind this approximates the same effect as cross-cutting between two locations to generate suspense in a filmed melodrama. After Fu Manchu arrives in the room, Petrie hurls the bunch of keys used by Káramanèh to free him into the villain's face and grabs the crossbar to make his escape. However, as he is about to jump from the window, Fu Manchu's gang, "the entire murder-group composed of units recruited from the darkest places of the East,"[186] attack Petrie. He saves himself by holding onto the crossbar and swinging back into the room where he kicks the man holding him in the head, splitting his skull. He then leaps through the window while holding the crossbar, "sweeping through the night like a winged thing…."[187] However, as he speeds towards the open window across the street he spies a "Burmese dacoit, a cross-eyed, leering being,"[188] clutching "a long curved knife [as he] waited-waited-for the critical moment when my throat would be at his mercy!"[189] To escape certain death Petrie throws his body back and extends his legs as he goes through the opening, striking the face of the dacoit. Although he suffers a leg wound ("I knew that the dacoit's knife had bitten deeply"),[190] he escapes by dropping into Museum Street where he hails a taxi to take him to the police pathologist at Harley Street. The story ends with Petrie's exclamation that "Merciful Providence had rung down the curtain; for tonight my rôle in the yellow drama was finished."[191] This passage would have been eminently suitable for any film serial.

Káramanèh

The moral context of Rohmer's Fu Manchu stories were based on Edwardian moral values. This is hardly surprising as Rohmer was an Edwardian author. Yet, it is not quite as simple as this as author William Patrick Maynard, and others, point to a tension in his fiction with regard to his presentation of "the East." While Fu Manchu is cruel, sadistic, and obsessive, he is also intellectually superior and, within his moral terrain, honorable. For example, at the end of one of Rohmer's most atmospheric stories, "Redmoat," which was published in *The Story-Teller* in December 1912 and revised to form chapters 7 to 9 in his first Fu Manchu novel, *The Mystery of Dr. Fu-Manchu*, Fu Manchu withdraws his attack on the Norfolk estate of the Rev. J.D. Eltham after Eltham, a "hero" in the Boxer Uprising, abandons his plan to return to China to resume his missionary work in Ho-Nan. Maynard concludes:

> Dr. Fu-Manchu acts with honour and shows himself superior to the imperialist British heroes…. It is Reverend Eltham who most clearly represents the proponents of the Yellow Peril even more than the colonialist Nayland Smith for it is Eltham who lacks empathy that is essential for bridging cultures. It is deeply ironic that Sax Rohmer's Fu-Manchu stories, long-derided as racist and jingoistic, actually represent a more enlightened view of the East and beneath the exotic mystery and thrills, their author repeatedly demonstrates that the differences between East and West are reconcilable.[192]

There are, on the other hand, notable acts of cruelty and sadism on the part of Fu Manchu, including the killing of his daughter and the impersonal dispatch of her body into a fiery furnace in *The Trail of Fu-Manchu* as well as the gleeful slaughter of police in *The Mystery of Dr. Fu-Manchu*, that offset his "honorable" acts. But it is a point worth making. I believe that Maynard's argument is much stronger in Rohmer's depiction of the major female character, Káramanèh, who was Dr. Petrie's love interest in the first three novels. She is Fu Manchu's slave born of Egyptian and European parentage and she functions, at various points in the first three novels, as femme fatale, a victim of a real-life social problem (slavery) who suffers from Fu Manchu's penchant for the whip and a constant savior figure rescuing Smith and Petrie on many occasions. Within the context of Edwardian values she is a complex, fascinating character. None of the Hollywood film versions had the courage to include her and they, unfortunately, present Petrie's lover as white, Anglo-Saxon and utterly conventional. Rohmer, on the other hand, defied reader expectations as an early chapter in the first Fu Manchu novel sets up a conventional heroine, Greba Eltham, the Reverend Eltham's daughter, as Petrie's likely partner. Rohmer quickly subverts these expectations and instead focuses on Káramanèh. She appears in Rohmer's first Fu Manchu story, "The Zayat Kiss," as a mysterious woman, somehow connected to Fu Manchu. After handing Petrie a perfumed envelope as part of Fu Manchu's scheme to kill Nayland Smith, she warns the young doctor "not [to] go near him [Smith] any more tonight."[193] Smith, however, is alert to Fu Manchu's machinations and explains to Petrie that the envelope has been saturated with the heavy perfume of a rare species of orchid that attracts a venomous, six-inch centipede. Smith's initial reaction to Káramanèh provides a clear contrast between the values of an aging misogynist (Smith) and Petrie, the young romantic. Smith tells the doctor, "She is one of the finest weapons in the enemy's armoury, Petrie. But a woman is a two-edged sword, and treacherous. To our great good fortune she has formed a sudden predilection, characteristically Oriental, for yourself. Oh, you may scoff, but it is evident. She was employed to get this letter placed in my hands."[194] Petrie, on the other hand, is immediately aroused by the exotic "otherness" of Káramanèh:

> A girl wrapped in a hooded opera-cloak stood at my elbow, and, as she glanced up at me, I thought I had never seen a face so seductively lovely nor of so unusual a type. With the skin of a perfect blonde, she had eyes and lashes as black as a Creole's, which, together with her full red lips, told me that this beautiful stranger whose touch had so startled me was not a child of our Northern shores.[195]

Káramanèh appears in the second Fu Manchu story, "The Clue of the Pigtail," published in *The Story-Teller* in November 1912 and it forms the basis of chapters 4 to 6 in *The Mystery of Dr. Fu-Manchu*. Her appearance this time, however, is even more morally problematic as she plays a crucial part in the murder of an undercover Scotland Yard policeman, Cadby. Smith and Petrie enter the story after a series of mysterious deaths in London's Limehouse district. The mystery emanates from the fact that each of the bodies have missing fingers. Their first stop in the investigation into Cadby's death takes Petrie to the dead policeman's rented rooms at Coldharbour Lane near the Brixton Police Station. Here the doctor interviews Cadby's landlady, Mrs. Dolan, who tells Petrie that there was a "terrible wailing at the back of the house last night."[196] She also tells him that that there is a young lady in Cadby's rooms. When Petrie asks her if she knows the woman, the exact nature of the relationship between Petrie and the woman is made apparent:

Mrs. Dolan grew embarrassed again.

"Well, Doctor," she said, wiping her eyes the while, "I do. And God knows he was a good lad, and I like a mother to him; but she is not the girl I should have liked a son of mine to take up with."[197]

Later, Dolan continues:

"I should never have allowed her in his rooms."[198]

The landlady's obvious disgust with the young woman as a woman of "lowly virtue" is interrupted by the sound of her attempting to escape. Petrie, however, corners her in one of Cadby's rooms: "She cowered against the desk by the window, a slim figure in a clinging silk gown, which alone explained Mrs. Dolan's distrust. The gaslight was turned very low, and her hat shadowed her face, but could not hide its startling beauty, could not mar the brilliancy of the skin nor dim the wonderful eyes of this modern Delilah. For it was she!"[199]

Knowing that Káramanèh is somehow involved in the young policeman's death, and that she had formed a sexual relationship with him, provokes considerable internal torment in Petrie:

It is with some shame that I confess how her charms enveloped me like a magic cloud. Unfamiliar with the complex Oriental temperament, I had laughed at Nayland Smith when he had spoken of this girl's infatuation. "Love in the East," he had said, "is like the conjurer's mango-tree; it is born, grows and flowers at the touch of a hand." Now, in those pleading eyes I read confirmation of his words. Her clothes or her hair exhaled a faint perfume. Like all Fu-Manchu's servants, she was perfectly chosen for her peculiar duties. Her beauty was wholly intoxicating. But I thrust her away.[200]

At this point in the narrative Petrie is utterly conflicted by Káramanèh:

At that moment I honestly would have given half of my worldly possessions to have been spared the decision which I knew I must come to … she was an Oriental, and her code must necessarily be different from mine. Irreconcilable as the thing may be with Western ideas … there remained that other reason why I loathed the idea of becoming her captor. It was almost tantamount to betrayal! Must I soil my hands with such work?

Thus—I suppose—her seductive beauty argued against my sense of right.[201]

Petrie's distrust, at this point in the narrative, prevents him from committing to her ("What should I do? What could I do?")[202] and this drives Káramanèh away as she is afraid to trust him. The readers are aware that she is not your conventional heroine—both in terms of race and also actions as she has, on Fu Manchu's behalf, performed deeds that, at least within both the moral strictures of Edwardian England and pulp literature of the period, would invalidate her as a suitable companion/love interest for the hero. As William Patrick Maynard writes, Fu Manchu's slave is "no English rose."[203]

Rohmer further complicates the moral context of his story by having, once again, Káramanèh betray Fu Manchu and save Petrie. After Smith and Petrie visit ShenYen's barber shop, an opium den where Petrie, after stumbling into a room, has his first sight of Fu Manchu who is sitting at a table. As Smith exhorts Petrie to shoot the Chinaman, Fu Manchu's hand slips down beside the table and the floor collapses under Petrie. The doctor falls into the Thames as the trap door through which he fell closes above him. His only means of escape appears to be a beam projecting a few feet above the water. However, this turns out to be an ingenious, sadistic trap set by Fu Manchu to maim his victims as two sword blades are riveted to the beam with their edges up. Unaware of this trap, Petrie sets off for the beam and as he is about to grab it, Smith intervenes by warning him not to touch it and continue swimming. Meanwhile, Káramanèh, dressed as a Chinaman with a pigtail, uses her wig to save Petrie from drowning by giving it to Smith who uses the false queue to pull Petrie to safety.

Rohmer deserves considerable credit to carry his Edwardian readers through the pros and cons regarding Káramanèh. Importantly, he resolves their affair not in the conventional way—by killing off either Petrie or Káramanèh. This would have appeased many readers at the time as well as the Lord Chamberlain's office in the United Kingdom who regularly prohibited productions that endorsed miscegenation. Importantly, Petrie resolves his inner conflict in the Arab slave's favor by marrying Káramanèh and settling down in her city, Cairo, not London.

The Villain in Melodrama

Fu Manchu illustrates the importance of the villain in melodrama. As Peter Brooks points out with regard to nineteenth-century theatrical melodrama:

> In the clash of virtue and villainy, it is the latter that constitutes the active force, the motor of plot. If to what we have said about drastic structures we add a consideration of affective structures, our starting point must be in evil. When contemporary audiences baptized the boulevard du Temple, site of the principal houses of melodrama, as the "Boulevard du Crime," they gave evidence of a recognition that, despite the ultimate triumph of virtue, it was the moment of evil triumphant that fascinated. The villain had the beau rôle, the one played by famous actors. The force of evil in melodrama derives from its personalized menace, its swift execution of its declarations of intent, its reductions of innocence to powerlessness. Evil is treachery in that it appears to unleash a cosmic betrayal of the moral order and puts all appearances into question.[204]

The villain drives the plot and creates excitement, as Christine Gledhill explains that it is the "villain ... [who] taps into the unthinkable, bringing it to the surface. That is what is exciting about melodrama: the villain breaks open the arena of moral certitudes, he challenges what is presumed to be the ethos by which we live; he challenges the moral order; he embodies the danger to it. In this respect, he's iconoclastic. And, I think that is what makes melodrama, what makes you sit at the edge of your seat."[205]

While Fu Manchu is more intelligent, ruthless, and resourceful than Nayland Smith, the British officer possesses the one attribute that ensures his place in melodrama as the hero—resilience. He struggles and struggles to overcome Fu Manchu's brilliance and, occasionally, enjoys limited success as Fu Manchu never succeeds in his ultimate aim of destroying white civilization. Providence always rescues Smith, as he reminds Alan Sterling in *The Trail of Fu-Manchu*:

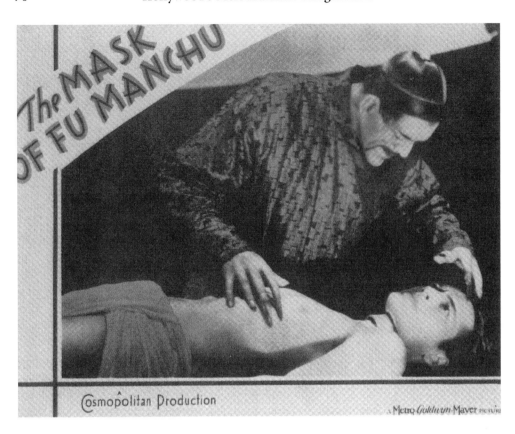

Boris Karloff as Fu Manchu touching Charles Starrett as Terrence Granville in MGM's *The Mask of Fu Manchu* (1932).

It was fate, I suppose, that made me an officer of Indian police. The gods—whoever the gods may be—had selected me as an opponent for—"Dr. Fu-Manchu," said Sterling.

He [Smith] brushed his hair back from his forehead; it as a gesture of distraction, almost of despair. Nayland Smith crossed to the buffet and from a tobacco jar which stood there, began to load his briar.

"Dr. Fu-Manchu. Yes. I know I have failed, Sterling, because the man still lives. But he has failed, too; because I have succeeded in checking him, step by step."

"I know you have, Sir Denis. No other man in the world could have done what you have done."[206]

Fu Manchu represents absolute evil. He is a sadist who whips his daughter, an opium addict, and exploiter of young men and women (Káramanèh and her brother Aziz), and, at times, a madman. In the first Fu Manchu novel, the aptly titled chapter "The Fungi Cellars," the police carry out a raid on Fu Manchu's Limehouse operations. As usual, the Devil Doctor outsmarts the police as Nayland Smith, Dr. Petrie and Inspector Weymouth watch in disbelief and horror as the Scotland Yard police officers walk into a trap in the fungi cellars where poisonous spores envelope the police officers and they die a painful death. As the men perish, Fu Manchu, "the greatest fungologist the world had ever known, ... a poisoner to whom the Borgias were as children,"[207] gleefully responds to their suffering:

Like powdered snow the white spores fell from the roof, frosting the writhing shapes of the already poisoned men. Before my horrified gaze, *the fungus grew*; it spread from the head to the feet of those it touched; it enveloped them as in glittering shrouds....

"They die like flies!" screamed Fu-Manchu, with a sudden febrile excitement; and I felt assured of something I had long suspected: that that magnificent, perverted brain was the brain of a homicidal maniac—though Smith would never accept the theory.

"It is my fly-trap!" shrieked the Chinaman. "And I am the god of destruction!"[208]

Rohmer's readers did not buy his stories for tales about Nayland Smith. It was Fu Manchu who appeared in the title and on the covers of his novels. And it was the author's ability to exploit their fears with descriptions of his Devil Doctor:

He came forward with an indescribable gait, catlike yet awkward, carrying his high shoulders almost hunched. He placed the lantern in a niche in the wall, never turning away the reptilian gaze of those eyes which must haunt my dreams for ever. They possessed a viridescence which hitherto I had only supposed possible in the eye of a cat—and the film intermittently clouded their brightness—but I can speak of them no more.

I had never supposed, prior to meeting Dr. Fu-Manchu, that so intense a force of malignancy could radiate—from any human being. He spoke. His English was perfect, though at times his words were oddly chosen; his delivery alternately was guttural and sibilant.[209]

Rohmer and Hollywood

After the third Fu Manchu book, *The Hand of Dr. Fu-Manchu*, published in 1917, Rohmer had no interest in continuing the character until the announcement by Paramount that they were buying the rights to his first book and would produce a film version, *The Mysterious Dr. Fu Manchu* (1929). Rohmer, with this commercial opportunity, had to return to Fu Manchu. Paramount followed their first film with *The Return of Fu Manchu* (1930) and *Daughter of the Dragon* (1931), all starring Warner Oland as Fu Manchu. Rohmer's publisher, Collier's, were keen for more stories and he signed a contract to renew the series.[210] However, the author's first attempt to rework the series into a contemporary thriller involving a self-styled Emperor of Crime who is ultimately revealed to be Fu Manchu's daughter did not satisfy Collier's and all traces of Fu Manchu were removed and his story appeared as *The Emperor of America*.[211]

The fourth Fu Manchu novel, *Daughter of Fu Manchu*, was published in 1931 and this was quickly followed by *The Mask of Fu Manchu* (1932) and *The Bride of Fu Manchu* (1933). In the gap between 1917 and *Daughter of Fu Manchu* fourteen years later, Rohmer made significant changes to his formula. This included a shift in the locale away from their English settings to more global locations, such as Egypt and Persia. Similarly, the deep seated, but largely insular, sense of paranoia in the early novels is broadened to more global threats. The motivation for this was, at least in part, the success of his books in the United States.

Unfortunately, Hollywood, with the exception of Republic's 1940 serial, largely botched their adaptations of his novels. Both Paramount and MGM emphasized the demented, albeit brilliant, side of his character but failed to develop a more subtle, more covertly sinister and multi-faceted villain. Paramount was also keen to eliminate the political and cultural aspect of Rohmer's fiction and any suggestion that Fu Manchu was connected to the Chinese Government. Hence Fu Manchu was transformed from an anti-colonialist zealot in their three films to a patriarch driven insane by the loss of his wife and son. Predictably, Káramanèh is nowhere to be seen as each film substitutes a conventional heroine—Jean Arthur in the Paramount films—as the love interest for Dr. Petrie.[212]

In 1929 Paramount cast Swedish born Warner Oland as Fu Manchu in the first talkie adaptation of a Rohmer novel. It was also filmed as a silent and it was released on August 10, 1929. Filmed during the awkward transition from silent to sound films, it is a dull, static and overly talky film, qualities never evident in Rohmer's novels. It begins in Peking during the Boxer Uprising where Fu Manchu is presented as a genial family man and

The first Hollywood appearance of Sax Rohmer's Fu Manchu in Paramount's *The Mysterious Dr. Fu Manchu* (1929) starring Warner Oland as the Devil Doctor. Also appearing: Neil Hamilton as Dr. Jack Petrie, Claude King as his father Sir John Petrie, William Austin as the comic relief, the butler Sylvester Wadsworth and Jean Arthur as Lia Eltham who was raised by Fu Manchu.

scientist. During the Uprising he agrees to look after a young baby, Lia Eltham, after her father dies. Fu Manchu, at this stage, is supportive of the imperial relief force and their attempts to quell the Uprising ("Do not fear, the white men are kind and generous"). However, after some Boxers take refuge in Fu's garden, overzealous Allied troops inadvertently kill Fu's wife and young son and Fu is suddenly transformed

Opposite, top: Jean Arthur, Neil Hamilton and O.P. Heggie as Inspector Nayland Smith in *The Mysterious Dr. Fu Manchu* (1929). *Bottom:* Neil Hamilton as Dr. Jack Petrie confronts Fu Manchu (Warner Oland) while Nayland Smith (O.P. Heggie) tries to hold Petrie back in *The Mysterious Dr. Fu Manchu* (1929).

into a demented, vengeful scientist vowing to murder officers of the Allied Expeditionary Force in order to compensate for every blood stained scale on his sacred dragon tapestry. This includes the entire Petrie family ("I have been blind. These whites are barbarous, devils, fiends!"). In this manner, screenwriters Lloyd Corrigan, Joseph L. Mankiewicz and Florence Ryerson, along with the uncredited George Marion, Jr., remove the Yellow Peril ethos and replace it with a revenge melodrama.

The film is also notable for introducing the mustache that is never found in the novels as well as inserting a degree of generic knowingness rarely evident in a Hollywood melodrama. After Fu Manchu gleefully traps Petrie (Neil Hamilton), Lia (Jean Arthur) and Nayland Smith (O. P. Heggie) near the end of the film he tells Petrie, "I'm afraid my somewhat weird and oriental methods may have misled your occidental mind into believing that this is nothing but a gigantic melodrama in which the detective's arrival at the last moment produces the happy ending." Of course, the ending is both conventional and melodramatic as Fu Manchu, seemingly, perishes after drinking a cup of poisoned tea. At this point he chuckles and points out to Nayland Smith: "after all, inspector, our story ended in the usual way."

Paramount quickly put a sequel into production with Warner Oland returning as Fu Manchu, Neil Hamilton as Jack Petrie, Jean Arthur as Lia Eltham and Australian born actor O.P. Heggie as Nayland Smith. *The Return of Fu Manchu* opened on May 2, 1930. Fu's resurrection is explained by a special potion that placed him in a state of cataleptic suspension and revives him during his funeral ceremony. Again, there is little of Rohmer's second novel in the film as the vendetta against the Petrie family continues. The only (slight) reference to Rohmer's novels occurs at the end when Jack Petrie is forced to operate on Fu Manchu after he suffers a bullet wound in a scene reminiscent of an incident in the third Fu Manchu novel, *The Hand of Fu-Manchu* (1917). The film, however, closes in a similar manner to the first film with Fu Manchu's "death" following his fall into the Thames holding an exploding grenade.

While the first two Fu Manchu films for Paramount were directed by Rowland V. Lee, screenwriter Lloyd Corrigan took over the direction of the third film, *Daughter of the Dragon*, released on September 2, 1931. The studio paid Rohmer $20,000 for the screen rights on March 23, 1931,[213] for his 1931 novel, *Daughter of Fu-Manchu*. Although the story had been serialized the year before in *Collier's*, and on radio between March and May 1930 in *The Collier's Hour*, Paramount's screenwriters Lloyd Corrigan, Sidney Buchman and, uncredited, Jane Storm took nothing from Rohmer's novel. They even changed the name of Fu Manchu's daughter from Fah Lo Suee to Ling Moy, as played by Anna May Wong. They also jettisoned Nayland Smith who was replaced by the incompetent Basil Courtney (Lawrence Grant) of Scotland Yard while introducing a Chinese detective Ah Kee, played by Japanese born actor Sessue Hayakawa in one of his last major American roles before leaving Hollywood. To make matters worse, they kill off Fu Manchu, for real, less than halfway into the film!

The plot continues Fu Manchu's machinations against the Petrie family from the previous films and the film is enlivened by the casting of Anna May Wong. Following Fu Manchu's death, she promises to keep her vow to kill Ronald Petrie (Bramwell Fletcher), the last of the Petrie's. This is complicated by the fact that Petrie, although he has a fiancé Joan Marshall (Frances Dade), becomes besotted with Ling

Moy. While this has some parallels to the fourth Fu Manchu novel, *Daughter of Fu-Manchu*, published in 1931, when Nayland Smith's new assistant Shan Greville, who is engaged to Lionel Barton's niece Rima, has a sexual relationship with Fah Lo Suee, Ronald Petrie's infatuation is much less interesting as he comes off as a buffoon. The plot also complicates his relationship with Ling Moy by the fact that Ah Kee also falls in love with her.

The film's ending takes place in a basement when Ling Moy puts aside her feelings for Petrie and threatens Joan with acid unless Ronald kills her. The politically correct, for 1931, ending sees Ah Kee murder Ling Moy before she can kill Petrie and then perish alongside her. Warner Oland also made one other appearance as Fu Manchu in a short comedy segment titled "Murder Will Out" in the portmanteau film *Paramount on Parade* (1930). The comedy skit also featured Clive

The third Fu Manchu film produced by Paramount *Daughter of the Dragon* (1931) starred Anna May Wong as Fu Manchu's daughter although the film changed her name from Fah Lo Suee to Ling Moy. Wong is excellent although the film had little to do with Rohmer's 1931 novel *Daughter of Fu-Manchu*. Bramwell Fletcher co-starred as Ronald Petrie along with Frances Dade as Joan Marshall.

Brook as Sherlock Holmes, William Powell as Philo Vance and Eugene Pallette as Sergeant Heath. Oland has great fun with lampooning the Devil Doctor and he shoots Vance in the bottom and Holmes in the heart before flying off screen. Oland soon left Paramount for Fox where he appeared in his most famous role, Charlie Chan, beginning with *Charlie Chan Carries On* (1931). He went on to appear in another fifteen Chan films before his death in 1938.

Rohmer's next novel, *The Mask of Fu-Manchu*, was serialized in *Collier's* from May to July 1932 and MGM bought the film rights. In what was described by its star,

Boris Karloff, as a chaotic production,[214] the studio clearly wanted to push the limits of the 1930 Production Code with as much aberrant sexuality and sadism as it could get away with. Fu Manchu is presented as a one-dimensional sadist from the very first image of Boris Karloff, his distorted face mirrored in a "nebularium," a large concave mirror. This grotesque introduction is reinforced by the sound of crackling electricity and a beam of light projected from his eyes. He subsequently drinks a bubbling concoction and Karloff then gives the audience an insane, knowing grin.

Production of the film took place from August 6 to October 21, 1932, and while the film retained Rohmer's basic premise regarding Fu Manchu's desire to acquire the magical scepter from El Mokanna's tomb in Persia to unite people in the

Boris Karloff as Fu Manchu with Myrna Loy as his daughter Fah Lo See and Charles Starrett as Terrence Granville in MGM's *The Mask of Fu Manchu* (1932).

East against the West, scriptwriters Irene Kuhn, Edgar Allan Woolf and John Williard made substantial changes that included shifting the locale from Persia to mountains on the edge of the Gobi Desert and Shanghai and substituting the more well-known Genghis Khan for El Mokanna. The half caste Shan Greville in the novel became all-American Terry Granville (Charles Starrett) in the film and Myrna Loy as Fah Lo See (as it was spelled in the film) was transformed from Fu Manchu's duplicitous daughter to, in her words, a "sadistic nymphomaniac" who shares her father's taste for sexual sadism.

It is a bizarre film that was banned for many years. Its emphasis on sadism, surprising for a MGM film, included multiple torture scenes filmed in the brightly lit MGM art deco style. This includes Sir Lionel Barton (Lawrence Grant) suffering the "torture of the bell," a constant clanging in his ears while deprived of food and water—at one point Fu Manchu offers him salt water. The archeologist Von Berg (Jean Hersholt) is nearly impaled by protruding metal spikes attached to two walls ("the silver fingers"), Nayland Smith (Lewis Stone) is left on an unstable plank in a crocodile infested pit, and the heroine Sheila Barton (Karen Morley) is about to be sold in an auction to the highest bidder before she is rescued. In an infamous scene, which precipitated Myrna Loy's decision not to accept future roles playing Orientals, she becomes sexually aroused at the sight of young Terence Manville stripped to the waist and being whipped at her orders by two large black men. When he resists the whipping his clothes are removed, except for a brief toweling costume around

The Mask of Fu Manchu (1932) with Boris Karloff as Fu Manchu and Myrna Loy as his daughter.

his waist, as she continues to seduce him. He is then manacled to an operating table and injected with a special serum that removes his resistance to all commands, sexual and otherwise, from both Fu Manchu and Fah Lo See.

The film climaxes in the Hall of Gods as Sheila is carried onto the stage in a "sacrificial bridal bed" while Fu Manchu extorts the "frenzied Orientals"[215] with the question "Would you all have maidens like this for your wives?" When he receives loud affirmation from the excited men, he orders them to "conquer and breed! Kill the white man, and take his women!" However, Smith breaks free from his crocodile infested prison, frees Terry and Von Berg, and they redirect Fu Manchu's electricity machine onto the screaming Orientals below. Terry then decimates Fu Manchu with Genghis Khan's sword. On the ship back to England, Nayland Smith throws the sword overboard.

According to Elizabeth, Sax Rohmer's widow, her husband did not like the film as he thought it crude and obvious.[216] It was, however, a commercial success, grossing $625,000 domestically and internationally. However, when the studio considered a sequel, there was opposition from the Chinese Consulate, and others.[217] The strict imposition of the Production Code after mid–1934 made a sequel impossible. When the film was re-released in 1992 on video a number of scenes involving racism and acts of sadism were deleted. They now have been restored.

On June 16, 1939, Republic signed a contract with representatives of Sax Rohmer for a serial based on Fu Manchu. Rohmer was paid $10,000 for the rights which prohibited a separate feature film. The contract gave the studio access to Rohmer's novels, including his 1939 novel *The Drums of Fu Manchu*. Scriptwriters Franklin Adreon, Morgan Cox, Ronald Davidson, Norman S. Hall, Barney A. Sarecky and Sol Shor, with uncredited work from Rex Taylor and W.P. Thompson, borrowed liberally from Rohmer's stories although, by far, the greatest influence on their script was MGM's 1932 feature *The Mask of Fu Manchu*. A notable absence, however, was the sexual sadism displayed by Fu Manchu's daughter. In the 1940 serial Fah Lo-Suee (Gloria Franklin) lacks any sexual interest in the equivalent male figure, young American archeologist Allan Parker (Robert Kellard). Both the 1932 MGM film and the 1940 serial focus on Fu Manchu's plan to conquer Asia and eradicate Europeans after establishing that he is the true heir to Genghis Khan. To unite the tribesmen Fu Manchu (Henry Brandon), and his secret terrorist organization the "Si-Fan" society, must acquire the Lost Scepter of Genghis Khan which can only be found

Chapter Ten ("Drums of Doom"), Republic's fifteen-chapter serial *Drums of Fu Manchu* (1940), arguably the best film adaptation of Rohmer's stories.

via the Dalai Plaque which is held by American Dr. James Parker (George Cleveland).

Fu Manchu's nemesis, Sir Dennis Nayland Smith (William Royle) of the British Foreign Office, is aware of Fu Manchu's master plan after recounting details to his friend Flinders Petrie (Olaf Hytten) of his recent visit to Asia where he noted that the Nihala Hills Tribesmen were waiting restlessly for the arrival of a new messiah in the person of Fu Manchu. Parker is murdered by one of Fu Manchu's dacoits, lobotomized warriors who serve Fu Manchu, and his son Allan joins Nayland Smith to stop Fu Manchu acquiring the Sacred Scepter from the tomb of Genghis Khan. Mary Randolph (Luana Walters) also becomes involved after her father, Professor Edward Randolph (Tom Chatterton), is kidnapped.

Unlike the Paramount feature films, the Republic serial presents a more complex Fu Manchu as it acknowledges that he normally acts within the parameters of his own moral code. In chapter 3 ("Ransom in the Sky"), for example, Fu Manchu is offended when Mary Randolph breaks the gas line of a plane after he has given his word that no harm will come to her if Allan exchanges the Dalai Scroll for her freedom. He tells Mary: "May I remind you that among my people honor is a sacred thing and those who defile it can expect no mercy." As a consequence, he and his Dacoit depart from the plane on the only parachutes. Minutes earlier, before Mary's deception, he was prepared to let Mary and Allan escape unharmed. The chapter ends with Allan forced to make a crash landing in the disabled plane in rugged terrain.

Chapter 5, "The House of Terror," is the screen's best presentation of Rohmer's emphasis on paranoia from a largely unseen enemy when Nayland Smith visits the remote estate of Professor Ezra Howard (John Dilson) during a violent storm. Smith wants to borrow the Kardac Segment, an artifact that will assist in locating Genghis Khan's tomb. Despite Nayland Smith's warning to Howard that if "Fu Manchu knew you had the Segment, this is precisely the sort of night he would select to move against you," the eccentric professor dismisses Nayland Smith's anxieties ("I don't fear the Fu Manchus of this world. My home has been specially built to thwart them"). Sitting in a semi-darkened room, with the sounds of wind and lightning, Howard's confidence ("Fu Manchu is welcome to attempt an entrance") is quickly exposed as foolish. After boasting that his grounds are patrolled by vicious dogs, the serial shows the image of a dead dog. A Dacoit silently enters the room after a violent gust of wind blows open the doors. Howard's servant Cardo (John Lester Johnson) and another dog are killed while Fu Manchu confidently strides through the rain and wind towards Howard's mansion. His arrival is signaled by the sound of drums. Hearing the drums, Nayland Smith, in a moment of British understatement, utters: "We're in for it." The chapter ends not with the usual action sequence but a sense of gothic malevolence that is conveyed by the lightning, sounds and composition. It concludes with Fu Manchu, body in shadow and face brightly lit, surveying the carnage around him with satisfaction.

The epilogue is unique for a film serial as the villain always died. This appears to be the ending in this serial as, towards the end of chapter 15, Fu Manchu seemingly dies when his car rolls off a mountain. This ending was used to show Fu Manchu's death in the 69-minute edited version of the serial which was released as a feature

William Royle as Dennis Nayland Smith and Robert Kellard as Allan Parker (background) watch Henry Brandon as Fu Manchu and John Merton as Loki with three Dacoits in *Drums of Fu Manchu* (1940).

film in 1943. The serial, however, presents a less conventional ending. After the High Lhama (Joe De Stefani) celebrates the victory over Fu Manchu and accepts the restoration of the status quo, the return of British rule, by praising the efforts of Nayland Smith and Parker ("It was their heroism that prevented the holy scepter from falling into the hands of the false prophet"), the epilogue shows Fu Manchu making a pledge to his idol Genghis Khan: "My plan to conquer this land, even as you conquered it, has been buried away in the rifle fire of alien soldiery. But there will dawn another day … a day of reckoning … when the forces of Fu Manchu will sweep on to victory. This I pledge you!" This ending was predicated on the expectation of a sequel, tentatively titled *Fu Manchu Strikes Again*. Here the Devil doctor would direct his attention to the Japanese. However, pressure from the Chinese Government and the American State Department terminated this possibility. Jack Mathis also argues that another factor involved protests from parent's and civic groups who claimed the serial terrified children.[218]

Melodrama's Sign of Virtue: "December 7"

Brooks argues that melodrama "exteriorizes conflict."[219] The most common form of melodrama, sensational melodrama, achieves this by dramatizing the persecution of innocence.[220] This, in turn, invokes a sense of indignation and a desire for retribution. Emotions that Robert Heilman argues are inherently pleasurable as they deflect consideration away from our own moral flaws so that we can focus solely on the battle between "us" and "them." Thus, Heilman maintains, the sense of indignation emanating from the polarization of the drama is stirring, exalting. It has a public function, he argues, as it concentrates energies for the rigors of combat:

> Whether for war or for its moral equivalents. It has a private function: as a unifier of emotions, it cures the painful divergency of feelings present in states of high self-awareness, and it is a preventive of the melancholic states that occur at the other end of the melodramatic spectrum. It is the ultimate unquestioning, unquestionable assertion of our own rectitude. Through it we soar into simple, untragic excitement.[221]

Following the Japanese attack on Pearl Harbor on December 7, 1941, "December 7" became a national sign of American virtue. It was used again and again in many mediums, especially the Hollywood combat film, as a form of explanation, an ethical sign. This is apparent in the terms used by President Franklin D. Roosevelt to explain the nature of the actions of the Japanese at Pearl Harbor to the American people.

On November 26, 1941, a Japanese task force left the Kurile Islands with the intention of decimating the American military forces on Oahu, the most populous island in Hawaii. The specific target was the naval base at Pearl Harbor which the Japanese believed to be a major obstacle to their southern expansion throughout Asia.[222] The Americans suffered damage to eighteen vessels including eight battleships, three light cruisers, three destroyers and four auxiliary craft. Nearly two-thirds of the naval

Pearl Harbor, December 1941, just prior to the Japanese attack.

Pearl Harbor, December 1941, just after the Japanese attack.

aircraft were destroyed, and 2,403 people were killed or missing with a further 1,178 wounded. The Japanese, on the other hand, lost only five midget submarines, a large submarine and twenty-nine planes out of an attacking force of three hundred and sixty aircraft. Sixty-four Japanese were dead or missing.[223] The damage was exacerbated by the fact that the Army Air Force aircraft were bunched together due to the fear of sabotage.[224]

The plan to attack the main strength of the United States naval force at Pearl Harbor was conceived by the Commander-In-Chief of the Japanese Combined Fleet, Admiral Isoroku Yamamoto. Yamamoto insisted that the final diplomatic note be delivered before the first shot was fired and he maintained that there was a significant difference between a "strategic surprise attack" and "a political sneak attack."[225] The final note was to have been presented three hours before the attack, but this was later reduced to one hour. However, a directive was issued prohibiting the use of a typist and the typing was left to the First Secretary and, following administrative mishaps, the note was finally delivered fifty-five minutes after the initial attack. The delay in the timing of the note never really concerned the Japanese government who considered it "strictly a formalistic bow toward the conventions. Tokyo had left no margin for error."[226]

The Japanese attack for the American people, on the other hand, represented a "deep emotional experience, indeed, a traumatic shock"[227] and Gordon Prange described the impact as a "mind staggering mixture of surprise, awe, mystification, grief, humiliation, and above all, cataclysmic fury."[228] There were two reasons for this. First it became immediately apparent to the American people that detailed preparations for the assault were carried out simultaneously with the expression of peaceful intentions from Ambassador Nomura and Special Envoy Kurusu in Washington. Secondly, the attack without a formal declaration of war incensed all Americans. This resulted in an intense sense of indignation[229] and greatly assisted the process of unification of the American people behind the war effort.

This was encapsulated by the opening lines of President Roosevelt's Address to Congress the day after the attack:

> Yesterday, December 7, 1941—a date which will live in infamy—the United States of America was suddenly and deliberately attacked by naval and air forces of the Empire of Japan.[230]

The phrase "a day which will live in infamy" was an inspired opening as it created an immediate moral context to view the Japanese attack. It was the essence of melodrama, the violation of innocence (the United States) by evil (the Japanese). This theme was constantly reiterated by Roosevelt:

> The United States was at peace with that Nation and, at the solicitation of Japan, was still in conversation with its Government and its Emperor looking toward the maintenance of peace in the Pacific. Indeed, one hour after the Japanese air squadrons had commenced bombing in the American island of Oahu, the Japanese Ambassador to the United States and his colleague delivered to our Secretary of State a formal reply to a recent American message. And while this reply stated that it seemed useless to continue the existing diplomatic negotiations, it contained no threat or hint of war or armed attack. It will be recorded that the distance of Hawaii to Japan make obvious that the attack was deliberately planned many days or weeks ago. During the intervening time the Japanese Government has deliberately sought to deceive the United States by false statements and expressions of hope for continued peace.[231]

The duplicitous nature of the Japanese actions was reiterated many times by President Roosevelt and others. For example, six days after his initial address to Congress the President gave a comprehensive historical survey of the relationship between the two countries in *A Message to the Congress Outlining the History of Relations Between the United States and Japan*. The theme was betrayal and violation: "We may acknowledge that our enemies have performed a brilliant feat of deception, perfectly timed and executed with great skill. It was a thoroughly dishonorable deed."[232]

Roosevelt emphasized the repeated attempts by the United States to prevent military action. However, we "did not know then, as we do now, that they had ordered and were even then carrying out their plan for a treacherous attack upon us."[233] He emphasized "for the record of history,"[234] that the Japanese reply to their most recent proposal was delivered "one hour after the Japanese had launched a vicious attack upon American territory and American citizens in the Pacific."[235] This, he maintained, "is the record, for all history to read in amazement, in sorrow, in horror, and in disgust."[236] He concluded that "no honest person, today or a thousand years hence, will be able to suppress a sense of indignation and horror at the treachery committed by the military dictators of Japan, under the very shadow of the flag of peace borne by their special envoys in our midst."[237]

Horror and disgust at this act of betrayal under the "very shadow of the flag of peace borne by their special envoys in our midst" invokes the melodramatic "*topoi*" involving a duplicitous usurper within "our midst." This is reminiscent of the actions of Count Romaldi in *A Tale of Mystery* and countless other theatrical and film melodramas. Roosevelt's response, in effect, presented the Japanese actions on

December 7 as the primal scene, "a moment of intense, originary trauma that leaves virtue stunned and humiliated"[238] where innocence (the United States) is forced to "undergo an experience of the unbearable."[239]

The melodramatic response within this context is to seek retribution. Although Roosevelt could have diffused this desire with a more comprehensive selection of facts,[240] he wanted to elicit a powerful sense of righteous indignation. For example, his message to Congress ignores the fact that the United States placed an embargo on high-octane gasoline along with a reduction of heavy oil exports to Japan and a freeze on Japanese assets in the United States some months before the Japanese attack. The Japanese considered these actions extremely provocative as their expansion southward was interconnected with the overall national policy. The oil embargo, as Gordon Prange writes, was perceived as a "slinging slap to the national psyche"[241] and encouraged the Japanese Naval General Staff to look seriously at the "Pearl Harbor project" as they estimated that the Japanese Navy would be crippled within two years and its industries disabled in less than half that time.[242] Instead, Roosevelt explained the attack in ethical terms involving "powerful aggressors who sneak up in the dark without warning"[243] and violate a nation at peace. The only possible response, he argued, was the use of force "directed toward ultimate good as well as against immediate evil."[244]

In this confrontation between good and evil, Roosevelt argued in his Address to Congress on January 6, 1942, the elimination of the aggressor was the only acceptable goal: "There never has been—there never can be—successful compromise between good and evil. Only total victory can reward the champions of tolerance, and decency, and freedom, and faith."[245] Prange argues that the nature of the Japanese actions generated a powerful sense of indignation that unified a nation that was divided before the attack. The success of Roosevelt and others in presenting the Japanese actions within an ethical context involving betrayal and duplicity within "our midst," had the effect whereby "American strength would be concentrated into an arrow point of resolution."[246] The public reaction to the Japanese attack according to Prange was also one of relief: "Through all the conflicting emotions ran a thread of relief—relief that Japan had taken the United States off the hook and made the decision for it; relief that the onus of aggression rested with the Axis; relief that Americans could stop the talk and get on with the real job; relief that the isolationship-interventionship cleavage had fused into unity."[247]

The nature and timing of the Japanese attack removed all doubt and provoked a singleness of purpose. As Secretary of State Henry Stimson recorded in his diary: "When the news that Japan had attacked us, my first feeling was of relief that the indecision was over and that a crisis had come in a way which would unite all our people. That continued to be my dominant feeling in spite of the news of catastrophes which quickly developed."[248]

The *New York Herald Tribune* also argued that the Japanese action brought a sense of relief as the "air is cleaner. Americans can get down to the task with old controversies forgotten."[249]

In the period from December 7, 1941, to the end of the Second World War, and beyond, "December 7th" and "Pearl Harbor" became moral signs in the American culture. It became a short-hand way of explaining the change in attitude and behavior for a character in films. When associated with the Japanese it was a sign of their duplicitous nature. A common technique was to insert a newspaper dated "December 7" into the drama, as in *Across the Pacific* (1942), with the headline "Hirohito Reply to Roosevelt Will Insure Peace.... Say Nomura and Kurusu. Special Envoy Kurusu Assure Tokyo Peace Efforts Will Succeed." A camera movement immediately destroys the veracity of this report by showing the date of the newspaper: "December 7, 1941."[250]

In opening moments of *So Proudly We Hail* (1943) an American convoy, including a group of nurses, cross the Pacific in December 1941. Relaxing on a warm, sunny, day on the deck of the ship Lieutenant Joan O'Doul (Paulette Goddard) interrupts her letter writing to ask, "what's the date?" A nurse replies, "Sunday. We had chapel." O'Doul's query is a transparent metaphor for the United States as a nation unaware of the Japanese threat, as reiterated in O'Doul's reply: "Thanks, I'll just head it eighteen shopping days to Christmas." The audience, on the other hand, fully aware of the significance of "Sunday the Seventh" as the film dissolves from the sunny deck to the sudden arrival of heavy black clouds, accompanied by an ominous musical chord on the soundtrack.

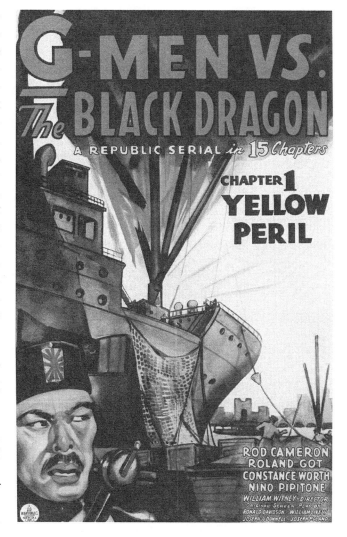

Chapter One ("Yellow Peril") of the 1943 Republic serial *G-Men Vs. The Black Dragon.*

Similarly, the written prologue in *Somewhere I'll Find You* (1942):

October 2, 1941
When we still had 83 shopping days until Christmas
... and 65 days until Pearl Harbor.

In *Bombardier* (1943), when one of the trainee airmen bursts into the military chapel with the news of the attack on Pearl Harbor, the rest of the group are occupied with their prayers. In the next scene the leader of the group walks up to a calendar on the wall and points to the date ("December 7, 1941") and tells his men: "Gentlemen, there's a date we will always remember, [pause] and they'll never forget!"

John Ford's December 7th

This recurring presentation of the violation of innocence by a duplicitous enemy is evident not only in feature films but also documentaries such as *December 7th* which was supervised by John Ford. The initial aim of the film was to present a "factual" account of the Japanese attack and it was initiated by the Secretary of the Navy Frank Knox who passed the project on

FIRST GREAT LOVE STORY OF OUR GIRLS AT THE FIGHTING FRONT!

CLAUDETTE COLBERT
PAULETTE GODDARD
VERONICA LAKE

So Proudly We Hail

A MARK SANDRICH PRODUCTION

with GEORGE REEVES · BARBARA BRITTON
WALTER ABEL and introducing SONNY TUFTS
Directed by MARK SANDRICH
Written by Allan Scott . . . . . . A Paramount Picture

So Proudly We Hail (1943), Paramount's tribute to the Red Cross nurses who sail for Hawaii just prior to the Japanese attack and, later, are trapped on Bataan in the Philippines. Claudette Colbert, seen with George Reeves, heads the nursing group which includes Veronica Lake and Paulette Goddard.

to William J. "Wild Bill" Donovan, head of the recently formed Office of Strategic Services. When John Ford's Field Photographic Unit was assigned the documentary Ford delegated the project to cinematographer Gregg Toland who worked closely with screenwriter Lieutenant Samuel G. Engel. While Donovan favored an explanation for the military debacle at Pearl Harbor[251] Navy officials wanted to deflect criticism of the lack of preparation and they preferred to focus on the rebuilding process.

Toland and special effects expert Ray Kellogg began work on the project in January 1942 and, after traveling to Hawaii, they assembled footage of the actual attack which was shot by Navy photographers, together with footage of the salvage operations. However, there was insufficient footage for a feature film so Toland and Engel employed Hollywood actors to perform scripted sequences while recreating the attack with members of the army deployed at Pearl Harbor and the nearby Hickam Air Force Base. Some of footage was directed by Ford until he was sent to Midway to film *The Battle of Midway* (1942) and Toland was left in charge. There were also miniatures filmed in Hollywood by Ray Kellogg along with simulated "interviews" with civilian personnel in Hawaii. After viewing the film the Joint Chiefs of Staff were appalled by the criticisms of the Navy along with a fear that suggestions of sabotage by Japanese Americans would foment racial tensions in Hawaii. The controversy reached the Secretary of War who decreed that the film would have to be approved by him before it could be released.[252] Eventually the Navy confiscated all the work prints and it was only resurrected twelve months later when Ford and editor Robert Parrish edited the negative into a short documentary that focused on the battle and its aftermath. Although the long version (82 minutes) of *December 7th* was kept from general release for some decades, the edited version won the 1943 Academy Award for Documentary Short Subject.

The 34-minute version of the film begins by showing "Uncle Sam" fast asleep as the narrator warns of the impending disaster:

> Warned of the fire licking across the ocean from without. Warned of the dangers that were threatening within. Tired from wrangling with conscience and fatigued after a long, dark night full of disturbing events that indeed the year 1941 was. He slept in the early Sabbath calm. Safe and secure behind its military ramparts....

The Ford/Parish edit removes the problematic aspects of Toland's version and the narrative is shaped in much the same manner as nineteenth-century theatrical melodramas, such as *Coelina, or the Child of Mystery* where the play typically opens with a presentation of virtue *as* innocence "taking pleasure in itself."[253] Innocence enjoys its moment of "false" security while the villain, the "troubler of innocence,"[254] prepares to strike. At the beginning of Ford's film the military are celebrating a field mass at the Kaneothe Naval Air Station as the priest is suggesting the type of gifts the servicemen might consider sending home to loved ones for Christmas. This tranquil setting is soon violated and the narrator calls it "the Axis brand of war: a stab in the back on Sunday morning!"

December 7th was unable to provide the final act, violent retribution against a duplicitous enemy. While sensational melodrama traditionally closes on a situation where ultimately evil is irredeemably eradicated and no "shadow dwells, and the universe bathes in the full, bright lighting of moral manichaeism,"[255] all *December 7th* and the combat films could do was promise this outcome. This occurs with the narrator's final exhortation: "Well, you may crow Mr. Tojo! You've done a good job of stabbing in the back. You've darkened our cities, you've destroyed our property, you've spilled our blood. Our faith tells us, to all this treachery there can be but one answer, a time-honored answer: 'For all that live by the sword shall perish by the sword.'"

A Parabolic Mode

"December 7" unified a divided nation determined through its desire to retaliate against "evil's moment of spectacular power."[256] The American cinema followed Roosevelt's lead as "Pearl Harbor" was transformed into a series of parables, all depicting the process of regeneration. For example, in Ford's *December 7th* the narrator interrupts his description of the damage inflicted by the Japanese at Pearl Harbor to highlight the "resurrection" of the minelayer the *Oglala*: "Who is this saucy little gal … the minelayer Oglala … given up and reported as lost … taken to dry dock this small dauntless craft was refitted and repaired. Now spanking new, a symbol of the fighting spirit of our men who build and man our ships, this veteran of World War 1 again takes up her battle stations. God speed old girl!"

The insertion of the story of the *Oglala* within the overall narrative reiterates Roosevelt's theme involving the resurrection of innocence. Roosevelt also included such stories in his frequent radio broadcasts to the nation. For example, his *Fireside Chat to the Nation* on April 28, 1942, he told three stories of, seemingly, different incidents. The first story highlighted the bravery of Dr. Cordyn M. Wassell[257] who remained behind with twelve wounded soldiers on Java as the Japanese advanced across the island. Knowing that they would be captured by the enemy, Wassell decided to get the men out and makeshift stretchers were constructed to transport the wounded men fifty miles to the coast where they boarded a small Dutch ship that was subsequently bombed and machine-gunned by Japanese planes until Wassell and the wounded men reached Australia. Roosevelt described Wassell as a "missionary, well known for his good works in China. He is a simple, modest, retiring man, nearly sixty years old, but he entered the service of his country and was commissioned a Lieutenant Commander in the Navy."[258] Wassell, as Roosevelt quotes from an official report, was "like a Christ-like shepherd devoted to his flock."[259] He was awarded the Navy Cross.

Roosevelt's second story involved the resurrection of the submarine the USS *Squalus* that was sunk off the English coast in the summer of 1939. It was raised from the bottom of the sea and restored to active service under a new name, the USS *Sailfish*. The renamed submarine, which included three men who went down with it in 1939, proceeded to sink a Japanese destroyer, torpedoed a Japanese cruiser and made two hits on a Japanese aircraft carrier. Roosevelt added that it is "heartening to know that the Squalus, once given up for lost, rose from the depths to fight for our country in time of peril."[260]

Roosevelt's last story continues the resurrection motif. An Army Flying Fortress in the western Pacific, part of a flight of five bombers on a mission to attack Japanese transports supplying troops to the Philippines, was halfway to its destination when one of the bomber's motors failed and the pilot lost contact with the other planes. By the time the fault was rectified and the bomber reached the target area, the other Flying Fortresses had already dropped their bombs and departed. In their wake, however, they had "stirred up the hornet's nest of Japanese "Zero" planes. Eighteen of these "Zero" fighters attacked our one Flying Fortress. Despite this mass attack, our plane proceeded on its mission, dropped all of its bombs on six Japanese transports which were lined up along the docks."[261]

On the return journey the bomber was subjected to a continuous battle with eighteen Japanese pursuit planes for 75 miles as the enemy simultaneously attacked both sides of the bomber. The crew managed to shoot down four Japanese planes despite the fact that the radio operator was killed, another gunner injured and the engineer's right hand was shot off. However, the remaining gunner alternately manned both guns and succeeded in bringing down a further three Japanese planes. During the battle one of the bomber's engines was destroyed, a gas tank was hit, the radio damaged, the oxygen system disabled, and only four out of the eleven control cables were working. Also the rear landing wheel was destroyed and both front wheels were damaged. However, the bomber, with two engines gone, survived and made an emergency landing at its base later that night. The mission, Roosevelt announced, "had been accomplished."[262] Soon, Roosevelt promised, "American Flying Fortresses will be fighting for the liberation of the darkened continent of Europe itself."[263]

The Combat Film 1942 to 1945

> RICK: Don't you sometimes wonder if it's worth all this? I mean what you are fighting for.
> LASZLO: We might as well question why we breathe. If we stop breathing we'll die. If we stop fighting our enemies, the world will die.—*Casablanca* (1942)
>
> We flee from the complexities of peace to the terrible simplicity of war.—
> Marquis Childs, *Yale Review*, number 36, September 1946

Hollywood immediately followed Roosevelt's lead and "December 7" was regularly inserted into feature films. For example, *A Yank on the Burma Road*, released by M.G.M little more than six weeks after the disaster at Pearl Harbor, traces the transformation of an "average" American, a taxi driver, from being a self-interested mercenary to a committed patriot. The change in his attitude after Pearl Harbor is outlined in the film's prologue:

> On December 7, 1941, Japan attacked the United States and engaged it in War.
> This is the story of one American who tackled Japan a little before the rest of us—and what he started the rest of the Yanks will finish!

The Navy Comes Through was released by RKO on October 27, 1942, ten months after the attack. The film begins with Lieutenant Sands (George Murphy) resigning his commission following his censure by a Court of Inquiry. The film then cuts from the corridor outside the Court to a close-up of a Japanese flag, followed by footage of Japanese planes attacking American ships in Pearl Harbor. This is accompanied by the closing section of President Roosevelt's December 8 Address to Congress ("I ask that the Congress declare, that since the unprovoked and dastardly attack by Japan....") along with footage of men at the recruiting stations. They include the formerly disgruntled sailor (Sands) re-enlisting in the Navy as an ordinary seaman. Sands, who was unjustly persecuted following an accident which resulted in his censure, is given a second chance. This melodrama, similar to many Hollywood films produced during this period, assimilates the personal into the social. As Sands battles

MGM's response to the Japanese attack on Pearl Harbor was *A Yank on the Burma Road*, released in New York on January 29, 1942. Barry Nelson stars as Joe Tracey, a New York cabbie escorting a convoy of trucks along the Burma Road. Along the way he meets Gail Farwood (Lorraine Day), the wife of an American traitor.

to establish his true identity, his resurrection becomes a parable for the United States now fighting for its own survival. This is achieved in the film's epilogue which takes place between Sands, and the man (Mallory) who inadvertently caused his censure at the beginning of the film, while watching a new batch of recruits:

> SANDS: Well, they will learn all right, and a lot more of them. When they get rolling they're going to be a tough outfit to stop.
> MALLORY: Awful tough!
> SANDS: You know there once was a pretty fair sailor by the name of John Paul Jones. He said….
> MALLORY: Yeah, I know, "We've just begun to fight."

Flying Tigers, released by Republic on October 8, 1942, and *Air Force*, released by Warner Bros. on February 3, 1943, follow the same pattern and rely on "December 7th" to explain the regeneration of a central character. In both films this takes the form of excerpts from Roosevelt's December 8 Address to Congress. *The Flying Tigers* follows the exploits of the 1st American Volunteer Group of the Chinese Air Force, a mercenary group of Americans that included Captain Jim Gordon (John Wayne) and Woody Jason (John Carroll) in the period immediately preceding the

Japanese attack on Pearl Harbor. The dual narrative strands concern the high casualty rates suffered by the Americans in their encounters with the Japanese along with the regeneration of Woody Jason who explains to other members of the American Volunteer Group that his motivation for fighting on behalf of the Chinese is purely financial:

> I know there's a war, but you fellas have no part of it. We are all out here for the same reason.
> Dough!

Other members of the group, including Gordon, are disgusted with his attitude and one pilot points out that "back home most of us would kill rattlesnakes whether there is a bounty on them or not." Jason counters with an isolationist argument: "I know but you're protecting your own home. This is not our home, it's not our fight. It's a business, and boy, I sure hope business is good."

RKO's story of the regeneration of navy lieutenant Tom Sands (George Murphy), intended as a parable for the revival of the United States after the Japanese attack on Pearl Harbor in *The Navy Comes Through* (1942).

Jason's self-interest results in the death of two colleagues. However, a Japanese atrocity, the bombing of an orphanage, marks the beginning of his regeneration. The full transformation occurs when Jason hears Roosevelt's December 8 Address and the final moments of the address are accompanied by a close-up of his face. He immediately reverses his previous pattern of behavior by participating in a dangerous mission that offers no financial gain. En route on the mission to destroy a Japanese bridge he uses a metaphor to explain his change of attitude:

> A whole, lot of us don't grow up, we stay kids and the most important thing to a kid is the street he lives on. It's his life, his whole world. That was me when I first joined up with you. Hong Kong, Shanghai, Chungking—they didn't mean anything to me, just a lot of names in a

Nurse Brooke Elliott (Anna Lee) with American flyer Woody Jason (John Carroll) watch a Japanese aerial attack with Chinese children in Republic's *Flying Tigers* (1942).

geography book, not towns where millions of people were being maimed and killed by bombs. Call them Texas, Maine or Michigan, that would have been different. They were my street. That's why I acted the way I did. Not because I was a heel but because I was still a kid.

Jason subsequently sacrifices himself during the mission by flying into a Japanese supply train after he is wounded.

Flying Tigers was completed before December 7, 1941. However, following the Japanese attack additional scenes were filmed that necessitated radical changes to the script. This change is most evident with regard to the leader of the group, Jim Gordon. For much of the film Gordon expresses a strong degree of anguish at having to send ill-equipped young pilots to their deaths. This is clear when Gordon collects the belongings of a young pilot. As he opens a drawer to put the dead pilot's articles away, a close-up reveals three similar packages. The camera captures his sense of grief as he conveys his sense of despair to his girlfriend, nurse Brooke Elliott (Anna Lee):

> GORDON: Quite a collection! [Gordon slams the dryer shut] Should've stayed in college where he came from. But he begged for a chance, begged like some kid asking to go to the circus. And I gave it to him
> ELLIOTT: What happened?
> GORDON: He didn't watch his tail, and outnumbered as usual.
> ELLIOTT: He did bring his ship back.

GORDON: Yeah, he did. But tomorrow or the next day there'll be somebody else in it, with three of them on his tail, or six or seven....

For much of the film Gordon is a divided character, conflicted by the military need to send men out to fight the Japanese versus his awareness that they are ill-equipped and outnumbered and that their chances for survival are not good. However, in the scenes filmed after December 7, this sense of internal discord and self-doubt disappears and by the time Roosevelt's December 8 Address to Congress is inserted any lingering sense of division is not evident. The film concludes with Gordon warmly welcoming a new recruit.

A similar pattern to the transformation of Woody Jason is evident in the Howard Hawks directed combat film *Air Force* (1943). Prior to the Japanese attack Joe Winocki (John Garfield) expresses his hostility towards the military and his desire to leave the service as soon as his enlistment on the *Mary Ann* expires. His superior officer, Captain Michael Quincannon (John Ridgely), fails to convince him that we "need you just like we need the whole gang. It takes all of us to make this ship function." However, they arrive in Hawaii just as the Japanese are attacking the island. Watching the battle from their plane, Quincannon urges his crew to take a "good look at Pearl Harbor, maybe it's something you'll want to remember." Winocki's response is immediate ("Damn them! Damn them!").

This instantly removes his desire to leave the service, as he tells Sergeant White (Harry Carey), the oldest and most respected member of the crew:

RKO's *Bombardier* (1943) traces the development of high level bombing on the enemy.

WHITE: Them Japs! They smear Pearl Harbor, smack Manila, raid Wake, Guam and Midway and still there ain't no war!

WINOCKI: And then they send a couple of oily gents to Washington with an olive wreath for the President while the boys back home slug Uncle Sam over the head with a crowbar.

WHITE: But Uncle Sam's a pretty tough old gentleman. You just wait until he gets mad!

WINOCKI: I hope you don't mind if I get slightly annoyed in the meantime.

WHITE: No, but I didn't expect it of you!

Selected passages from Roosevelt's December 8 Address are inserted as the *Mary Anne* approaches Wake Island and the men listen to Roosevelt's description of the damage inflicted by the Japanese. Roosevelt's pledge that "always will our whole Nation remember the character of the onslaught against us. No matter how long it may take us to overcome this premeditated invasion, the American people in their righteous might will win through to absolute victory" is accompanied by a close-up of Winocki's face. The trajectory of Roosevelt's address, from indignation to resistance to "inevitable triumph—so help us God," sets the pattern for the film.

Air Force, similar to many other films, closes with images of B-17s embarking on another mission accompanied by Roosevelt's voice promising retribution: "We shall hit him and hit him again wherever and whenever we can reach him, for we intend to bring this battle to him on his home ground." The film's epilogue reiterates the promise of melodramatic retribution: "This story has a conclusion but not an end ... for its real end will be the victory for which Americans ... on land, on sea and in the air ... have fought, are fighting now, and will continue to fight until peace has been won."

The Combat Film in 1945

In 1945, the final year of the Second World War when the threat to the survival of the United States had disappeared, there was a noticeable shift in the combat films released that year. The dramatic focus of these films changed from the external threat, a bipolar fight between "us" and "them," (the Allied Powers versus the Axis powers), to a focus on "us." While the emphasis in the combat film in 1942 and 1943 was on a desire for retribution, the 1945 combat film focused more on self-doubt and psychological torment. This shift followed the publication of long casualty lists along with first hand reporting of the war by correspondents such as Ernie Pyle. Pyle, one of the preeminent war journalists, captured this shift in his 1943 account of the Tunisian campaign in North Africa when he wrote that the exhilaration and "intoxication" generated by war is ultimately false.[264] He was supported by other war correspondents such as Richard Tregaskis who reported on the battle in the Solomon Islands in his book *Guadalcanal Diary*. Pyle, Tregaskis and others refused to present the war in terms of moral absolutes. They refused to romanticize it. Instead, Pyle wrote:

That is our war, and we will carry it with us as we go on from one battleground to another until it is all over, leaving some of us behind on every beach, in every field. We are just beginning with the ones who lie back of us in Tunisia. I don't know whether it was their good fortune or their misfortune to get out of it so early in the game. I guess it doesn't make any difference, once a man has gone. Medals and speeches and victories are nothing to them any more. They died and others lived and nobody knows why it is so. They died and thereby the rest of us go on and on. When we leave here for the next shore, there is nothing we can do for the ones beneath the wooden crosses, except perhaps to pause and murmur, "Thanks, pal."[265]

This shift, Pyle's "version of experience," was not a repudiation of melodrama but a change to a different emphasis within the melodramatic discourse. It approximates what Brooks describes as the "melodrama of consciousness,"[266] where the "melodrama of external action—the suspenseful menace, pursuit, and combat—are all past."[267] As Pyle explained:

It may be that war has changed me, along with the rest. It is hard for anyone to analyze himself. I know that I find more and more that I wish to be left alone, and yet contradictorily I believe that I have a new patience with humanity that I've never had before. When you've lived with the unnatural mass cruelty that mankind is capable of inflicting upon itself, you find yourself dispossessed of the faculty of blaming one poor man for the triviality of his faults. I don't know how any survivor of war can ever be cruel to anything, ever again.[268]

Howard Hawks's *Air Force* (1943). A dramatization of a true incident involving an American bomber arriving at Pearl Harbor just as the Japanese attack is taking place.

Objective Burma! *(1945)*

The filming of *Objective Burma!* took place at, among other places, the Los Angeles County Arboretum & Botanic Garden and the Providencia Ranch, between May 1, 1944, and August 26, 1944. It was premiered in New York on January 26, 1945. However, when the film was released in the United Kingdom in September that year, the British press took strong exception to the film's assumption that America played a major role in the Burma campaign.

Warner's *Objective Burma* (1945) with George Tobias as Corporal Gordon and James Brown as Sergeant Tracy.

In reality the campaign was fought almost entirely by British, Indian and Commonwealth troops. After the British Prime Minister Winston Churchill joined in the controversy, the film was shelved in Britain until 1952 when it was released with a pro–British introduction and an apology. *Objective Burma!* was the first Hollywood combat film produced during the Second World War to move away from the jingoistic presentation of war and focus more on the culpability of the American military command and less on the external threat from the Japanese. Every combat film released between 1942 and 1944 focused on unity of purpose between the fighters on the ground and the military hierarchy. Not so *Objective Burma!* The film follows the attempt of a small number of American paratroopers to get back to their base and how this is frustrated, and sabotaged, by military command, led by Colonel Carter (Warner Anderson).

Objective Burma! was directed by Raoul Walsh and starred Errol Flynn as Captain Nelson. The script by Ranald McDougall and Lester Cole was based on Alvah Bessie's original story. Both Cole and Bessie were subsequently sent to prison for one year as members of the Hollywood Ten and they were also blacklisted in Hollywood. The film was nominated for three Academy Awards including Bessie for Best Writing, Original Story. The story begins with a small unit of American paratroopers sent to Burma with orders to destroy a Japanese radar station. This is accomplished early in the film, leaving the bulk of the story, most of the 142-minute film, to focus on their attempts to return to their base. As each attempt fails a rift develops between the combat group and the command center as the audience, not the combat soldiers, learn that Colonel Carter is prepared to sacrifice the paratroopers in the interest of the overall military strategy. Instead of directing them back to the base, he decides to use them as decoys to draw the Japanese away from the major Allied invasion of Burma. After studying reconnaissance photos of three dead Americans at the third supply drop, he calls off the search for the men and this, seemingly, condemns them to capture or death. Tired, hungry and angry, the unity of the group begins to fracture until Mark Williams (Henry Hull), a middle-aged newspaper reporter accompanying the paratroopers, collapses. The men, however, refuse to abandon him. This provides a counterpoint to Carter's decision that the men are expendable.

Nelson splits his command into two groups with plans to meet at a new rendezvous point. However, when he and his men arrive at the new destination they discover that the other group has been butchered by the Japanese. This, briefly, takes the film back to the tenor of the earlier combat films as the men pledge to "wipe all those Japs off the face of the Earth." This desire for retribution subsides quickly as the men focus on their own survival. After many frustrations, their loyalty to Nelson begins to wear thin. After a futile, and grueling, climb to Carter's latest destination point, when Nelson asks them to dig in and set up defenses, they refuse and just stare at him. Both bewildered by their refusal and sympathetic to their bitterness, he tells them, "What's the matter with you. What did you expect to find up here anyway? I don't like this any better than you do, but we had orders to come here and we're going to stay here even if we rot waiting."

The paratroopers, reluctantly, follow Nelson's order without any real hope for their survival. Although Carter's tactics of using the men as a diversion is successful in the overall Burma strategy, the small group is forced to fight for their lives in the darkness. After successfully repelling the Japanese they confront the cost the next morning. One of the soldiers notices the body of a member of the group, Fred Hollis (William Hudson), and his bitter reaction provides a response that would never have been countenanced in the earlier combat films: "So much for Mrs. Hollis' nine months of pain and twenty years of hope!"

This is reiterated in the film's closing moments when Nelson confronts Carter by telling him that most of his command is dead:

> CARTER: You have no idea how important blowing up that radar station was to us.
> NELSON: [He puts his hand in his jacket and pulls out a large handful of tags representing the men killed during the mission] Here's what it cost! Not much to send home, is it? A handful of Americans [referring to the tags as he hands them over to Carter].

The film's epilogue reiterates the film's prevailing theme involving the human cost of military success. This shows in Nelson's anguish. As he enters the plane that will take him back to his base, he looks back to the area where his men died and a brief camera movement captures his torment.

A Walk in the Sun *(1945)*

Based on Harry Brown's 1944 novel *A Walk in the Sun,* the film was directed by Lewis Milestone with an excellent screenplay by Robert Rossen. It was filmed on the Agoura Ranch (California) and the Twentieth Century–Fox ranch between October

24, 1944, and January 1945. It premiered on December 3, 1945. While the 1943 allied invasion of Italy, specifically the beach landing at Salerno, provides the military backdrop, the film focuses on a platoon of American soldiers and one minor mission: to occupy a farmhouse so as to facilitate the destruction of a nearby bridge. The platoon has little knowledge of, or even interest in, the success or otherwise of the overall campaign. They just want to survive the war. One of the main narrative strands concerns the impact that leadership has on a succession of men. In earlier combat films, such as *The Navy Comes Through*, *Air Force*, *Crash Dive* (1943), *Action in the North Atlantic* (1943) and *Gung Ho* (1943), the mantle of leadership strengthens the individual and intensifies his patriotic duty. In *A Walk in the Sun* this is reversed as each leader suffers self-doubt and psychological torment due to the responsibilities of the position.

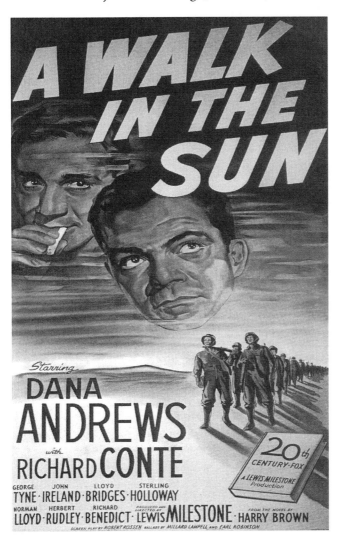

During the landing at Salerno the young lieutenant in charge of the platoon is wounded by a shell fragment. After landing on the beach Sergeant Pete Halverson (Matt Willis), the senior sergeant, arranges for Sergeant Eddie Porter (Herbert Rudley) to take charge while he goes to inform the captain of the lieutenant's injury. After both Halverson and the lieutenant die, Porter reluctantly assumes command and leads the men on a six-mile march to their destination, a farmhouse. However, during the trek Porter suffers a nervous breakdown forcing Sergeant Bill Tyne (Dana Andrews) to take over.

Director Lewis Milestone's *A Walk in the Sun* (1945), an adaptation of Harry Brown's novel which follows a platoon of American soldiers who, after landing at Salerno in Italy, have to capture a farmhouse. The film focuses more on the psychological effects of war rather than combat with the enemy. The film stars Richard Conte as Private Rivera and Dana Andrews as Sergeant Bill Tyne.

There are only two

encounters with the enemy as the film focuses more on Tyne's psychological battle with himself. This culminates in the assault on the farmhouse and Tyne's slow crawl towards it is presented in a series of tight close-ups of his face, intercut with lap dissolves from his point of view, accompanied by his voiceover. During this slow movement, where the enemy are not shown, he encounters the dead body of one of his men, Rankin (Chris Drake), whereupon he repeats the ironic phrase passed from soldier to soldier throughout the film: "Nobody dies! [Tyne continues to crawl across the field towards the farmhouse] Nobody dies! We've come a long way, a long six miles…. My head's spinning, everything's spinning, that house [zip pan to the farmhouse], the fields [the fields are spinning], the sky [Tyne turns over and looks up at the sky which is also spinning]."

Unlike earlier combat films which celebrated the importance of each mission, *A Walk in the Sun* eliminates the military importance of the mission to focus on the men. There is even a touch of irony in the form of Private Windy Craven's (John Ireland) "make believe" letters back home. At one point he composes a make believe letter from one of the dead soldiers, Tinker (George Offerman, Jr.), to his mother: "Dear Mum. I'm now asleep against a wall somewhere in Italy. It isn't very comfortable but a man has to lie where he can these days. If you ever get to Italy you must come and see me for I am always going to be here." Later, after the successful completion of their mission, Windy composes another ironic "letter" to his sister: "Dear Frances, we just blew a bridge and took a farmhouse. It was so easy, so terribly easy." On another occasion one of the men, Sergeant Ward (Lloyd Bridges), while waiting for a reconnaissance patrol to scout the road ahead, explains that the soil around here is no good: "Maybe too many soldiers have been walking on it. They've been walking on it for a long time. That's what always happens to a country when soldiers walk on it."

Ward's comment and Windy's "letters" functions as parables. But not the regeneration parables told by President Roosevelt after the Japanese attack on Pearl Harbor. When Sergeant Porter finally breaks down and is unable to lead the platoon, Ward picks up a handful of dirt and remarks "poor dirt, poor country." This is followed by Windy's explanation (to himself) as to the nature of Porter's breakdown.

> You're crying, Porter. You're crying because you are wounded. You don't have to be bleeding because you are wounded. You've just had one battle too many. Yeah, you are out of it now. No more guesswork waiting and wondering for you. You've built yourself a foxhole up here [Windy places a thumb to his forehead]. Ain't nothing in the world will make you come out of it. Go ahead Porter, keep crying, we understand.

Windy's ironic letters and asides are encapsulated by the film's title, *A Walk in the Sun.* This film, in an unconventional epilogue, closes with a ballad that provides another ironic commentary on the "success" of the mission: the capture of just one small farmhouse, and the deaths that resulted. It will not go down as a major event in military history and will pass unnoticed in the context of the overall war. The "poets" will not write of their deeds and children will not celebrate their "success" in song. Instead it was just a little walk in the warm Italian sun. Although it was not an easy thing, the ballad notes, it will be celebrated by poets and children in the future. Of course, this is deeply ironic as the taking of the farmhouse will pass undetected by history. No poets, no children. The film's overt use of irony threatens its melodramatic basis as irony, as a fictional mode, is the antithesis of melodrama. As Northrop Frye explains, irony "is born of the low mimetic; it takes life exactly as it finds it. ... the ironist fable without moralizing, it has no object but his subject."[269] Tragic irony, Frye argues, invokes a sense of alienation from society.[270]

Ernie Pyle's The Story of G.I. Joe (1945)

Ernie Pyle's The Story of G.I. Joe was a box office and critical success with four Academy Award nominations, including best screenplay (Leopold Atlas, Guy Endore and Philip Stevenson), best supporting actor (Robert Mitchum), Best Music Scoring and Best Song ("Linda"). The film was based on descriptions recorded by Pulitzer Award winning war correspondent Ernie Pyle in his newspaper column. Excerpts from his columns were subsequently collected in his books, *Here Is Your War* (1943) and *Brave War* (1944). The production was initiated by producer Lester Cowan when he approached the War Department in September 1943 seeking approval and cooperation for a war film that focused on infantryman fighting in North Africa. In November 1943 he submitted an outline based on material from Pyle's *Here Is Your War* followed by filming, mainly battle sequences, in the desert under the direction of Leslie Fenton in March 1944. After a few weeks the production was shut down for script revisions while Cowan sought a new director.

In September William Wellman, after repeatedly refusing to be involved, agreed to direct the film. Robert Mitchum, who was largely unknown at the time, was cast as Captain Walker after impressing Wellman with his test scene that depicted Walker's emotional breakdown following news of more casualties. Mitchum, who was currently serving in the Army, was allowed to count the time spent on the film towards his military service. The Army also allocated 150 veterans of the Italian campaign to the film.

Ernie Pyle spent two weeks in Hollywood working on the script during the early stages of the production. Filming ended in January 1945 although Mitchum was brought back for retakes on April 25, 1945. It premiered on June 18, 1945, two months after Ernie Pyle was killed at Iejima on April 18 during the invasion of Okinawa. Reviews for the film were universally positive and General Dwight D. Eisenhower described it as the greatest war film he had ever seen. William Wellman also regarded it as his best film although he refused to watch it after its release as it brought back too many painful memories of the soldiers who participated in the filming that had subsequently died in battle after filming finished. *The New York Times* reviewer described the film as a "hard hitting, penetrating drama of the footslogging soldier," and elevated the film to its "ten best" list for 1945.[271] The *Daily Variety* reviewer said that the "picture is screened with unequivocal realism. There is no hokum. No flag waving. No synthetic sentimentality. No bombast."[272]

The casting of real-life soldiers, who are listed in the credits as "the combat veterans of Africa, Sicily and Italy," as well as actual newspaper correspondents, impressed reviewers. Aside from Burgess Meredith as Pyle, the cast comprised little known actors (at that time) such as Robert Mitchum as Captain Walker, ex-boxer Freddie

Steele in the key role as Sergeant Warnicki, who eventually breaks down with battle fatigue, even director Wellman's wife Dorothy Coonan Wellman who, after a 12-year absence from the screen, appeared in the brief role as Lieutenant Elizabeth "Red" Murphy who marries one of the infantrymen, Private "Wingless" Murphy (Jack Reilly). Murphy, like many of Walker's command, dies (off-camera) after a battle-ground marriage ceremony. Meredith as Pyle was also transformed into a close facsimile of the war correspondent. This was accomplished by shaving Meredith's head and applying wrinkles to his face. Pyle wrote in his column in February 14, 1945, that they "made him up so well that he's even uglier than I am, poor fellow."[273]

Cinematographer Russell Metty eliminated any semblance of glamor with his stark compositions. This included the studio sequences such as a bombed out Italian church that provided the setting for one of the few fighting scenes in the film. The cramped, dirty sets included the ruins of an Italian town as well as the muddy caves and makeshift quarters for Walker's command at Monte Cassino. Here the Americans suffered heavy casualties due to the decision by the command not to bomb a monastery used by the Germans positioned on the top of a hill who, in turn, directed their artillery at the Americans. Only Eisenhower's intervention, after many deaths, reversed the order.

Sam Fuller, future screenwriter and celebrated director, served as a soldier with the 1st Infantry Division fighting the same route out of North Africa and he praised the film for its "feeling of death and mass murder."[274] Yet there are very few actual combat scenes. Men are shown heading towards the battlefield. Only some return. The few battles in the film are not choreographed in the usual Hollywood style but are presented as bloody and chaotic defeats, such as the defeat inflicted on the (largely) new recruits of Company C, 18th Infantry, U.S. Army at the Battle of Kasserine Pass near the beginning of the film. Even in the victories, such as Monte Cassino, the emphasis is on the cost. Except for a relatively brief sequence in an Italian church-yard depicting a skirmish involving Walker, Warnicki and three Germans, the enemy is not seen.

The film begins with C Company, 18th Infantry, about to join a convoy to engage the enemy in Tunisia. In a melodramatic touch, to denote the men as "innocent," a young puppy ("Arab") is found by one of the soldiers. While this incident has its basis in fact, as a small black and white female named "Squirt" served as mascot to the Company, Arab is seen throughout the film as she is passed among the surviving members of the Company. After Walker initially rejects their request to take the puppy with them, a young recruit is shown holding her in the truck as it moves towards the front. However, he becomes the first casualty, killed off-screen, when an enemy plane attacks the convoy.

The men move from the disaster at the Kasserine Pass, the site of the first major American defeat of the Second World War, to their arrival in Italy. Under Walker's command, they move from one battleground to the next. Eventually the survivors are transformed from callow recruits to, in Walker's words, "tough killers." But we see little evidence of this as the battle scenes, involving rapid editing, darkness, explosions and flares, are presented as chaos. In Italy the men are shown "flinching, huddled against a small blasted wall as mortars explode close by, turn hollow-eyed and mechanical as they progress through this terrain, begin sleepwalking , stiff-legged in their exhaustion."[275]

As the casualties mount, Walker's psychological state deteriorates until he shares a bottle of grappa (what Walker describes as "Italian moonshine") with Ernie Pyle late one night close to Christmas in his "quarters," a muddy hovel in the remains of a bombed out building. The scene begins with Walker sitting by a pile of papers as he tries to summon the energy to write to the families of men who died that day. He begins composing a fictional "letter" about a deceased soldier to his mother: "Dear Mrs. Smith. Your son died bravely today…." He then breaks down and explains to Pyle that it "ain't my fault they get killed." Nevertheless, he feels like a "murderer." His anguish is compounded by the fact that he is forced to welcome the "new kids" ("that's what gets you") knowing that most of them will not survive very long. Disgusted by the "number of hills to be taken," Walker tells Pyle that if "only we could create something good out of all this energy, all these men."

The film ends with the death of Walker. The screenwriters closely followed the details in Ernie Pyle's famous newspaper column, "The Death of Captain Waskow," published on the front page of the *Washington Daily News* (where the entire edition sold out). It was subsequently reprinted in *Time* magazine and also featured in a war bond drive. Captain Henry T. Waskow of the 36th Division's Company B 143 Infantry, died on December 14, 1943, at San Pietro Infine in Italy. Pyle, however, does not witness Walker's death, only his body. After leaving the group for some time, he returns after Cassino has been taken and comes across the men as five mules are shown bringing down dead soldiers from a skirmish on a hill. The bodies, draped over wooden saddles with legs dangling over the other side of the mules, are lifted off and placed on the side of the road. The men, initially, seem disinterested as this is a regular occurrence. However, when one of them (Dondaro) notices Walker's body, he places him gently on the ground. He waits until other men have expressed their grief before unsuccessfully attempting to straighten Walker's uniform. He then takes Walker's hand and strokes his face.

Walker is denied a heroic death. It happens off-screen and for the men not close to him, he is just another casualty in a long line of casualties. As Pyle remarks in the film, "the G.I. lives so miserably and dies so miserably" and Walker's death is a testament to this. The film concludes as Dondaro and the other men, including Pyle, move on the next battle. It closes with Pyle's voice-over which accompanies an effective melodramatic moment as thousands of military crosses are superimposed on the hill behind Pyle:

> That is our war. And we will carry it with us as we go from one battleground to another until it is all over. We will win and I hope we can rejoice with victory but humbly. That all together we will try, try out of the memory of our anguish to reassemble our broken world into a pattern so firm and so fair that another great war can never be possible. And for those beneath the wooden crosses there is nothing we can do except pause and murmur "thanks pal."

Critics were universal in their praise of the film. They stressed that *The Story of G.I. Joe* was different from other combat films produced during the Second World War. Terms like "realistic" and "tragedy" were invoked in an effort to distinguish it. In *The Story of G.I. Joe* the spirit of blame, the righteous anger that permeated the post Pearl Harbor films, is replaced by a pervasive sense of sadness and loss. James Agee, in his review of the film, described it as "a tragic and eternal work of art."[276] He pointed out that nobody "is accused, not even the enemy; no remedy is indicated."[277]

Two

The 1930s Western

The thirties B-Western is the one place in the history of the Hollywood genre that doesn't ignore the historic failure of small farming in America. Put it this way, it is impossible not to claim that the B-Western, for all its crackpot plots and incompetent production values, is more sophisticated and even more "intellectual" than the vastly more pretentious and straight-faced A-Western—Scott Simmon.[1]

In 1927 Dora H. Stecker, from Cincinnati, addressed the National Conference on Social Work on the subject of "Some Desirable Goals for Motion Pictures." Stecker's paper crystallized the concerns of regional and rural audiences with regard to their inability to tailor the distribution and exhibition of Hollywood films to meet local needs. Stecker complained that the marketing practices of the major studios affected thousands of smaller communities and neighborhoods all across America. She pointed out that it was in the smaller urban or rural centers where the problems of socialization by the motion picture was more acutely manifested because it was here that traditional social norms were affected to a much greater degree.[2] Stecker pointed out that while the larger cities only contributed one-fifth of the American population, the influence of this urban sector on the content of the film industry was "overpowering."[3] This, she maintained, was evidenced by the "disproportionate influence of the first-run, downtown movie house on the films shown at suburban theatres."[4] Of the 17,836 theaters in the United States in 1927, 1,720 were first run, 3,140 were downtown while 12,700 were neighborhood, provincial or rural theaters. However, as the studios were fully aware, 25 percent of all rental income came from the relatively small number of downtown theaters. Stecker's concern was that the type of films catering for inner city theaters did not always meet the needs of rural and neighborhood audiences. This problem was compounded by the industry policy of block booking as it largely prevented many neighborhood, provincial and rural theaters from selecting "suitable" films for their audience.[5]

Block booking meant that any exhibitor not affiliated with a studio was often forced to take an entire "block" of films from a studio or distributor. This practice was based on a calculated pricing policy that raised the rental cost of a single film to a prohibitive level. It forced independent exhibitors to purchase a group/block of films where the average price was far more reasonable. The main impact of this practice was felt by local, independent theater owners operating in urban neighborhoods as well as provincial and rural areas. As Garth Jowett points out, the ramifications of

First National's 1925 film *Chickie* was a box-office success in urban centers but poorly received in rural and provincial areas. *The Lexington Leader* (Kentucky) described the film as totally unsuitable. The film starred Dorothy Mackaill as a young stenographer who has a baby out of wedlock with Barry Dunne (John Bowers), a law clerk.

this practice were not only economic but social. Many reform groups, women's organizations, including some people in the federal government, considered block booking as a key component in the fight against unsuitable films as it "stymied attempts at local control."[6]

Gregory Waller's book length study of commercial entertainment in Lexington, Kentucky, between 1896 and 1930 confirms Stecker's anxieties. Waller points out that in the 1920s the six downtown theaters in Lexington exhibited a "good measure of variety."[7] Yet, with the coming of sound, "Lexington saw a major overhaul of the local film exhibition business."[8] The Orpheum, which had been in continuous operation since 1912 as a "second-rank picture show,"[9] with an ever changing program of westerns, comedy shorts and serials (with as many as five different serials each week),[10] and without "all-star feature films"[11] (viz. major studio productions), closed its doors in April 1930. This left only two Lexington cinemas, the Ada Meade and the Opera House to program "westerns thrillers," serials and action films, the type of film favored by the local audience.

A new independent cinema, the State, opened in April 1929. However, six months later its owners leased both the State and the Kentucky to the Publix Theaters

Dorothy Mackaill in Warner's *Safe in Hell* (1931). Directed by William Wellman, Mackaill plays a woman who flees to a Caribbean island after killing the man who raped her and forced her into prostitution. *Safe in Hell* is another film that provoked outrage in rural and provincial areas.

Corporation, a subsidiary of Paramount Studios.[12] These theaters were among five hundred theaters acquired by Paramount between September 1929 and May 1930 as it sought to expand "its domination of film exhibition in the South."[13] This concentration of ownership weakened the ability of provincial cities such as Lexington to adjust its programming to the values and preferences of the local community.

The population of Lexington, a bi-racial city, grew from 26,00 in 1900 to 45,000 in 1930 and debate over movie content, and all forms of "commercial entertainment," was, at times, intense, especially during the various Sabbatarian campaigns that aimed to close all forms of amusements on the Sabbath. In 1915 demands for censorship intensified following the screening of Universal's *Hypocrites*, directed by Lois Weber, as the film featured the "figure of an undraped woman."[14] This, and other "controversial" films, inspired the *Leader*, one of Lexington's two daily newspapers, to publish an editorial, headed "Wanted—A Local Moving Picture Censorship,"[15] in its 27 February 1916 edition:

> Within the last two weeks there have been at least three pictures, probably more, exhibited in Lexington which should not have been countenanced and they belong to a class of attractions which, if not abandoned in respectable communities, will do serious damage....

When a young man takes a young woman to see a motion picture which he cannot discuss with her fully and frankly—if she is the right sort of a woman—it is about time he was changing his place of entertainment, and certainly a picture of this character is not a fit object to be displayed to hundreds of morbidly curious boys and girls.[16]

The editorial in the *Leader* was supported by several letters from the local board of education. The release of Fox's *The Serpent* (1916), written and directed by Raoul Walsh and starring Theda Bara, was also singled out by the board as "typical" as they claimed that the film "climaxed with a quasi-incestuous 'sexual act' and a suicide." These calls for censorship were strengthened by the decision of the Supreme Court in 1915 that ruled that moving pictures were merchandise and not protected by the First

Columbia's 1927 domestic melodrama *Stolen Pleasures*, a "Thrilling Drama of Foolish Wives and Husbands," involved two couples who separate after a domestic dispute.

Amendment. The Court's decision in Mutual Film vs. Ohio upheld the right of prior censorship and paved the way for local censorship boards. In 1933 there were eight state censorship boards: Florida, New York, Massachusetts, Kansas, Ohio, Pennsylvania, Virginia and Maryland. However, the "sphere of influence"[17] of these eight boards extended beyond these states. Thus, films censored in Ohio were shown in West Virginia and Kentucky.

In Lexington the *Leader* never lost its misgivings about the "dangerous 'jazz environment'"[18] of commercial amusements, especially the movies. When, for example, First National's 1925 melodrama *Chickie* was released, the *Leader* expressed its outrage as it could not be "discussed frankly and without reserve by a respectable young man and modest young woman in the presence of the parents of the young woman."[19] *Chickie* is a lost film that starred Dorothy Mackaill[20] as Chickie, a young stenographer, who is initiated into the high society world of millionaire Jake Munson (Paul Nicholson). At one of Munson's parties Chickie has a sexual relationship with Barry Dunne (John Bowers), a young law clerk. Following a misunderstanding when Dunne and his companion Ila (Olive Tell) find Chickie in Munson's apartment, a disillusioned Dunne leaves for London, closely followed by Ila. Meanwhile Munson withdraws his marriage proposal to Chickie after she tells him she is not a virgin. Pregnant, Chickie writes to Dunne in London but Ila intercepts the letter, destroys it and then writes to Chickie, falsely claiming that she is married to Dunne. Chickie becomes a mother and Dunne, after learning of Chickie's predicament, returns home and marries her.

Films such as *Chickie* served to inflame the *Leader* as the paper argued that the problem was a "national problem, not something particular to

Fox's popular series of films featuring ex-marines Harry Quirt (Edmund Lowe) and Jim Flagg (Victor McLaglen) who battle each other over Pepper (Lupe Velez), a nightclub entertainer, in *Hot Pepper* (1933). *Variety* described the film as a "little dirtier and a little rougher" than the earlier films featuring Quirt and Flagg.

Lexington."[21] Many studio films such as *Chickie* were considered "unfit for consumption"[22] in provincial towns and rural areas as they represented, according to an editorial in the local paper, "what is lowest and basest in human nature."[23] These towns, Stecker and others argued, wanted to select their own films. And they did not want "sophisticated" melodramas such as *Chickie*. In the late 1920s and early 1930s these protests from provincial areas became more pronounced and it was a factor in the formation of the Production Code in 1930. They preferred sensational melodramas, especially series westerns starring Tom Keene, George O'Brien, Buck Jones, Ken

In Fox's *Hot Pepper* (1933) Quirt (Edmund Lowe, left) and Flagg (Victor McLaglen, right) chase after Pepper (Lupe Velez) who spends part of the film in a satin sheet. Rural audiences were not impressed. A Midwest exhibitor declared the film as too "hot for small town patronage catering to respectable people and family trade."

Maynard, William Boyd, Gene Autry, Tex Ritter, and the Three Mesquiteers. But the major Hollywood studios were, with a few exceptions, not interested in this market as the profit margins were small.

The 1930s series western has received scant scholarly attention. These films were either ignored or treated with contempt. This includes academic studies by Jane Tompkins,[24] Lee Clark Mitchell[25] and Robert Murray Davis.[26] Perhaps the conventional view of the series/B western is summed up Richard Koszarski, in Volume 3 of the *History of the American Cinema*, titled *An Evening's Entertainment: The Age of the Silent Feature Picture 1915–1928*, in his section on "Drama and Melodrama: The Genre Film." He writes that the early cinema "continued to operate in the melodramatic tradition that had worked so well during the nickelodeon era."[27] In this context he, incorrectly, views melodrama as "old-fashioned" as only a few directors during this period, such as King Vidor, Erich von Stroheim, and William deMille, are able to transcend its limitations and "offer a vision of life more complex and multidimensional than that found in UNCLE TOM'S CABIN (1918), BLUE JEANS (1918), or WAY DOWN EAST (1920)."[28] With regard to the western (the "most popular of silent genres"),[29] he bemoans the fact that Tom Mix had, by the 1920s, eclipsed William S. Hart's popularity "by substituting a circus rider's bag of tricks for the dour realism

Ann Harding and John Boles star in RKO's *The Life of Vergie Winters* (1934), a melodrama involving adultery between a married politician and a milliner. A Midwest exhibitor complained that it "may be ok for the large cities [but] it's bad medicine for our business." Another exhibitor in a small town in Michigan reported taking "a terrible licking on the picture."

offered by Hart. The change in public taste was predictable because Westerns had moved from the serious plateau of the early DeMille pictures to a genre intended for children. The form ultimately became so degraded that Westerns were the only genre segregated from the balance of a studio's product line (as in '…and eight westerns')."[30]

None of this is true. The western in the 1920s and the series western in the 1930s were not produced for children, although they probably enjoyed the genre. The target audience was adults in small towns and rural areas. The "dour realism" of William S. Hart was no more "realistic" than Tom Mix's "circus rider's bag of tricks." Hart mostly worked in films that were sentimental melodramas. Mix, on the other hand, was a successful exponent of sensational melodrama. The publication of Peter Stanfield's *Hollywood, Westerns and the 1930s: The Lost Trail* in 2001 and, the following year, *Horse Opera: The Strange History of the 1930s Singing Cowboy* along with Scott Simmon's *The Invention of the Western Film: A Cultural History of the Genre's First Half Century* finally provided a scholarly approach to this neglected area. This neglect, Stanfield points out, was due to the fact these films were considered "from the perspective of a middle-class aesthetic."[31] This, he argues, is an "inappropriate criteria"[32] as they were always going to fall short of "bourgeois notions of taste, where the demand is for narratives and characters that conform to prevailing discourses of realism."[33]

Stanfield utilizes contemporary trade publications and newspaper reviews, cultural studies such as Michael Denning's *Mechanic Accents: Dime Novels and Working Class-Culture in America,* along with a broad selection of films, to provide an important corrective to studies of the 1930s western. He establishes a clear dichotomy in the production and exhibition of westerns in the 1930s. The content and form of the westerns preferred by rural and small-town audiences differed markedly from that favored by audiences who attended the large first-run theaters in urban centers. While the major studio westerns were preoccupied with variations of the "myth of the frontier," the clash between the wilderness and civilization and stories based on nation building, the series western ignored such concerns. Instead they dramatized rural/small town

William S. Hart directed and starred in *The Cold Deck* (1917), a sentimental melodrama with Hart as "Level" Leigh, a professional gambler, who keeps his profession a secret from his sister who is an invalid. To raise money for his sister's care he holds up a stagecoach.

fears and anxieties arising out of modernity, industrialization[34] and the Depression. Hence stories involving dispossession, dislocation, gender anxieties, the "end of the west" and the conflict between capital and labor appeared regularly. As the decade proceeded there was a shift in these concerns, most notably with regard to the role of the Federal government in rural communities. This provoked significant formal and thematic changes to a sub-genre based on populist values that were, in general, fiercely individualistic. As the economic situation in the United States improved late in the decade, and, especially, after America's entry into the Second World War, the series western was no longer overly concerned with dispossession and dislocation. Instead, it addressed a different set of anxieties and desires.[35]

In essence what you have in the 1930s was two types of western melodramas.

Both types shared the same dramatic structure, melodrama. The narrative in each type was predicated on a bipolar structure involving the clash between good and evil. Each presented the violation of virtue by a powerful villain. And each closed their stories with an unequivocal presentation of poetic justice. Yet, within this aesthetic framework the ideological concerns of each type was markedly different. This dichotomy extended not only to the narrative focus but also exhibition and marketing practices. This was discussed in the Introduction of this book with regard to the 1932 George O'Brien series western *Mystery Ranch*. The decision of New York's Winter Garden Theater to retitle the film *The Killers* was motivated by the theater's determination to hide the fact that the film was a fifty-six-minute George O'Brien series western.

Tom Mix in the western melodrama *The Fighting Streak* (1922). Mix, as blacksmith Andy Lanning, is framed for murder until his girlfriend Ann Withers (Patsy Ruth Miller) engages a lawyer to clear his name.

However, during the screening of the film the patrons, and reviewers, soon discerned the truth and reacted accordingly. This prompted a warning from one reviewer to exhibitors to be "careful with this one" and focus on the "class of your patrons that are not so sophisticated in their picture demands" and who prefer "thrills, action, danger, daring heroism, and a typical Western-hero romance."[36] To distinguish between the series western and A budgeted westerns, the studios often promoted their expensive westerns with major stars as anything but westerns. This resulted in advertising campaigns utilizing vague descriptors such as "outdoor dramas" or "romance."[37] On the other hand, series and B westerns were promoted, primarily in rural areas and small towns, as westerns. These films, as Stanfield points out, had a "predetermined audience that the film companies recognized in their more direct, limited and unambiguous marketing campaigns."[38]

The series western, along with the film serial, are prime examples of sensational film melodrama. Sensational melodrama, with its emphasis on spectacle, visceral thrills and performance (stunts, comedy, music) within a binary mode of address, clear-cut characters and predictably moral resolutions was an ideal aesthetic form to address specific concerns to rural, small town and provincial audiences. In other words, sensational melodrama provided an aesthetic framework that appealed to rural and small-town audiences while assimilating concerns, anxieties and desires specific to this audience. As discussed with the 1940 version of *Law and Order*, it offered a comforting form with familiar actors, repetitive plots and recurring the-

Tom Mix starred in Fox's adaptation of Zane Grey's *Riders of the Purple Sage* (1925).

matic concerns that were resolved according to the values favored by this audience.

Without mentioning melodrama, Stanfield documents the appeal of this type of melodrama to an audience that did not place great value on narrative causality and narrative logic involving psychologically complex characters.[39] Instead of coherence and introspection they wanted the "spectacle of stunts, trick riding, buffoonery, fist-fights, and so forth [which] created a pleasurable stalling of the inevitable plot trajectory."[40] These intrinsic aspects of sensational melodrama enhanced the pleasure of the film for an "intended audience … [who] values the exhibition of performance (which disrupts an 'invisible' unfolding of narrative events linked through cause and effect)."[41] While Koszarski argued that the B and series western "ultimately became so degraded that Westerns were the only genre segregated from the balance of a studio's product line (as in '…and eight westerns')," Stanfield counters this by pointing out that this is precisely the reason why studying the series western is important as "Hollywood clearly recognized that these westerns had a distinct audience, which is why the production was 'segregated,' not because it was 'degraded.'"[42]

The series western was characterized by what Scott Simmon describes as the "surrealism" of the 1930s B western.[43] There was a deliberate lack of historical verisimilitude as these films assimilated Hollywood's version of the historical west (including familiar studio western towns, cowboy clothes, guns, saloons and the locations such as the Iverson Ranch) with representations of 1930s America that included contemporary women's fashions, hairstyles, cars, telephones, trains, planes, boats, skyscrapers, 1930s music and dancing. Simmon cites *The Man from Utah* (1934), a low budget John Wayne western, where stagecoach

Tom Mix in Fox's *Hard Boiled* (1926), an action melodrama promoted as "Riding with Youth in the Wide Open Spaces."

riders are subjected to a holdup while traveling to watch John Wayne compete in a 1930s rodeo.[44] Thus, he argues, "the B-Westerns seem irresponsibly cavalier about the era in which they are set."[45] The cowboy heroes, with their flamboyant costumes, were not perceived as "naturalistic figures in a fictional equivalent of the world inhabited by its audience but are instead its fantasized substitutes who act out the audience's fears and desires."[46] This mixture was not, Stanfield points out, off-putting to its audience of "men, women, and children from small town, rural and urban neighborhoods, working-class families that were habitual consumers of cinema that wanted what [Michael] Denning calls a 'magical, fairy tale transformation of familiar landscapes and characters,' where everything that is wrong is turned right. This is precisely the world that series and singing westerns envisioned."[47] A world where conflicts between labor and capital were always resolved in favor of the working man and woman.[48]

The "surreal" form of the series western had a specific aesthetic function to mask the contemporary concerns embedded in these films. For example, one of the most extreme examples of this bizarre mixture of the "historical" west and 1930s America can be found in the Gene Autry westerns produced in the mid- and late 1930s. This "surrealism" allowed them to "deal overtly with issues engendered by the Great Depression and the New Deal. They make no claim to represent the West authentically, but they do invoke the economic, social, and cultural issues that affected his core constituency."[49] The plots in these films, along with most series westerns, were concerned with both cultural changes arising out modernity's challenge to Victorian values as well as specific economic issues emanating from the Great Depression. Hence, stories again and again focused on the tension between social changes and traditional (populist) values as well as specific economic issues involving rural dislocation, dispossession and the tensions between capital and labor.

John Wayne, Ray Corrigan and Max Terhune as the Three Mesquiteers in Republic's *Overland Stage Raiders* (1938). The "surrealism" of the series western is evident in this film which features a Greyhound bus, cattle rustled off a train, cowboys on horses and John Wayne parachuting out of a plane co-owned by Louise Brooks. This was Brooks's last film in a career that included the leading role in G.W. Pabst's *Pandora's Box* (1929).

As sensational melodramas these films addressed questions such as how to live, who are the victims and who is persecuting them. While the answers provided were utopian in nature, they documented the anxieties and desires of a specific group of Americans in the 1930s. To make these films palatable to this audience the films employed the pleasures of sensational melodrama with its comforting mix of music, action, comedy, spectacle and retribution. In the face of widespread drought, soil erosion, rural over production, falling agricultural prices, widespread unemployment, labor unrest, and the abandonment of rural properties, the series western dramatized how the failing farm or ranch can magically be transformed into an economically viable unit through the elimination of rustlers. Or through the discovery of precious minerals or oil. Or the restoration of water rights by the building of a dam and irrigation systems. Or the elimination of gangsters causing industrial unrest. In other words, the world of melodrama transposed these concerns into social allegories and their audience recognized them as such.[50]

Gun Smoke *(1931) and* Cross Fire *(1933)*

Ben Singer's study of sensational theatrical melodrama reaffirms Brooks's conclusion that "melodrama portrayed the individual's powerlessness within the harsh and unpredictable material life of modern capitalism ... it [also] served a quasi-religious ameliorative function in reassuring audiences that a higher cosmic moral force still looked down on the world and governed it with an ultimately just hand."[51] It flourishes, Singer argues, in times of social and economic upheaval, in a "world of unprecedented cultural discontinuity and social atomization,"[52] by addressing modern anxieties in an allegorical form. Hence it provides "reassurance of ultimate divine protection and fortifying faith in simple, immutable moral verities."[53] Its role is to reaffirm the virtues of traditional society as it cannot, Brooks argues, "figure the birth of a new society—the role of comedy—but only the old society reformed."[54] This, as a representative example of sensational melodrama, was the function of the series western.

Paramount promoted their 1931 western *Gun Smoke* with the tagline that the film was "A 'WESTERN' that's different!" Nothing could be further from the truth. The ideological basis of *Gun Smoke* was entirely consistent with other series westerns produced during this period. In essence, the film argues for a return to "traditional" western values after modernity, in the form of gangsters, descends upon a small town in Idaho. The advertising posters promoted the film showing the star Richard Arlen in full cowboy costume alongside a cowboy riding in a western setting. Below Arlen is the villain William Boyd who is presented in direct contrast to the cowboy. He is wearing a business suit while smoking a cigarette. This summarizes the film. Arlen represents tradition, the "innocence" of small-town life (Bunsen, Idaho) while the gangster imports a system of corrupt values that threaten this small town. In essence, the poster dramatizes the populist fear of big city corruption—represented by five men in suits firing automatic guns.[55]

The film begins with gangster boss Kedge Darvis (William Boyd) and his gang traveling by train from Boston after killing members of a rival gang. Darvis decides to hide out in the small town of Bunsen and take what is valuable from the town before moving back to Boston. His choice of Bunsen, aside from the fact that it is a remote small town, comes from an invitation from people in Bunsen to visit the town as they are looking for investors from the East and will offer concessions to them. As

Darvis tells his men, "We're capitalists." The locals greet Darvis and his men with a marching band and a welcoming committee. This is headed by the film's heroine, Sue Vancey (Mary Brian), who desperately wants to modernize Bunsen. To this end she hosts Darvis and his men at her ranch. Sue, eager to impress the prospective investors, tells Darvis that although we are still "primitive out here … we are doing our best to keep up with the times."

The opposition to Darvis and his "investors" comes from the film's hero, Brad Farley (Richard Arlen). In direct contrast to the gangsters, who arrive by train, Farley makes a spectacular (western) entry, guns blazing, as he rides down the main street with his men. Farley, with his colorful cowboy clothes, horse and six guns, provides a visual contrast to the drab urban clothes worn by the gangsters. However, Farley's desire to retain traditional values and reject the "businessmen" is opposed by Sue. This causes a major rift between them as she disapproves of his "primitive" cowboy ways. When she tells Farley that Darvis is "up to date, modern," he tells her that he does not "like businessmen."

> SUE: Do you call hunting wild horses a man's job?
> BRAD: Well, maybe no. But I've never seen any cripples make a success out of it!
> SUE: Oh, I know it's hard work. But that isn't the point. Don't you understand that [your] … time has gone by in this country…. You waste your time doing things that had to be done in the Old West.
> BRAD: The Old West was a pretty good country, Sue. And some pretty good people came out of it.
> SUE: Oh, I know but things are different now, Brad.

Sue is impressed by the "sophistication" of the gangster which includes his musical skill at the piano, a talent that elicits a sneer from Farley. This follows Farley's warning to the citizens of Bunsen:

> Maybe they'll put up a lot of factories and use all of the water in our creeks for power, and our trees for paper pulp, and our kids to run the machines for them. Maybe, if we pay them enough, they'll put up a lot of tall buildings, so that we can't see the sun for the smoke of the chimneys. And all of the cowboys left in this country will get jobs driving trucks and we'll all be just as tame, dirty and crowded as a lot of them places back east…. I want to keep this country the way it always been: big, clean and roomy. So the people who like it can have it to live in and those who don't like it that way can get out!

Darvis's attempt to seduce Sue comes to an abrupt end after the gangster discovers the existence of a lucrative gold mine near Bunsen. After murdering the mine's elderly owner, "Strike" Jackson (William V. Mong), he imprisons Sue and the rest of her employees at her ranch. He then imports gangsters from the city to work Jackson's mine while placing Bunsen under his brutal control, killing anyone who resists him. After more killings, Tack Gillup (Charles Winninger), Sue's foreman, escapes with the assistance of the ranch cook, Wong (Willie Fung). In retaliation Darvis orders the execution of Wong while Tack alerts Brad Farley who is rounding up wild horses in the mountains. Farley vows vengeance by telling his men that "they [Darvis and his men] have come back to where killing was invented!" The West!

After exhausting the gold from Jackson's mine, and worried that Gillup will bring help, Darvis and his gang leave Bunsen after taking Sue and her employee Hempsey

Tom Keene and Betty Furness in RKO's *Cross Fire* (1933). Another celebration of traditional western values.

Dell (Louise Fazenda) along as hostages. He warns the town that he will kill the two women if anyone follows them. Undeterred, Farley and his cowboys kill the remaining gangsters in Bunsen before setting off after Darvis and the women. In the action climax to the film Farley unleashes a herd of wild mustangs on the frightened gangsters and throws Darvis from a high cliff during a fight while the rest of the gangsters are shot or killed in a landslide. A chastened Sue reunites with Farley and urges him to stay the way he is ("I want you just as you are").

Two years after the release of *Gun Smoke* RKO released a similar film *Cross Fire,* the last entry in its twelve film Tom Keene series. Otto Brower directed it for executive producers Merian C. Cooper and David Lewis while studio head David O. Selznick was also involved in the production. The cinematographer was Nicholas Musuraca with Max Steiner in charge of the music that included an unusual jazz score over the opening credits. The script by Harold Shumate reaffirmed the ideological thrust of *Gun Smoke* by celebrating the "tried and true" values of the Old West. The budget for this above average series western was a minuscule, for a major studio, $26,000 and the film grossed a respectable $98,000.[56]

Cross Fire begins in the early years of the First World War, before the United States entered the War, in the small rural community of King City. Tom Allen (Tom Keene) manages the Sierra Mining Company on behalf of five elderly citizens:

rancher Daniel Plummer (Lafe McKee), Judge Whitney T. Wilson (Jules Cowles), blacksmith Charlie Rudorph (Thomas Brower), who is also mayor of King City, the local doctor, Milas P. Stiles (Nick Copley) and banker John Wheeler (Charles K. French). Tom, eager to get involved in the war, enlists as an ambulance driver where he meets an expatriate Chicago man, Ed Wimpy (Edgar Kennedy), in Paris who is driving a taxi after a failed business venture.

Back in King City, banker John Wheeler discovers that Bert King (Edward Phillips), the man Tom left behind to operate the mine, has been colluding with an Eastern crook, Kreuger (Stanley Blystone), to divert profits from the mine into their bank accounts. Before Wheeler can notify his partners, King murders him and frames Daniel Plummer for the killing. After Sheriff Jim Wells (Murdock MacQuarrie) arrests Plummer, Charlie Rudorph erupts and tells the other men: "These up to date methods of settling things don't settle well with me. I propose we go back to the tried and true methods that were good enough when us fellows were starting to settle this country. ... You ain't forgot how to shoot, have you?" Rudorph, Wilson and Stiles stage a jail break and extricate Plummer. They head for the hills where they rob cash payments from the mine. The imagery involved in the robberies reinforces the film's central theme as the elderly men, dressed as cowboys on horses, are shown robbing cars driven by gangsters in city clothes. After each robbery the men leave a receipt.

Following the Armistice in Europe, Tom returns to King City and accepts the job of deputy sheriff so that he can assist Plummer and the others. When he rides out to their camp in the hills and arrests Plummer, the elderly rancher asks Tom: "Have you turned modern too!" After they arrive back in King City they discover that Bert King, as mayor, has fired Jim Wells and replaced him with Kreuger as sheriff. King also appoints his own (corrupt) judge to handle Plummer's trial. All appears to be lost until Wimpy overhears King planning to lynch Plummer by setting a trap for the four elderly men when they try to rob King's latest shipment of money from the mine. The film's climax is a mixture of the modern and the traditional with the old timers on horseback trapped by gangsters using a machine gun while Tom and Wimpy ride to the rescue in Wimpy's taxi cab. Tom disarms the machine gun, captures King after a fist fight, and the elderly men are exonerated after Kreuger, whom King shot trying to escape, turns against his boss and explains that King murdered Wheeler. The film ends with Tom marrying Plummer's daughter Pat (Betty Furness).

Both films valorize values from the past. Both also express a deep hostility to corporate capitalism. In this manner films such as *Gun Smoke* were allegories on the state of the nation.[57] Stanfield, following the research of cultural historian Michael Deming on the dime novel, points to the "master plot" that runs through most 1930s series westerns. They were narratives "of a betrayed but finally saved republic."[58] It was, Stanfield argues, a "narrative conceit that owed much to the magnification of social divisions engendered by the Great Depression. Both series westerns and dime novels act out reconciliation of the contradictions between the needs of the individual and the demands of living and working in a modern economy."[59] These were not part of the 1930s gangster cycle. Instead, the gangster represented the dangers of rapid modernization. His association was with murder (Darvis and his men kill a rival gangster in the opening minutes of the film), greed, materialism and urban corruption as these films provided a "salutary warning of what can transpire if society does not check the rush to embrace the new."[60]

The series cowboy differed from his counterpart in A budgeted western produced by the major studios. He was not as an "agent of progress who will be superseded by the arrival of the modern world in the form of organized society—the predicate of the frontier myth. Instead, the cowboy operates in … series Westerns as a figure able to forestall and moderate progress."[61] This can be seen in film after film.[62] For example, in the Charles Starrett series western *The Cowboy Star* (1936), Starrett plays Spencer Yorke, a disen-

The series western cowboy epitomized by Charles Starrett, who starred in 131 low budget westerns for Columbia between 1936 and 1952.

chanted Hollywood cowboy star who travels back to his home in Taylorsville, Arizona. After purchasing a ranch under an assumed name to protect his privacy, he falls in love with a local woman, Mary Baker (Iris Meredith). However, his tranquil lifestyle is disrupted by Johnny Simpson (Marc Lawrence) and his gangsters who are hiding in nearby Ghost Town, a deserted assortment of abandoned buildings. After Simpson's men capture Jimmy Baker (Wally Albright), Mary's younger brother, and shoot Mary's father, Sheriff Clem Baker (Ed Pell, Sr.), Yorke is galvanized into action. In the film's climax he gains control of the gangster's machine gun and kills two of them before knocking Simpson to the ground. In a surprise twist at the end of the film, Yorke and his bride Mary leave Taylorsville and return to Hollywood where he will resume his film career—a nice rejection of the Wister/Rooseveltian notion that promoted the "frontier" as the ideal place to live.

Rural and Small-Town Audiences in the 1930s

While rural and provincial audiences relished the repetitive world of the series western, the major studios were, for the most part, not interested in this type of western.[63] This disdain extended to big city newspaper critics. In an article on "horse operas" in *The New York Times* published on August 4, 1935, the writer argued that in these types of westerns the hero always overcomes all obstacles in the pursuit of justice in plots often concerned with conflict arising from "irrigation rights, railroad rights of way, dams and mines."[64] Characterizations, he pointed out, were shallow and the "plot gets started and, as soon as possible, gets violent. Such things as innuendoes, psychological problems and anti-climaxes worry not the producer of the Western. Hate is hate, love is love and the shooting must start quickly. The hero must conduct himself in a high class manner, A1 manner and must not gamble, smoke or drink."[65] Despite the mocking tone of the article, the writer highlighted some of the major attributes of the series western. As Stanfield notes:

> The Manichaean world of the western that this writer describes is set forth for a [urban] readership that has little knowledge and probably little regard for the form. The emphasis on the western's rejection of characterization, innuendo, and psychological problems separates the "horse opera" from middle class drama.[66]

This patronizing attitude occasionally found its way into films produced by the majors, such as Warner's *The Cowboy from Brooklyn* (1938) which starred Dick Powell as urban drifter Elly Jordan who is forced to assume the role of singing cowboy Wyoming Steve Gibson. This propels him to radio stardom under the guidance of an overbearing promoter, Roy Chadwick (Pat O'Brien). The main joke in the film emanates

(From left) Johnnie Davis, Dick Powell, Priscilla Lane, Pat O'Brien and Dick Foran in Warner's send up of the singing western in *Cowboy from Brooklyn* (1938).

Fast talking agent Roy Chadwick (Pat O'Brien) points towards his client Elly Jordan (aka Wyoming Steve Gibson) with Sam Thorne (Dick Foran, center, in hat) looking on in *Cowboy from Brooklyn* (1938).

from the fact that Jordan has a fear of animals and it takes hypnosis and the love from a young woman, Jane Hardy (Priscilla Lane), to cure him. An even more savage parody was Warner's film adaptation of the Broadway hit *Boy Meets Girl* (1938). The film starred James Cagney and Pat O'Brien as renegade studio writers Robert Law and J.C. Benson, who concoct a western featuring the studio's resident cowboy star, Larry Toms (Dick Foran), a gormless fool who is upstaged by an infant. Foran's character is called the "idol of illiteracy" and the parody was made even more relevant by casting Dick Foran as the inept western star. Foran, in reality, had just concluded his series of 12 low budget singing westerns for the studio. The film's "humor" is based on presenting the audience who attended series westerns "as intellectually stunted, [and it] measures the patronizing distance of Warner Bros. from the genre's audience, which was better served by Republic Pictures."[67]

This dichotomy was not just geographical but also cultural. The market for westerns was economically, culturally and geographically circumscribed, predetermined by class, geography and ideologies. As Stanfield notes, the series western had a "predetermined audience that the film companies recognized."[68] When *Variety* reviewed *Gun Smoke* on April 29, 1931, the reviewer described the film as a "combo gangster-western [that] should fare better in the small towns than in the met [metropolitan] centers." The reviewer, in a back-handed compliment, conceded that the film has "an entertainment value," but, for "sophisticated" urban audiences, the "story

An attempt to overcome singing "cowboy" Wyoming Steve Gibson's (Dick Powell) fear of animals in *Cowboy from Brooklyn* (1938).

is too naively presented to be realistic fare." The review also singled out the importance of the film's closure: "If a righteous ending means something to reformers and the small town element there can be no squawk with this picture." One presumes that "naive" story refers to the film's strict moral polarization of the drama while the importance of a "righteous" ending to small town audiences meant an ending in accordance with their populist values. The inverse of this point of view was the assumption that these features involving a rigid bipolar dramatic structure, ethically defined characters and a "righteous ending" would not appeal to audiences in the urban first run theaters.

An exhibitor in 1935 who operated both a first run theater for major studio productions as well as a neighborhood theater reserved for B films and series westerns reinforced the notion that there were two types of western melodramas in the 1930s, each with a different audience. This exhibitor decided, after glowing reports from other exhibitors, to screen *In Old Santa Fe* (1934) starring series cowboy star Ken Maynard in his more prestigious theater. But just as the Winter Garden in New York changed the title of *Mystery Ranch* to *The Killer* to hide the fact that it was a series western, this exhibitor removed Maynard's name from the marketing of *In Old Santa Fe*. His motivation for screening this Ken Maynard western was based on positive reports from other exhibitors who celebrated the film's seven-minute musical performance by radio stars Gene Autry and Smiley Burnette. The exhibitor commented that if it had "not been for the glowing tributes paid to this film by fellow exhibitors we would have relegated this film to our 'B' house and then forgotten about it. However, after reading reports on it we made a radical departure from our almost set policy of playing everything except [series] Westerns at our A house and booked it. It took some clever selling and the elimination of Maynard's name from the billing to put it over."[69]

Similar praise for Autry and Burnette was received from other exhibitors. H.M. Johnson from the Avon Theater in Avon Park, Georgia, wrote in June 1935: "I have recently made a point not to review westerns, as they are pretty much the same sort and it is useless to review them. However, I'll have to say a good word for this western. It drew better than average business and pleased. Created a lot of comment. Play it on Saturday."[70] In July 1935 another exhibitor, in Montpelier, Ohio, praised the film as a "fine outdoor picture."[71]

After deciding not to renew Tim McCoy's contract in 1929 MGM never made another series western. After the Rin-Tin-Tin series concluded at Warners the studio, except for the Dick Foran series of twelve singing westerns from 1935 to 1937, also avoided them. Paramount dropped Richard Arlen in the early 1930s leaving only Universal and RKO to continue with series westerns. Aside from the financial incentives of the major studios to focus on the urban first-run theaters, they were unable to match the low budgets of the independent producers because of their high overhead costs. For example, the independents were not saddled with the financial responsibilities of maintaining a large studio complex as well as an extensive distribution system. Paul Seale points out that independent producers in the early 1930s could produce a western for as little as $3,000 although a $10,000 to $15,000 range was more common.[72] The closest the majors came to matching these budgets were twelve westerns starring Tom Keene, produced by RKO between 1931 and 1933. The budgets for *Come On Danger!* (1932) and *Cross Fire* (1933), for example, were $31,000 and $26,000 respectively and although both films generated reasonable profits, with grosses of $106,000 and $98,000 at a time when the majority of the higher budgeted RKO films were failing to produce a profit,[73] the majors normally wanted a higher return on their investment.

While the frontier myth was, rarely, of interest to the series western, its paradigm of civilization and savagery found favor with the (sporadic) production of big budget westerns from the major studios in the 1930s. All of the major studios produced A budgeted westerns during the silent period. A slump in the production of prestige westerns, beginning in mid–1927, resulted in studios divesting themselves of well-known western stars such as Buck Jones and Tom Mix at Fox and MGM's sole western star Tim McCoy. As they always did in times of financial stress, the majors retreated to their profitable first run market in major cities and neglected the demands of their rural and provincial markets for westerns and outdoor adventures. This changed with the resumption of the threat of antitrust litigation[74] and the need to appease provincial and rural areas. Hence, the majors resumed (limited) production of A budgeted westerns at the end of the 1920s despite technical fears of outdoor filming with cumbersome sound equipment.

The commercial success in 1929 of *In Old Arizona* at Fox and *The Virginian* at

Paramount, along with the 12-chapter serial *The Indians Are Coming*, starring Tim McCoy, at Universal in 1930, restored studio confidence in the western. Particularly surprising was the financial success of *The Indians Are Coming*, the first all-talking serial, with a reported box-office gross that exceeded a million dollars and play dates in prestigious first run theaters such as the Roxy Theatre in New York. This serial convinced executives at Universal that there was still a market for outdoor serials and it was possible to film a sound western on location despite reservations from the studio's sound engineers.[75]

The resumption of the production of prestige westerns, however, was short-lived. With the suspension of the threat of antitrust litigation and the consequent elimination of any need to satisfy the demands of the

Warner Baxter as the Cisco Kid, Dorothy Burgess as the duplicitous Tonia Maria and Edmund Lowe as Sergeant Micky Dunn in Fox's popular "south of the border" melodrama *In Old Arizona* (1928).

less profitable rural and provincial markets, together with the disastrous financial impact of the Depression on the studios following the stock market crash in October 1929, they basically ignored the western in the 1930s except for a limited revival of production in 1936–37. The financial pressures on some major studios was exacerbated by over-expansion in theater construction and real estate investments. This lack of confidence in A-budgeted westerns was exacerbated by commercial failure of three prestige westerns in 1930–31: *Cimarron*, *The Big Trail* and *Billy the Kid*. Hence, for some years, the majors eschewed location filming in favor of studio-filmed movies where costs could be kept under tight control.[76] In the period from 1930 to 1939 the major studios released 428 westerns, but most of these films were B westerns. The number of A budgeted westerns was only 44, and in terms of the overall decade production was sporadic with only two A westerns in 1932, one in 1933 and none in 1934.[77] This created an opening in the rural/small town market for Poverty Row companies such as Monogram and even smaller companies such as Superior, Willis Kent, Freuler/Monarch, KBS/World Wide, Majestic Pictures, Allied, Reliable/William Steiner, Aywon, Supreme, Ambassador, Spectrum, Trop Productions, Beacon, Imperial, Empire, and SecurityPictures.

While the number of A budgeted westerns for the decade was fewer than fifty, the number of B/series westerns produced by independent companies was 624 films.[78] When you add this to the 384 B/series westerns produced by the majors, the number of B/series westerns in the decade exceeded one thousand films.

Although many of the smaller independent companies failed to survive the depression, the demand for westerns and serials did not abate from regional markets. This resulted in the formation of Republic Pictures in 1935. Republic incorporated smaller studios such as Majestic and Liberty Pictures along with larger production companies such as Mascot and Monogram. Mascot was a notable acquisition because it included the studio's lease of the former Mack Sennett studio that occupied 20.1 acres along with a 503-acre backlot. Under the control of Herbert Yates, the founder of Consolidated Laboratories, a large film processing company, Republic acquired

John Wayne in Republic's *The Oregon Trail* (1936). Wayne's first western for Republic, *Westward Ho* (1935), was also the studio's first feature release. Wayne was under contract to Trem Carr at the time and the studio paid Carr $1750 for his services. In 1938 Republic secured Wayne's release from Carr and the actor signed a contract for eight films per year for five years. However, John Ford's *Stagecoach* (1939) changed his status from series western star to film star.

not only studio facilities and a large backlot but also the contracts of directors and filmmakers as well as actors such as Gene Autry and John Wayne.[79]

The advent of Republic was important for the series western, as well as the serial, as the quality of low budget westerns improved greatly when the studio acquired many filmmakers experienced in low budget productions, especially at Mascot. Republic had a financing and distribution advantage compared with the independents. And it also had Gene Autry, and the phenomenal success of his singing westerns enabled the studio to impose its own block booking practices on exhibitors. If theaters wanted the season's output of Autry westerns they also had to take Republic's other productions, sight unseen.[80] In terms of content, Republic's westerns, with a few exceptions,

Republic secured Gene Autry when Nat Levine's Mascot Pictures was absorbed into Republic in 1935. *The Singing Cowboy,* released in May 1936, was his seventh film for the studio.

did not address the frontier myth. Instead they focused on issues specific to rural, small-town and provincial audiences interested in tensions created by the Depression and by social changes impacting on their traditional values.

It would be a mistake, however, to regard the audience in the 1930s for the series western as consisting of children and adolescent boys.[81] This view was perpetuated by middle-class critics and older viewers reminiscing about their Saturday matinee experiences in the late 1940s and early 1950s when the series western, because of changes in the industry after the Second World War, was in rapid decline due to sparse budgets and the erosion of their traditional market due to the production of television westerns. This was not true of the 1930s when the series western often played the top half of a movie program in the popular weekend schedules of rural and small-town theaters, as well as urban neighborhood theaters attended by working class families that migrated to large cities from rural districts throughout the decade in search of work. It was these rural/small town workers migrating to the cities, as Stanfield argues, who "experienced the hardships of the Great Depression and felt the economic pressures to adapt to new ways of living."[82] And it was this audience who responded most strongly to the series western, a "cultural form that was marketed to an economically disenfranchised audience."[83]

Although there was a gradual shift in the values and recurring message of the series western as the 1930s progressed, dispossession remained a fixture of these films. The rapid growth in mechanization, such as the introduction of tractors and machine powered combines, decimated the demand for rural labor[84] in the period after 1900. Farmers, forced to compete by acquiring expensive technology, often suffered when they were unable to meet the mortgage payments when the demand for their products declined. Bankruptcy followed. The Depression exacerbated this situation along with disastrous weather conditions and damaging soil erosion. In the 1930s more than 25 percent of Americans still lived on farms but there was a massive migration from rural districts into towns and cities throughout the decade.[85] Between 1929 and 1932 net income in rural areas fell by 70 percent yet the farm, ranch or small town remained the ideal.[86] And the series western addressed this dream in an allegorical form.

Depression Allegories: One Man Law (1932) and The Trail Drive (1933)

Thematically *One Man Law* and *The Trail Drive* have nothing in common with the A budgeted films of the period—such as *In Old Arizona* (1929), *The Virginian*, *Cimarron* (1931), and *The Big Trail* (1930). For one thing, these low budget westerns were profitable. The A budgeted westerns, on the whole, were not. Both *One Man Law* and *The Trail Drive* bypass the frontier myth and focus on rural poverty, dispossession and the evils of eastern capitalism. Both films were produced and released in the worst years of the Depression and both highlight the desperation of rural communities within an aesthetic framework (sensational melodrama) that promised hope, retribution and justice.

By March 1933, the presidential inauguration date of Franklin D. Roosevelt, there were between fourteen and sixteen million Americans unemployed.[87] Mark Roth, writing on the Busby Berkeley/Warner Brothers musicals of the early 1930s, points out that it "is critical commonplace to refer to the 1930s musicals as 'escapist.'"[88] Roth disputes these claims and rejects concepts such as "escapism" to describe these films. Instead he argues that rather than being "escapist" in the sense of a value free experience, which is impossible, "these musicals are essentially political."[89] He also includes the gangster film as "two major film genres to explore this crisis. Each in its own way tried to come to terms with the effects of the worst economic crisis ever experienced by Americans."[90] The same could be said of the series western.

Both *One Man Law* and *The Trail Drive* are populist fables that dramatize the restitution of property (*One Man Law*) and justice for impoverished cattle ranchers (*The Trail Drive*). The enemy is mercenary eastern capitalism preying on small independent farmers and ranchers. The "message" is absorbed into the familiar attributes of sensational melodrama, action in the form of gunfights and fistfights, broad comedy, romance, a turkey shooting competition (*One Man Law*) and spectacular stunts (*The Trail Drive*). In both films the cowboy hero undergoes the same experience—after seemingly betraying his local community he struggles to reintegrate himself until his true state, his virtue, is publicly recognized. In the process property is restored and justice achieved.

One Man Law

There was a special bond between the series western cowboy star and his audience. Many of these actors provided not only a comforting presence but also a moral context to understand the film. Their screen persona rarely changed and the companies and studios were careful to project an image that would coincide with the values of rural and small town audiences. This value system, and the emphasis on performance and spectacle, coalesces in *One Man Law* in the film's opening image—the hero's gun firing at a target in a shooting contest, a contest he wins. Next, he disarms a dangerous drunk, followed by a comedy sequence involving deputy Hank (Harry Todd) who chases a turkey across the fields. The introduction of the villain, Jonathan P. Streeter (Robert Ellis) and his associate Dye (Harry Sedley), soon follows. Both men are seated in a buggy, not on horses, and both are wearing Eastern clothes. An elegant suit. These attributes, along with their Chicago background, immediately establishes them as the villains. For the rest of the narrative these melodramatic character types are placed in a familiar narrative which traces virtue's struggle for public recognition as the plot is concerned with the restoration of property stolen from small landowners by eastern interests.

Filming took place between October 21 and November 3, 1931, at the Walker Ranch in Placerita Canyon, Newhall, California, as well as the Paramount Ranch in Agoura, California which served as the town of Grass Valley, Nevada. The film was released on January 11, 1932. The film begins at a county fair in Grass Valley, a small town in Nevada where cowpuncher Brand Thompson (Buck Jones) wins a number of turkeys in a sharp shooting contest. The prizes at the fair were donated by Jonathan P. Streeter, a land promoter living in nearby Ropersville but originally from Chicago. Streeter schemes with his offsider Dye to cheat the locals out of their land. He persuades them to live and work on properties owned by him without giving them the security of a title to the land. After they have increased the market value of his property through hard work, he sells the properties to people in Chicago after dispossessing the locals from land promised to them. When Ed Grimm (Murdock MacQuarrie) and Sorenson (Richard Alexander) ask Streeter for titles to their properties early in the film, the developer enlists the support of Thompson to validate the land promoter's honesty. To persuade Thompson to work for him Streeter, with the assistance of Stubb (Ernie Adams), a crooked racehorse owner and jockey, cheats Thompson out of the one thing he loves most—his horse Silver. To achieve this Stubb enters a race horse in Grass Valley's annual horse race knowing that the entry is restricted to "cow horses," such as Brand's horse Silver. Stubb then goads Thompson (he calls Silver a "grey goat") into betting everything he owns, including Silver, on the outcome of the race. When Stubb's horse wins, Thompson, emotionally distraught, is forced to hand Silver over to Stubb who, in turn, gives it to Streeter. Streeter then offers Silver, and the job of sheriff, to Thompson. Overjoyed at the chance to regain Silver, Thompson accepts the offer.

Thompson is deceived by Streeter from the outset. When the locals come questioning Streeter's character and the delay in giving them titles to their land, Thompson chides them for questioning the character of the land developer:

> THOMPSON: Well, I'd rather have Jonathan P. Streeter's word than most men's bond.
> You folks ought to be ashamed of yourselves for doubting a man like him.
> He's the one citizen we have trying to make something out of this valley.

Thompson's validation of Streeter's moral character reassures the locals and they return to their properties—without their titles. Meanwhile Thompson develops a relationship with Grace Duncan (Shirley Grey), a young woman living with her even younger brother, Tommy (Wesley Giraud), on a farm without a title. They meet after he rescues her from Carver (Albert J. Smith), a jail escapee. Thompson's relationship with Grace, and the settlers of Grass Valley, is shattered after people with legal titles arrive from the East claiming properties sold to them by Streeter's agents in Chicago. Thompson, who has been out of town chasing bandits, is greeted with hostility from Grace and the other citizens after he arrives back in town. He discovers that more than half the people of Grass Valley have been dispossessed and the community turns against him. This places him in a moral bind. As sheriff he is required to enforce the law and evict Grace, Ed Grimm and his other friends. To make matters worse, Thompson's deputies, including his friend Hank, resign in protest, leaving him alone with only the support of the local judge, Judge Cooper (Edward LeSaint).

Distraught, Thompson invites Ed Grimm to shoot him when he comes to evict him as his mental condition deteriorates. The local community continue to reject him, including Grace who tells Thompson:

> I've nothing to discuss with a bully, hired by a thief to protect him with his gun....
> You're worse than Streeter, far worse. There's nothing lower than a traitor.

Thompson's problems worsen when a vigilante group, led by Sorenson (Richard Alexander), is formed to fight Streeter (and Thompson). Thompson tells Judge Cooper (Edward LeSaint) that he should resign and lead the vigilantes against Streeter. However, the judge tells Thompson that "we need to pray for a break." Their prayers are immediately answered when Stubb informs Thompson of Streeter's scheme to cheat him at the county race by bringing in a ring-in. He also tells Thompson that Streeter now refuses to return Stubb's horse, which is worth $900, and that he hit Stubb over the head with a money box. Judge Cooper declares that Streeter has committed grand larceny and assault and battery and instructs the sheriff to arrest him before he escapes over the county line with the money from the sale of the properties to an eastern syndicate.

Before Thompson can arrest Streeter, Sorenson's vigilantes throw him in jail. Grace, however, relents and releases Thomson after telling him that "I have no reason to believe you … somehow I can't help myself." Thompson rides after Streeter and just as the villain is about to cross the state boundary between Nevada and California, Thompson captures him and takes him back to the Grass Valley jail. As the vigilantes approach the jail, preparing to hang Streeter, the crooked developer panics and buys back the deeds from the Chicago immigrants and gives the titles to the Grass Valley ranchers. In the film's epilogue, Thompson is reunited with Grace.

The film was reviewed in *Variety* on February 16, 1932, and the reviewer wrote: "Wherever they like western pictures this should click for it gets off to a flying start and holds the pace consistently, spaced nicely with comedy bits but in the main tending strictly to business." The review, while providing an outline of the plot, focused on the film's main selling point: "Nothing particularly new to either plot or development, but it has been directed to gain maximum action and with suspense well sustained … the action builds steadily and the complications are easy to follow." The reviewer also highlighted the fact that the film is "mostly outdoors and includes a corking horserace unusually well photographed, several solo and mob rides, plenty of menace." As a consequence, the reviewer argued, the film's main appeal would be to rural exhibitors.

The Trail Drive

Less than two years later after release of *One Man Law* Universal released *The Trail Drive* on September 4, 1933. The film starred Ken Maynard[91] and it was his third film for Universal and one of his best. The story is similar to *One Man Law* and the allegorical references to the Depression are clear. It begins with starving ranchers waiting outside Sweetwater, Texas, with their cattle herds for buyers. However, no buyers are forthcoming, including Jameson (Lafe McKee), their usual buyer. Compounding their problems, the local bank refuses to extend credit to the desperate ranchers. Even the villain, "Honest" John (William Gould), appears to be caught up in the lack of sales and his well-respected foreman Ken Benton (Ken Maynard) is puzzled as to why Jameson and the other buyers are refusing to purchase cattle from the Sweetwater ranchers. Honest John, however, has a swindle in operation and he proposes to the ranchers that he will purchase their cattle without paying them any money. Instead he offers to establish his own bank and pay the cattlemen in scrip, which they can redeem for goods from his stores in Sweetwater. He also reassures the ranchers that his men will drive the cattle across the border to New Mexico where they can expect sales at much higher prices. Afterwards, he promises to buy back the scrip for cash. Uncertain as to the validity of Honest John's offer, the ranchers ask Benton whether he can be trusted. Benton reassures them of John's honesty and tells them he will lead the cattle drive to New Mexico. However, when the ranchers attempt to exchange the scrip for goods in Sweetwater they discover that John has reneged on his promise and the scrip is worthless. The ranchers' sense of betrayal is compounded after Jameson, the cattle buyer, finally tells them that Honest John's plan was a scam as his men, led by John's henchman Blake (Bob Kortman), prevented Jameson from purchasing their cattle.

Unaware of Honest John's scheme, Benton, followed by Virginia (Cecilia Parker), leaves the cattle drive and rides back to confront John in Sweetwater. However, the villain is warned that Benton is coming and sets a trap after capturing Virginia. Benton escapes John's trap after he is tied to a wooden towel rack on a door in John's room. He manages to loosen the hinges of the door and with the door fastened to his back, falls backward out of a second-floor window onto the rump of a horse below the window. The horse, carrying Benton with the door fastened to his back, rides wildly down the main street until Benton is able to free himself by falling off the horse. Benton rescues Virginia and rushes back to the cattle drive to stop it crossing into New Mexico as the ranchers will lose control of their cattle once they cross the border. This fails and Benton discovers that John has sold the cattle to buyers waiting in New Mexico. Benton confronts John and, as in the ending of *One Man Law*, convinces the villain to relinquish the money he acquired by the sale or face hanging by the irate ranchers. John reluctantly acquiesces and is subsequently murdered by Blake while Ken and Virginia plan their future together.

Ken Maynard, the star of *The Trail Drive*, was an expert horseman having toured as a stunt rider in wild west shows since 1914. The film exploits his horse-riding skills, notably during the film's climax when he chases Honest John on horseback. With the villain in a buckboard, and an outlaw gang following Benton, the hero swings off to the side of his horse and fires back at the gang until they fall away. He then transfers from his horse to Honest John's buckboard and the two men fight it out while the vehicle is traveling at high speed. Eventually, the buckboard's chassis breaks away leaving Ken riding two horses while battling Honest John. Close-ups of the action show, for at least some of the time, Ken riding two horses at once while long shots of the fight allow stuntman Cliff Lyons to stand-in for the star. It is filmed so seamlessly by director Alan James and cinematographer Ted McCord that it is impossible to differentiate between Ken and the stuntman. The net effect is a lengthy, extremely spectacular climax.

There is also a cattle stampede, augmented by Universal's extensive library of stock footage from the silent period, a gunfight in a saloon, songs (Ken sings around the campfire accompanied by his banjo), a square dance, a chaste courtship between Ken and Virginia, which includes her warning to Ken when he tries to kiss her in the dark out on the prairie that "somebody might see us," and broad comedy routines involving Ken's sidekick Thirsty (Frank Rice) and his courtship of Aunt Martha (Fern Emmett). Martha's frustration with Thirsty's lack of romantic attention erupts when she tells Ken that Thirsty has not attempted to make love to her once, "not that I would want him to," but "a man his age ought to keep in practice." Ken then advises Thirsty to close his eyes when making love to Martha and "think of the Widow Jones." The epilogue shows Ken with Virginia and Thirsty with Aunt Martha against a scenic background.

The Myth of the Frontier: The Virginian

Whereas the series/B western throughout the 1930s focused on contemporary issues such as the conflict between labor and capital, the effects of new technology, the widespread dispossession and dislocation in rural areas and the inroads of modernity, the A budget westerns dramatized various manifestations of the frontier myth while celebrating America's manifest destiny. Virtually all studies of the 1930s western, including Will Wright's *Six Guns and Society,* focus on the dialectic opposition between "savagery" and "civilization." This formed part of a familiar scholarly discourse involving the cowboy's ability to transform the "wilderness" into "civilization." Jim Kitses,[92] Peter Wollen,[93] John Cawelti[94] and, especially, Richard Slotkin[95] endorse a view first put forward in Henry Nash Smith's 1950 publication *Virgin Land: The American West as Symbol and Myth.*[96] Smith's two oppositional myths, the "garden" and the "desert," proved attractive to scholars interested in exploring the "frontier myth as a means of imagining the American West in history and fiction."[97] Jim Kitses, for example, argues that

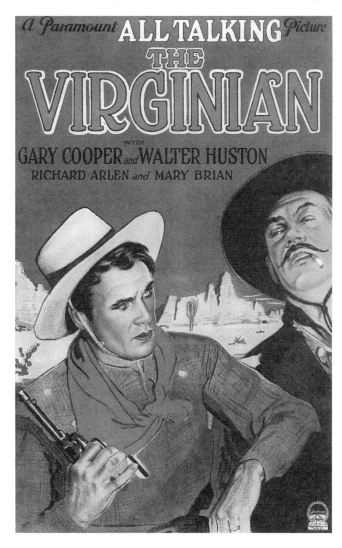

a structuralist grid focused around the frontier's dialectical play of forces embodied in the master binary opposition of the wilderness and civilisation [and] ... the centrality of ... its frontier mythology to the American cinema.

The cornerstone of the Western, this scaffold of meanings grounds the genre in issues of American identity at both individual and national levels. Focused by Henry Nash Smith's seminal study, *Virgin Land*, these oppositions capture the profound ambivalence that dominates America's history and character. Was the West a garden threatened by a corrupt and emasculating East? Or was it a

Gary Cooper as the Virginian and Walter Huston as the villain Trampas in Paramount's *The Virginian* (1929).

Gary Cooper, Mary Brian and Walter Huston in *The Virginian* (1929).

Desert, a savage land needful of civilising and uplift? Filtered through the classic plots, stereotypes and conflicts of the genre, this dialectical scheme positions the Western hero between
the nomadic and the settled, the savage and the cultured, the masculine and the feminine. This
interplay of ideas accounts for the charged racial and sexual dynamics of the genre, wherein the
Indian and the woman can be constructed principally as archetypal agents that define the hero's
direction.[98]

This centrality of the frontier myth to theories of American exceptionalism, its
character and its institutions, can also be traced to a confluence of ideas and images
developed by Theodore Roosevelt, historian Frederick Jackson Turner, artist Frederic
Remington and author Owen Wister in the late nineteenth century. Wister's vision of
the "aristocratic cowboy" first appeared in "The Evolution of the Cow Puncher," an
essay written in conjunction with Remington and published in the September 1895
edition of *Harper's New Monthly Magazine*. However, Wister's major impact came
with the publication in 1902 of his novel *The Virginian*, followed the next year by a
theatrical adaptation, co-written with Kirk LaShelle. In many ways, it was the theatrical adaptation that toured for the next decade, rather than the novel, that had the
most impact as it formed the basis of the first four film versions, released in 1914,
1923, 1929 and 1946.

Roosevelt, Remington and Wister emphasized the special power of the frontier
as a "liminal space where a return to a more primitive state helps in the process of
purifying and revitalizing an overcultivated secular soul."[99] These men were racialists

who promoted the idea of a "natural aristocracy" of Anglo Saxon men, not women, who would firmly lead the mob, a group they deeply feared. In "The Evolution of the Cow-Puncher" Wister promulgated his notion of the cowboy as a direct descendant of the English aristocracy, a man redeemed by frontier life. Only Anglo Saxons, he concluded, could survive in the "clean cattle country" as it requires a "spirit of adventure, courage and self-sufficiency; you will not find many Poles or Huns or Russian Jews in that district."[100] Or, African Americans or any other non–Anglo Saxons in Wister's world.

The influence of Wister's novel on the ideology, iconography and narrative development of the A budgeted western in the pre–Second World War years cannot be denied. Richard Slotkin, for example, cites Wister's *The Virginian* as the paradigm text of the western film genre,[101] a romantic vision of the lone (superior) cowboy confronting evil in a deserted street.[102] Wister's novel, often regarded as the first "serious" western novel, was an immediate success, going through 15 reprints in the first year of publication, and by 1920 it had sold more than a million copies. The Virginian, who has no name, is introduced early in the story:

> Lounging there at ease against the wall was a slim young giant, more beautiful than pictures. His broad, soft hat was pushed back; a loose-knotted, dull-scarlet handkerchief sagged from his throat; and one casual thumb was hooked in the cartridge-belt that slanted across his hips. He had plainly come many miles from somewhere across the vast horizon, as the dust upon him showed. His boots were white with it. His overalls were grey with it. The weather-beaten bloom of his face shone through it duskily, as the ripe peaches look upon their trees in a dry season. But no dinginess of travel or shabbiness of attire could tarnish the splendor that radiated from his youth and strength.... Had I been the bride, I should have taken the giant, dust and all.[103]

To Wister the cowboy was a special kind of man, a descendant from Anglo Saxon aristocracy fashioned by the special qualities of the frontier. Although he represented the people, he was above them as Wister had little faith in working class men and women. His elitist views included a convoluted notion of equality in a democracy. They emerge in *The Virginian* when the narrator describes the hero in the second half of the novel, chapter XIII. The Game and the Nation—Act First:

> There is no doubt of this: All America is divided into two classes,—the quality and the equality....
>
> It was through the Declaration of Independence that we Americans acknowledged the ETERNAL INEQUALITY of man. For by it we abolished a cut-and-dried aristocracy. We had seen little men artificially held up in high places, and great men artificially held down in low places, and our own justice-loving hearts abhorred this violence to human nature. Therefore, we decreed that every man should henceforth have equal liberty to find his own level. By this very decree we acknowledged and gave freedom to true aristocracy, saying, "Let the best man win, whoever he is." Let the best man win! That is America's word. That is true democracy. And true democracy and true aristocracy are one and the same thing. If anybody cannot see this, so much the worse for his eyesight.[104]

Peter Stanfield describes *The Virginian* as an "embourgeoisement of the western—a middle class appropriation of the cowboy who had previously entertained the masses in such déclassé forms as the dime novel. The series western

Gary Cooper and Walter Huston in *The Virginian* (1929).

reclaimed the cowboy for the mob—that inchoate mass of working-class men and women that members of America's elite, such as Wister, so vocally damned and feared."[105]

The film adaptations of Wister's novel follow the author's notion of the regenerative powers of the frontier. This is encapsulated in the transformation of his heroine, Molly Stark Wood, who travels from Bennington, Vermont, to take up a teaching position at Bear Creek, Wyoming. Her initial harsh reaction to, and eventual acceptance of, frontier life provides the narrative arc for the audience to share. This is articulated in the 1929 and 1946 versions after the Virginian orders the hanging of his close friend Steve when he is caught cattle rustling. The Virginian's act of lynching his best friend was disliked by William S. Hart, who acted in the stage version of the story in 1907 and 1908. Hart told Wister that he failed to understand western life as the Virginian would have protected Steve and diverted the ranchers away from him. Frontier loyalty, Hart argued, was more important than some "murky vision of abstract justice."[106] Wister rejected Hart's advice as he was a fierce advocate of capital punishment and the act of hanging Steve was the firm hand that had, in Wister's world, to be applied to the lower classes as the survival of society depended on the efforts of "natural aristocrats"—like the Virginian.

Molly, a representative of Eastern "civilized" views, is appalled by the Virginian's decision to hang Steve and she decides to leave the Virginian and her teaching position at Bear Creek and travel back to the East. In the 1929 and 1946 films

Gary Cooper and Mary Brian in *The Virginian* (1929).

versions Molly's decision provokes a hostile response from her friend and mentor. In the 1946 version, Mrs. Taylor (Fay Bainter), the wife of the local judge, tries to persuade Molly not to leave by pointing out that the Virginian had no choice: "he was in charge" and if "we don't put the fear of God in these lawbreakers you couldn't teach school … our lives would not be worth anything." Molly, unconvinced, tells Mrs. Taylor that it was "horrible." Taylor, however, counters by arguing that "it was his duty." When Molly describes the Virginian's actions as "lynching," Taylor becomes outraged and tells Molly that there are no policemen, courts or jails out here and "we have to do things in our own way." Molly, however, rejects this view and describes the Virginian's actions as "downright murder." As she tells Mrs. Taylor, she fears that if she remains in Wyoming she will become "callous, hard and lose all sense of decency."

> TAYLOR [ANGRY]: It's the law I tell you. The only kind we've got and I'm grateful for it. We are building a country out here and there's no place for weaklings—men or women. If that's the way you feel you had better get out!

Molly soon changes her mind and is reunited with the Virginian until Trampas, at the end of the film, challenges the Virginian to a shootout on their wedding day. Again she decides to leave and again she changes her mind and marries the Virginian after he kills Trampas.

The turning point in *The Virginian* (1929) comes when the Virginian has to hang his friend Steve (Richard Arlen), at right in the black shirt, along with Jim (Jim Mason) at left and Pedro (Charles Stevens), for cattle rustling.

Bob Custer as the disgraced Eastern socialite Jack Steel who redeems himself in the West in J.P. McGowan's *The Manhattan Cowboy* (1928). Steel is seen battling the villain Slim Sergeant (Charles Whittaker).

The Regenerative Power of the Frontier:
Manhattan Cowboy *(1928)/* The Texas Rangers *(1936)*

Manhattan Cowboy begins with Jack Steel (Bob Custer) returning to his wealthy family home in New York late at night with two girls and a male friend. Steel, dressed in the stolen taxi starter uniform from the Midnight Club, is drunk. He is pursued by the angry taxi starter and a policeman and they threaten Jack with criminal charges including assault and battery, grand larceny and disturbing the peace. Unperturbed, Jack expects his father John Steel (Lafe McKee), as usual, to take care of the problem. As Jack tells his anxious mother: "Don't worry, Mother, it is only the taxi starter from the Midnight Club. Dad will take care of him." This time, however, John Steel refuses to protect his son from criminal charges by refusing to pay for the "wrecked taxis, torn clothes and bruised bodies." Amazed, Jack's laughter suddenly stops after his father tells the cop to take his son to jail. Jack's mother, however, intercedes and persuades her husband to protect their son. John Steel agrees and tells her that he will give Jack one more chance as long as he does everything he says. This involves reporting to the Duncan Ranch in Wyoming operated by Steel's close friend Bud Duncan (John Lowell).

John Steel sends a letter to his friend Duncan explaining:

> My good-for-nothing son Jack has been kicking over the traces lately. Riding the range kicked all of the foolishness out of you and me in our younger days so I am sending the boy out for you to kick the same foolishness out of him.
> p.s. Don't spare him.

Immediately, the West has a positive effect on Jack as he channels his energies into saving Bud's daughter Alice (Mary Mayberry) from ranch ruffians. He subsequently rescues her after she loses control of her wagon. To achieve this Jack has to make a spectacular jump from his horse onto Alice's wagon. This prompts Bud to say that Jack appears to be a "chip off the old block" as he reminds him of John Steel in his younger days. Jack's regeneration includes romancing Alice and stealing her from the swarthy villain, Slim Sergeant (Charles Whittaker), as well as rescuing her from Sergeant and his two cohorts, Mack Murdock (Mack V. Wright) and Tex Spaulding (Cliff Lyons). After beating up Sergeant in a fight over Alice, Bud writes to Jack's father and tells him that his son has responded well to western life, the "smell of the sage brush, the squeak of the saddle leathers and the clatter of pony's feet." In the film's climax, Jack, again, saves Alice by pole vaulting onto the roof of Sergeant's shack and proceeds to knock down all opposition. The film ends with an epilogue showing Jack placing an ornamental cross, that has passed from generation to generation in his mother's family, around Alice's neck.

The Texas Rangers

Paramount's 1936 western *The Texas Rangers*, released in the same year of Texas' Centennial celebrations, was (very) loosely based on incidents taken from Walter

Prescott Webb's 1935 history *The Texas Rangers: A Century of Frontier Defense*.[107] This reformation story follows the fortunes of three bandits, Jim Hawkins (Fred MacMurray), Henry B. "Wahoo" Jones (Jackie Oakie) and Sam McGee (Lloyd Nolan). After they split up to evade the law following a stage holdup, Hawkins and Jones join the Texas Rangers hoping to continue their life of crime from inside the organization. Love, in the form of Amanda Bailey (Jean Parker), an orphan boy, David (Bennie Bartlett), and an Indian attack combine to transform Hawkins and Jones. They, like the audience, come to understand the important role the Texas Rangers played in bringing civilization to a savage frontier. This theme is expounded not only in the moral regeneration of Hawkins and Jones from outlaws to committed Rangers but in the film's declamatory speeches by Major Bailey (Edward Ellis), the head of the Texas Rangers.

This theme is clearly articulated in the film's prologue which celebrates the role of the Rangers in making "life safe" and ensuing "progress" through their "unyielding courage." Soon after Hawkins and Jones enlist, Bailey tells the Rangers that he received a telegram from Austin:

> Men, the Indian troubles have broken out again. They are on the warpath. Murder, deprivation…. We've got to subdue them and put them on the reservation for good. I know what is on your minds. The odds against every Ranger company will be fifty to one. But if Texas is to be a State. If families are to build homes. If there is to be any future for our peoples, the sacrifice of lives will be worth it [close up of Jones and Hawkins].

Although the odds are fifty to one, and the Rangers become trapped on a hillside, Hawkins manages to bring reinforcements in a last-minute rescue of the remaining Rangers.

Bailey celebrates the rescue with another speech to his men. "Now that we have placed the Indians on the reservation for good, the people can look to real progress. A state marching forward to its rightful destiny!" He warns, however, of the danger of crooked cattle and crooked judges. Hawkins tracks down his former partner, McGee, after McGee murders Jones. The film ends with Bailey's oration at the funeral of Henry B. Jones (supplemented by images of Rangers who lost their lives riding across the screen and a male choir on the soundtrack):

> The men who have died for Texas have not died in vain. Unsung though their names may be in future years. It shall be known that in the turbulent years of a state's transformation, it was their deeds of individual sacrifice, their acts of dauntless courage, that made possible for the changing of a lawless frontier into a civilized land. These are the men called Texas Rangers. Moulded in the crucible of heroic struggle, guardians of the frontier, makers of the peace.

"New Frontiers": American Populism and Roosevelt's New Deal[108]

There was a shift in emphasis in the series western towards the end of the 1930s. While this sub-genre remained fiercely populist in its prevailing system of values, this ideology incorporated a change with regard to the role of the Federal Government. Earlier in the decade films such as *Gun Smoke* and *Cross Fire* promoted a strong individualistic ethos that precluded government officials, corporations and eastern financial interests. This under went a change with a cycle of films, produced mainly by Republic studio, that promoted the benefits of the Federal government for rural communities. Big business, corporations, unions and corrupt local officials remained the enemy. This is not only evident in *Under Western Stars,* which was discussed in the Introduction, but other Republic produced films.

As Scott Simmon points out:

> With little qualification then, the B western can be rightly labeled "Populist"—both in the sense that the political movement was understood in the 1890s and in the looser sense of the 1930s, a decade in which New Deal farm policies adopted many of the earlier People's Party demands.[109]

Republic, the key studio servicing the needs of small town and rural communities from the mid–1930s was a studio that aligned itself with the ideals of "Roosevelt's New Deal through their support of self-help combined with government assistance."[110] Gene Autry, in his autobiography, confirmed the nexus between the studio and Roosevelt's economic program:

> I did not engage, for the most part, in such mundane activities as saving the old homestead or chasing bank bandits. While my solutions were a little less complex than those offered by FDR, and my methods a little more direct, I played a kind of New Deal Cowboy who never hesitated to tackle many of the same problems: the dust bowl, unemployment, or the harnessing of power. This may have contributed to my popularity with the 1930s audiences.[111]

Under Western Stars

In *Under Western Stars* the film's solution to removing the water corporation's monopoly power involved a combination of self-help, the function of the cowboy hero (Roy Rogers), and support from Federal politicians. The problems facing the local ranchers in the film, and many people in the audience watching this film in 1938, is established in the opening images which show a dust storm ravaging the countryside as newspapers report: "DUST AND DROUGHT SWEEP SOUTHWEST," "RANCHERS ASK U.S. AID," "CATTLEMEN FIGHT FOR WATER." This is followed by a gunfight between the disgruntled ranchers and the black shirted security guards hired by the water company. This is resolved by Roy and his (comedic) offsider Frog Millhouse (Smiley Burnette) although they are subsequently arrested by the local sheriff. On the way back to Sageville, Roy and Frog sing the first of seven songs in the film, "Send My Mail to the County Jail." In Sageville, Mayor Biggs (Earl Dwire) fines Roy one dollar and urges him, as the son of a congressman, to run for Congress. Roy, opposed by the local representative, William P. Scully (Dick Elliott) who is a stooge for the water company, is easily elected and goes to Washington to lobby for Federal support for the ranchers.

In Washington Roy's initial attempts to meet with the influential Congressman Edward H. Marlowe are frustrated by the head of the water company, John D. Fairbanks. This changes when Fairbank's daughter Eleanor suggests that Roy host a western party at a local country club. Here, as described in the Introduction, Roy sings the highly emotive song "Dust" accompanied by newsreel images of the devastation, supposedly, in Sage County. Marlowe and the other politicians are so moved by Roy's presentation they agree to offer their support once they verify the conditions by traveling to Sage Valley. However, in Sageville they learn, courtesy of a leak from Fairbanks, that Roy used footage of another state suffering similar problems in his Washington presentation and they withdraw their support. As Marlowe, his wife (Dora Clement) and his secretary Tom Andrews (Alden Chase), drive out of the area through the stark, barren volcanic rocks (filmed in the Alabama Hills near Lone Pine), they are ambushed by cowboys who take their car, leaving them only horses for transportation. Without food and only a little water they hear a group of cowboys (Roy and his friends) singing nearby and they walk to their campsite. Desperate for water, Roy takes them on a tour of the local area until a dust storm forces them to seek shelter with an impoverished local rancher who shares her sparse water supply with the politicians. Next morning, after the dust storm has receded, Marlowe agrees to support Roy's water bill. However, Mayor Briggs arrives to tell Roy and Marlowe that some of the ranchers are about to take matters into their own hands by dynamiting the water corporation's dam. Marlowe warns Roy that if this happens he will, again, withdraw his support. Roy saves the day by diverting a wagon loaded with dynamite from hitting the wall of the dam.

The reviews for *Under Western Stars* were surprisingly positive for a series western. *Variety's* reviewer, "Hurl," praised the film for its "timeliness of utility-company theme for exploitation" and that it was "plausible sage stuff that will hold the adult mind as well as the credulous kiddies." However, in another reminder that the industry considered the series western as suitable only for small town and rural exhibitors, the reviewer warned exhibitors that the film had "limited [potential in generating strong box-office returns in urban centers] 'because of the cacti stigma.'"

New Frontier

The need for Federal assistance was reiterated in John Wayne's final low budget western, *New Frontier*, which was part of the Three Mesquiteer series produced by Republic. In the film Wayne's function is to reconcile the ideological contradictions between populism's emphasis on individualism and role of the Federal government. The film begins with a montage of Civil War action and the written prologue: "Impoverished by civil war and faced with the painful labor of reconstruction, thousands of Americans cut the old ties and took the immigrant trail to the free lands of the far west —and a new beginning." Forced by economic circumstances, Major Steven Braddock (Eddy Waller) takes his family west after the Civil War and establishes a new community which he names New Hope Valley. The fifty-year celebration of the establishment of New Hope begins with a reenactment of the Pony Express, as carried by Stony Brooke (John Wayne), Tucson Smith (Ray Corrigan) and Rusty Joslin (Raymond Hatton), the Three Mesquiteers. The reenactment includes a "fake" Indian attack by white men dressed as Indians, a dance and banquet where Braddock, in a contemporary (1930s) town meeting, asks the citizens of New Hope to bow their heads in prayer: "The Lord has been so good to us that He hasn't left us much to ask for. Unless it's this. Keep us safe, O Lord … and if it's all right with You, we'd like to keep on just as we have in the past."

Braddock's prayer is interrupted by the arrival of a politician, assemblyman William Proctor (Harrison Greene) and M.C. Gilbert (LeRoy Mason) who represents the Metropole Construction Company. After Proctor announces that New Hope Valley has been condemned and a dam will be constructed to flood the valley to supply water to the large urban center of Metrapole, Braddock, much like Brad Farley in *Gun Smoke* eight years earlier, extols the virtues of the Old West and expresses his implacable opposition to any change. New Hope's legal challenge to stop the dam fails when the presiding judge, Judge Lawson (Reginald Barlow), orders that the dam must proceed as it represents the "greatest good for the greatest number."

John Wayne with Raymond Hatton and Ray Corrigan, the Three Mesquiteers, in *New Frontier* (1939). Phylis Isley, who was more famous later as Jennifer Jones, was the female lead.

To compensate for their loss the government sends checks to the citizens of New Hope. While most residents of New Hope destroy the checks, the Three Mesquiteers, who understand the need for a new dam, keep the $3200 check and Tucson Smith comments that it represents generous compensation for their ranch.

When Gilbert and Proctor send their henchman Harmon (Jack Ingram) to forcibly remove people from their properties, the Mesquiteers intervene on the side of the residents and Harmon and his men are arrested. After their defeat on the battlefield Proctor and Gilbert concoct a phony real estate scam to move the residents out of their homes and they trick the Three Mesquiteers into supporting their plan to sell (barren land) at Devil Acres to the residents of New Hope where they promise to transform the land by the construction of miles of pipeline to carry water through the mountains. However, as the residents of New Hope move out of their properties, the Three Mesquiteers ride ahead and discover abandoned pipes and they realize they have been tricked. Gilbert merely wanted to remove the New Hope residents so that he can flood their valley and complete his dam. The Mesquiteers ride back and warn the New Hope citizens that Gilbert is unleashing flood waters and the film climaxes in a battle between the construction workers and New Hope residents. They stop the flooding after Stony Brooke knocks Gilbert off the wall of the dam.

The ending of the film, however, creates a dilemma. The actions of the Three Mesquiteers are irrelevant as stopping the flooding is pointless as it fails to resolve the plight of the New Hope citizens who cannot return to their former homes as they have been condemned. At the same time they cannot settle in Devil Acres as the land is barren. This dramatic gap is, surprisingly, addressed by the actions of the Federal government, not the cowboy hero. This is conveyed through a series of headlines in the *New Hope Courier*:

> Land Swindlers Convicted. Proctor and Dodge Sentenced to Ten Year Imprisment.

Next headline:

> Devil Acres Reclaimed. Government Complete Pipe Line.

Despite the brevity of this resolution, it is government action, not the actions of the Three Mesquiteers that removes the obstacle so that the former residents of New Frontier can settle on fertile land at Devil Acres, tentatively renamed "New New Hope."

Wyoming Outlaw

Actions by the Federal government also provide the resolution in the Three Mesquiteer western, *Wyoming Outlaw*. The film was co-scripted by Jack Natteford and Betty Burbridge, who also wrote *New Frontier* with Luci Ward. It is, arguably, the most subversive series western ever produced in Hollywood as it makes no attempt to mask the ideological tensions in the film. Peter Stanfield describes the film as "the most overt commentary in Republic's output on the issues raised by the Depression and its effects on the rural population."[112] Its historical setting is a mixture of the traditional western iconography and representations of 1930s America as it assimilates 1930s fashions, automobiles and jitterbug dancing in the small town of Mesquite with horses, six-guns, cowboy clothes and the familiar Republic western set.

The film begins with Stony Brooke (John Wayne), Tucson Smith (Ray Corrigan) and Rusty Joslin (Raymond Hatton) driving their cattle through Wyoming when a dust storm forces them to take refuge in an abandoned farmhouse. While waiting for the storm to subside, Brooke picks up an old newspaper, dated March 9, 1918, and explains to Smith and Joslin how once prosperous farmers during the early years of the First World War were reduced to poverty in the years immediately after the War. Brooke:

Looks like the World War's to blame [for the abandoned farm].... Listen to this [Brooke reads from the newspaper].... "Overseas demand sends wheat prices new high. Panhandle country turns from cattle range to wheat fields. In this country alone eleven thousand acres of grassland are being plowed under this spring. Nora Higgins made a profit of over eighty dollars an acre last season and will plant three thousand acres this year. Luke Parker has just completed a fine home for his family and paid cash for an expensive automobile."

Brooke explains that millions of farmers were ruined at the end of the War when wheat prices plummeted. For farmers the Depression did not begin in 1929 but a decade earlier, caused largely by policies adopted by Herbert Hoover, the U.S. Food Administrator, who encouraged a massive increase in wheat farming. This resulted in the conversion of cattle land into farmland. After the War an oversupply of American

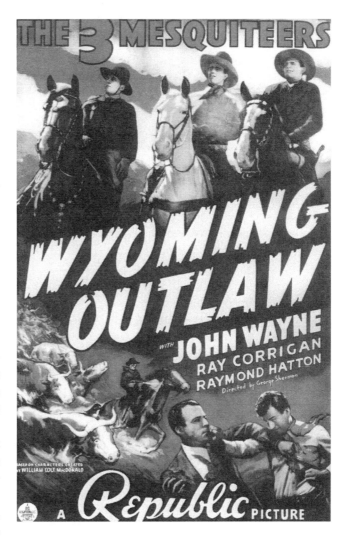

Raymond Hatton, John Wayne and Ray Corrigan in *Wyoming Outlaw* (1939). Wayne battles crooked local politician Joe Balsinger (LeRoy Mason) without much success. As in *New Frontier*, it takes the intervention of the federal government to resolve the problem.

wheat, along with a dramatic fall in European demand, caused economic ruin for many farmers. Not only did prices plummet but the conversion of cattle country to wheat farms resulted in soil erosion, leading to a dust bowl.

When the dust storm recedes the Three Mesquiteers head into Mesquite for supplies. Along the way they notice that one of their cows has been carried away on the shoulders of a rustler on foot. In Mesquite, Brooke meets a young woman, Irene Parker (Adele Pearce),[113] and protects her from the advances of Joe Balsinger (LeRoy Mason), the chairman of the local Public Works Program. Brooke walks Irene home from the dance across barren fields to the Parker house where he finds Tucson and

Rusty are waiting for him with Irene's parents, Luke (Charles Middleton) and Mrs. Parker (Katherine Kenworthy). At this point the film returns to the 1918 newspaper report by Stony as Luke Parker is the man mentioned in the article: "Luke Parker has just completed a fine home for his family and paid cash for an expensive automobile." Now, in the 1930s, he has been reduced to poverty, unable to borrow money ("Did you ever try to borrow money on a thousand acres of dust and sand?") and unable to work following an accident. And Luke's son Will (Donald Barry) is the young man who rustled the steer from the Mesquiteers' herd.

The film focuses less on the Three Mesquiteers and more on the plight of the Parker family, notably young Will Parker who is a bitter youngster. The Mesquiteers try to assist him by employing him on their cattle drive. This fails when Will's criminal record prevents him from working in a national park. His bitterness deepens when he is arrested for violating Federal game laws after killing a deer in the national park to feed his family. His father Luke is also a victim of a swindle after he used his lifesavings to buy 1,000 acres of infertile land. When he tries to return to work on the local council, the villain Balsinger blackmails his wife into paying a "contribution" to his political campaign with the promise of a job for her husband. After she pays the money, Balsinger tells her that the only available position for her husband is a return to day labor on the road gang, a job that Luke is physically incapable of doing. Brooke comes to the realization that the only possible solution for families such as the Parkers is a government enquiry into Balsinger's corrupt public welfare scam. However, the government inquiry is disrupted after Balsinger lures Stony into a fight and he is subsequently arrested for destroying Balsinger's office. With the Mesquiteers rendered impotent, the townspeople succumb to Balsinger's intimidation and refuse to testify at the hearing.

The film's narrative has created an almost impossible scenario as the heroes are unable to help the Parkers. Will's escape from jail triggers a large manhunt by the police and media, a sequence very similar to the climax in *High Sierra* (1941) when gangster Roy Earle (Humphrey Bogart) is trapped on Mount Whitney by the police. Produced two years before *High Sierra*, *Wyoming Outlaw* shows the hostile, unfeeling reaction of the media to Will's plight. In a scene that predates the 1941 film, a radio reporter describes the widespread hunt for Will. After evading capture, Will hitches a ride with a cynical, and unsuspecting, reporter. He then reveals his identity to the reporter and tells him that "everything is a lie in this Dust Bowl!"

The film ends in a downbeat manner, a rarity for a series western. The final scene shows Will's death. After a final visit to his parents he returns to Mesquite and captures Balsinger and both men die in front of the local bank. The film's epilogue tries to restore some sense of justice through a series of newspaper headlines. The *Wyoming Post* reports:

New Homes Given Dust Bowl Victims

A close-up of the subheading shows:

Public Relief Committee Relief Racket

Stanfield argues:

Will's "radicalism" is contained by this ending, which has a beneficent State authority stamp out corruption and offer a helping hand to the distressed (an ending not dissimilar to the following year's *Grapes of Wrath*). But this cannot wipe out the image of a barely potent Three Mesquiteers whose best efforts have been unable to save Will or bring the bad men too book by legal means.[114]

Wyoming Outlaw is an extremely aberrant series western. Not only does the cowboy hero fail to save Will,[115] he is unable to alleviate the problems facing the Dust Bowl farmers. It is left to the government to do this.

Wyoming Outlaw, as Scott Simmon points out, "spells out the economic sympathies of the B-Western with rare directness. What Populists had long contended was not merely that farmers have a special value … but also that farmers have an obligation to act politically and the right to expect special government response to their hardships. Its more surprising that the Western promotes this second idea, especially if we come expecting the genre's apparently unqualified love of individualist gunfight solutions."[116] The film does "not … cover over the contradictions of its Populist logic."[117]

Films such as *Under Western Stars, Wyoming Outlaw, New Frontier,* along with a host of other series western including *Heart of the Rockies* (1937), which includes child abuse within its plot involving poaching and the illegal use of the national park land by a corrupt mountain community, deserve consideration for their ability, unlike the A budgeted westerns, to assimilate specific cultural and economic issues of interest to regional audiences. As Stanfield points out:

> Despite their circumscribed critiques, series westerns of the 1930s address themselves to issues of class struggle and division that surfaced during this turbulent decade, at least as much as the more prestigious films of the major studios. The critically disparaged and apparently simplistic genre of the series western has, in its own way, more to say about the social disruptions of capitalism in crisis than such better-known films of the era as *Mr. Deeds Goes to Town* [1936] or *The Grapes of Wrath* [1940].[118]

Honor (1926), part of a series of films featuring Lightnin' the police dog and Eileen Sedgwick as a special agent who appears in this scene with Hal Water and Walter Lowery.

Charles Jones, before he changed his name to Buck Jones, starred in Fox's 1923 melodrama *Snowdrift*. The heroine was played by Irene Rich and the villain by Lalo Encinas. This still approximates the style of the tableau in nineteenth-century theatrical melodrama.

Buck Jones in Fox's *Against All Odds* (1924).

The visceral appeal of sensational melodrama. Action and romance in Fox's production of *The Desert Outlaw* (1924) starring Buck Jones and Evelyn Brent. Brent went on to star in films directed by Josef von Sternberg such as *Underworld* (1927) as "Feathers" McCoy and *The Last Command* (1928).

The Wolf Man, a 1923 Fox melodrama. Believing he has murdered his fiancé's brother while under the influence of alcohol, Gerald Stanley (John Gilbert) flees England for Quebec. After a drinking spree, Stanley kidnaps Elizabeth Gordon (Norma Shearer). When pursued, he leaps into a canoe for a wild ride down the rapids. Eventually his innocence is established and Elizabeth falls in love with him.

The violation of Terrence Granville (Charles Starrett) by Fah Lo See (Myrna Loy) in *The Mask of Fu Manchu* (1932).

Viola Dana stars in *Naughty Nannette,* a 1927 romantic melodrama distributed by Joseph Kennedy's Film Booking Office (FBO).

WILLIAM FOX
PRESENTS
Tom Mix
IN
"CHASING THE MOON"
DIRECTED BY EDWARD SEDGWICK

Tom Mix is Dwight Locke in *Chasing the Moon* (1922). In this bizarre melodrama Locke's hand is poisoned and he goes to Russia and Spain in search of the antidote. Eva Novak co-stars as his girlfriend Jane Norworth.

Richard Arlen as cowboy Brad Farley and William Boyd as the gangster Kedge Darvis who takes over a small town in Paramount's *Gun Smoke* (1931). The poster highlights Farley's western heritage and Darvis's corrupt urban image.

Buck Jones and Shirley Grey in Columbia's *One Man Law* (1932).

Ken Maynard, William Gould and Cecilia Parker in Universal's *The Trail Drive* (1933).

Gloria Swanson as Sadie Thompson with Lionel Barrymore as the religious zealot Alfred Davidson in *Sadie Thompson* (1928), directed by Raoul Walsh.

William Powell as Philo Vance and Mary Astor as Hilda Lake in *The Kennel Murder Case* (1933), the best of S.S. Van Dine's novels featuring Vance.

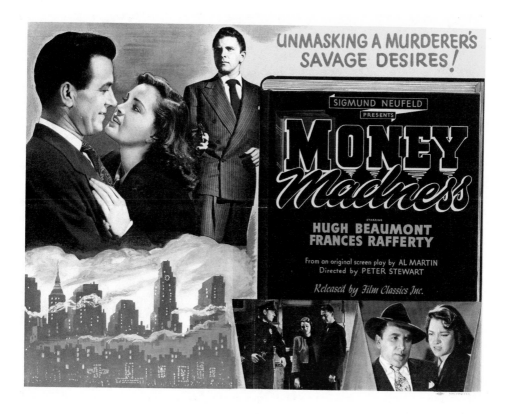

Hugh Beaumont, Frances Rafferty and Danny Morton in *Money Madness* (1948).

RKO's 1938 adaptation of Leslie Charteris's 1935 novel *The Saint in New York* with Louis Hayward as Simon Templar (the Saint) and Kay Sutton as the femme fatale Kay Edwards. The film provided a bridge between the gentlemen detectives of the 1920s and 1930s and the 1940s hardboiled screen detective.

Brian Donlevy, Alan Ladd and Veronica Lake in Paramount's 1942 version of *The Glass Key*.

Tom Conway, Kim Hunter and Jean Brooks in Val Lewton's *The Seventh Victim* (1943).

Robert Young as the adulterer Larry Ballentine in RKO's *They Won't Believe Me* (1947).

The comatose Jeff Cameron (Robert Mitchum) is increasingly dependent on femme fatale Margo Lannington (Faith Domergue) in *Where Danger Lives* (1950).

THREE

The "Half Lights"
of W. Somerset Maugham

Elemental tastes like to have their heroines and their heroes unmistakably heroic. They like to know which characters to admire and which to dislike. The gallery gets a kick out of hissing the villain. Maugham has a literary trick of drawing his people in half lights composites of good and bad.... There isn't a character in the play you can really admire or actively hate. This is all very confusing to the gallery clients who want to hiss the villain.—*Variety*, *The Letter*, March 13, 1929

On November 10, 1927, Gloria Swanson, the producer and star of *Sadie Thompson*, which was based on W. Somerset Maugham's 1921 short story "Miss Thompson," arranged for a sneak preview of the film in San Bernardino. After the screening Swanson, who had invested heavily in the film, nervously read the responses passed in from the audience. The first card:

Acting was wonderful but as a church member think religion should be left out of pictures.[1]

Swanson responded by smiling nervously as she was reminded that "even if they don't like it, they know what it is. It doesn't matter whether you call Davidson Reverend or Mister; the public isn't fooled."[2]

The second card praised the film, "She's good picture's good," as the responses varied from positive to outrage:

Enjoyed it more than any picture I've ever seen.
Wonderful. Way ahead of the play at the Biltmore.
Splendid. Don't cut a scene.
Sadie should have used the razor on Davidson's neck.

However there were a number of responses who objected to the film's ending:

Marvelous acting, great photography. But the ending was a let down. Sadie should turn out either good or bad.
Wonderful. The downfall of the minister may bring the money in but let him show he's a real Christian by relenting and let Sadie go to Sidney [*sic*].

Others objected to the film's depiction of the fundamentalist Christian missionary, Mister Davidson:

Not interested in that type of woman unless a REAL Christian gets hold of her.
Gloria's acting was the only good thing about it. Such terrible clothes. Why is it necessary to show the Minister's downfall?

Disgusting.
A slam on a Christian nation.

Four years later another version of Maugham's short story was released with the title of the Broadway play, *Rain*. It failed badly at the box-office with an estimated loss of nearly $200,000. It was the only film starring Joan Crawford during this period which failed at the box-office and it was a setback to her career. Part of the reason for this was a backlash from the "hinterlands,"[3] provincial and small-town audiences who objected to the film's attack on the clergy as well as its hedonistic celebration of a fun-loving prostitute from the red-light district of Honolulu. An exhibitor in Nampa, Idaho wrote: "A flop. Stupid beyond words."[4] Another in Rochester, Indiana, objected to the immoral tone of the film: "Companies should not be allowed to release pictures of this kind." A similar response came from one in Monroe, Georgia, who put it quite bluntly: "If this is a small town picture, then I'm a bricklayer."[5] In Erie, Pennsylvania, an exhibitor pointed to the poor audience reaction to the film from his customers: "It's hard to realize that a star of Crawford's caliber means so little at the box office.... Audience reaction was very bad, so I had to pull the picture before the end of the run. This picture will hurt this star."[6]

Rain was exactly the type of "sophisticated" metropolitan melodrama that regional, rural and small-town audiences disliked.[7] As discussed in Chapter Two, the preference in this market was for sensational melodramas, such as the series western. This problem, as noted earlier, was exacerbated by block booking practices which meant that exhibitors were often forced to block a book of films sight unseen. The end result of this, as discussed earlier with regard to provincial cities such as Lexington, meant that "rural and small town exhibitors would have to show films that their audience often found distasteful, particularly those films that had characters that were immoral."[8] There was a clash between the economics of exhibition and the conservative values evident in this market:

> Films that had played to appreciative audiences in first-run metropolitan theaters were not guaranteed a similar reception in small-town and rural America. This is why Harry Brandt, president of the Independent Theatre Owners of America, released his infamous 1938 list of leading female stars—Katherine Hepburn, Joan Crawford, Greta Garbo, Marlene Dietrich— who were "box-office poison." Nevertheless, because the major studios realized the majority of their income from first-run metropolitan theaters where the stars were popular, they continued to produce "sophisticated urban dramas" and oblige the independent exhibitors to rent them.[9]

The 1930s Hollywood western, as discussed in the previous chapter, could be separated into two sub-genres (the series western and the A budgeted studio western) with significant cultural and formal differences between each sub-genre. However, both were representative of sensational melodrama with its bipolar, Manichaean world of clear-cut characters, clear differentiations between virtue and evil and their assumption of an ethical world of justice and retribution. The "sophisticated" metropolitan melodrama was altogether different. This type of melodrama has been variously described as "modified melodrama,"[10] "drawing room melodrama"[11] and "melodramas of passion" by Michael Walker when distinguishing it from "action melodrama."[12] In "melodramas of passion," writes Walker, "the concern is not with the external dynamic of action but with the internal traumas of passion (the emotions), audience involvement being held and articulated through the 'agonies and ecstasies' of intense personal feelings and relationships."[13]

Frank Rahill argues that this form of melodrama developed somewhere between the middle of the nineteenth century and the 1870s and 1880s. Its dramatic focus was the

> "heart" [which] became the target of playwrights rather than the nervous system, and firearms and the representation of convulsions of nature yielded the center of stage to high-voltage emotionalism, examination of soul-states, and the observation of manners…. Something like subtlety was attempted here and there in characterizations, with the result that stock types lost some of their rigidity. Increasingly as the century wore on heroines were to be discovered who were less than blameless, especially in love, villains who were more to be pitied than censured when all the evidence was in, and even heroes who refused to fight![14]

Singer, in discussing the shift of sensational melodrama from the theater to the cinema at the end of the first decade of the twentieth century, noted that in this type of melodrama there were few, if any, "spectacular sensation scenes" as these were more "'upscale … talkative' … milder melodramas … geared for middle-class audiences."[15] It is sufficient to say, as Williams points out, that there "are melodramas that emphasize pathos and melodramas that emphasize action, there are melodramas of repression and sublimation—all the genres that [André] Bazin once praised for their 'classical ripeness' exist in the mode of melodrama."[16] All confirm the existence of a moral legibility, a fictional world dedicated to confirm not only the existence of a clear set of ethical/cultural values but also endorse melodrama's dictum that the world has meaning, that it is not an arbitrary universe. On the other hand Maugham's fiction and plays challenged this. While he regularly utilized the character types and the dramaturgy of melodrama, notably themes involving the claustration of virtue and the use of suspense, to involve his audience before inverting their expectations and repudiating traditional notions of poetic justice. His thematic strategies, often masked by the surface of reality, were determined to reject conventional notions of moral legibility, thus violating melodrama's domain of operative spiritual values.[17]

"The Letter"

Maugham's short story "The Letter" was first published in 1924 in Hearst's *International Magazine* and subsequently collected, along with five other stories, in 1926 for *The Casuarina Tree*. The inspiration for the stories came from Maugham's six-month travel in the Federated Malay States in 1921 and "The Letter" was a dramatization of an actual event that occurred in 1911. In 1907 William J. Proudlock, a teacher at a school in Malaya, married Ethel Charter. In April 1911 William was away from home dining with a friend when Ethel, alone in their house, killed William Crozier Steward, an engineering consultant. Ethel emptied her gun into Steward and he stumbled onto the verandah of the Proudlocks' bungalow. At the subsequent trial Ethel claimed self-defense by arguing that Steward tried to rape her. The trial judge found her guilty and sentenced Ethel to death. Public sentiment, however, was on her side and after a successful appeal to the Sultan of Selangor she was released five months after the trial. After the trial William Proudlock attempted, unsuccessfully, to sue the police for their handling of the case. After leaving Malaya, Ethel and William separated and Ethel died in an asylum with psychological problems.[18]

Maugham was told the details of the case from Ethel's lawyer, Courtenay Dickinson, and while the case provides a broad template, Maugham changed many aspects. This includes his invention of the incriminating letter that causes Leslie Crosbie considerable grief. The 1924 short story was reworked by Maugham into a play, first performed on February 24, 1927, at the Playhouse Theatre in London followed by a Broadway production at the Morosco Theatre on September 26, 1927. Two years later Paramount adapted Maugham's story for the first film version starring Jeanne Eagels and in 1940 the most well-known version directed by William Wyler and starring Bette Davis was released by Warner Brothers. There are many differences between Maugham's story, the theatrical versions and the first two film versions. Each retains, in different ways, Maugham's presentation of racism in the local (British) community as well as the destructive effects of sexual repression. Significantly, in terms of its melodramatic basis, the 1940 film version was rendered "moral" by Joseph Breen and his application of the principle of morally compensating values. This had the effect of eliminating the morally problematic elements evident in the 1929 film version.

The Short Story

The story begins in the office of Leslie Crosbie's lawyer, Howard Joyce, after she shot and killed Geoffrey Hammond. Joyce is discussing the case and upcoming trial with Robert Crosbie, Leslie's husband. Although it is told in third person, the point of view is limited to Joyce. Despite being a close friend, Joyce does not hold a high opinion of Crosbie's mental capacities: "he could hardly be described as intelligent."[19] Joyce, however, is intrigued by Leslie's reaction to the killing. Initially he is impressed by her composure and the fact that she never deviated from her initial account of the events leading up to, and including, the shooting. Leslie, as described by Maugham, was "in her early thirties, a fragile creature, neither short nor tall, and graceful rather than pretty. Her wrists and ankles were very delicate, but she was extremely thin, and you could see the bones of her hands through the white skin, and the veins were large and blue. Her face was colorless, slightly sallow, and her lips were pale.... She was a quiet, pleasant, unassuming woman.... She was the last woman in the world to commit murder."[20]

Joyce recounts Leslie's version of the story and her insistence that Hammond attacked her (he began "kissing her passionately"[21]). In a confused state, "through a mist of horror and fear ... [while] he held her in his tempestuous embrace,"[22] she grabbed a revolver from the desk and shot him six times. Joyce is mystified by the fact that four of the shots were fired close to the body and this was the "last thing you would have expected from this quiet and demure woman."[23] However, he rationalizes her actions by concluding that "you can never tell what hidden possibilities of savagery there are in the most respectable of women." He has no doubt that she will be acquitted as it is known that Hammond was living with a Chinese woman, a fact Joyce intended to raise at the trial. This, he anticipated, would rob Hammond of "any sympathy which might have been felt for him. We made up our minds to make use of the odium which such a connection cast upon him in the minds of all respectable people."[24]

Complications arise when Ong Chi Seng, Joyce's Chinese legal clerk, tells him of the existence of a letter that was written by Leslie on the day of Hammond's death. In the letter she urged Hammond to visit her that night:

> R. Will be away for the night. I absolutely must see you. I shall expect you at eleven. I am desperate, and if you don't come I won't answer for the consequences. Don't drive up.
> L[25]

This creates a degree of angst for Joyce ("Vague suspicions troubled him")[26] and he decides to confront Leslie. She, initially, denies that she wrote the letter. However, after realizing that it was useless to lie any further, she faints. When she recovers Leslie exploits Joyce's affection for her husband by telling him that the letter will destroy him. Joyce responds by pointing out that this would be a criminal act: "Do you think it's so simple as to secure possession of an unwanted piece of evidence? It's no different from suborning a witness. You have no right to make any suggestion to me."[27] Nevertheless, he relents and agrees to obtain the letter after telling Robert of its existence. He also tells him he will be forced to purchase it if he wants to save his wife from a guilty verdict:

> Crosbie did not speak. His large, red face bore an expression of complete bewilderment, and Mr. Joyce was at once relieved and exasperated by his lack of comprehension. He was a stupid man, and Mr. Joyce had no patience with stupidity. But his distress since the catastrophe had touched a soft spot in the lawyer's heart, and Mrs. Crosbie had struck the right note when she asked him to help her, not for her sake, but for her husband's.[28]

After learning of the cost in acquiring the letter—$10,000—Crosbie is devastated as it will ruin him financially. He insists on accompanying the lawyer to a Chinese shop and after Joyce receives the letter Robert keeps it.

The trial proceeds without the letter and the jury's verdict of acquittal is accompanied by a "great outburst of applause"[29] in the courtroom. At the post trial "celebration" party, Robert suddenly leaves the party to return to his rubber plantation after a short chat with his wife. Leslie returns to the party and tells Joyce that her husband knows she was having an affair with Hammond. She then proceeds to recount the events leading up to the shooting. The turning point in her argument with Hammond occurred when he admitted that he was living with a Chinese woman and that "she [the Chinese woman] was the only woman who really meant anything to him, and the rest was just pastime."[30] Leslie subsequently seized a revolver and continued to fire until there were no bullets left:

> Her face was no longer human, it was distorted with cruelty, and rage and pain. You would never have thought that this quiet, refined woman was capable of such fiendish passion. Mr. Joyce took a step backwards. He was completely aghast at the sight of her. It was not a face, it was a gibbering, hideous mask.[31]

Leslie regains her composure when Mrs. Joyce calls her from another room. Although a trifle pale, she "was once more the well-bred and even distinguished woman." The story ends with Leslie telling Mrs. Joyce: "I'm coming Dorothy dear. I'm sorry to give you so much trouble."[32] Leslie gets away with murder, Joyce is not punished for acquiring the letter and misleading the jury and Robert Crosbie remains the victim as he is financially ruined and forced to live with a wife who cuckolded him.

The 1927 Play

Maugham adapted his short story into a play and it was first performed at the Playhouse Theatre in London. Gladys Cooper produced and starred in the play which ran for 60 weeks. Later that year Katherine Cornell appeared as Leslie Crosbie in the Broadway production which opened at the Morosco Theatre and ran for 104 performances. Not only did both plays differ from the short story, there was also a crucial difference between the London and Broadway productions.

The play, unlike the short story, opens in the sitting room of the Crosbies' bungalow:

> When the curtain rises the sound of a shot is heard and a cry from HAMMOND. He is seen staggering towards the verandah. LESLIE fires again.
> HAMMOND: Oh, my God!
> He falls to the ground. Leslie follows him, firing, and then standing over him, fires two or three more shots in rapid succession into the prostrate body.[33]

After the Assistant District Officer (Withers) arrives, followed by Robert Crosbie, Leslie gives her account of the events where she claims that Hammond "tried to rape her."[34] However, when Robert tries to comfort her, she tells him, "don't touch me."[35]

All versions include the fact that Hammond's reputation was damaged at Leslie's trial when it is revealed that he had been living with a Chinese woman for the past eight months:

> JOYCE: It's strange how angry that's made people. It's turned public opinion against him more than anything.
> CROSBIE: I can tell you this, if I'd known it I'd never have dreamed of letting him come to my place.[36]

Joyce anticipates the "jury will accept this as proof that Hammond was a man of notorious character"[37] and Leslie will be acquitted. As in the short story, Joyce's legal assistant complicates matters by informing the lawyer of the existence of an incriminating letter which Joyce takes to the jail and confronts Leslie with it. After initially denying writing it, Leslie confesses and asks Joyce to obtain it. Again, the lawyer is conflicted by her request ("I've always thought I was by way of being an honest man. You're asking me to do something that is no different from suborning a witness")[38] and tries to explain to Leslie that he has a "duty not only to his client, but also to his profession."[39] Leslie, on the other hand, is only concerned with her own fate and exploits Joyce's affection for her husband.

The next section represents a significant deviation from the short story. Joyce persuades Robert to authorize him to obtain the letter without letting on how much it will cost. Also, Robert, in the play, does not travel with Joyce to the Chinese quarter of Singapore, an opium den, to obtain the document. This sets up the tension in the final scene when Robert learns of contents of the letter. Scene II, act III, occurs after Leslie has been acquitted and is sitting with Joyce and his wife in their bungalow:

WITHERS: I shall never forget the shout that went up when the jury came in and said: "Not guilty."

MRS. JOYCE: It was thrilling, wasn't it? And Leslie absolutely impassive, sitting there as though it had nothing to do with her.[40]

The play, unlike the short story, withholds knowledge of the contents of the letter, and the cost paid by Joyce, from Robert until the final scene. It also adds an additional aspect concerning Robert's plan to use his savings to buy his own property in Sumatra. When he discovers that Joyce was forced to use his entire savings to acquire the letter, he is devastated ("that's everything I have in the world. It reduces me to beggary").[41] Slowly he begins to understand that his wife was not telling the truth. This is confirmed when Leslie confesses that "Geoff Hammond was my lover."[42]

Distressed, he listens while she recounts the events leading up to Hammond's death. Nevertheless, he, offers to send her back to England, an offer she refuses. After telling her that, even after all this, he still loves her, Robert leaves the room. Joyce tells Leslie that he [Robert] will forgive her while Leslie admits she can never love her husband. The play, unlike the short story, imposes a form of retribution upon Leslie.

JOYCE: It's not easy to live with a man you don't love. But you've had the courage and the strength to do evil; perhaps you will have the courage and strength to do good. That will be your retribution.

LESLIE: No, that won't be my retribution. I can do that and do it gladly. He's so kind, he's so tender. My retribution is greater. With all my heart I still love the man I killed.

CURTAIN[43]

The London production made an additional alteration. After attending a few rehearsals, Maugham decided to rewrite the ending by inserting what he called a "throwback,"[44] or what is more commonly known today as a flashback. Leslie's recounting of events leading up to the shooting as "the stage darkens for a moment"[45]:

HAMMOND (VIOLENTLY): If you want the truth you must have it. Yes, the Chinawoman is my mistress, and I don't care who knows it. If you ask me to choose between you and her, I choose her. Everytime. And now for God's sake leave me alone.

LESLIE: You cur!

She seizes the revolver and fires at him. He staggers and falls, The lights go out, and the stage is once more in darkness.[46]

The flashback ends and the play concludes in the manner described above with Leslie telling Joyce that her retribution is that with "all my heart I still love the man I killed."[47] However, when the play was staged on Broadway they jettisoned the flashback and it was performed as originally written by Maugham.

The 1929 Film

Paramount's 1929 adaptation of Maugham's story would have been banned had it been released after Breen's revisions to the Production Code in mid–1934. Unlike Wyler's 1940 version, the 1929 film violated the Code's basic premise: "No picture shall be produced which will lower the moral standards of those who see it. Hence the sympathy of the audience shall never be thrown to the side of crime, wrong doing, evil or sin." The Paramount version also violated specific tenets of the Code relating

Broadway actress Jeanne Eagels in Paramount's *The Letter* (1929).

to murder: "Brutal killings are not to be presented in detail; Adultery: 'must not be explicitly treated, or justified, or presented attractively' and Miscegenation (sex relationships between the white and black races) is forbidden."

The 1930 Code incorporated the prohibitions in the pre–Code formulation, the "The Don'ts and Be Carefuls of Motion Picture Producers and Directors of America, Inc.," that were promulgated as Rule 21 of the Code of the Motion Picture Industry adopted at a trade practice presentation held by the Federal Trade Commission in New York in October 1927. This included "miscegenation," "sympathy for criminals" and the "sale of women" that "shall not appear in pictures produced by members of this Association, irrespective of the manner in which they are treated."[48] When Father Daniel Lord and Martin Quigley formulated the 1930 Production Code the list of topics film producers had to avoid included all of the issues listed in the 1927 "The Don'ts and Be Carefuls." This was done at the request of Will Hays and reflected the MPPDA's experiences with the various state boards.[49] However, the 1927 list did not have the support of regulatory institutional mechanisms to enforce its prohibitions. Hence producers bypassed them. In 1927, for example, the MPPDA did not regularly review screenplays or completed features during this period.[50] This began to change in 1928 when Jason Joy was sent from New York to, among other things, monitor scripts before they went into production. However, it was not until 1931 that the submission of scripts was made "mandatory."

The "frenzied filming of Broadway plays,"[51] as in the case of *The Letter,* proceeded unhindered by "The Don'ts and Be Carefuls." While the credits for the film state that the 1929 version was based on Maugham's stage play, a closer analysis shows that there are substantial deviations. The narrative trajectory of the 1929 Paramount film, unlike the short story, the play and the 1940 film, is chronologically linear. Hence, we know from the start that Leslie (Jeanne Eagels) murdered Hammond (Herbert Marshall). Similarly, her motivation, a mixture of sexual repression and racial jealousy is, unlike the other versions, spelled out explicitly in the 1929 film.

After the opening images that establish that Leslie lives with husband Robert Crosbie (Reginald Owen) on the British Interstate Rubber Company Plantation, a few miles from Singapore, he tells his wife that he is going into Singapore to exchange his rifle. Leslie, working on her lace knitting, listens while Robert extols her virtues:

ROBERT: It's only wives like you can make these Godforsaken places bearable,
LESLIE: Seven years on a rubber plantation, with no company except natives and a lot of
    dowdy planters' wives.
LESLIE: Yes, Robert. That ought to be a test for the good wife.

After Robert leaves, Leslie writes a note to Geoffrey Hammond pleading with him to visit her that night ("Robert will be away for the night…. I am desperate and if you don't come, I won't answer for the consequences…"). The note is delivered to Hammond who is shown sitting in his bedroom with his Chinese mistress, Li-Ti (Lady Tsen Mei). This does not appear in any other version as they are clearly in a sexual relationship. Hammond, on his bed with Li-Ti, reads an excerpt from Oscar Wilde's "Ballad of Reading Gaol" to her, a carefully chosen passage that anticipates the events to follow. Wilde's poem concerns a prisoner about to hang for killing his wife:

Yes, each man kills the thing he loves.
By each let this be heard
The coward does it with a kiss.
The brave man with a sword.

Hammond then lies to Li-Ti about the contents of Leslie's note. Later, he also lies to Leslie:

LESLIE: Geoffrey, will you swear to me that she is not your mistress?
HAMMOND: Certainly.
LESLIE: On your honor?
HAMMOND: On my honor
LESLIE: It's a lie!
HAMMOND: All right, then. It's a lie. In that case, why don't you let me go?

During her trial, Leslie does not hesitate in condemning Li-Ti as coarse and common (accompanied by a close-up of Li-Ti's reaction) during her testimony. Joyce (O.P. Heggie), her lawyer, exploits the racism of the expatriate British colony. As he explains, Hammond, "living with a Chinese woman, robbed him of any sympathy for him that might be felt in the minds of all respectable people."

Perhaps the most crucial change made by Garrett Fort in his screenplay, other than the closing minutes, is the stipulation inserted by Li-Ti that Leslie must collect

Jeanne Eagels as Leslie Crosbie and Australian-born Oliver Peters Heggie (always billed as O.P. Heggie) as her suspicious lawyer Howard Joyce in *The Letter* (1929).

the letter in person from her. Instead of Joyce and his legal assistant One Chi Seng (Tamaki Yoshiwara) buying the letter as in the play, Leslie must confront Hammond's vengeful mistress alone. The films replaces the opium den in the story and play with a brothel owned by Li-Ti. These changes intensify Leslie's humiliation as she is taken into a room where young prostitutes are caged behind bamboo bars waiting for customers to choose them. When Leslie tries to hasten the exchange, Li-Ti tells her there is no hurry as both women watch a customer surveying the girls and then, after rejecting them, inspecting Leslie in the same manner—much to Li-Ti's enjoyment. When Leslie objects, Li-Ti taunts by telling her that "white lady very proud. But not too proud to share same man with Li-Ti." When she continues to torment Leslie by pointing out that Hammond had a number of "love names" for her, Leslie calls Li-Ti a "vile yellow thing like you." The Chinese woman retaliates with "cheap woman, liar woman, murder woman" before pushing Leslie into the corner of the room. This proves too much and Leslie prepares to abandon the meeting until Li-Ti reminds her that all of Singapore will laugh at Robert. She then throws the letter on the ground forcing Leslie to kneel at Li-Ti's feet to pick it up: "white woman at Chinese woman's feet." The prostitutes laugh and point at Leslie's humiliation.[52]

The film's final scene, between Robert and Leslie, one of Hollywood's more subversive endings, deviates from the other versions. In the short story and play Robert seemingly forgives Leslie as she resumes her place in the colony's social hierarchy. While the play injects a degree of retribution (with "all my heart I still love the man I killed"),[53] the 1929 film is devoid of retribution, justice and any semblance of an ethical universe. The film refuses to apportion guilt and innocence. After Robert learns of Leslie's affair with Hammond, and the fact that she murdered him in a fit of frustrated sexual desire and racial jealousy, he is not prepared to forgive her. He tells her that he "gave her my name" and he worked and starved to make a future for both of them. Leslie, unlike in the play, refuses to cower before Robert's onslaught and is unrepentant over her actions. She tells him:

> You brought me out to this filthy place, Godforsaken place and you kept me here for seven years living among dirty natives and dowdy planters' wives. My youth going. Eating my heart out with loneliness, trying to make a go of it. And I did try for your sake. And what did I get from you. Nothing! Nothing! Your whole life was wrapped up in rubber.

When Robert tells her that rubber was his business so that he had "money to give you the things you wanted," Leslie then justifies her actions by pointing out that she was flesh and blood and what "I wanted was love, affection, happiness. You took everything for granted" and thought only of rubber. "All night I had to listen to you talk of rubber. Rubber! Rubber! Rubber!" So, she tells him, when someone came along and "talked of love and romance and music" it was little wonder that she fell into his arms. Defiantly, she challenges him: "And it's done now. So what are you going to do about it?" While in the play Robert offers to send her back to England, the film pointedly rejects this option. After she asks him "why don't you send me away?"

> ROBERT: Send you away! You're not going anywhere. There is no money to send you away [Robert grabs her roughly]. You are going to stay here, right here in this house with your memories!
> LESLIE: Ah! So I am to be punished. I am to be punished, am I?
> ROBERT: [shouting at her] Right!
> LESLIE: I am going to live in this house with my memories. Very well, all right, if your smug respectability is going to punish me, and that is my punishment, I am to remain here in this house with my memories. All right, I'll give you something to remember. I, with all my heart and soul, still love the man I killed. [wide eyed, with a hint of madness] Take that. With all my heart and all my soul, I still love the man I killed.

The film ends by fading to black leaving Robert shocked and Leslie defiant.

While most critics, including Glenn Erickson in his review of the DVD release,[54] praised the film, few, if any, noted the important difference between the ending of the 1929 film and all other versions of this story. Erickson, for example, claimed that the film concluded as a "straight stage adaptation."[55] Eighty years earlier *Variety*'s review of the film, published on March 13, 1929, also claimed that while it was a "gripping drama,"

> any summary of the picture must record that the merits of the screen production belong to the original play … and the filming has contributed only atmospheric details. That is to say the production is entirely a transcription of a stage work.

Both are incorrect. While the play closes on a whimper, with Robert's acceptance of Leslie and her determination, as a victim, to "try to do everything in the world to make him [Robert] happy," Leslie, in the 1929 film, has no intention of making

Robert happy. Nor does she accept Robert's "punishment" of forcing her to remain with him. Instead, as the film closes, we are left with her defiant stance that he will have to live with a woman that still loves the man she killed. A far different proposition than the endings in the short story, play, and the 1940 film.

Eagels,[56] a stage actor, as opposed to a film actor, brings her theatrical training to the role with her clear enunciation and an ability to thrive in the film's long takes and static staging by French director Jean de Limur. As there are little visual distractions, the film basically hangs on Eagels' performance and the actress does not disappoint. Her cool reserve is shown in the opening scene with her husband as she waits for him to leave so she can to invite her lover to see her. Eagels' nervous energy and repressed sexuality erupts into savagery, culminating in her violent stabbing motion as she fires each bullet into Hammond's body. In the next scene, however, she regains her composure so she can convince the jury that she acted only in self-defense. This shift in her demeanor captures the essence of Maugham's story regarding the inner tensions and frustrations of a "respectable" planter's wife, tensions that emerge during her recounting the events leading up to the killing ("gibbering, hideous mask")[57] and her ability to regain her composure and become the "well-bred and even distinguished woman."[58]

The film's final scene, the confrontation between Robert and Leslie, allows Eagels to expose the hypocrisy and patriarchal control inflicted on wives in the British colony—and her determination to break free of such constraints. While the film suggests a bleak future for Leslie and Robert, her final stance, reinforced by her body language, is one of defiance—not one of repentance. She does not seek Robert's forgiveness and she refuses to be made ashamed of her adulterous behavior. Her only regret is that Hammond is dead.

The Letter *(1940): Breen's Principle of Compensating Moral Values*

> We have read with great care the playscript of The Letter, by W. Somerset Maugham. In the development of this story we have the murder of the lover; all the sordid details of the illicit sex relationship between the married woman and her lover; and the very pointed and very numerous references to the second mistress of the murdered man, who is characterized as a Chinese woman…. Because of all this, we could not, of course, approve a motion picture, based on this story.
>   Memo from Joseph Breen, Director of the Production Code Administration, to Jack Warner, April 18, 1938.[59]

Bette Davis was a huge fan of Eagels having watched her on Broadway. However, her interpretation of Leslie Crosbie differs greatly from Eagels' presentation in the 1929 film. Much of this was due to the restrictions imposed by Breen on Howard Koch's script. The film opens with Leslie shooting Hammond, thereby denying the possibility that she shot him in self-defense. Despite repeated claims that the 1940 version "is startlingly true to the source material,"[60] this is not true. Breen's systematic application of the principle of moral compensating values changed this into an ethical melodrama, something the 1929 film was not.

The principle of moral compensating values existed prior to the changes in the interpretation and implementation of the Production Code in 1934. It was one of the determining censorship principles after the Production Code was proclaimed in 1930 when the Studio Relations Committee (SRC) was charged with the responsibility of regulating Hollywood films. It was used by the SRC to pass moral judgments on "immoral" characters through devices such as denunciation scenes. However, as Lea Jacobs points out, the "single most important means of doing this was some form of final retribution."[61] Prior to 1934 producers and the SRC favored indirect modes of representation to suggest what could not be explicitly shown. This included the use of techniques such as ellipsis.

Bette Davis as Leslie Crosbie in William Wyler's 1940 adaptation of W. Somerset Maugham's short story *The Letter*. Gale Sondergaard was Leslie's nemesis Mrs. Hammond, the wife of the man Leslie murdered.

In Paramount's 1933 film *The Story of Temple Drake*, an adaptation of William Faulkner's novel *Sanctuary*, an ellipsis is used when the film, following the novel, has to present a rape scene involving an impotent male who uses a corn cob to penetrate the heroine. Instead of a literal depiction, which state censors would have cut, the lights go out at the moment the rape occurs as a woman's scream is heard. The film then cuts to another scene. Negotiations took place between the producer, and James Wingate, representing the SRC, as to whether an image of a corn cob could be included. In 1934 Breen outlawed indirect means of representation such as the use of an ellipsis.[62] These prohibitions extended to nonverbal aspects including set design, costume and performance. Anything, in fact, that Breen regarded as "low tone"[63]:

> Low tone alone may render a whole production unacceptable. The location of scenes and the conduct, the demeanor, the attitude of the players enter very much into the question of the flavor of the appeal of the right or wrong presented.[64]

Thus the vague suggestion of a brothel in Howard Koch's screenplay for *The Letter* was immediately pounced on by Breen. Not only was the term "prostitution" eliminated, the PCA watched the set design, the performance and the "atmosphere" to ensure that no suggestion of a brothel crept into the production.

Adultery, while not totally outlawed, was addressed at a meeting of the MPPDA in New York on June 13, 1934, when Breen tabled a pamphlet titled "A Code to Govern the Making of Motion and Talking Pictures, the Reasons Supporting It and the Resolution for Uniform Interpretation." As Mark Vieira notes, the "new Code required that evil be identified as such by a major character in the film, and that it be punished, promptly and thoroughly."[65] The outcome of this meeting was to give Breen enormous power in determining what would appear on the screen. While he employed many of the devices used by the SRC, he signaled an important change in the application of the principle of compensating moral values. In the annual PCA report for 1936 he argued that the "narrative as a whole should offset or compensate for the character's transgressions."[66] Not just at the end of the film. This was to be achieved, Breen stressed, through "a list of compensating moral values" which included a "voice of morality" that extended throughout the film and it included suffering, punishment and the regeneration of the transgressor.[67] Lea Jacobs:

> Prior to 1934, the Studio Relations Committee had advocated the use of all these devices. What distinguishes Breen's administration, then, is that he was in a position to require a relatively more extensive *elaboration* of them. Thus, for example, the heroine's deviations from the familial norm were not only condemned in isolated scenes of denunciation, but condemned more unobtrusively, through the working out of the plot.[68]

In his report Breen argued that screenplays should not be valued solely on the position established at the point of closure. Just to have the "principals simply and suddenly marry in the final scene after leading an alluring life of sin throughout the play" was not enough.[69] Censorship after 1934 was more systematic as "there was a more far-reaching transformation of offensive material."[70] Breen wanted to make it difficult for audiences to "pinpoint with certainty" when transgressions took place.[71] He insisted that producers work to reshape the narrative so as to heighten the "instability of meaning."[72] This meant that audiences could never really point to a moment in the film where "offensive acts" took place as the narrative both denies the possibility of such action while, at other times, allowing the suggestion that "something" may have taken place at some indeterminate time. When such transgressions were apparent, his interpretation of the principle of compensating moral values was deployed to systematically condemn the transgressor throughout the entire narrative—through dialogue, costume and performance.[73] Thus, Jacobs argues, "Pressure was constantly and "invisibly" exerted throughout the production process. And the power of censorship, especially after 1934, extended to the most delicate filiations of the text."[74]

The changes implemented by Breen had a profound effect on the textual determination of Hollywood films for the next decade—until, at least, *Double Indemnity, Gilda* and other films that devised ways to undercut and bypass his system of censorship. In 1940, however, his application of the principle of compensating moral values, which demanded that a "voice of morality" permeate the entire narrative, had a profound effect on Wyler's film.

These changes imposed by Breen mandated not only an unhappy ending for Leslie but, unlike the other versions, her demise. Yet even this was not sufficient to overcome what Breen considered moral transgressions in the screenplay. His aim was to extend the effect of the unhappy ending throughout the entire film.[75] In other words, to punish her throughout the story. Hence, there was no way in which he would accept Maugham's ending to his short story with Robert forgiving Leslie and her assimilation back into "respectable" society. Even the play's melodramatic employment of retribution at the closure, where she will have to live with a man she does not love while longing for her dead lover, was not sufficient, in Breen's mind, to compensate for her adultery and committing murder. She was not only a murderess, but also an adulteress and while the Code allowed some (limited) reference to adultery, as it was "sometimes necessary plot material, [it] must not be explicitly treated, or justified, or presented attractively." Thus, in the post 1934 world of the revised Production Code, Breen was careful to deny audience sympathy or understanding for Leslie. Or even provide any possible (ethical) justification for committing adultery and then killing Hammond—unlike the 1929 film.

There is in the 1940 film no comparable scene from the 1929 film when Leslie retaliates after her husband tries to punish her for the affair. As she tells him in the 1929 film: "You brought me out to this filthy place, Godforsaken place and you kept me here for seven years living among dirty natives and dowdy planters' wives. My youth going. Eating my heart out with loneliness, trying to make a go of it. And I did try for your sake. And what did I get from you. Nothing! Nothing! Your whole life was wrapped up in rubber." Instead, when Robert confronts Leslie in Wyler's film and demands to read the letter, she wearily agrees to let him see it, and then admits she had been conducting an affair with Hammond for years and that she murdered him. Her rationale for her behavior is cold and precise and racially motivated as it includes her description of Hammond's Eurasian wife, whom she calls "that native woman," "with those hideous bangles, that chalky, painted face, those eyes like a cobra's eyes. But I couldn't give him up."

Unlike the 1929 film where Robert responds to Leslie's admission of infidelity with a determination to punish her, his counterpart in Wyler's film leaves the room a broken man as Joyce and Leslie reason that he is going to forgive her. Humiliated, he rejoins the post-trial celebration party and extols the virtues of his wife, with more than a touch of irony, after boasting to his friends that they plan to move to their own plantation in Sumatra ("There will be the two of us, but my wife's a good sport. I can always count on her. She's not afraid of anything. And we'll have each other. That's the important thing, isn't it"). Although Robert knows that his dream of economic independence and marital happiness has been shattered by Leslie's actions, he rejoins her in the bedroom of the Joyce house where she offers him a way out ("You should have the sort of wife you really deserve"). Robert, however, reiterates his love for her:

> ROBERT: If you love a person, you can forgive anything. [she embraces him] So, what about
>   you? Can you go on?
> LESLIE: I'll try. I'll really try.
> ROBERT: That isn't what I am asking.
> LESLIE: I'll do everything in my power to make you happy.

ROBERT: That's not enough, unless, Leslie, tell me now, this minute, do you love me?
LESLIE: Yes, I do.

After kissing Robert and asking for his forgiveness, Leslie suddenly pulls away and, in an amazingly sadistic action, tells her husband that she cannot maintain the pretense of loving him:

LESLIE: No, I can't. I can't!
ROBERT: Leslie, what is it? Leslie, what is it?
LESLIE: [with emphasis] With all my heart, I still love the man I killed!

At one point in Wyler's film she seems to be heading in the same direction of Maugham's play, which ends with her preparing to resume her marital life with a man she does not love. Suddenly, she reverses this, not as an act of defiance, as Robert has declared his forgiveness with no hint of retribution on his part, but as an act of cruelty as she looks straight into her husband's eyes as she declares her love for Hammond, an action that caused Bette Davis such anguish that she walked off the set rather than deliver the lines as Wyler had directed. While objecting to his instructions, as she felt the way she delivered the line, looking straight into her husband's eyes, was sadistic and unwarranted, her respect for Wyler eventually prompted her return to deliver the line the way he wanted it delivered.[76]

Wyler's interpretation, however, was exactly what Breen wanted—to strip any vestiges of audience sympathy for Leslie. While many critics point to the similarities between the films, and Maugham's story and play, there are critical differences which reveal how the system of censorship imposed by the PCA after 1934 affected the level of representation and, of course, meaning in the 1940 film. Its ideological function was a reiteration of conservative values, a means of social control. In comparing various scenes from the 1929 film and the 1940 film it is reasonably easy to illustrate the prevailing values of the 1940 film as it negotiated its way through the censorship obstacles imposed by the PCA's interpretation of the Code. For example, the presentation of Leslie's shooting of Hammond in the 1929 film emphasizes Leslie's hysterical reaction to Hammond's rejection of her in favor of his Chinese mistress. Her repeated firing of the gun consists of a series of stabbing movements as if her rage and sexual repression manifests itself in an attempt to violate his body. In the dramatic opening to the 1940 film, Wyler opens with a tracking shot past a rubber tree with its slow expulsion of white liquid, past the thatched hut containing the workers who are relaxing at night until the sound of a gunshot from inside the Crosbie bungalow. The film cuts to the low angle image of a man (Hammond) staggering onto the veranda of the bungalow followed closely by a woman (Leslie) holding a smoking gun. In a cold, calculated manner she pursues her victim and shoots him a second time as the sound of the shots awakens the dogs and the workers. Hammond falls down the steps as Leslie, devoid of emotion, follows him while continuing to fire her gun until it is empty. After six shots she lowers the gun as the camera tracks into a close-up of her unemotional face. While the audience is denied the events leading up to the shooting at this stage, she is not presented as a victim. Her self-control is evident and in the next few moments she orders one of the workers to get inside while sending for her husband: "Tell him there has been an accident and Mr. Hammond is dead." She goes into her bedroom. After Robert (Herbert Marshall) returns with lawyer Howard Joyce (James Stephenson), Leslie, although she claims she is "dreadfully faint," shows little emotion following such a traumatic event. Instead, she inquires about Joyce's wife Dorothy (Frieda Inescort) and his niece Adele Ainsworth (Elizabeth Earl) who is visiting from England. The first warning to Joyce that something is wrong with Leslie's claim of self-defense occurs when the lawyer is told by District Officer Withers (Bruce Lester) that Hammond's body is "riddled with bullets."

Leslie gives Withers, Robert and Joyce her account of the events leading up to the shooting, based on Hammond's behavior as some kind of "madman" who repeatedly declared his love for her:

> Oh, it's horrible, I can't go on…. He lifted me in his arms and started carrying me. … I seized the gun as he came towards me. I heard a report and saw him lurch towards the door. Oh, it was all instinctive. I didn't even know I fired. Then I followed him out to the veranda. He staggered across the porch, grabbed the railing, but it slipped through his hand and he fell down the steps. I don't remember anything more, just the reports one after another till there was a funny little click and the revolver was empty; it was only then I knew what I'd done.

Both Withers and Robert believe her account of the events with the District Officer telling Leslie that "may I say that I think you behaved magnificently. I'm terribly sorry that we had to put you through the ordeal of telling us all this. It's quite obvious the man only got what he deserved." After the head boy disappears, to inform Mrs. Hammond of the killing, Leslie, seemingly unperturbed by the events, cooks a meal for the men. Soon, however, Joyce's suspicions return after viewing Hammond's body:

> JOYCE: When I was looking at Hammond's body [Leslie reacts]. Oh, I'm sorry, dear, but this is a question that's bound to come up.
> LESLIE: Yes, what is it?
> JOYCE: It seems to me that some of the shots must have been fired after he was lying on the ground.
> LESLIE: Oh, I know that it was so terribly cold-blooded, but I was so terrified. Everything was confused and blurred. I didn't know what I was doing.

Although the audience does not have the information available in the 1929 version, it can be inferred from the way the shooting occurred, by a cold, unemotional woman, her statement to Joyce is at odds with her account that she does not "remember anything more" and that "everything was confused and blurred." In other words, there is sufficient evidence that the audience, like Joyce, should be wary of Leslie's claims that she is a victim and the killing was in self-defense. These doubts are accentuated by Bette Davis's complex rendering of her character which is in accord with Breen's determination that Leslie must not be presented in a sympathetic manner. This initial perception of a cold, calculating woman steadily builds until the appearance of the incriminating letter confirms she is lying.

Davis gives a subtle performance, using both facial reactions and body language, to reinforce the perception that behind Leslie's calm, cold facade, there is another, more sinister side to her character. This is reinforced by Wyler's use of the moon, a motif suggested by screenwriter Howard Koch, that gives the film a gothic sensibility by invoking the realm of dark, repressed emotions. In this way, the moon becomes the film's "moral voice." As Koch later recalled, images of the moon were used to suggest a suppressed sense of guilt behind her "facade of protested innocence."[77] This, combined with recurring images of Leslie's lace-making, provides a network of moral signs throughout the film. For example, at the start of the film the moon disappears behind dark clouds just prior to Hammond's murder. Later, while packing her clothes to accompany Withers to jail, she looks up at the moon from her bedroom window as the shadows from the window slats form intricate patterns across her face and body to suggest a visual form of emotional repression and physical containment. Again, in another striking moment near the end of the film, as Leslie is drawn into the dark tropical garden of the Joyce compound, a place where she will die, Wyler's camera returns to her lace-making and the moon to give the film a sense of visual unity. After Leslie's death, the camera cranes over the wall of the compound to show the reception party inside the house. This is followed by the film's final dissolve into the shadows of Leslie's bedroom where the wind suddenly catches the abandoned lace shawl as the moon, once again, moves behind a bank of dark clouds. Screenwriter Koch later claimed that the initial intention was not to show Leslie's death and leave her demise to the audience's imagination as she walks towards Hammond's dagger wielding widow. Breen, however, insisted that everybody be punished—literally. This included not only Leslie but the widow and her accomplice. To this end the police suddenly arrive without any kind of motivation. Wyler opposed this ending as he thought it quite silly.[78] But, at the insistence of the PCA, he had to film it in accord with Breen's demands.

The use of Leslie's lace-making motif was a little different as it was also found in Maugham's story and play, as well as the 1929 film. In the 1940 film it was used to bypass Breen's determination to systematically condemn Leslie. Knowing full well that Breen would readily censor any literal depiction of her deep-seated need for a sexual/romantic affair, the lacemaking is a metaphor for her loveless marriage as well as her sense of frustration with the social demands of plantation manager's wife. While Robert, in the play, is pleased by Leslie's skill in this regard, as he tells Withers: "My wife is rather a dab at lace-making."[79] Koch and Wyler extend the metaphoric implications of her lace making and it becomes a key image in the final moments of the film. It suggests a sense of sadness, of missed opportunities, when the billowing lace shawl, draped over a chair, is illuminated by the moon. Thus, while Leslie is literally permitted to vent her sexual and social repressions at her husband in the 1929 film, the 1940 film, through the use of her lace-making, is able to provide the same message, albeit in an oblique manner.

Aside from her final scene between Leslie and Robert, the major set piece in *The Letter* is Leslie's recovery of her incriminating letter from Hammond's widow. After Robert authorizes Joyce to purchase the letter, not knowing its contents or cost, Leslie and the lawyer travel to Chinatown where Mrs. Hammond, as a condition of sale, insists on Leslie's attendance. This sequence, not found in either Maugham's short story or play, represents a tour de force moment of acting, lighting, composition and editing. While denied the brothel of the 1929 film, Wyler's version begins with Joyce lying to his wife and Robert as to the reason for their visit to Chinatown. And Joyce makes Leslie feel guilty about his participation in the sale: "Maybe it's my own sense of guilt, but I have an unpleasant feeling that I'm going to be made to pay the piper for what I'm doing tonight. I'm jeopardizing my whole career and I have to rely on your discretion." Unmoved, without any sense of guilt, Leslie continues with her lace-making:

> JOYCE: It [her lace-making] must take enormous concentration and patience.
> LESLIE: I find it soothing.
> JOYCE: You mean it takes your mind off other things?
> LESLIE: Is that a legal question?
> JOYCE: You're not an ordinary client, Leslie.
> LESLIE: You've been watching me all evening.
> JOYCE: I'm responsible for you to the Court.
> LESLIE: No, that isn't it. You've been, what, trying to read my thoughts.
> JOYCE: I'm trying to understand you.
> LESLIE: Why? Because I'm so—so evil. That's it, isn't it?

Joyce objects to Leslie's flippant reaction to the news that she will have to travel to the Chinese quarter in Singapore to purchase the incriminating letter:

> LESLIE: I've always wanted to visit the Chinese quarter. I hear it's a bit creepy. Of course I'd have chosen other circumstances for a visit.
> JOYCE: Be flippant about your own crimes if you want to but don't be flippant about mine.

While the 1929 version is extremely literal in its presentation of the retrieval of the letter, both versions emphasize a sense of racial revenge as the key motivation for the behavior of Hammond's mistress/wife. The 1940 film, denied the censorship freedoms of the 1929 film, employs composition, sounds, body language and lighting to convey the same meaning. In the 1929 film, as described above, the setting is a nightclub and brothel with young girls held in a bamboo cage awaiting customers. This provides the context to intensify Leslie's humiliation as a customer scrutinizes her in the same manner in which he surveyed the young prostitutes. While Leslie's encounter with Li-Ti in 1929 is emotionally bruising, with the Chinese woman determined to extract as much humiliation as possible in her efforts to degrade her, racial retribution also becomes the dominant motif in Wyler's film. Wyler and Koch, for example, highlight the fact that the exchange takes place behind Chung Hi's General Store. While waiting to move to the room where Mrs. Hammond (Gale Sondergaard) resides, Leslie is intrigued with a pair of ornamental Chinese daggers, one of which will be used to kill her at the end of the film. Ong (Sen Yung), Joyce and Leslie move to another room which, instead of a brothel, has suggestions of an opium den where Chung Hi (Willie Fung) is shown smoking a pipe as they enter. The pipe, in turn, generates copious smoke which leads Joyce, uncomfortable with the whole situation, to ask Ong to open the window to clear the air. This action causes the chimes in the room to make a sound that unsettles Leslie. Compounding her unease, reinforced by Tony Gaudio's low key chiaroscuro lighting with its alternate areas of light and shade, Leslie and Joyce wait for Mrs. Hammond to arrive. When she does arrive, without dialogue, the power relationships are clearly drawn with Gale Sondergaard's domination of the scene, aided by low angle compositions to convey her disdain for her husband's lover. Leslie's humiliation is intensified by two further requests. The first, conveyed from Mrs. Hammond, who speaks only Malay and Chinese, to Ong, insists that

Leslie remove the shawl covering her head. Secondly, that the English woman walk over to her. Chung Hi, anticipating these requests, compounds Leslie's humiliation by laughing at her, a similar moment to the 1929 film when the young prostitutes laugh at Leslie's discomfort. This is the primal moment, the lowest point for Leslie, with the statuesque Gale Sondergaard positioned above Bette Davis as she throws the letter onto the floor near her feet, forcing Leslie to kneel down to collect the document. The scene ends, after Leslie and Joyce have left the room, with a long shot held on the austere face of the Eurasian woman, a clear indication that this is not the end of the matter.

Breen's interpretation of the rule of compensating moral values, which decreed that a calculus of retribution be deployed to punish the guilty while declaring sympathetic characters innocent,[80] was a significant factor in shaping the narrative of the 1940 version. As noted above, while Leslie escapes judicial punishment in the short story, play and 1929 film, there was no possibility of this happening in 1940. Smaller, but significant, changes included the transformation of Hammond's Chinese mistress into his Eurasian wife. But the dual layer of the 1940 film, with, on one (literal) level, the film having to fulfill Breen's insistence on the absolute punishment of Leslie and, on another level, rendering this a little more complex through Wyler's imagery, transformed the film into a moral melodrama, unable to match the subversive power of the 1929 film because of Breen's rigorous system of censorship. Denied any semblance of Leslie's defiant confrontation with her vengeful husband in the 1929 film, or the more oblique punishments meted out to Leslie in the short story and play, Breen's prohibitions play a significant part in determining the kind of melodrama he was prepared to sanction. Interestingly, the only character who escapes his "calculus of retribution," and the character who remains the most morally conflicted person in every version, is Howard Joyce the lawyer. As Robert reminds him late in the 1940 film, after he has secured a committal, for Leslie:

> ROBERT: Buying that letter was a criminal offense, wasn't it?
> JOYCE: Well, it's not the sort of thing a respectable lawyer does in the ordinary way of business.
> ROBERT: It was a criminal offense!
> JOYCE: Yes, it was. I might be disbarred for it.
> ROBERT: Then, why did you do it? You, of all people. What were you trying to save me from?

Joyce, as it turns out, despite having reservations about Robert's intelligence and judgment, is shown to be the only person who cares about the cuckolded plantation manager.

Sadie Thompson *(1928)*/Rain *(1932)*

> In any discussion of frankness and censorship in Hollywood, the play *Rain* inevitably comes up. Written by John Colton and Clemence Randolph, it was based on a wonderful story by W. Somerset Maugham entitled "Miss Thompson," in which a sadistically puritanical minister named Davidson in the South Seas tries to reform a prostitute named Sadie Thompson. Instead of saving Sadie, however, he falls prey to her charms and kills himself, and

Sadie leaves for Sydney with a lovable marine named Handsome to find a
better life. Jeanne Eagels had played Sadie when *Rain* was on Broadway.
Raoul [Walsh] … had never seen it, but I had twice, the second time in
order just to study Jeanne Eagels, who for the run of the play was that
rarest of phenomena—a great actress in a great role that suits her perfectly
… every producer had secretly dreamed of filming the work. But everyone knew that the Hays Office would never give the nod. The two major
problems with filming *Rain*, as Raoul said, were that the minister in it was
a secret lecher and the heroine talked like a sailor on leave. Such things
might be all right for theater audiences, Hollywood censors felt, but movie
audiences must be spared.—Gloria Swanson[81]

One of the major tasks of the "Formula," as set up by Will Hays in 1924, was to
prohibit the filming of "a certain type of play"[82] and, according to Swanson, "*Rain*
was at the top of the list."[83] The fact that the central character, Sadie Thompson, was
a prostitute and that the villain is a clergyman who succumbs to his lust for Sadie
meant that Maugham's story, as well as the play, directly violated Hays's "Formula."
Maugham's short story "Miss Thompson" was published in the April 1921 issue of the
American literary magazine *The Smart Set*. Just as Maugham developed the framework for "The Letter" from an actual event, "Miss Thompson" emerged out of a
real-life character and a set of events involving the author. In late 1916 and early 1917
he went on an extensive sea voyage that included stops in Hawaii, Samoa, Fiji, Tonga,
New Zealand and Tahiti. The first port was Honolulu and the ship arrived on November 14, 1916. Maugham stayed three weeks while waiting for the arrival of another
ship, the *Sonoma*, a small steamship heading to Australia. During his time in Honolulu Maugham and his traveling companion Gerald Haxton visited the red-light district of Iwilei. The night before they were due to sail, there was a police raid in Iwilei
and as the *Sonoma* was about to sail Miss Sadie Thompson boarded the ship in a
hurry. Sadie, a prostitute working in Iwilei, was fleeing from the law.[84] At sea Sadie
antagonized some of the passengers, including an American missionary and his wife
and a doctor and his wife, with loud music from her gramophone and "drunkenly
keeping open house in her cabin for the ship's crew."[85] On their arrival in Pago Pago,
a measles outbreak confined Maugham, Haxton, Sadie, the missionary couple, the
doctor and his wife to a "squalid boarding house" where the monsoonal rain forced
the inhabitants to remain indoors most of the time. Sadie refused to tone down her
activities and the missionary eventually complained to the governor about her "bra-
zen behavior."[86]

Maugham's lifelong passion for travel to exotic places in his constant search for
inspiration for his short stories, a genre in which he became a skillful protagonist,
was perfectly realized in "Miss Thompson." His practice of making frequent note-
book jottings formed the basis for the story, a talent recognized by James Michener
when he wrote that "Rain," the retitled "Miss Thompson," was prerequisite reading
for anyone contemplating writing a story with a South Pacific setting:

[Before] I start to do any writing about this vast area I usually take down "*Rain*" and reread
those first three paragraphs to remind myself of how completely one can set a physical stage in
a few absolutely correct observations. I hold those passages to be about the best beginning of a
mood story extant.[87]

The genesis of "Miss Thompson" was four short paragraphs written in 1916 with Maugham's description of Mr. and Mrs. Woodrow, the missionary couple, and their encounter with Sadie Thompson. This included their time on the *Sonoma* from Honolulu to Pago Pago, together with the six weeks spent in the guesthouse in Pago Pago. Right from the start Maugham adopted a hostile view of the intrusive, intolerant proselytizing practices of the two missionaries. He wrote of Mrs. Woodrow:

> [She] spoke of the depravity of the natives in a voice nothing could hush, but with a vehement, unctuous horror; she described their marriage customs as obscene beyond description. She said that when first they went to the Gilberts it was impossible to find a single "good" girl in any of the villages. She was very bitter about the dancing.[88]

On the other hand, Maugham was a little more generous in his initial reaction to Sadie, whom he described as "pretty in a coarse fashion ... she wore a white dress and large white hat, and long white boots from which her calves, in white cotton stockings, bulged."[89] This enabled Maugham to fashion an "emotional collision" imbued by his "loathing of intolerant religiosity and his unillusioned view of the weakness of human nature."[90] The result, as the reviewer in the *Saturday Review* concluded, was a "sheer masterpiece of sardonic horror."[91]

In "Miss Thompson" Maugham was able to exploit the emotive, moral and social ramifications of melodrama while presenting a tale that challenged the cultural values and preconceptions of western society in the late nineteenth century and early twentieth century. It truly is one of the more devastating and subversive short stories that, as Maugham noted, was "as shocking in print as censorship at that time would permit."[92] Maugham devised a tale where virtue is threatened and violated by evil—the basis of all melodrama. Yet his representation of virtue, a prostitute, and his representation of evil, a fundamentalist minister of religion, inverts what most people would consider virtuous and evil at that time.

Maugham's story is told from the point of view of Dr. Macphail, who is traveling with his wife to take-up a position in Apia. During their voyage to Pago Pago they form a casual ship-board relationship with two missionaries, Mr. and Mrs. Davidson, who are returning to their mission on an island north of Samoa. Maugham's description of Mrs. Davidson is very transparent:

> She was dressed in black and wore round her neck a gold chain, from which dangled a small cross. She was a little woman, with brown, dull hair very elaborately arranged, and she had prominent blue eyes behind invisible pince-nez. Her face was long, like a sheep's but she gave no impression of foolishness, rather of extreme alertness; she had the quick movements of a bird. The most remarkable thing about her was her voice, high, metallic, and without inflexion; it fell on the ear with a hard monotony, irritating the nerves like the pitiless clamour of the pneumatic drill.[93]

Her unforgiving attitude to local customs matched her physical attributes: "She spoke of the depravity of the natives in a voice which nothing could hush, but with a vehemently unctuous horror."[94] Her husband, on the other hand, was tall with "great eyes flashing out of his pale face"[95] and a powerful sense of self-righteousness expressed through the "fire of his gestures and in his deep ringing voice"[96]: "I expect to have my work cut out for me. I shall act and I shall act promptly. If the tree is rotten it shall be cut down and cast into the flames."[97] His eyes were "large and tragic"[98] and he was "not a man to whom any intimacy was possible."[99] On the other hand, Sadie is presented as coarse, but harmless and playful. She provides a stark moral contrast to two self-righteous missionaries: "She was twenty-seven perhaps, plump, and in a coarse fashion pretty.... She gave Macphail an ingratiating smile."[100]

When an outbreak of measles confines the missionaries, the Macphails ,and Sadie to a two-story frame house owned by a local trader, Joe Horn, the Reverend Davidson directs his attention to Sadie, especially after Sadie gives a farewell party to some of the ship's crew and the music from her gramophone disturbs the missionaries. Her "sins" are compounded the following night when she invites a couple of sailors to her room. Davidson concludes that she must be from Iwilei, the red-light district which he describes as the "plague spot of Honolulu."[101]

After attempting to confront Sadie and the sailors, ending in his humiliating ejection from her room, Davidson becomes obsessed with saving Sadie's soul. Initially, she rejects Davidson's advances, even taunting him with a transparent indication of her "profession" when she replies to his invitation to see her: "Miss Thompson's compliments, as long as Rev. Davidson don't come in business hours she'll be glad to see him."[102] The turning point comes when Davidson convinces the local governor to force Sadie to sail on the next ship, which is sailing for San Francisco in five days. Sadie counters with her offer to leave for Sydney few days later. As we discover later, Sadie cannot return to San Francisco as she is facing a three-year jail sentence there.

Sadie's predicament only intensifies Davidson's efforts to "save" her and he eventually wears down the young woman as the "pitiless rain fell, fell steadily, with a fierce malignity that was all too human."[103] Maugham, throughout the story, utilizes the rain as both a sexual and gothic metaphor that heightens Sadie's sense of claustration in the small boarding house. Relentlessly and systematically Davidson breaks down her resistance, reducing Sadie to a pitiful victim ("She was cowed and broken"),[104] totally dependent on her "savior." However Davidson's efforts of "reforming" Sadie also have a decided effect on him, as his wife explains to Macphail:

> "This morning he [Davidson] told me that he's been dreaming about the mountains of Nebraska," said Mrs. Davidson.
> "That's curious," said Dr. Macphail.
> He remembered seeing them from the windows of the train when he crossed America. They were like huge mole-hills, rounded and smooth, and they rose from the plain abruptly. Dr. Macphail remembered how it struck him that they were like a woman's breasts.[105]

Buoyed "'up by a wonderful exhilaration' ... [in] tearing out by the roots the last vestiges of sin that lurked in the corners of that poor woman's heart,"[106] Davidson rejoices in Sadie's "rebirth," as he recounts to his wife and the Macphails one evening: "her soul, which was as black as night, is now pure and white like the new-fallen snow."[107]

Maugham, however, refuses to present Davidson's "reformation" of Sadie in a positive manner. Instead, he slowly imbues his South Seas story with an atmosphere of gothic terror, presenting Sadie as the victim of Davidson's persecution:

> The days passed slowly. The whole household, intent on the wretched, tortured woman downstairs, lived in a state of unnatural excitement. She was like a victim that was being prepared for the savage rites of bloody idolatry. Her terror numbed her. She could not bear to let Davidson

out of her sight ... she hung upon him with slavish dependence. ... She could not bear much longer the vague terrors which now assailed her.... Meanwhile the rain fell with a cruel persistence. You felt that the heavens must at last be empty of water, but still it poured down, straight and heavy.... Everything was damp and clammy.[108]

On the morning of Sadie's forced evacuation from Pago Pago, Macphail is awakened by the owner of the boarding house and asked to accompany him to the beach where the doctor discovers Davidson's body at the water's edge. The missionary's throat was cut "from ear to ear and in the right hand was still the razor with which the deed was done."[109] When he returned to the boarding house he discovers that Davidson left Sadie's room at 2:00 a.m. and had not been in bed all night. Suddenly he hears Sadie's gramophone, which had been silent for many days, playing a "loud and harsh"[110] ragtime tune, followed by the sight of Sadie chatting with a sailor:

> A sudden change had taken place in her. She was no longer the cowed drudge of the last days. She was dressed in all her finery, in her white dress, with the high shiny boots over which her fat legs bulged in their cotton stockings; her hair was elaborately arranged; and she wore that enormous hat covered with gaudy flowers. Her face was painted, her eyebrows were boldly black, and her lips were scarlet. She held herself erect. She was the flaunting queen that they had known at first.[111]

As Macphail and Mrs. Davidson passed by, Sadie "collected the spittle in her mouth and spat"[112] at the missionary's wife. Still puzzled as to why Davidson committed suicide, Macphail asks Sadie:

> She [Sadie] gathered herself together. No one could describe the scorn of her expression or the contemptuous hatred she put into her answer.
> "You men! You filthy, dirty pigs! You're all the same, all of you. Pigs! Pigs!"
> Dr. Macphail gasped. He understood.[113]

The subversive nature of "Miss Thompson" emerges from the way in which Maugham employs a melodramatic structure to dramatize a moral dilemma, the raison d'être of melodrama. The basis of the story involves the persecution of a victim, Sadie, by a villain, Davidson. This ethical dilemma follows a conventional melodramatic trajectory with evil insinuating itself in the "space of innocence" until driven out, only to return triumphant with virtue almost completely subjugated. Finally, evil is eradicated and innocence is free to resume the patterns of behavior evidenced in the first act. As Maugham describes in "Miss Thompson," this "wretched, tortured woman"[114] escapes the "terrors which ... assailed her"[115] when Davidson finally succumbs to "the mountains of Nebraska."[116]

Sadie Thompson (1928)

Maugham's depiction of innocence as a prostitute dressed in shiny boots "over which her fats legs bulged," with her painted face, black eyebrows and scarlet lips, was even more stark considering the post Victorian period when he was writing this tale. This was a time when ministers of religion were held in high regard and prostitutes in low regard. Ministers of religion were protected by point 10 in the list of prohibitions passed in 1927 in the "The Don'ts and Be Carefuls" of Motion Picture Producers and Directors of America, Inc. which instructed that "ridicule of the clergy" was specifically forbidden, a clause that was retained in the 1930 Production Code: "Ministers of religion in their character as ministers of religion should not be used as comic characters or as villains."

In November 1920 Maugham arrived with Gerald Haxton in Hollywood, a place he was to return to again and again for the next three decades. While Maugham was an extremely successful playwright, his attempts at screenwriting were not successful.[117] Yet interest from Hollywood in his stories gradually escalated to the point where there have been nearly 100 film and television adaptations, the most of any English language writer.[118] Nevertheless, he had little interest, other than financial, in the film industry and found most directors, producers and actors, except Charlie Chaplin, shallow and boring. Before leaving Hollywood, a fellow guest at his hotel, John Colton, a young American playwright, asked Maugham for something to read. Maugham offered him the galley proofs of the yet unpublished "Miss Thompson." When Colton approached Maugham the next morning at breakfast asking if he could adapt the story for the stage, Maugham, who had received a number of rejections from publishers for the story, agreed to Colton's offer of nothing for the rights but a fifty-fifty split on any profit.[119] Following the publication of "Miss Sadie Thompson" in the magazine *Smart Set*, the story immediately attracted offers for the film and play rights. Nevertheless, Maugham stuck by his handshake agreement with Colton and the resultant play, retitled *Rain*, co-written by Colton and Clemence Randolph, opened on Broadway at the Maxine Elliott's Theatre on November 7, 1922, and continued for 608 performances until May 31, 1924. Jeanne Eagels played Sadie Thompson and the play and Eagels' performance attracted enthusiastic reviews. It was followed by touring companies throughout the United States and it eventually grossed more than $3 million.[120] In 1925 Basil Dean staged the play in the United Kingdom at the Garrick Theatre.

In 1926, after more than a decade in the film industry, Gloria Swanson left Paramount and joined United Artists where, with the support of Joseph Schenck, she set up her own production company, Gloria Swanson Productions Inc. After the completion of her first production, *The Love of Sunya* (1927), which was filmed in New York, Swanson decided to return to Hollywood and the newly built UA studios for her next film which, at that time, had not yet been selected. The tough, uncompromising Joe Schenck, president and chairman of the United Artists board, wanted Swanson to play it safe and film *The Last of Mrs. Cheyney,* a successful romantic comedy that starred Ina Claire a couple of years earlier on Broadway. Swanson, however, resisted Schenk's request as she felt the "gushy story sounded a bit too formula to me."[121]

Swanson, in her search for a new film project, began screening recent Hollywood films and one film, *What Price Glory?* (1926), attracted her attention. Consequently, she invited the film's director, Raoul Walsh, to visit her and he suggested a film adaptation of *Rain*. Initially, Swanson resisted Walsh's idea as she could not visualize how they could get the film past Will Hays until she remembered that Hays's Formula only mentions plays, not short stories. Also, to bypass the prohibitions on profanity and ridicule of the clergy, Swanson and Walsh decided to omit any profanity in the film, although Swanson can be seen mouthing "son of a bitch" a number of times, and the Reverend Davidson would become Mister Davidson. With regard to Sadie's vocation as a prostitute, which was prohibited under item 17, "The sale of women, or of a woman selling her virtue," they decided to overcome this by treating "it with taste."[122]

After Walsh and Swanson concluded that most Hollywood producers would love to do a film adaptation of the stage play (*Rain*), but were scared that Hays would veto the film, Swanson devised a strategy to lunch with Hays and pitch him the short story, "Miss Thompson," without ever mentioning that the play *Rain* was based on Maugham's story. They also agreed to change the Reverend Davidson to Mister Davidson and that Gloria Swanson Productions (GSP) would, through a Los Angeles broker, buy the rights to the short story and the play to prevent any other producer filming Maugham's story or Colton's play. As GSP was not a member of the MPPDA, and not signatory to the Formula, technically, the company was not bound by any prohibitions imposed by the Formula. To protect Swanson, Joe Schenck agreed to hold the rights to the play.

Swanson's strategy, initially, was successful as Hays, who had not heard of Maugham's short story, gave Swanson permission to film "Miss Thompson" providing the clergyman was transformed into a civilian. Hays, who had heard of Maugham, agreed that some of his "works are classics"[123] which gave Swanson and Walsh another loophole if they were challenged. After receiving news in the form of a coded telegram ("VERY HAPPY TO ADVISE YOU ARE NOW THE OWNER OF THE TWO MOLEHILLS OF NEBRASKA WHICH COST YOU SIXTY THOUSAND"),[124] Walsh and Swanson continued working on the film's script. After discreetly placing an announcement in the newspapers that "Gloria Swanson's second production for United Artists would be based on Somerset Maugham's story 'Miss Thompson,'"[125] all hell broke loose after somebody realized that Swanson was going to play "Sadie Thompson in *Rain*, in defiance of the Hays Office ban."[126] The furor was compounded by the threat of legal action from the attorneys for Maugham, Colton and Randolph and Sam Harris charging the Los Angeles broker with misrepresentation as the initial asking price for the play was $100,000.

The most serious problem facing Swanson was a "virulent two-page telegram signed by a list of studio chiefs and representatives of every big chain of theaters in the country charging us with endangering the entire film industry and hinting at foul play and retribution."[127] At the same time Joe Schenk received a strongly worded letter from Will Hays urging Schenk that if the film went ahead, not to allow exhibitors to distribute the film.[128] Swanson, tired of the hypocrisy from producers who also wanted to produce a film based on *Rain*,[129] told Schenk that part of the opposition to her project was based on gender: "Because I'm a woman. They refuse to recognize me as a producer. They expect you to handle me like a silly, temperamental star. Well, I'm not going to let them get away with it."[130]

Swanson sent a telegram to the studio heads and theater chain owners telling them that it was possible to produce a film based on Maugham's story in a "clean manner without offending the clergy"[131] and that she had already invested $200,000 in the production at a time when she was in no financial condition "to sacrifice this amount of money."[132] The next morning she received a telegram from Marcus Loew, chairman of the board of Loew's Incorporated Theatres and Metro-Goldwyn-Mayer, reassuring Swanson that if Hays had, initially, approved the project he would support her. He followed this with a subsequent telegram telling her: "I will do all in my power to straighten out the situation."[133] Loew's intervention proved crucial as he wielded great power within the industry.

After securing Lionel Barrymore to play Mr. Davidson from MGM and Raoul Walsh as director from Fox, they had trouble casting the role of Sadie's suitor Handsome O'Hara until Swanson persuaded Walsh to take the role although he had not acted in front of a camera for eight years. Their next problem was a cameraman. Their initial choice, George Barnes, was forced to withdraw after a week when Sam Goldwyn decided to invoke a clause in his contract and recall him for another film. The production was interrupted while they tried a number of cameramen but they could not replicate Barnes's style. As the unit was about to head for Catalina for location filming in a couple of days, Swanson was in a bind as postponing the film would also mean losing Walsh and Barrymore, who were committed to other films. Even Mary Pickford's favorite cameraman Charles Rosher could not satisfy Swanson and Walsh who felt that his "sharp, clear images did not blend at all with the shadowy, impressionistic style that George Barnes had set for the picture in the first days of shooting."[134] Again, Marcus Loew came to Swanson's rescue and he gave orders to his studio, MGM, to give Swanson anyone she wanted. She selected Oliver Marsh, thereby saving the film for her.[135]

The film went well over budget and when Swanson returned from location to undertake reshooting scenes in the studio, Joe Schenk called her into his office and tried to discipline her. Again, Swanson felt that it was primarily a gender issue and she told Schenk:

> When Irving Thalberg reshoots a third of a picture, you call him a genius. When Sam Goldwyn does it, you say he's maintaining his reputation for quality. But when I do it, you treat me like a silly female who can't balance her check book after a shopping spree.[136]

Rather than beg Schenk for more money, Swanson sold her farm in Croton-on-Hudson to finance the completion of the film. This, as it turned out, was a wise decision as the film was a critical and financial success.

Swanson's film retained Maugham's presentation of Sadie as a victim and Davidson as the villain while, following Colton's play, introducing a new character, Sergeant Timothy O'Hara, as Sadie's love interest. It is his function in the film/play to soften Maugham's confrontational ending. While the short story ends with Sadie returning, unrepentant, to her former life as a prostitute, the "flaunting queen they had known at first,"[137] the film ends with Sadie a reformed character planning to marry her lover, O'Hara, and start a new life in Sydney, thousands of miles away from the red-light district of San Francisco. Although she utters Maugham's famous line: "You men are all alike—pigs—PIGS," she soon retracts it by telling O'Hara that there was "nothing personal in that remark—old partner." Continuing in this vein she forgives Davidson after learning of his death and the film ends in a conventional manner. In the film's final line, she replies to O'Hara's pledge to her that he will soon be out of the service by telling him that "I'd wait a million years for you."

There are other changes in the film. Gloria Swanson's Sadie is not Maugham's

GLORIA SWANSON

Made in U.S.A

in "Sadie Thompson"

BASED ON THE STORY BY W. SOMERSET MAUGHAM
DIRECTED BY RAOUL WALSH
UNITED ARTISTS PICTURE

"Worldly woman, mend your ways!"

Lionel Barrymore as Alfred Davidson begins his campaign to "reform" and dissuade Sadie Thompson (Gloria Swanson) from her hedonistic lifestyle in *Sadie Thompson* (1928).

Sadie. In the short story she is "plump ... in a coarse fashion pretty ... [with her] fat calves in white stockings bulged over the tops of long white boots."[138] Swanson, on the other hand, is first seen with the camera focused on her rear as she leans over the ship's railing and then makes an electrifying entrance into Pago Pago as the four-foot eleven inch actress sashays down the gangplank, attracting the attention of a group of bored marines, wearing a tight jacket trimmed with a dazzling white fur collar, tight skirt, long hat with a foot-long feather and a parasol slung over her shoulder. Walsh's camera shows her jacket's piping to form two arrows pointing up as well as "down to the main attraction."[139] With her characteristic flashing white teeth and her sensual walk, Swanson's character, although colorful, is certainly not "plump" or "coarse." She is also a more complex character than Maugham's victim. While both women are prostitutes, Swanson's Sadie is racked with uncertainties with regard to the possibility of life and marriage after years of prostitution. In the short story, Sadie readily embraces a return to life as a prostitute. Her trajectory is from fun loving prostitute to victim to prostitute. On the other hand Sadie's trajectory in the film is from fun loving prostitute to, initially, a defiant woman racked by self-doubt as Davidson intensifies his psychological pressure on her until, completely broken, she rejects O'Hara's last minute attempt to rescue her from the pious missionary. It is not until Davidson succumbs to his own weakness that she is saved from her tormentor. And free to marry O'Hara.

Sadie's transformation is, in many respects, the familiar melodramatic tale of regeneration. A comparison of her hard-boiled view of the world at the start of the film to her final position is illuminating. At the beginning of the film she expresses her world view in a written response to a crew member seeking a comment in his autograph album: "Smile, Bozo, smile for no matter how tough it is today it's bound to be worse tomorrow. Sadie Thompson." At the end of the film she eschews the life of a prostitute and eagerly embraces the prospect of married life with O'Hara. On the other hand, Davidson's attitude remains unrelentingly consistent with his written comment in the autograph album: "The knife of reform is the only hope of a sin-sick world, Alfred Davidson." When he falters and succumbs to the temptations of this "sin-sick world," suicide is his option.

Sadie Thompson[140] was a financial success with an estimated gross of $1 million in the United States and $7 million internationally, although Swanson failed to garner most of the financial rewards as Joe Kennedy, who disliked Swanson playing a prostitute, persuaded the actress/producer to sell the full distribution rights to Joe Schenk.

Sadie (Gloria Swanson) rejects her boyfriend Sergeant Timothy O'Hara (Raoul Walsh, restrained at left) when he attempts to extricate her from the sinister control of the religious zealot Alfred Davidson (Lionel Barrymore, right) in *Sadie Thompson* (1928).

He warned Swanson, after the film had received wide critical praise, that "exhibitors were already showing signs of being leery .... even before it was released."[141] It was going to be a hard film to sell as "religious groups all across America, from the Catholics to the Baptists, were still going to find it pretty hot stuff."[142] When Swanson objected to his criticism and told Kennedy that it "is a sort of masterpiece,"[143] he told her that even "though the Hays Office passed it, they'll never approve it or recommend it." Reluctantly, Swanson followed Kennedy's advice. She was, however, nominated for an Academy Award for Best Actress along with George Barnes for Best Cinematography.

Rain (1932)

> Contrary to the mythology of "Pre-Code cinema," the early 1930s was in fact a period of increasing moral conservatism in American culture, in which the movie industry, along with other institutions of representation, failed to keep pace with a growing demand for a "return to decency" in American life. The protests about movies by women's organisations and Parent-Teacher Associations was a moral panic expressing class and cultural anxieties at a time of social, economic and political uncertainty; movie content was the site of this moral panic, rather than the cause of it.—Richard Maltby[144]

Rain did not lack for talent. Celebrated cinematographer Oliver Marsh was borrowed from MGM for the film as he had worked on *Sadie Thompson*. Director Lewis Milestone and screenwriter Maxwell Anderson also had impressive credentials following their success with *All Quiet on the Western Front* (1930). Anderson's screenplay also intensified Maugham's critique of religious fundamentalism.[145] After boarding house owner Joe Horn (Guy Kibbee) discovers that Alfred Davidson (Walter Huston) and his wife (Beulah Bondi) are staying with him following a cholera outbreak in Pago Pago, he tells Sergeant O'Hara (William Gargan) that "if there is anything I hate it's reformers." Horn warns O'Hara and the marines: "You had better watch yourselves ... they'll [Davidson and his wife] break your back to save your souls." Later, when walking through a native village with Dr. Macphail (Matt Moore):

HORN: I hear life is terrible back home in the States now.
MACPHAIL: How so?
HORN: Everybody's been made to behave.
MACPHAIL: Yeah, we live in the day of the new Commandment: "Thou shalt not enjoy yourself!"
HORN: I saw it coming twenty years ago. That's why I left Chicago.

As the two men walk through the village, Horn extols the pleasures of the uninhibited lifestyle of the natives as the "last remnant of an earthly paradise." He has no time for religious reformers like the Davidsons, who want to destroy this lifestyle: "That's my quarrel with reformers, they won't let it alone."

This conversation prefigures Davidson's decision to save Sadie's soul—even after she offers to reform and change her way of life by starting a new life in Sydney with O'Hara. Davidson, not satisfied, demands punishment for her crimes in

San Francisco that, she claimed, she did not commit. However, it is Sadie, the victim, who is finally saved by Davidson's inability to control his own urges. In the last section of the film, just as in the short story and the 1928 film, Sadie is psychologically imprisoned by Davidson's relentless pursuit of her "soul." As Horn explains to O'Hara when the marine comes to rescue her: "She's [Sadie] like a victim they have trussed up to sacrifice to some bloody idol."

Rain is more faithful to Maugham's story than Swanson's adaptation—despite the "happy ending" with Sadie leaving for Sydney to start a new life with O'Hara. This "happiness" is tempered by the last image in the film—Mrs. Davidson sobbing with her face buried in her hands. While Gloria Swanson presents Sadie as a well-dressed party girl and her vocation as a prosti-

Joan Crawford as Sadie Thompson in *Rain*, Lewis Milestone's 1932 remake of the W. Somerset Maugham short story.

titute is buried beneath Swanson's determination to appear glamorous, Joan Crawford's Sadie highlights her profession, as evidenced by her entry into the film. In a series of fragmented images to emphasize the link between her body and her material success, the first image shows her right wrist encased by jewelry. This is followed by a matching image of her left wrist wearing an ornate watch and numerous bracelets while holding a white glove. Next, her right foot followed by her left foot in white, high heeled shoes and patterned stockings with a band wrapped around her leg near the top of her ankle. The climax of these images is a startling close-up of Crawford's heavily made up face, including bright lipstick, a cigarette dangling from her mouth with pearls around her neck, a beret and a fur stole. Defiantly, she looks directly at the marines who are staring at her. In a line taken from the earlier film, she tells them: "Make the best of things today as they can be worse tomorrow."

Sadie, after telling the marines that she likes them, forms an instant attachment to O'Hara. He responds by telling Sadie that he is "very pleased to meet a lady"—a line which elicits laughter from the men. The film leaves little doubt that Sadie is a prostitute. This is confirmed by Davidson after he surmises that she worked in Iwelei. As a consequence, he tells his wife that he "is not going to have this house turned into a brothel," a line taken from Maugham's story although Maugham stopped before the word "brothel" was used.[146]

After Davidson torments Sadie in much the same gothic manner as the earlier film, and after he commits suicide, Sadie prepares to leave the boarding house dressed in the same manner and filmed in the same sequence of images

Joan Crawford in *Rain* (1932).

as when she entered the film. She is accompanied by music on her gramophone. In other words, as in Maugham's story, she is returning to her life as a prostitute. However, the film's epilogue, the final scene, matches the 1928 film's and becomes a sentimental melodrama detailing Sadie's "reformation" and her plans to marry O'Hara and live in Australia.

This ending did not soften the angry response of Crawford's fans to the film. Crawford, in later years, claimed that *Rain* was her worst film. The reason for this has less to do with the film itself than with the reaction of her fans which threatened her status as a "star" at MGM. The film damaged her carefully crafted persona built up by a series of roles in romantic melodramas.[147] Even when *Rain* was re-issued in 1939, to exploit Crawford's success in *The Women*, it again failed at the box-office. Crawford, in later life, had nothing positive to say about the film: "I hope they burn every print of this turkey in existence.... I don't understand to this day how I could have given such an unpardonable performance. All my fault, too—Milestone's direction was so feeble I took the bull by the horns and did my own Sadie Thompson. I was wrong every scene of the way."[148]

Dirty Gertie from Harlem U.S.A. *(1946)*

In the early 1940s Spencer Williams[149] directed a series of low budget all-black race films for Texas-based producer Alfred Sack. These films were distributed in cinemas reserved for African American audiences. Singer, dancer and model Francine Everett (the film's credits incorrectly list her as Francine Everette) stars as Gertie La Rue, who is invited to the Caribbean island of "Rinidad" to headline a variety performance at the Paradise Hotel. Throughout the film she is described as a stripper from Harlem, as well as a singer and dancer. Her nickname is "Dirty Gertie" because of her ability to attract, and reject, men. On the "island" (the film was shot in Dallas, Texas) she attracts the attention of two military men, one she calls "Tight Pants" (Hugh Watson) and the other Big Boy (Shelly Ross). She also has other admirers including Diamond Joe (Don Wilson), the owner of the hotel, and two missionaries, Jonathan Christian (Alfred Hawkins) and Ezra Crumm (David Boykin). The missionaries object to Gertie's flirtatious nature and her "lascivious" nightclub act which includes a mild strip where, effectively, she only removes her gloves.

Although the film's credits claim that the film was based on an original script by True T. Thompson, it "borrows" from Maugham's short story as the two missionaries pray for, and try and save, Gertie's soul. However, the final reel deviates from Maugham's story by introducing a vengeful ex-boyfriend from Harlem, Al (John King), who murders Gertie in the closing moments of the film. This completely repudiates the subversive nature of Maugham's story of a prostitute who becomes the victim of a hypocritical, vindictive clergyman. Instead, *Dirty Gertie from Harlem U.S.A.*, reinforces the prevailing (1940s) morality by punishing Gertie for her lifestyle.

Miss Sadie Thompson *(1953)*

In May 1953 Rita Hayworth, José Ferrer, Aldo Ray and a large contingent of actors began filming the fourth version of Maugham's short story on Kaua'i island and, specifically, at Hanalei Bay in Hawaii. The film, a Columbia production with direction by Curtis Bernhardt, was based on a script by Harry Kleiner for producer Jerry Wald. The screenplay transformed Maugham's story into a quasi-musical that included the energetically sensuous musical number "The Heat Is On." This number showcased Hayworth's skill as a dancer while she mimed to the vocals by Jo Ann Greer. Other songs included the Academy Award nominated "Blue Pacific Blues" and "Hear No Evil, See No Evil." This last song, performed by Sadie to a gathering of children from the local village, is a bizarre selection considering the film's depiction of her as a "party girl."

Kleiner's script follows the outline of Colton's play with a couple of additional scenes and some subtle changes in the characterizations. This includes the softening of Davidson's character who, initially, defends Sadie's right to live in the Horn Hotel and General Store to his wife Margaret (Peggy Converse). He changes his mind, however, after recalling that he saw Sadie in the Emerald Night Club in a disreputable part of Honolulu when he accompanied a police raid to the premises. From this, he surmises, she is a prostitute although the film does little to confirm his assessment. Sadie, on the other hand, insists that she was only a singer in the club. Hayworth's costume, a white blouse and red dress, does nothing to confirm Davidson's theory as it is much less suggestive than Joan Crawford's outfit in *Rain*. The other notable change is Sadie's insistence that the reason she cannot return to San Francisco is

Rita Hayworth as Sadie Thompson and José Ferrer as Alfred Davidson in Columbia's *Miss Sadie Thompson* (1953).

because she was innocently implicated in a stabbing murder—not the morals charge facing Sadie in the 1928 and 1932 versions.

José Ferrer's Alfred Davidson lacks the messianic fervor that characterized Lionel Barrymore and Walter Huston in the earlier versions. His sudden rape of Sadie appears perfunctory and poorly motivated compared to the other versions. The 1953 film includes an additional scene not found in the earlier versions where Sergeant Phil O'Hara (Aldo Ray) accepts Davidson's account of Sadie's past, and his claim that she worked as a prostitute. As a consequence, O'Hara withdraws his offer of marriage: "how could I marry you. You're dirty!" At the close of the film he apologizes to Sadie.

Despite these, and other attempts, to emasculate Maugham's story, including an additional scene where Dr. Macphail (Russell Collins) warns Sadie not to confuse

Davidson's actions with what he preached just because he failed to live up to his own ideals, *Miss Sadie Thompson* was still banned in a number of American states over objections to the film's suggestion of prostitution and its hostile depiction of religious fundamentalism.

Maugham and Sensational Melodrama

Somerset Maugham was fully conversant with the structures of melodrama. In 1908 one of his plays, *The Explorer: A Melodrama in Four Acts* was finally performed after a number of rejections. Earlier, in need of money, he converted the play into a novel, an exercise he despised. After its publication he told a friend that he did not like it and described it as his "worst book."[150] The play, and the novel, were suggested by the adventures of the African explorer H.M. Stanley, the man who gained fame when he found David Livingstone. However, Maugham had no taste for sensational melodrama: "The people were too heroic for me to live with…. I vomited daily at the exalted sentiments that issued from their lips, & my hair stood on end at the delicacy of their sense of honour."[151]

Four

Film Noir, Virtue, the Abyss and Nothingness

As a single phenomenon, *noir*, in my view, never existed. That is why no one has been able to define it, and why the contours of the larger *noir canon* in particular are so imprecise. Many of the features associated with *noir*—the use of voice-over, and flashback, the use of high contrast lighting and other "expressionist" device, the focus on mentally, emotionally, and physically vulnerable characters, the interest in psychology, the culture of distrust marking relations between male and female characters, and the downbeat emphasis on violence, anxiety, death, crime and compromised morality— were certainly real ones, but they were separable features belonging to separable tendencies and trends which traversed a wide variety of genres and cycles in the 1940s and early 1950s.[1]—Steve Neale, *Genre and Hollywood*

Questions of phenomenology aside, film history is as clear now about *film noir* as ever: it finds its existence as obvious as Borde and Chaumeton did forty years ago. If observers of *film noir* agree on anything, it is on the boundaries of the classic period, which begins in 1941 with *The Maltese Falcon* and ends less than a score of years later with *Touch of Evil*.[2]—Alain Silver and James Ursini, eds., *Film Noir Reader*

Film noir is a discursive critical construction. It cannot be verified by reference to studio documents as the term "film noir" was unknown in Hollywood until, at least, the 1960s. It is not a genre, as it crosses many Hollywood genres. It is not a movement, a cycle, a clearly defined visual style, a tone or a mood. Yet it exists. Although most writers agree on the noir "canon" (*The Maltese Falcon, Double Indemnity, Out of the Past,* etc.), there is always disagreement with regard to the "outriders," the films on the edge and why, or why not, they should be included. The great majority of films discussed in this chapter are mainstream noir films. However, there are a few exceptions including *Sensation Hunters* (1945), *The Macomber Affair* (1947), *The Man from Colorado* (1948) and *Money Madness* (1948).

John Huston's 1941 adaptation of Dashiell Hammett's novel *The Maltese Falcon* and Billy Wilder's adaptation of the James M. Cain novella *Double Indemnity* are important for a host of reasons. Because Wilder's film was a commercial and critical success, it was influential in convincing the studios to produce A budgeted hard-edged crime and suspense films. Yet Wilder realized during the editing of *Double Indemnity* that if it was released in the form in which he filmed it, the film might not attract a wide audience. Hence he eliminated the stark, overpowering gas chamber

183

sequence that closed the film in favor of melodramatic pathos. A similar pattern can be discerned throughout the 1940s as producers jettisoned source material, from novels, short stories and even shooting scripts, to return to melodrama. This is true, for example, in John Huston's last-minute change to the ending of *The Maltese Falcon*. Perhaps the most extreme example is Universal's 1947 adaptation of the Dorothy Hughes novel *Ride the Pink Horse*.

It is not the intention of this chapter to define "film noir." That is the road to madness. Instead I will consider a wide range of films generally labeled "noir" to demonstrate the protean quality of melodrama, its ability to incorporate shifting cultural changes into its aesthetic. On the whole, however, film noir is not a subversive form that presented a world devoid of moral meaning. What can be said is

Fred MacMurray, Barbara Stanwyck and Edward G. Robinson in Billy Wilder's *Double Indemnity* (1944). The critical and commercial success of Wilder's adaptation of James M. Cain's 1936 novella was important in convincing the major studios to undertake hard-edged crime films with major stars.

that crime/suspense film in the 1940s moved well beyond the bipolar world of sensational melodrama to morally complex presentations of victims and perpetrators. In some films, victims are perpetrators.[3] Many crime films, such as *Double Indemnity, The Postman Always Rings Twice, Gilda, Pitfall, Apology for Murder, The File on Thelma Jordon, Human Desire* and *Crime of Passion,* also removed the comforting, mediating function of heroes, especially detective heroes, and forced the audience to consider their own moral position as they followed protagonists who violated the prevailing moral norms. Some films, not a lot, went further by abandoning the world of melodrama by redefining the meaning and role of virtue. In *The Seventh Victim, Detour, Decoy, Out of the Past, Money Madness, Criss Cross* and *Angel Face* virtue is exposed as a "nothingness," a culturally empty concept in a world devoid of meaning.

The "Ethically Irrational Universe"

Robert Porfirio's 1976 article "NO WAY OUT: Existential Motifs in the Film Noir"[4] pointed to the presence of "existential" motifs in a number of 1940s films. While he claimed that this represented a general attitude rather than a specific school of thought, he argues that there was a "special affinity of the *film noir*"[5] for this "aspect of existentialism."[6] Existentialism, he maintains, "is an outlook which begins with a disoriented individual facing a confused world that he cannot accept. It places an emphasis on man's contingency in a world where there are no transcendental values or moral absolutes, a world devoid of meaning but the one man himself creates."[7] In support of his argument he cites a sampling of film titles such as *Cornered, One Way Street, Caged, The Dark Corner* and *In a Lonely Place.*[8] If this was true, and this chapter will argue that on the whole it is not, then film noir represents a major deviation from Hollywood melodrama.

Porfirio's thesis is shared by other writers who maintain that film noir was characterized by its depiction of a cruel, meaningless world. While the fiction of Dashiell Hammett is often cited as a key determinant in this approach, few, if any, Hollywood detective films had the courage to replicate the bleak vision found in Hammett's *The Maltese Falcon* and *The Glass Key.* Certainly not the Hollywood adaptions. Rather than Hammett and the hard-boiled detective tradition, a more appropriate literary genre was the gothic. As Paul Skenazy writes with regard to Cain's "extravagant melodramas of violence and passion"[9]:

> Cain writes tales of people haunted by the consequences of desire. His work seems an outgrowth of Poe's tales of horror, rather than tales of ratiocination that are the source of detective tradition. As in Poe's world, Cain's characters unconsciously pursue their own punishment. ... They are helpless before forces they have unleashed but cannot contain. Fate becomes a kind of conscience projected outward onto the world, taking material form in an appropriate retribution. Like Poe, Cain's characters seem to watch in horrified wonder as the pendulum inches its way towards them, the walls of their prisons slowly but surely close in on them. ... Like figures in a Gothic tale, Cain's characters watch as their unconscious feelings are made real and given the substance of a living nightmare. The test they face—and fail—is to give structure to this madness. This sense of coherence is what, in the detective novel, the detective achieves through his discoveries, explanations, accusations, and retelling of events. The suspense in the best of Cain's work comes from the terror of feelings that pull one out of accepted patterns of action to leave one vulnerable.[10]

In Cain's most popular novel *The Postman Always Rings Twice*, Skenazy writes that there is "no stable moral basis, no middle ground of sympathy, from which to condemn the lovers. Frank and Cora are all one has left."[11] Crime novelist James Lee Burke extends this argument by pointing out that Cain's characters "believed with the fervor of religious converts that failure to achieve the American Dream, in matters of both money and the heart, was a form of secular sin. So, in a perverse way, unbeknown to themselves, his characters commit crimes to satisfy a value system that was invented for them by others."[12] Similarly, Geoffrey O'Brien points out that Cain was a "chronicler of the gratuitousness of fate,"[13] in both the sexual and criminal spheres. In a typical Cain story someone opens a door at random, or is thrown off a "hay truck about noon,"[14] and the character's destiny is fixed. While that person may realize what is happening, they appear powerless to stop it—"until the final inevitable moment—the point where they click off neatly, leaving you with the void."[15] Melodrama, on the other hand, denies the existence of such a void as its basic function is to repudiate any sense of "ethical irrationality."[16] What is an ethically irrational, or arbitrary, world? This is best captured in Hammett's Flitcraft parable in *The Maltese Falcon*.

"The Flitcraft Parable"

In 1946 Dashiell Hammett was sitting on the lawn in the backyard of his estranged wife's house in West Los Angeles with his daughter Jo. Out of nowhere he began telling his twenty-year-old daughter of a local businessman living in Tacoma who nearly died on his way to lunch when a beam from a construction site came crashing down onto the street, barely missing his head. Although the man was badly shaken he escaped physical injury except for a scrape on his cheek. However, the accident had a profound effect on him as he "felt as if someone had taken the lid off life and let him look inside."[17] As Jo Hammett recounts the story, the businessman had been, up to that point, "leading a nice, orderly, reasonable life with a wife, two sons and a successful business. He'd been content because he'd believed that the world was a nice, orderly, reasonable place. Now he saw that that was an illusion."[18] Instead, he reasoned, the world was chaotic, people "lived and died by pure chance. It was a random universe."[19] By living in an orderly way he had "gotten out of sync with it."[20] Consequently, in an attempt to get in step with the universe, he abandoned his wife and children and his business and left Tacoma. Years later he was found living in Spokane in much the same manner as he did in Tacoma, with a similar business, two children and a wife "who was more like the first than not."[21] He was not sorry for what he did and he did not consider it strange that he, after some years, eventually drifted back to the same kind of life he lived in Tacoma. And, Jo Hammett remembers, that was the part of the story her father relished, that the businessman had "gotten used to beams falling, then when they did not fall, he got used to that, too."[22]

Jo said her father told the story as if he had just heard it, not as a parable from his novel. She also remembered his delight in telling the story "as if it were a gift he had received that was just right. As a boy he had wanted to find the Ultimate Truth—how the world operated. And here it was. There was no system except blind chance. Beams falling."[23] Hammett's parable, concerning the random or arbitrary nature of the universe, is central to his crime fiction, particularly *The Maltese Falcon* and *The Glass Key*. Both novels end on a note of personal despair as ethical meaning has been drained from the story. There is no joy or even pathos—only a chilling presentation of nihilism. Melodrama is the antithesis of this as the mode projects a sense of excitement, a reassurance. As Christine Gledhill reminds us in melodrama, "things matter, feel 'real,' and justify existence."[24]

Sometimes people conflate, or confuse, moral complexity in noir films with notions that the universe is devoid of meaning. The former, moral complexity, is not difficult to establish. The latter, presentations of an arbitrary or ethically irrational world, as this chapter will argue, are relatively rare. Moral complexity is not antithetical to melodrama. Presentations of a world devoid of meaning are. This is not to deny the challenge noir films presented to both Hollywood's and America's conventional expectations of ethical behavior. This is evident in the response of Steven Marcus when he viewed Huston's film in 1941 as a twelve-year-old. Marcus, later a distinguished literary scholar, was both intrigued and bewildered:

> What was striking about the event was that it was one of the first encounters I can consciously recall with the experience of moral ambiguity. Here was this detective you were supposed to like—and did like—behaving and speaking in peculiar and unexpected ways. He acted up to the cops, partly as a ruse. He connived with crooks, for his own ends and perhaps for some of theirs. He slept with his partner's wife, fell in love with a lady crook, and then refused to save her from the police, even though he could have. Which side was he on? Was he on any side apart from his own? And which or what side was that? The experience was not only morally ambiguous; it was morally complex and enigmatic as well.[25]

Marcus's reaction perfectly captures how a film such as *The Maltese Falcon* abandoned the stark bipolar world of the 1930s crime film. But this does not necessarily extrapolate to an ethically arbitrary world. First, however, I will document that shift from the comforting world of the pre 1940 detective, the gentleman/amateur detective tradition, to the pervasively corrupt world of the hard-boiled detective. In some ways, the shift was from the Manichaean world of sensational melodrama to melodramas of ethical choice. Melodrama, as has been argued throughout this book, functions as a "genre-generating machine."[26] It does not, as Gledhill and Williams argue, determine the "specificity of locale, character type, décor, or situation that characterizes specific film genres."[27] There are no fixed or specific moral values. It portrays a "felt sense of justice that operates differently within different generic worlds"[28] that can be "played out in innumerable ways."[29]

Epilogues and Happy Endings

More than thirty years ago David Bordwell wrote: "Few conventions of the Hollywood cinema are so noticeable to its producers, to its audience, and to its critics as that of the happy ending."[30] Its significance was not just formal but also ideological, as producer and director J. Stuart Blackton noted:

> The happy ending is the natural heritage of a happy, democratic nation…. Let us therefore not deride the happy endings, but give thanks to the motion pictures for spreading the spirit of Happiness and Optimism throughout our Land and for bringing Hope and Cheer and a glimpse of the Brighter side to the whole civilized world.[31]

Bordwell argues that although the happy ending was a "fixture of Hollywood filmmaking of the classical period (1918 to about 1960),"[32] its success, or otherwise, depended on whether it was adequately motivated.

According to Frances Marion's 1937 screenplay manual *How to Write and Sell*

Film Stories, at the point of closure, the final link in the causal chain of events, the characters "must be extricated in 'a <u>logical</u> and dramatic way that brings them happiness.' The unmotivated happy ending is a failure, resulting from a lack of craft or the interference of other hands."[33] There is, however, not just one phase but two in this narrative process. The first phase, familiar to melodrama, was the "untying," the overcoming of the obstacle/achieving the narrative goal/the solution of the problem.[34] The second, and final, phase, which may be brief, was the epilogue, the moment of final stability where the "characters' futures are settled."[35] Accordingly, Frances Marion writes, the film should not end until "the expected rewards and penalties are meted…. The final sequence should show the reaction of the protagonist when he has achieved his desire. Let the audience be satisfied that the future of the principals is settled."[36] Thus, Bordwell concludes: "Both the resolution and the epilogue constitute the film's ending, and both must be motivated."[37] In some cases the genre can motivate an ending not adequately motivated by the film's internal logic. Thus the detective film should, Bordwell argues, have a happy ending while the gangster film carries an expectation of an unhappy ending.[38] If we extrapolate Bordwell's argument, a downbeat ending in film noir does not necessarily mean an ending lacking in poetic justice.

Four Films Starring Glenn Ford: Framed *(1947),* Human Desire *(1954),* Gilda *(1946) and* The Man from Colorado *(1948)*

Three of these films appear in most studies of film noir. *The Man from Colorado* appears in very few, if any. Yet, thematically, it is consistent with other melodramas released in the immediate years after the Second World War.

Framed

Author, film historian and television presenter (TCM) Eddie Muller (the "Czar of Noir") maintains that *Framed* "is that kind of film that we talk about when we try to describe what film noir is all about…. Yes, there is an incredibly dangerous femme fatale in this movie. James M. Cain could successfully sue for royalties on this movie. This is the classic bump-off-the-spouse kind of deal."[39] *Framed* is also included in the influential *Film Noir: An Encyclopedic Reference to the American Style.* Robert Porfirio argues that the "plot line owes much to the middle-class milieu first created in literature by James M. Cain."[40] It is also described by writer Derek Winnert as an "intriguing and effective 1947 low-budget B-movie film noir crime thriller,"[41] while Hans J. Wollstein in his *AllMovie* review cites the film as a "thrilling example of 1940s film noir at its best."[42] Lisa Marie Bowman begins her online review of the film by describing the plot line: "1947 film *noir, Framed,* is the story of a loser." It will, she claims, "be enjoyed by those who appreciate the shadowy landscape of an old school film *noir.*"[43]

The plot involves a familiar mid– to late 1940s noir prototype, a veteran returning to civilian life trying to find work as a mining engineer. The film begins in a spectacular manner as Mike Lambert (Glenn Ford), working as a fill-in, or temporary, truck driver, tries desperately to control his truck after the brakes fail on a mountain road. He manages, after nearly driving over the edge a number of times, to steer the truck down the main street of a small town where he crashes into the fender of miner Jeff Cunningham (Edgar Buchanan). Without any money, Lambert is sentenced to ten days in the local jail. However, local waitress Paula Craig (Janis Carter) pays his fine and, after Lambert drinks himself unconscious, helps him secure a room in the local hotel. Paula's "kindness" is part of an elaborate embezzlement scheme to kill Lambert and steal $250,000 from the local bank which is managed by Steve Price (Barry Sullivan), Paula's boyfriend. However, Paula, motivated

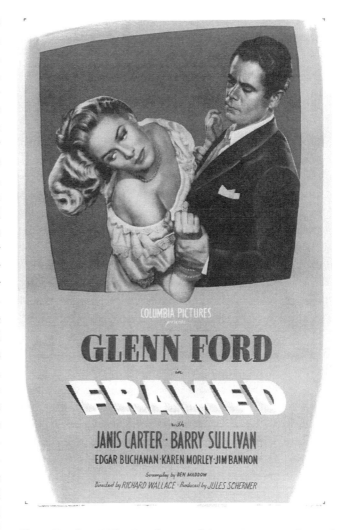

Glenn Ford as Mike Lambert and Janis Carter as the evil Paula Craig in Columbia's *Framed* (1947). The poster is misleading as Craig is in control of Lambert for much of the film.

by greed, betrays Price and kills him instead of Lambert. She subsequently frames miner Jeff Cunningham for Price's murder. The film is resolved in a conventional manner after Lambert becomes suspicious and exposes Paula as the killer.

The presence of a beautiful, scheming blonde femme fatale who deceives the gullible hero immediately, in some reviews, renders this film a "classic film noir." Adam Lounsberry in the online site *Film Noir of the Week* argues that Lambert is "a classic noir character—smart and resourceful, but bullheaded and cursed with a single fatal flaw. In Mike's case, its his habit of getting blackout drunk at all the wrong times, a condition he accepts the way other men accept the weather ('I told you I never remember what I do after a couple of drinks')."[44] Yet *Framed* is a conventional melodrama with a powerful villain who violates an innocent victim. Paula controls the narrative for much of the film until she is exposed by the hero. Lambert is not morally conflicted, nor is he especially estranged from society. He merely wants a job and a woman he can trust. Although he is financially rewarded in the epilogue, he rejects the money and leaves town.

Human Desire

Fritz Lang's 1954 film *Human Desire*, a loose adaptation of Émile Zola's 1890 novel *La Bêta humaine*, was previously filmed in 1938 by Jean Renoir. It is a more morally complex melodrama than *Framed*. There are superficial similarities between the two films as *Human Desire* involves a beautiful woman who seduces an "innocent" man, a Korean War veteran, so that he will murder her abusive husband. However, *Human Desire* refuses, unlike *Framed,* to polarize the drama into simple presentations of good and evil. While Columbia studio head Harry Cohn and executive Jerry Wald wanted a simple melodrama involving a duplicitous, sensual woman and a victim, a fall guy, director Fritz Lang and screenwriter Alfred Hayes had other ideas. Yet you can see the remnants of Cohn's intention in the film's advertising campaign showing Glenn Ford behind Gloria Grahame, gripping her bare shoulder with one hand and the side of her head with his other hand, with the tagline:

SHE WAS BORN
TO BE BAD....
TO BE KISSED....
TO MAKE TROUBLE!

Human Desire was filmed between 14 December 1953 and 25 January 1954 under its working title *The Human Beast,* the English title of Renoir's 1938 film. Cohn kept a close eye on the project as he was wary of the source material which he considered too pessimistic and anti-social.[45] Prior to the start of the filming a meeting was called with Lang, screenwriter Alfred Hayes and studio executive Jerry Wald to solve a number of disagreements which included the focus of the film. Who, for example, was the "human beast"? Was it a film about "three complex and tragic characters" or a more conventional narrative depicting the machinations of an "alluring but monstrous femme fatale"?[46] Lang and Hayes won out as the "erotic woman," Vicki Buckley (Gloria Grahame), is more victim than villain.

Human Desire is generally dismissed as one of Lang's lesser films. Although it is a melodrama with a victim and a villain, the film is less clear who is the victim and who is the villain. Certainly Vicki Buckley's abusive husband Carl (Broderick Crawford) is a villain. But Harry Cohn and Jerry Wald expected this to also include Vicki. To this end, and in a concession to Cohn, the film includes a "good" girl, Ellen Simmons (Kathleen Case). But Lang and Hayes are far more interested in the morally complex Vicki, the "bad girl." The film begins with railroad engineer Jeff Warren (Glenn Ford) returning to work after more than three years fighting in Korea. He is welcomed back into his railroad community by co-driver Alec Simmons (Edgar Buchanan), Simmons's wife Vera (Diane DeLaire), and their daughter Ellen who has a crush on Jeff. When the assistant yard manager Carl Buckley (Broderick Crawford) is fired, he asks his wife Vicki to persuade John Owens (Grandon Rhodes), a wealthy customer of the railroad company, to pressure the company to reinstate him.

Gloria Grahame as abused wife Vicki Buckley and Glenn Ford as disenchanted train driver Jeff Warren in Fritz Lang's *Human Desire* (1954), a loose adaptation of Émile Zola's 1890 novel *La Bêta humaine*. The poster shows Warren grabbing Vicki's hair and shoulder, one of the few times in the film when he displays any passion for life in his railway community.

Initially Vicki is adamant that she does not want to be involved with Owens as he was her mother's employer when she was a young girl. Eventually, after constant pleading from Carl ("you said once he liked you"), she agrees to travel to the city with Carl and see Owens, provided she can visit the businessman alone. Carl, suspicious of Vicki's five hour "meeting" with Owens, brutally attacks her after she returns and forces her to confess that to get Carl's job back she had sex with the businessman. Enraged, Carl makes Vicki write a note asking if she can join the businessman in his railway car. When Owens opens the door, Carl murders him with a knife.

After the killing, Carl and Vicki are unable to re-enter their compartment on the train as Warren is standing in the vestibule between Owens's room and their room. Carl, who knows Warren, cannot afford to be seen and, once again, Vicki is forced to assist her husband by diverting Warren's attention. Warren, who prior to meeting Vicki on the train, appears listless and bored with his life and his job, is suddenly rejuvenated and asks her to come with him to an empty railway compartment where they can smoke. Once inside, he tells her:

JEFF: I'll leave the door open just in case.
VICKI: In case what?

[Jeff leans close to Vicki and lights her cigarette]
JEFF: In case one of us gets nervous.
VICKI: Do I look nervous?

The movement of the train throws them together. They kiss and Warren, with a self-satisfied grin, watches Vicki walk back down the corridor.

Jeff is presented as a flawed hero. His problems get worse after he lies to protect Vicki at the inquest into Owens's murder. He then begins an adulterous relationship with her, much to the disgust of the film's "voice(s) of morality," Alec Simmons and his daughter Ellen. Alec warns Jeff that this is a small town and you cannot get away with romancing a married man's wife as it "ain't right." The affair intensifies, especially after Vicki shows Jeff the bruises on her body from Carl's beatings. Vicki, unable to leave Carl while he retains her incriminating note to Owens, tells Jeff the true story of what happened on the train. This marks a change in their relationship as Jeff suspects that she told him the story just to make him complicit:

> JEFF: You had to tell me about the murder, didn't you? You had to tell me because you knew I would be involved in it just as deep as you are.

When she attempts to hold him, Jeff pushes her away. Although they reconcile, his enthusiasm begins to wane until Vicki tells him that Carl has been fired and intends to sell the house and leave town. As Carl still retains her note to Owens, she will be forced to leave with him. After Vicki intimates that the only way out of their problem is to murder Carl, Warren follows the drunken husband home from the local bar, across the railroad tracks where he picks up a wrench. A high angle shot shows Jeff closing in on Carl and as he is about to strike, a train passes between the men and the camera. The film cuts to Vicki waiting anxiously at home for Jeff to return. When he does, he tells her that he couldn't murder Carl. Instead he took him to the railway office for treatment.

> VICKY: You couldn't kill him!
> JEFF: It's all wrong, Vicki. The whole thing's been wrong from the beginning.
> VICKI: You feel! Your conscience didn't stop you from making love to me, did it! It didn't bother you when I was in your arms. What about your feelings then! I guess it's only people like Carl who can kill for somebody they love.
> JEFF: I would have done anything for you.
> VICKI: Except that!
> JEFF: Yes, except that.

When she points out that he [Jeff] killed men during the Korean War, he tells her that he couldn't murder a helpless drunk: "That takes a different kind of killing." Vicky replies: "And a different kind of man!" After Jeff accuses her of having "no decency," he leaves despite her pleas that she loves him and will go to the police to confess her part in Owens's death. Defeated, she tells Jeff, "I'm no good." The film, at his point, makes a substantial moral shift in establishing Vicki as the victim of child abuse. She tells Jeff how Owens raped her when she was sixteen years old and that she thought it would be different with Jeff as she could trust someone she loved. Jeff, however, rejects her pleading and tells her, "I can't tell whether you're lying or not. And I don't care. This is finished." When Vicki tells Jeff that he is all she has in the world, he coldly pushes her away and then gives her the incriminating note she wrote to Owens, the note he removed from her drunken husband.

The climax occurs on the train with Vicki leaving town with her husband while Jeff and Alec are driving the train. Carl, drunk, enters Vicki's carriage and pleads with her to stay with him ("I'm all washed up"). He even offers her the note, which he does not have. Vicki rejects him by telling Carl that she is still in love with Jeff even though he walked out on her. She also confesses that when she was sixteen, she encouraged Owens to have sex with her as she wanted to replace Owens's wife and live in his big house. However, she tells Carl: "He [Owens] wasn't quite the fool you are. He knew what I was after. And you know what. I admired him for it. If I had been a man I would have behaved exactly as he did!"

Carl strangles Vicki while Jeff, unaware of what is taking place in Vicki's carriage, contemplates going to the local dance that night, presumably with Ellen.

Vicki is many things in this film. She is both femme fatale and victim. She is coded as "sexual" in an early scene where she is shown lying on her bed with one exposed leg in the air as Carl arrives home and she shows him her new pair of stockings. She is also a victim who initially resists Carl's pressure to meet with Owens to get his job back. In a vain attempt to counter pressure from Carl to see Owens, she offers to return to work, an offer her husband refuses ("I don't want my wife working. I didn't marry you to take care of me"). She is also an abused wife and a victim of child abuse.

The "hero," Jeff, is also trapped. He suffers from a sense of ennui, spending a lot of his time idly watching the railroad tracks from the engine or lying on his bed smoking. Only his illicit relationship with Vicki brings him alive. As Duncan Gray observes:

> And as Glenn Ford wanders about through the first act of the film, it can be easy to surmise that, somewhere between the source material and Columbia's wariness towards it, the character turned into an all-American empty shell. He is the salt-of-the-earth man with a boy-next-door grin: steady, capable and always ready with a good humored response that's as friendly as it is banal.... But then watch his eyes in the first scene he shares with Gloria Grahame, who asks him to have a drink to lure him away from a crime scene. As he walks behind, the boy-next-door grin takes on the quality of a leer.... He remains an unreflective blank slate, only reaching peak spontaneity when, mid-kiss with Grahame late in the film, he grabs a handful of her hair and clenches.[47]

Jeff's "relationship" with Ellen parallels Carl and Vicki in terms of their age difference. Jeff appears to be about 20 years older than Ellen. Lang emphasizes that Ellen is not a suitable partner for Jeff. The difference between the two women is made clear with a dissolve from one, Vicki, to the other, Ellen. When Vicki leaves Carl in the cellar after he refuses to burn her note to Owens, the scene ends with her walking up the stairs. The camera remains on Vicki's rear as she walks away before cutting to Ellen, dressed, child-like, in the kimono Jeff brought back from Japan. While Vicki is presented as a sexually mature woman, the costuming and the casting emphasize Ellen's immaturity. She is not a viable alternative. Hence the film's contrived attempt to present an upbeat epilogue, with Jeff's inclination to go to the local dance, is undercut by Lang who refuses to present the conventional Hollywood fadeout showing the hero and the heroine together.

Vicki becomes the focus of the film and she, as Duncan Gray points out, "is one of the more vivid and fascinating souls inside Lang's machines, bouncing up against the walls. She wants to get out, to leave those walls behind her, to end the film on her own terms even if it means ending the film alone."[48] Despite the studio's hopes that she would be presented as a conventional femme fatale, she is the film's "most self-possessed figure," trapped between "Ford's blankness and Crawford's impotent fury."[49] Vicki best understands how the world functions,[50] having to navigate the flawed men in her life. Gloria Grahame's nuanced performance is described by Gray as "remarkable, reactive, and then eruptive."[51] Her eyes, he points out,

> register a potent unspoken discomfort when men touch her or make a pass at her, and there are times when the overriding sense is that she'll say whatever needs to be said to make an encounter end quickly. "Most women are unhappy," Grahame tells Ford during their affair. "They just pretend they aren't." To which all Glenn Ford can do is offer that useless smile and say, "That's not true."[52]

Vickie is, however, more than just a victim. At the climax of the film, sick of Carl's drunken attempt to maul her, she erupts and tells him that she loves Jeff and that he rejected her. She also goads her husband by telling him that she wanted Jeff to kill him—but he refused. And, to reverse the moral point of her earlier story about Owens raping her as a teenager, she tells Carl that she encouraged Owens as she wanted to live in his large house and get rid of his sick wife. Even though she was only sixteen, and there is no excuse for Owens's behavior, Vicki refuses to be perceived as a victim and tells Carl that Owens was not the fool he (Carl) was, as he "knew what I was after." "And you know what," she continues, "I admired him for it." Thus, Gray concludes, Vicki, "badgered beyond patience, … cops to every femme fatale cliché she's been accused of, then caps it off by saying that if she 'had been a man,' she would have used women exactly the same way men used her. It's the moment the film has been building to for ninety minutes, and in that final, fatal phrase—'If I had been a man'—there is a defiant sense of inequity, an outburst of truth more cathartic to her than sex or murder. Because the world of the film, and indeed the film itself, will hold her transgressions to a separate standard."[53]

Gilda

Eight years before *Human Desire*, Glenn Ford co-starred in one of Columbia's most successful films, *Gilda*. The key creative figure was Columbia writer/producer Virginia Van Upp. In January 1945 Van Upp achieved a rare distinction when she was appointed executive producer at the studio, a difficult feat in the male dominated studio system at that time. She was second in command to the head of the studio, Harry Cohn. Her role was to supervise the preparation and production of twelve to fourteen big-budgeted films each year. One of her first productions in her new position was *Gilda*, based on E.A. Ellington's original story. Van Upp not only supervised various drafts of the screenplay, written by Jo Eisinger, Marion Parsonnet and, uncredited, Ben Hecht, she also wrote, uncredited, a substantial portion of the screenplay herself—including the film's upbeat epilogue. The first draft, submitted on 16 November 1944, was rejected by Joseph Breen and the PCA on the grounds that it depicted illicit sex and adultery without any semblance of compensating moral values. A revised screenplay was submitted on August 24, 1945. Again Breen rejected it. Nevertheless, filming began on September 4 and continued until December 10, 1945. Revisions were resubmitted on September 8 and Breen approved the production, with a few quibbles,[54] on September 11. After filming was completed, the PCA, without Breen, reviewed the film and it was granted a seal of approval on February 25, 1946. Within the history of Hollywood censorship after the tightening of the Production Code system in mid–1934, the PCA's decision to give *Gilda* their seal of approval was a significant moment as the film represented a direct challenge to Breen's dictum that the appropriate moral values must permeate the entire narrative, not just the epilogue.

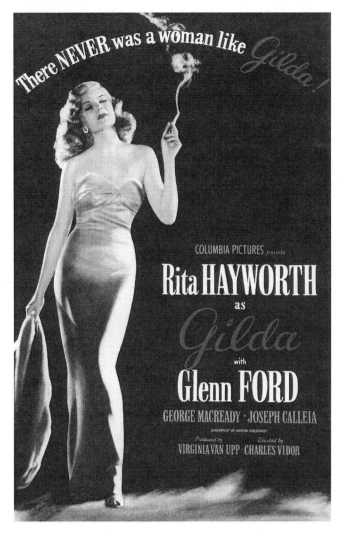

Rita Hayworth in Columbia's *Gilda* (1946) which cleverly bypassed most of censor Joseph Breen's objections to the film.

The film begins with Johnny Farrell (Glenn Ford), a drifter similar to Cain's opportunistic Frank Chambers in *The Postman Always Rings Twice*, in trouble in a waterfront gambling game in Buenos Aires. After winning money, he is confronted by a robber in a dark alley. He is rescued by a middle-aged man with his "little friend," a walking cane that abruptly transforms into an erect weapon with a phallic steel tip. Farrell's mysterious savior, middle-aged Ballin Mundson (George Macready), suggests the young man join him and Farrell is soon, in effect, in a kept relationship with his wealthy benefactor. Director Charles Vidor and cinematographer Rudolph Maté employ low angle camera compositions and subtle editing, along with the not-so-subtle visual metaphor of Ballin's "cane," to convey the real nature of Farrell's relationship with Ballin. Mundson even compares Farrell with his phallic cane: "Johnny," Mundson explains, "is almost as sharp as my other friend, but he will kill for me." Johnny replies, "That's what friends are for." Many years later Glenn Ford acknowledged that there was a concerted effort by the filmmakers to bypass Breen's opposition to any film he considered contained suggestions of "sexual perversion."

The relationship between Mundson and Farrell is threatened when Mundson, while on a business trip, marries Gilda. The prospect of regularly seeing a woman who had an affair with him some time ago unsettles Johnny. His condition deteriorates when Mundson orders the young man to "look after" Gilda, a situation she exploits to the full as she teases her frustrated ex-lover with her supposed infidelities in Buenos Aires. Johnny's psychological disintegration is exposed in his narration. After watching Gilda with her husband he explains: "I wanted to hit her. I wanted to go back and see them together with me watching." Although Gilda enjoys Farrell's torment, she gradually realizes that her husband has his own peculiarities, especially when he tells her that "hate can be a very exciting emotion. Very exciting. Haven't you noticed that … there's a heat in it that one can feel. Didn't you feel it tonight…. I did! It warmed me. Hate is the only thing that had ever warmed me." In this perverse scene, effectively played by George Macready, Mundson, dressed in a flamboyant dressing gown over his formal costume, sits on edge of their bed. Director Charles Vidor places Mundson, in shadow, deep in the foreground of the frame to show his domination of Gilda as his body divides her into two parts.

Mundson seemingly dies two-thirds into the film although a brief insert shows him surviving a plane explosion after parachuting from the damaged craft. Mundson's "death" clears the way for Johnny to court and marry Gilda. However, she soon discovers that Johnny is even crazier than Mundson. His marriage to her was a ruse to control and punish for her "adulterous affairs." On their wedding night she discovers a large photograph of Mundson in their room. Distressed, she tells Johnny that this "isn't decent." He throws the word "decent" back into her face as his narration reiterates his deep-seated psychosis:

> She didn't know then what was happening to her. She didn't know then what she heard was the door closing on her own cage. She hadn't been faithful to him when he was alive but she was going to be faithful now that he was dead.

Obsessed with his debt to Mundson, Johnny systematically tortures Gilda by denying her any sexual contact with him, or other people. To achieve this he assigns Munson's casino employees to watch her day and night. Distressed by Johnny's neglect, she tells him: "You wouldn't think that one woman could marry two insane men in one lifetime, would you?" Gilda tries to get away, fleeing to Montevideo where she intends filing for divorce. In Montevideo she meets an attorney, Tom Langford (Don Douglas), who is seemingly infatuated with her. He tells Gilda to return to Buenos Aires and file for an annulment as her marriage was never consummated. Accepting his advice, she returns to Buenos Aires, only to learn that Langford was working for Johnny. Gilda, in an attempt to humiliate Johnny, sings the torch song "Put the Blame on Mame," while gyrating her hips and undertaking a strip tease (she only removes her gloves) in front of excited patrons in the casino. When she invites two eager men in the audience to assist her, Johnny, who is watching her, erupts with rage. The film's "surface plot" involving former Nazi agents who seek a patent for Tungsten is quickly resolved and one of the casino's employees, Uncle Pio (Steven Geray), stabs Mundson in the back with his own walking stick just as he is about to shoot Gilda and Farrell. In the epilogue Johnny and Gilda prepare to leave Buenos Aires for life together in the United States.

The film's final moments, with Johnny suddenly assuming some semblance of "normality," is poorly motivated. It is an extreme example of a melodramatic deus ex machina. It represents one of Hollywood's more obvious violations of Frances Marion's advice in her 1937 screenplay manual *How to Write and Sell Film Stories* that the characters "must be extricated in a logical and dramatic way that brings them happiness." While the film's brief epilogue endorses the prevailing ethical norms of the 1940s, a "normal" heterosexual romance along with a celebration of marriage and domesticity, the episodic narrative for the great bulk of the film is devoid of any consistency with regard to its presentation of virtue—depending on whether Gilda's "transgressions" are to be believed. Each of the central characters, Gilda, Johnny and Mundson, take turns in extracting pleasure through acts of cruelty. The only semblance of an explanation for this, and it is barely plausible, is that once the couple are able to extricate themselves from the "depravities" of an "alien" culture (Buenos Aires), they somehow will resume a "normal" life back in the United States.

Van Upp's upbeat epilogue was, in effect, a cynical attempt to bolster the film's chances at the box office while also appeasing Breen and his objections concerning the film's depiction of "illicit sex and adultery without compensating moral values."[55] On the whole, however, the film cleverly bypassed Breen's prohibitions by following his advice to producers in the 1930s that "illicit acts" should always be rendered in an oblique manner so that audiences could never really point to a moment in the film where "offensive acts" took place. Hence the narrative should deny constantly the possibility of such actions while, at other times, admitting the possibility that they occurred. The filmmakers took this advice and, in process, made it almost impossible for Breen to object to the ramifications of its oblique presentation, as in the following dialogue exchange:

> JOHNNY: Get this straight. I don't care what you do. But I'm going to see to it that it looks all right to him [Mundson]. From now on, you go anywhere you please, with anyone you please. But I'm going to take you there and I'm going to bring you home. Get that? Exactly the way I'd pick up his laundry.
> GILDA: Shame on you Johnny. Any psychiatrist would tell you your thought-associations are very revealing…. All to protect Ballin—who do you think you are kidding, Johnny?

This shift in Hollywood's more problematic presentation of morality was detected by French critics such as Nino Frank[56] and Jean-Pierre Chartier[57] in the summer of 1946. After viewing a relatively large number of Hollywood films produced between 1940 and 1946, films not screened in France during the first half of the 1940s due to the German occupation, they realized that something had changed. For Chartier, however, this change was not necessarily for the better as he noted in 1946:

> "She kisses him so that he'll kill for her." Emblazoned on the movie posters, over a blood stain, is description of Billy Wilder's *Double Indemnity*. The same line would work just as well for Edward Dmytryk's *Murder, My Sweet*. It would hold true again for *The Postman Always Rings Twice* which is currently a big hit in the US. We understood why the Hays Office had previously

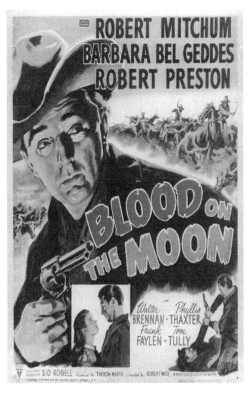

Left: Teresa Wright and Robert Mitchum, as the psychologically traumatized Jeb Rand, in Raoul Walsh's *Pursued* (1947). *Right:* Robert Mitchum and Barbara Bel Geddes in Robert Wise's *Blood on the Moon* (1948), part of a cycle of postwar "noir westerns."

forbidden film adaptations of James M. Cain's two novels from which *Double Indemnity* and *The Postman Always Rings Twice* are drawn. It is harder to understand, given this censor's moral posture, why this interdiction was lifted, as it's hard to imagine story lines with a more pessimistic or disgusted point of view regarding human behavior.[58]

The Man from Colorado

The Man from Colorado was part of a short cycle of westerns[59] produced soon after the end of the Second World War that transferred the maladjusted hero, a familiar character in urban noir films, to the western. The film's screenplay by Robert D. Andrews and Ben Maddow, from a story by Borden Chase, focused on a familiar western plot involving a greedy capitalist, "Big" Ed Carter (Ray Collins), who cheats the local miners out of their claims while they are fighting for the Union in the Civil War. The "noir" aspect involves the film's focus on the psychological disintegration of a war "hero," Colonel Owen Devereaux (Glenn Ford).

The film begins on the final day of the Civil War as a strong force of Union soldiers, led by Devereaux, corner a small band of Confederate soldiers at Jacobs Gorge in Colorado. When the Confederates try to surrender by flying a white flag, Devereaux ignores their surrender and opens fire with his artillery, killing all except one enemy soldier. A close-up of Devereaux, with Glenn Ford uncharacteristically presented with wavy hair, a touch of grey, and a grim visage, records his reaction to the slaughter. Devereaux later learns that the killing took place after Jefferson Davis's surrender and he feigns dismay at the news. In his tent that night he records his reaction to the killing in his diary. As the tormented Devereaux, the painful tone of Glenn Ford's narration is reminiscent of his voice-over in *Gilda*. His narration records his reaction to the slaughter as recorded in his diary:

> I killed a hundred men to-day. I didn't want to. I couldn't help myself. What's wrong with me? I'm afraid—afraid I'm going crazy.
> No, it was the war that's all. But the war's over—now. I can stop. I'm safe. God is helping me.

Devereaux collapses with his head in his hands on his desk only to quickly recover when close friend, Captain Del Stewart (William Holden), enters his tent. Earlier, Stewart found the Confederates' white flag near one of their bodies and suspects that Devereaux deliberately murdered them.

Both men return to the same town in Colorado where they, especially Devereaux, are celebrated for their contribution in the war. Both men are in love with the same woman, Caroline Emmett (Ellen Drew). Caroline chooses Devereaux and they marry. He accepts an appointment as Federal judge to the territory and Stewart reluctantly becomes his Federal Marshal on the understanding that Devereaux will never use his gun again. Devereaux, however, is unable to control his bloodlust and when the sole Confederate survivor of the Jacobs Gorge massacre confronts him, Devereaux knocks him to the ground and shoots him a number of times in front of Stewart and Doc Merriam (Edgar Buchanan). Devereaux continues to support Carter

Opposite, bottom: **Joel McCrea, Veronica Lake, Donald Crisp, Don DeFore, Preston Foster, Arleen Whelan and Charles Ruggles in André de Toth's "noir western" *Ramrod* (1947).**

Left: William Holden, Ellen Drew and Glenn Ford in *The Man from Colorado* (1948). *Right:* Ellen Drew as Caroline Emmett married to the psychologically disturbed ex-army colonel Owen Deveraux (Glenn Ford) in *The Man from Colorado* (1948).

against the working-class miners and when the judge hangs young Johnny Howard (Jerome Courtland), who he mistakenly believed robbed Carter's Great Star Mining Company, Stewart joins the miners in their fight against Carter's corporate interests. Just prior to the film's action-based climax, Caroline finds Devereaux's diary which exposes his mental instability. She joins Stewart and they hide out in town until Devereaux's madness, provoked by his long-time fear that Caroline will leave him for Stewart, finally erupts and he burns the entire town down. Devereaux dies when the side of a building falls on him and the epilogue shows Stewart leaving for Washington to help the dispossessed miners regain their properties—after promising Caroline he will return to her.

Glenn Ford's Devereaux is similar to the character he portrayed in *Gilda*. While *Gilda* offers no explanation for Johnny's psychosis, *The Man from Colorado* tentatively suggests Devereaux's psychological problems are caused by the war. After the massacre at Jacob's Gorge Devereaux blames the war for his behavior. This is never confirmed and it is possible that the war gave him a license to act on his sadistic impulses. Perhaps the historical context of the film's release provides the explanation missing from this film. *The Man from Colorado* was produced in 1947, a time when many ex-military personnel were trying to adjust to life back in the United States. During this period there were a number of films in different genres that focused on this issue. They included "problem films" such as *The Best Years of Our Lives* and *Till the End of Time* as well as urban thrillers such as *The Blue Dahlia* (1946), *Somewhere in the Night* (1946), *Crack-up* (1946), *The High Wall* (1947), *Crossfire* (1947), *Ride the Pink Horse* (1947) and *The Crooked Way* (1949).

The Investigative Thriller

One of the key changes in the Hollywood cinema detected by Nino Frank in 1946 was the decline of the classical detective in favor of the hard-boiled variety. As Frank noted with regard to the crime film, the emphasis on ratiocination receded, or virtually disappeared, and was replaced by a focus on "criminal psychology"[60]:

> This sort of film has now notably changed in the U.S. following the course of popular litera-ture where the preeminence of S.S. Van Dine has ceded to that of Dashiell Hammett. Since Poe, since Garboriau, and since Conan Doyle, we've become familiar with the formula for detec-tive stories: an unsolved crime, some suspects, and in the end the discovery of the guilty party through the diligence of an experienced observer. This formula has long been perfected: the detective novel (and film) have substituted for the Sunday crossword puzzle and become over-shadowed by boring repetition.[61]

The Classical/Amateur Detective

Classical detective fiction is one of the most optimistic of genres. It presupposes, according to Nevins, "that in most respects all is right in the world, and that the few patches of darkness are illuminable by the light of human reason. The murder of Sir George in the library of his ancestral manor is but a momentary aberration, a glitch. Once the detective has organized the clues into a rationally harmonious mosaic, the guilty person is exposed and the world is restored to its Edenic innocence."[62]

Hammett, who began publishing crime stories in 1923, was well aware of the conventions and style of the "Golden Age of Detection," or classical detective fiction, a form he despised. This type of detective fiction emphasized the process of "ratio-cination," the systematic application of logic to solve a crime. It can be traced back to Edgar Allan Poe and three short stories he published in the 1840s featuring Che-valier C. Auguste Dupin, an eccentric, super-intelligent gentleman detective. Poe's first story, "The Murders in the Rue Morgue," was published in *Graham's Lady's and Gentlemen's Magazine* in April 1841. The second story, "The Mystery of Marie Roget," where the term "ratiocination," meaning stories of logical deduction,[63] appears three times, was published in *Snowden's Lady Companion* in November 1842 and the third story, "The Purloined Letter," in the *Gift* in October 1844. The second story, "The Mystery of Marie Roget," was an early example of the locked room mystery which became a staple of crime fiction during its golden age after the First World War. Rati-ocination is an essential element, as Dupin outlined while walking the streets of Paris in "The Mystery of Marie Roget." He emphasized the importance of the cerebral pro-cess where the detective logically and systematically sorts through the facts of the case to reach a logical solution, a solution not reached by the inept police. Arthur Conan Doyle's Sherlock Holmes, E.C. Bentley's novels, G.K. Chesterton's Father

Brown stories, A.A. Milne, Ngaio Marsh and especially Agatha Christie continued this tradition.

To take one of hundreds of possible examples, Christie's first crime novel *The Mysterious Affair at Styles*, published in 1921, featured the Belgian detective Hercule Poirot. In the story a series of murders occur at a country manor. This, a familiar closed setting, was a common feature of the classical detective story where the number of suspects could be limited by an enclosed location—an island, a ship, a remote area and so on. After the police interrogate the suspects, the (superior) amateur detective investigates until the climax when the suspects are assembled and the detective, after recounting the events leading up the crime, or crimes, exposes the murderer. A reviewer in the *Observer* in May 1958 described this kind of detective fiction as "cosy," a non-confrontational, comforting form where crime is presented as a social aberration and not as endemic to society.

In the United States the most popular practitioner of this form of crime fiction in the 1920s was S.S. Van Dine, the pseudonym of Williard Huntington Wright and the creator of Philo Vance. Wright was born in Charlottesville, Virginia, in 1887. After his expulsion from Harvard for bringing a glass of absinthe to lectures, he pursued a career as a poet and literary scholar and worked, for a time, as literary critic for the *Los Angeles Times* where he was dismissive of crime and detective novels. After he was sacked as editor of the upmarket literary magazine *Smart Set,* Wright's mother sent him to Paris for treatment for his opium addiction. While in solitary confinement he read a number of detective novels. He decided he could do a better job and embarked on a new career as S.S. Van Dine, the creator of Philo Vance, the debonair, aristocratic detective who first appeared in 1926 in *The Benson Murder Case.* Wright was influenced by British writers such as H.C. Bailey, the creator of Reggie Fortune, and Dorothy Sayers and her amateur detective Lord Peter Wimsey. Vance was a dilettante

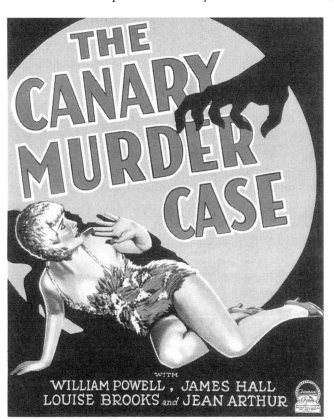

Paramount's *The Canary Murder Case* (1929) was based on the second Philo Vance novel by S.S. Van Dine which was published in 1927. The film starred William Powell as Vance.

William Powell as S.S. Van Dine's detective Philo Vance with Louise Brooks as Margaret O'Dell (the "Canary") in *The Canary Murder Case* (1929).

and aesthete who often brought his knowledge of art, music, and philosophy into the investigation. He differed from Sherlock Holmes, Miss Jane Marple and other classical detectives in his reliance on psychological insights to solve crimes.

The Benson Murder Case, Wright's first detective story, was an immediate success and the first edition sold out within a week. His next novel *The Canary Murder Case* was serialized in *Scribner's Magazine* in 1927 and it was even more successful. This was followed by the equally successful *The Greene Murder Case* in 1928 and *The Bishop Murder Case* in 1929. By the late 1920s Van Dine was the most successful author of detective fiction in the United States and in 1930 it was estimated that he had sold more than a million copies. Hollywood soon took an interest and in 1928 Paramount purchased the rights to *The Benson Murder Case* as well as *The Canary Murder Case* and *The Greene Murder Case*. William Powell was cast as Vance in the first film, *The Canary Murder Case*, and although it began production as a silent film the studio inserted a few brief talkie scenes and some sound effects. In 1930 Van Dine sold the rights to *The Bishop Murder Case* to MGM and Basil Rathbone was cast as Vance in a stilted tale where Vance tracks down a killer known as "the Bishop" who murders according to the Mother Goose nursery rhyme (the original title was *The Mother Goose Murder Case*).

In 1932 and 1933 Van Dine worked on his best novel, *The Kennel Murder Case*, which was published in 1933. Warner Brothers purchased the rights and the film was released on October 28, 1933, with William Powell returning as Vance in the best screen adaption of a Van Dine novel.[64] Both novel and film begin at the Long Island Kennel Club where Vance is showing his beloved Scottish Terrier. However, after Sir Thomas MacDonald's (Paul Cavanagh) prize-winning dog is killed and suspicion falls on wealthy businessman Archie Coe (Robert Barrat), Coe is found dead in his bedroom. As the bedroom door is locked from the inside, Coe's death is ruled a suicide although Vance suspects murder. In this variation of the traditional locked room mystery there are multiple suspects—including Coe's ward Hilda Lake (Mary Astor), who resents Coe's strict control of her inheritance; MacDonald, who not only lost his dog but is frustrated by Coe's opposition to his romance with Hilda; Raymond Wrede (Ralph Morgan), Coe's secretary who also loves Hilda and resents Coe's interference to his plans; Doris Delafield (Helen Vinson), Coe's mistress, who was planning to

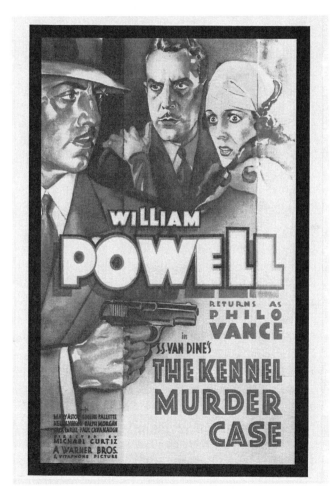

run away with art dealer boyfriend Eduardo Grassi (Jack La Rue), who also had a motive in murdering Coe as the businessman had cancelled an important art sale after catching Doris with Grassi; Coe's "cook" Liang (James Lee), who had been illegally purchasing rare Chinese works of art on the mistaken understanding that Coe would not sell them; and, finally, Coe's butler Gamble (Arthur Hohl), who has a criminal record. Coe's murder is soon followed by the death of Coe's brother Brisbane (Frank Conroy), who also hated his brother and planned to murder him.

The screenplay by Robert N. Lee and Peter Milne, with the adaptation by Robert Presnell, follows Van Dine's novel although the film benefits from director Michael Curtiz's skill in breaking up long-winded dialogue sequences with

William Powell as Philo Vance in the screen's best presentation of S.S. Van Dine's detective in Warner's *The Kennel Murder Case* (1933) with Mary Astor as Hilda Lake and Paul Cavanaugh as Sir Thomas MacDonald. The director was Michael Curtiz.

William Powell as Philo Vance and Mary Astor as Hilda Lake in *The Kennel Murder Case* (1933).

dramatic compositions and a determination not to allow the story to become static and ponderous. The authorities, represented by District Attorney Markham (Robert McWade) and Sergeant Heath (Eugene Pallette), are, at best, bewildered and, at times, a hindrance to Vance's investigation. After an attempt on the life of Sir Thomas MacDonald, Doris's Doberman Pinscher is found wounded from a blow on its head. Vance, with the assistance of an impressive small-scale recreation of the Coes' mansion and the surrounding houses, explains how the murder occurred. He then provokes a situation whereby Sir Thomas and Wrede quarrel over Hilda and when Wrede instinctively reaches for the incriminating poker to attack Sir Thomas, the Doberman is released and recreates his attack on the murderer. Vance solves the crime and Hilda and Sir Thomas are now free to marry.

The Kennel Murder Case was successful at the box office with an estimated profit of almost $400,000.[65] After Powell left Warner Brothers for MGM, Warren William was cast as Vance in Warner's *The Dragon Murder Case* (1934), while MGM followed with *The Casino Murder Case* (1935) starring Paul Lukas as Vance. Lukas was then replaced by Edmund Lowe for *The Garden Murder Case* (1937) while Paramount reworked *The Greene Murder Case* as *Night of Mystery* (1937) with Grant Richards as Vance. However, by the end of the 1930s Vance was no longer a top box office draw and by the time of *The Gracie Allen Murder Case* (1939), starring radio comedienne Gracie Allen and Warren William as Vance, Van Dine's books were no longer best sellers.

The melodramatic structure of the classical detective formula represents a strand of sensational melodrama. While devoid of the spectacle and visceral thrills, it is populated by characters who have no interior or psychological depth, Brooks's "drama of pure psychic signs."[66] Interest primarily resides in the detective's investigation and the formulaic outcome where he/she exposes the guilty party. Above all else, the detective is a superior figure, an intellectual superman compared to the police and just about everyone else—Vance took this aspect to the extreme with his clothing, often wearing a monocle and chamois gloves. In *The Benson Murder Case* Markham asks Vance if he intends wearing a green carnation as this was often a symbol of homosexuality. Vance's foppish quality was epitomized by his pretentious speech patterns and choice of words ("Really, y'know, Markham old thing … you should study the cranial indications of your fellow man more carefully—vultus est index animi"—from *The Greene Murder Case*).[67] His expertise on Japanese and Chinese prints, as well as tapestries, ceramics, and even Tanagra figurines, polo, pedigree dogs, chess, archery, golf, fencing and Egyptology,[68] irritated contemporary commentators such as the poet Ogden Nash who wrote:

> Philo Vance
> Needs a kick in the pance.[69]

The most popular detective in Hollywood in the 1930s was Charlie Chan. Based on the character created by Earl Derr Biggers, he appeared in a long series of films produced by Twentieth Century–Fox. Chan first appeared in print in the novel *The House Without a Key* which was serialized in the *Saturday Evening Post*, beginning on 24 September 1925. In his stories Biggers abandoned the conventional racist stereotype of the sinister Asian. He presented Charlie as an amiable, courteous and highly intelligent detective who delivered his trademark aphorisms in stilted English. Although Chan was not the central character in *The House Without a Key*, he was well received by the public and played a more central role in Biggers' next story, *The Chinese Parrot*. Similarly, in early film adaptations of Biggers' novels Chan was relegated to a minor role. It was not until Fox purchased the rights to the stories and cast Swedish-born actor Warner Oland as Charlie Chan that the series took off. The first film, *Charlie Chan Carries On* (1931), based on the fifth Chan novel, was a commercial success, initiating a long running of series of films throughout the 1930s with Charlie's name inserted in the title of more than 20 films. The films evolved into a predictable formula with Chan gathering the various suspects together where he exposed the guilty party with his trademark accusation: "You are murderer." After Oland's death in 1938, after 16 films as Chan, the series began to lose its popularity and the studio ended the series in 1942 with *Castle in the Desert*. While the character continued in a low budget series at Monogram from 1944 to 1948, it no longer commanded a large audience.

An associated sub-genre to the detective tradition, and an even clearer example of sensational melodrama, was that of the adventurer, a regular feature of the dime novels that flourished between 1860 and 1915. The earliest example was "Malaeska, the Indian Wife of the White Hunter" by Mrs. Ann S. Stephens in 1860. This story was published in the first paper covered series of books called *Beadle's Dime Novels*. The earliest stories in the dime novel were mainly frontier and western stories although by the 1880s they were supplanted by detective and mystery stories. The first dime novel detective story, "The Ticket-of-Leave Man," was published in 1865 in a Boston story paper.[70] Nick Carter, who first appeared in the September 18, 1886, issue of the *New York Weekly*, was a favorite during this period. As a clean-cut action hero Carter battled New York's underworld, especially his nemesis Doc Quartz. Carter existed long after the demise of the dime novel with a long career in the pulps, movies, radio and television.[71]

This was also the era of the pulp magazines which featured a wide range of sub-genres: westerns, romance, sports action, adventure, science fiction, sex and crime. Today they are mostly remembered for "hard-boiled" crime writers such as Carroll John Daly, Dashiell Hammett, Paul Cain, Frederick Nebel, Frederic Davis, Raoul Whitfield, Cornell Woolrich, Raymond Chandler and many others. A popular variation on the hard-boiled detective was Leslie Charteris's The Saint. While there are echoes of Philo Vance in The Saint, with his superior lifestyle, he was more of an adventurer for hire than detective. His stories were popular in both Britain and the United States and in 1932 Charteris went to the United States to work for Paramount on the script for the 1933 film *Midnight Club* staring Clive Brook and George Raft. While in America he began work on a Saint novel that was more hard-boiled than his previous books. *The Saint in New York* appeared in an abridged version in the September 1934 edition of *The American Magazine*. The complete novel was published in January 1935 in both the UK and the USA, becoming a bestseller. Gary Dobbs, in his introduction to a recent edition, noted, "I couldn't believe how gritty the book was, and just how hardboiled a character Simon Templar was."[72]

The inspiration for the novel came from the time Charteris spent drinking in the speakeasies in New York at the end of the Prohibition period. RKO bought the film rights in May 1936 but objections from Joseph Breen delayed filming until February 21, 1938. RKO initially cast Fredric March as Simon Templar, Joan Fontaine as the femme fatale Kay Edwards with John Cromwell as director. The long delay resulted in many changes. Ben Holmes replaced Cromwell, South African born and English educated actor Louis Hayward replaced March and Kay Sutton replaced Fontaine. The cinematographer was Joseph August, assisted by Frank Redman. August was an expert in low key lighting and while this 1938 film was not the first to employ this style of lighting, it was not a regular feature of crime films until the early 1940s.[73] Charles Kaufman and Mortimer Offner's screenplay follows Charteris's novel closely with only a few minor changes, mainly to dilute the novel's presentation of Templar as a heartless killer. For example, the novel shows Templar killing gangster Jake Irbell in cold blood as he leaves the courthouse; the film, on the other hand, changes this sequence by justifying the killing as Irbell (Lester Dorr) is about to murder Inspector Fernack (Jonathan Hale). In both mediums Templar carries out the killing dressed as a nun, which subsequently caused censorship problems for the film in some areas.

The Saint in New York is a tough crime film described by critics as "hard-boiled" with *Variety* praising the film in its 1938 review as a "rugged gangster melodrama." With a budget of $128,000, it grossed more than $460,000 leaving the studio with an overall profit of nearly $200,000. This resulted in RKO initiating a series of Saint films starring, at first, George Sanders as Templar. RKO changed the style from hard-boiled to the 1930s gentleman tradition by presenting the Saint as an affluent amateur, forever chasing women. This provoked outrage from the author. RKO, tired of criticisms from Charteris and tired of paying royalties to him, soon changed the name of their series from the Saint to the Falcon. The most interesting of the Falcon films was the attempt to assimilate the conventions of two different detective traditions, the gentleman detective and the hard-boiled sleuth, into a 63-minute series film *The Falcon Takes Over* (1942), the first film adaptation of Raymond Chandler's novel *Farewell, My Lovely*.

The Hard-Boiled Detective

Throughout the 1930s the hard-boiled detective gradually replaced the gentleman detective. In the April 1933 issue of *Black Mask* magazine, the magazine's editor Joseph Shaw outlined the (melodramatic) qualities he sought in his detective:

> Vigorous minded, hard in a square man's hardness; hating unfairness, trickery, injustice, cowardly underhandedness, standing for a square deal and a fair show in little or big things, and willing to fight for them; not squeamish or prudish, but clean, admiring the good in man and woman; not sentimental in a gushing sort of way, but valuing true emotion, not hysterical, but responsive to the thrill of danger, the stirring exhilaration of clean, swift action—and always pulling for the right guy to come out on top.[74]

Six years earlier, soon after he became editor of the magazine, Shaw wrote an editorial in the June 1927 edition describing the type of detective fiction he favored:

> This subject embodies mental and physical conflict in man's most violent moods. Its stories are essentially stories of suspense and action, with the thrill of chasing, the terror of pursuit, the triumph of successful analysis and the dread of discovery. They touch at the very heart of human emotion.[75]

Frank Krutnik argues that the hard-boiled detective represented an "'Americanisation' and masculinisation of the classical detective"[76] where the emphasis is not the "safeguarding of 'normal' society, … [but] the affirmation of the hero as an idealised and undivided figure of masculine potency and invulnerability."[77] To support his argument he cites John Huston's 1941 adaptation of *The Maltese Falcon,* based on Dashiell Hammett's 1930 novel.

Dashiell Hammett and *The Maltese Falcon*

Between 1923 and the summer of 1928, when he began work on *The Maltese Falcon*, Hammett wrote forty-eight stories and two novels, experimenting with a variety of literary styles, characters and plots. He considered *The Maltese Falcon* a departure from his *Black Mask* stories as he believed that "serious writing" could not include a series character such as the Continental Op, his first detective. In a letter to Blanche Knopf (wife of publisher Alfred Knopf) dated March 20, 1928, just after *Black Mask* published the last installment of *Red Harvest*, Hammett expressed his ambitions for *The Maltese Falcon*:

I'm one of the few—if there are any more—moderately literate people who take the detective story seriously. I don't mean that I necessarily take my own or anybody else's seriously—but the detective story as a form. Some day somebody's going to make "literature" of it ... and I'm selfish enough to have my hopes, however slight the evident justification may be.[78]

In *The Maltese Falcon* he reworked characters and incidents from the earlier stories.[79] From his 1924 story "Who Killed Bob Teal," published in *True Detective Magazine* in November 1924, Hammett took the story of a detective who is hired and then murdered by his client to cover up another crime. In "Who Killed Bob Teal" the Op is given the facts of the case from his supervisor at the Continental Agency, the Old Man, who tells the Op that one of his detectives, Bob Teal, was shot at close range after instructions from a client (Ogden) to shadow his business partner:

> He was shot with a .32, twice, through his heart. He was shot behind a row of signboards on the vacant lot on the northwest corner of Hyde and Eddy Street, at about ten last night. ...from the condition of Teal's clothing and the position in which he was found, I would say there was no struggle.[80]

The Op subsequently exposes Ogden as the murderer along with his accomplice Mae Landis, who Hammett describes as a "plump woman who could lie with every semblance of candor, and laugh when she was tripped up, [and who] wasn't interested in anything much beyond her own comfort."[81]

Hammett reworked this segment in *The Maltese Falcon* to show Spade's indifference to the news of his partner's death. When a 2:05 a.m. phone call wakes Sam up, and he is told that his partner Miles Archer has been shot, he orders a taxi to Bush Street. Policeman Tom Polhaus tells Spade that "I figured you'd want to see it [Archer's body] before we took him away."[82] After providing a few details, including the fact that Archer was killed at close range ("the blast burned his coat"),[83] Polhaus invites Spade to come down and look at Archer's body. When the detective refuses, Polhaus "looked back at Spade with surprised small eyes."[84] He then tells Spade that Archer's gun was tucked away on his hip and had not been fired and his overcoat was buttoned. After Polhaus asks some questions, Spade tells him not to "crowd" him and that he was going to break the news to Miles's wife Iva—which is a lie. Surprised by Spade's unemotional response ("Tom, scowling, opened his mouth"),[85] he tells Spade:

> "It's tough, him getting it like that. Miles had his faults same as the rest of us, but I guess he must've had some good points too." "I guess so," Spade agreed in a tone that was utterly meaningless, and went out of the alley.[86]

Spade phones his secretary, Effie Perine, to notify Iva and he also instructs her to keep Iva, his mistress, away from the office. He then returns to his apartment and begins drinking Bacardi. When the street doorbell rings Spade, expecting Iva, mutters "Damn her" and stands "scowling" at the prospect of a visit from his mistress. However, his face brightens when he discovers that his visitors are two policemen.

From "The Girl with the Silver Eyes,"[87] a Continental Op story published in 1924, Hammett extended and reworked the climax to the story for the last scene between Spade and Brigid in *The Maltese Falcon*. The female protagonist in the short story is Jeanne Delano. Her eyes, the Op reports, "were wide-set and of a gray shade that wasn't altogether unlike the shadows on polished silver."[88] In the climax to the story the Op is torn between allowing Jeanne to escape punishment and handing her to the police. In this delicate balance, Delano's callous treatment of her victim, Porky Grout, tips the scales against her:

> Porky Grout, whose yellowness was notorious from Seattle to San Diego, standing rigidly in the path of a charging metal monster, with an inadequate pistol in each hand. She had done that to Porky Grout—this woman beside me! She had done that to Porky Grout, and he hadn't even been human! A slimy reptile whose highest thought had been a skinful of dope had gone grimly to death that she might get away—she—this woman whose shoulders I had gripped, whose mouth had been close under mine![89]

The Op almost loses his self-control, a rarity in an Op story:

> My fingers went deep into the soft white flesh of her shoulders. Her head went further back, her eyes closed, one hand came up to my shoulder.
> "You're beautiful as all hell!" I shouted crazily into her face, and flung her against the door.
> It seemed an hour that I fumbled with the starter.... The girl straightened herself up in the seat again, and sat huddled within the robe I had given her.[90]

The Op regains control and tells Delano that she is a liar and a murderer. After they drive into Redwood City, the Op could not look at her while she is booked by the police. The story ends with her asking if she might speak privately with the Op:

> We went together to a far corner of the room.
> She put her mouth close to my ear so that her breath was warm again on my cheek, as it had been in the car, and whispered the vilest epithet of which the English language is capable. Then she walked out to her cell.[91]

Hammett continued to experiment with detective fiction until the end of the 1920s and the publication of *Red Harvest*, *The Maltese Falcon* and *The Glass Key*. In a revealing moment, his world view was articulated in the Flitcraft parable. Whereas the classical detective assumes that life is orderly, sane and rational, Hammett's detective understands it is not. The premise of his fiction assumes a world that is devoid of ethical meaning, an inscrutable, ethically irresponsible and arbitrary universe—something that the two Warner Brothers adaptations of *The Maltese Falcon*[92] were not prepared to replicate.

Endings and Epilogues: *The Maltese Falcon* (1931 and 1941)

The 1931 version, produced in a different censorship context to the 1941 film, is closer to the gentleman detective style with Spade (Ricardo Cortez) solving the crime with information withheld from the audience. Early in the film, after Spade leaves the police scene near Archer's body, he is shown, but not heard, quietly speaking to a Chinese man standing nearby. Nothing more is made of this until the final minutes of the film when a newspaper report is used during Brigid's trial. The newspaper states that "Samuel Spade, private detective, caused a sensation at the trial when he produced Le Fu Gow, Chinese merchant, the only eye-witness to the Archer killing who positively identified Miss Wonderly as the murderess."

Huston's 1941 version was unable, due to Breen's censorship prohibitions, to show two scenes from the novel. They are included in the 1931 film. The first one

Warner's first adaptation of Dashiell Hammett's *The Maltese Falcon*. It was released in 1931 with Ricardo Cortez as Sam Spade, J. Farrell MacDonald as Det. Sgt. Tom Polhaus, Bebe Daniels as the duplicitous Ruth Wonderly and Robert Elliott as the belligerent Det. Lt. Dundy.

shows Spade leaving Miss Wonderly in his bed early in the morning so that he can search her hotel room. The second occurs when he forces her to take all of her clothes off so that he can find out whether she stole $100 from the villain Casper Gutman. The other major omission, from both versions, is the Flitcraft parable.

Production of the film began on Monday June 9, 1941, with a budget of $381,000 and a filming period allocation of 36 days. While this was a tight schedule for a first-time director, the budget and filming period indicates that it was not intended as a B film. Huston's preparations were meticulous as he sketched out each scene before filming began and he also shot the script in sequence. Over three days and a long Saturday night in the middle of July, Huston filmed the final confrontation between Sam Spade (Humphrey Bogart) and Brigid O'Shaughnessy (Mary Astor). On July 18, following the burning of the studio "ship," the *La Paloma*, on the back lot and a brief scene between Spade and Casper Gutman (Sydney Greenstreet) on Stage 19, the picture officially closed.

The film's climax involved the five principal characters: Spade, O'Shaughnessy, Gutman, Wilmer, and Cairo. It was one of the last sequences to be filmed and it consumed almost 20 minutes of the film's 100-minute running time.[93] This began with them waiting for the arrival of the Maltese Falcon, the discovery that it is a fake and the final confrontation between Spade and O'Shaughnessy. It ends with Spade

Ricardo Cortez as Sam Spade and Otto Matieson as Joel Cairo in *The Maltese Falcon* (1931), directed by Roy Del Ruth.

handing her over to Dundy and Polhaus. As producer Henry Blanke wrote to Hal Wallis, this consisted of one "solid sequence of thirty-five pages of script and every member of the cast is in it."[94] The climactic confrontation between Spade and Brigid involved eight pages of dialogue, three long days of filming as the actors repeated the scene again and again to match the change of camera angles. Finally, the film's epilogue, with Brigid looking "like a sleepwalker" according to the screenplay directions, "led off by the law."[95] This final scene took seven takes to satisfy the director.[96]

After controlling the events for much of the film, Spade's vulnerability is exposed in the final moments. His determination to survive, and not be a "sap," becomes the deciding factor in his decision to turn Brigid in. There are, however, significant differences between the novel and Huston's version. For example, Spade tells her in the novel that he is going to survive and that she is going to take the fall: "One of us has got to take it, after the talking those birds [Gutman and Cairo] will do. They'd hang me for sure. You're likely to get a better break."[97] Huston omitted this passage. Similarly, after Brigid tells Spade in the novel that he should know whether he loves her or not, Spade replies:

"I don't. It's easy enough to be nuts about you." He looked hungrily from her hair to her feet and up to her eyes again. "But I don't know what that amounts to. Does anybody ever? But suppose I do? What of it? Maybe next month I won't. I've been through it before—when it lasted that long. Then what?"

Huston replaces Hammett's pragmatic cynicism with the more romantic response from Spade: "Maybe I do [love you]."

Frank Krutnik argues that Huston's version functions as an "unproblematic validation of the detective as masculine hero."[98] He points out that Spade persistently triumphs over a "parade of characters who seek to deceive and threaten him."[99] He is, according to Krutnik, the "embodiment of self-sufficient phallic potency."[100] This, Krutnik continues, is "most vividly at the end of the film, when the detective determines where the burden of guilt shall fall—setting up the woman ... as the 'fall-guy' to the law.'"[101] This, however, ignores the effect the decision to turn Brigid in has on the detective. His torment is evident in his appearance (loose tie, button undone) and body movements (head

Humphrey Bogart as Sam Spade and Mary Astor as the femme fatale Brigid O'Shaughnessy in John Huston's *The Maltese Falcon* (1941).

lowered, shoulders slumped, wide-eyed). After he tells her he "won't play the sap for you," she declares her love for him:

> BRIGID: Oh, How can you do this to me, Sam? Surely, Mr. Archer wasn't as much to you as....
> [Spade, distressed, walks away and slumps in a chair. He explains that when a man's partner gets killed he's supposed to do something about it. Also, because he is in the detective business, it is bad business to let the killer get away with it. Finally, he explains, he has no reason he can trust her. Staring into space, he continues]:
> SPADE: All those are on one side. Maybe some of them are unimportant. I won't argue about that. But look at the number of them. What have we got on the other side? All we've got is that maybe you love me and maybe I love you.
> BRIGID: You know whether you love me or not.
> SPADE: Maybe I do. I'll have some rotten nights after I've sent you over, but that'll pass.
> [Spade stands up and pulls Brigid roughly towards him]

(From left)Humphrey Bogart as Sam Spade, Peter Lorre as Joel Cairo, Mary Astor as Brigid O'Shaughnessy and Sydney Greenstreet as Casper Gutman in *The Maltese Falcon* (1941).

SPADE: If all I've said doesn't mean anything to you, then forget it, and we'll make it just this. I won't because all of me wants to, regardless of consequences and because you've counted on that with me, the same as you counted on that with all the others.
[Spade responds to Brigid's kiss as the doorbell rings and Spade tells the police to come in]

Brigid enters the lift with the police as Spade walks away. However, Huston's script, in accordance with Hammett's novel, contained a final scene. This takes place in Spade's office where he tries to explain to his secretary, Effie (Lee Patrick), why he turned Brigid in. Effie, unconvinced, stands by the window, mouth twisted, eyes reproachful:

EFFIE: You did that Sam, to her?
SPADE: She *did* kill Miles, Angel....
EFFIE: Don't, please—don't touch me.

A doorknob rattles in the corridor. Effie goes out to see, comes back, and announces Iva Archer. The story ends as Spade, with a shiver, prepares to reunite with his mistress, his dead partner's wife.

SPADE: Send her in.[102]

This effectively replicates the epilogue in Hammett's novel aside from some additional material:

EFFIE: "I know you're right. But don't touch me now—not now."
Spade's face became pale as his collar.[103]

The novel concludes with Effie:

She said in a small flat voice: "Iva is here."
Spade, looking down at his desk, nodded almost imperceptibly, "Yes," he said, and shivered. "Well, send her in."[104]

Despite including this epilogue in his shooting script, Huston never filmed it. In an Inter-Office Communication at Warner Brothers, dated July 19, 1941, unit manager on *The Maltese Falcon* Al Alleborn, wrote that filming was completed on the 34th shooting day, two days ahead of schedule with a budget outlay of $327,182, which was $54,000 under budget. In his memo Alleborn noted that yesterday, Friday, the Huston company had a 2:00 p.m. shooting call, having worked until 2:30 a.m. the night before on Stage 19. The first shot was undertaken at 3:35 p.m. and the filming completed at 2:00 a.m. with 14 camera set-ups and nearly 8 pages of dialogue completed. Alleborn declared that "the picture is finished, as stated above, but, at Blanke's and Huston's request we eliminated the ending, as written in the script, which takes place on Stage 3 in SPADE'S OFFICE. These gentlemen feel they can cut the picture without this ending, and if necessary they can always get BOGART. Their feeling, however, is that the picture will not need the ending written for SPADE'S OFFICE."[105]

Instead they returned a week later with additional filming to complete the revised ending which appears in the release print. This shows Brigid, Dundy (Barton MacLane) at her elbow, moving towards the door while Spade remains behind with Tom Polhaus (Ward Bond) and the fake statue. The actors were required to return to the studio to film a line added by script supervisor Meta Wilde, also known as Meta Carpenter Wilde. Later, Huston claimed it was Bogart's idea[106]:

POLHAUS: [picking up the statue] Um, [its] heavy. What is it?
SPADE: The stuff that dreams are made of.

If they had filmed the final scene in Huston's script, with Spade preparing to see his mistress, the film would be much different. By eliminating this scene, as Ann Sperber and Eric Lax point out:

The final note, rather than amorality, was of honor among detectives. Find your partner's killer even if it means sending over your lover; be true to your code even if it means breaking your heart. Spade has done the Right Thing.[107]

This decision to eliminate Hammett's epilogue satisfied one of Joseph Breen's initial objections to the film. In a memo dated May 27, 1941, he notified Jack Warner that Huston's final script "could not be approved under the provisions of the Code because of several important objectionable details."[108] These included any indication of an "illicit sex affair" between Spade and Brigid and Spade and Iva, especially any scenes showing "physical contact between Iva and Spade," any suggestion that Cairo is "a pansy," especially any indication of "lavender perfume," "high-pitched voice" and the deletion of scenes "21 and 115 where Cairo should not appear effeminate while rubbing the boy's [Wilmer] temple," the "fade-out of Spade and Brigid is unacceptable because of the definite indication of an illicit sex affair. There must be no indication that Brigid and Spade are spending the night together in Spade's apartment," "Spade's speech about the District Attorneys [sic] should be rewritten to get away from characterizing most District Attorneys as men who will do anything to further their careers. This is important," "nothing suggestive in Spade's eyeing of Brigid," "no flavor of a previous sex affair [between Spade and Brigid]," and the "action of Spade putting his hand on Effie's hip must not be offensive."[109] Breen's last objection confirms that Hammett's epilogue was included in the final draft submitted to the PCA.

The reviews for Huston's film were uniformly good. *Variety* applauded the film as "one of the best examples of actionful and suspenseful melodramatic story telling in cinematic form" in their October 1, 1941, review. The term "melodrama," or "melodramatic," is used three times in the review, which noted that the film was a remake of the 1931 film with Ricardo Cortez and Bebe Daniels. The review concluded by noting that the film "is an A attraction in its class, and will hit biz of the same kind in all bookings." However, Warners did not treat the film as an A attraction, as producer Henry Blanke complained to Hal Wallis: "I should think that the company after ... discovering what they had in their possession would go a little after this picture but ... it 'sneaks in'—and in spite all this makes a success."[110] The failure by the studio to promote the film also mystified Bosley Crowther in his October 4 review in *The New York Times*. Crowther began his review by pointing out that "Warners have been strangely bashful about their mystery film 'The Maltese Falcon.'" Crowther, normally a hostile critic of genre films, described the film as "supremely hardboiled" although he viewed the film as "a combination of American ruggedness with the suavity of the English crime school—a blend of mind and muscle—plus a slight touch of pathos." On October 13, author, film critic and art historian Richard Griffith, in a review titled "'Maltese Falcon' Rated Top 'Number' in New York" wrote that although the "biting performances of Bebe Daniels and Ricardo Cortez made the 1931 film memorable," the "new version is the best because it is the most cynical, depraved and brilliantly melodramatic. There isn't an honest motive among the entire cast—which is why we accept the characters as real people."[111] Hammett, particularly, enjoyed Griffith's response as he sent a copy of the review to his wife. Long time *Los Angeles Times* film critic Philip K. Scheuer also celebrated the film as the "finest detective-mystery movie ever turned out by a Hollywood studio" and he noted that "you've never seen a detective like Sam Spade. ... In private practice, not above a shady deal or two."[112] Despite a lack of advertising, the film fared well at the box office, grossing $967,000 domestically and $805,000 internationally.[113]

The Glass Key *(1935/1942)*

Hammett's favorite novel, *The Glass Key*, was published in London on January 20, 1931, three months before its American release. Julian Symons considered it the "peak of Hammett's achievements":

> Constant re-reading of it offers fresh revelations of the way in which a crime writer with sufficient skill and tact can use violent events to comment by indirection on life, art, society, and at the same time to compose a novel admirable in the carpentry of its structure and delicately

intelligent in its suggestions of truth about human relationships. As a novel *The Glass Key* is remarkable, as a crime novel unique.[114]

The Glass Key was filmed twice, in 1935 and 1942. The story is set in an unnamed city, possibly Baltimore, where Ned (Ed in the films) is a fixer for the man who controls the city, construction company owner Paul Madvig. Paul, obsessed with Janet Henry, supports the reelection of Janet's father, Senator Henry. As Henry is standing on the reform ticket, this brings him into conflict with Shad O'Rory (Nick Varna in the 1942 film) and his gambling interests. Henry also opposes the relationship between his son Taylor and Paul's daughter (Paul's sister in the 1942 film), Opal. When Ned finds Taylor's body on the sidewalk outside his house, suspicion soon falls on Paul, especially after a series of anonymous letters accuse Paul of Taylor's murder. Ned, to protect Paul, destroys an incriminating note but, in the process, is kidnapped by Rusty and Jeff, O'Rory's thugs, who take him to a warehouse where he is brutally beaten. Jeff, who is described by Hammett as an "apish man,"[115] exhibits sexual pleasure in punishing Ned's broken body.

Ned escapes after setting a mattress on fire and after several days in hospital he discovers that Opal has turned against her father and threatens to accuse him of murder in *The Observer,* a newspaper controlled by O'Rory. To prevent the publication of Opal's accusations, Ned manipulates Eloise Mathews into making love to him which results in her husband, Clyde Mathews, committing suicide. This allows Ned to destroy the document giving O'Rory control of *The Observer.* Ned's friendship with Paul deteriorates, especially after he tells Paul that Janet Henry was only using him to get her father re-elected, and that she is responsible for the incriminating notes sent to the district attorney. In an attempt to get information from Jeff about O'Rory's criminal activities, Ned invites Jeff to a private room for a drinking session. After O'Rory intervenes, Jeff strangles him while Ned watches. The film concludes with Ned exposing Senator Henry as the murderer. In novel's final moment, Ned, cruelly, tells Paul that he is leaving the city with Janet. Paul is devastated.

Ned Beaumont, the novel's "hero," has no moral boundaries, no commitment to society. His only loyalty is to Madvig and he even destroys that in the final moments of the novel. Hammett refuses to sentimentalize or glorify Beaumont. Although Beaumont, mockingly, describes himself as an "amateur detective," as he does expose the murderer at the end of the novel, he acknowledges to Janet Henry that, in reality, he is a "gambler and a politician's hanger-on."[116] In the prologue to the novel Hammett describes Beaumont as a "moustached, cigar puffing ward heeler's hanger-on, he had a penchant for only money and mares, especially when the two were closely related."[117] Hammett's view of the Madvig controlled city, and Beaumont's amoral behavior, represents Hammett's view of life as devoid of ethical meaning. It is a corrupt world where money and power rule.

The "sickness" of the city is paralleled in the novel by a "sickness" of the soul as sado-masochism becomes one of the novel's dominant motifs. Twice, Beaumont, in an irrational attempt to help Madvig, places his body at the service of the sadistic "ape," Jeff. The first-time results in a brutal beating in a dingy warehouse with Jeff violating the helpless Beaumont. When Rusty tells Jeff to ease off ("'Jesus, Jeff, you'll croak him'")[118] Jeff tells him, after kicking Beaumont, "'You can't croak him.

He's tough. He's a tough baby. He likes this.' He bent down, grasped one of the unconscious man's lapels in each hand, and dragged him to his knees.' Don't you like it,
baby?' he asked and, holding Ned Beaumont up on his knees with one hand, struck
his face with the other fist."[119] Later, "the apish Jeff knocks aside Ned Beaumont's
upraised hand and pushes him down on the bed. 'I got something to try.' He scooped
up Ned Beaumont's legs and tumbled them on the bed. He leaned over Ned Beaumont, his hands busy on Ned Beaumont's body."[120]

   Later in the novel, Ned, again trying to save Madvig, "solicits" Jeff in a bar:

> Jeff swaggered over to Ned Beaumont, threw his left arm roughly around his shoulders, seized
> Ned Beaumont's right hand with his right hand, and addressed the company jovially: "This is
> the swellest guy I ever skinned a knuckle on and I've skinned them on plenty." He dragged Ned
> Beaumont to the bar. "We're all going to have a little drink and then I'll show you how it's done.
> By Jesus, I will!" He leered into Ned Beaumont's face. "What do you say to that, my lad?"
>   Ned Beaumont, looking stolidly at the ugly dark face so close to, though lower than, his, said:
> "Scotch."
>   Jeff laughed delightedly and addressed the company again: "You see, he likes it. He's a—" he
> addressed, frowning, wet his lips—"a God-damned massacrist, that's what he is." He leered at
> Ned Beaumont. "You know what a massacrist is?"
>   "Yes."[121]

Both film versions, 1935 and 1942, include Ned's beating in the warehouse as well
as the sequence later in the story where Ned goes upstairs with Jeff. While the reference to "massacrist" (masochist) was censored by the PCA, there is enough in
both novel and film to reveal Ned's penchant for pain. In the scene over the bar, for
example, Ned tries to get information out of the inebriated Jeff. However, he is interrupted by the arrival of O'Rory in the 1935 film and Varna in 1942. When Jeff takes
offense at O'Rory/Varna's attempt to curb his drinking and loose talk, he lunges at
his boss, accidentally knocking the single overhead light in the room. Rory/Varna, in
an attempt to protect himself, pulls a gun from his pocket, but Ned takes it away and
calmly watches Jeff murder the defenseless gangster.

   The 1935 film, in an almost iconic example of "noir" lighting, depicts the killing with a chiaroscuro lighting effect as Ned's face alternates between dark shadow
and bright light as the single light swings across the room. Director Frank Tuttle and
editor Hugh Bennett in the 1935 film clearly implicate Ned in the murder as they cut
between Ned's impassive gaze and Jeff slowly strangling O'Rory. The sexual basis of
the act is clear. In 1942 director Stuart Heisler and editor Archie Marshek achieve
exactly the same effect.

   Earlier in the novel, and repeated in the 1942 film, Ned provokes the suicide
of newspaper owner Clyde Mathews, by making love to his wife while her husband
waits anxiously upstairs. However, a significant omission in both films is Janet's
dream, a parallel to the Flitcraft parable in *The Maltese Falcon*. It occurs late in the
novel when, following a comment from Ned that he had a dream about her the previous night that "I don't much like,"[122] she smiles and asks him, "Surely you don't
believe in dreams." Ned replies, "I don't believe in anything, but I'm too much of a
gambler not to be affected by a lot of things."[123] Janet demands to know what "was
this dream that makes you mistrust me?"[124] After he tells her a story involving a large
rainbow trout that she throws back into the river, Janet reciprocates by telling him

This scene from Paramount's 1935 version of Dashiell Hammett's *The Glass Key* is an early example of the high contrast chiaroscuro lighting often associated with film noir in the 1940s. (From left) Guinn Williams as Jeff, George Raft as Ed and Irving Bacon as the waiter. The scene culminates with Ed impassively watching the inebriated Jeff strangle his boss Shad O'Rory (Robert Gleckler).

about her dream. They, Ned and Janet in the dream, were lost in the forest and after walking some distance they came to a little house. When they peered through the window they saw a large table piled high with food. After knocking on the door of the house and receiving no answer, they found a key under the doormat. However, when they opened the door, they discovered hundreds and hundreds of snakes "sliding and slithering" towards them. After slamming the door shut they climbed onto the roof and Ned leaned down and opened the front door. The snakes then poured out of the house and slithered off into the forest, allowing Janet and Ned to enter the house, use the key, lock the door and eat the food: "I woke sitting in bed clapping my hands and laughing."[125]

Later in the novel, however, Janet admits that she lied about the ending of her dream. The dream was a nightmare as the key was made of glass and it shattered when they opened the front door: "She shivered. 'We couldn't lock the snakes in and they came out all over us and I woke screaming.'"[126] This, of course, explains the title of the book. However, both films replace Janet's dream with a literal explanation, a personal rebuke from Beaumont to Madvig. When Ed warns Paul that he is being used by Janet Henry and her father, and after the election, when they have no further use of him, Madvig will learn that their hospitality will be like the "key" to their house, a glass key.

Hammett uses the closing moments, the epilogue, in this novel to achieve the same effect as the final moment in *The Maltese Falcon*. To present a world devoid of meaning, a bleak nihilistic universe, the one positive constant in the novel, the relationship between Ned and Madvig, is cruelly destroyed. In the novel's final moment, Madvig tries to persuade Ned to stay as his fixer. However, Beaumont coldly announces that Janet is leaving the city with him. Madvig, unaware of Ned's interest in Janet, is both surprised and devastated:

> Madvig's lips parted. He looked dumbly at Ned Beaumont and as he looked the blood went out of his face again. When his face was quite bloodless he mumbled something of which only the word "luck" could be understood, turned clumsily around, went to the door, opened it, and went out leaving it open behind him.
> Janet Henry looked at Ned Beaumont. He stared fixedly at the door.[127]

Both film versions of *The Glass Key* jettison Hammett's ending and replace it with an upbeat epilogue. The 1935 film reunites Ed with Paul, and, without much motivation, suddenly converts Opal, Paul's daughter, into a convenient romantic partner for Ned. The tone of the 1942 film is similar as it suddenly eliminates the hostility between Ed and Paul. It ends with Madvig giving his blessing to Ed's courtship of Janet, Madvig's ex-fiancée.

George Raft and Emma Dunn in *The Glass Key* (1935).

The Gentleman Detective and the Hard-Boiled Private Eye: The Falcon Takes Over *and* Murder, My Sweet

The Falcon Takes Over

After the financial success of *The Saint in New York*, RKO embarked on a series of low budget films starring George Sanders as Simon Templar. In the process the studio shed the hard-boiled presentation of Templar to return to an American variation of the gentleman detective, exemplified by the casting of English educated Sanders with his distinctive British upper-class accent as the Saint. After terminating the Saint series, RKO effectively revived it with their Falcon series. The Falcon was created by Michael Arlen, the pen name of author and screenwriter Dikran Kouyoumdjian. The sleuth's only appearance in print was the short story "Gay Falcon" which was published in *Town and Country* magazine in 1940. RKO bought the rights and it provided the (loose) basis to the first Falcon film, *The Gay Falcon*, released on October 24, 1941. In virtually every respect, including the casting of George Sanders as a wealthy playboy with an eye for the ladies, this was a continuation of the Saint series under a different title. The similarities between the series were reinforced by the casting of Wendy Barrie, the Saint's love interest in *The Saint Takes Over* (1940) and *The Saint in Palm Springs* (1941) as well as the Falcon's love interest in the first two Falcon films, *The Gay Falcon* and *A Date with the Falcon* (1941). The emphasis in both series was on comedy and romance as each took a light-hearted approach to crime and murder.

The third Falcon film, *The Falcon Takes Over*, is the most interesting as it tries to assimilate two detective traditions, the gentleman detective and the hard-boiled detective, into the one sixty-three-minute film. After the encouraging sales for Chandler's first novel, *The Big Sleep*, the author began work on his second novel, which was eventually titled, against his publisher's wishes, *Farewell, My Lovely*. This was published in April 1939. The initial title was *The Girl from Florian's*. As he did with his first novel, and did again with subsequent novels, Chandler "cannibalized" characters and events from his short stories. In this case, "The Man Who Loved Dogs" (1936), "Try the Girl" (1937) and "Mandarin's Jade" (1937). At the start of the story Philip Marlowe encounters an ex-convict, Moose Malloy, outside Florian's, a disreputable nightclub for African Americans. Moose's ex-lover, Velma Valento, worked as an entertainer at Florian's when it was a burlesque house for white patrons. Moose, just released from jail after serving eight years for bank robbery, lost contact with Velma while he was in jail and he wants Marlowe to find her. When the manager of the nightclub objects to Malloy's entry, he pulls a gun. Moose subsequently kills him with one blow of his arm. In his search for Velma, Marlowe visits Florian's widow Jesse who attempts to deflect the private detective's attempt to find her.

Marlowe, unable to find Valento, takes another case involving Lindsay Marriott, who is trying to regain a valuable jade necklace. At night he accompanies Marriott to Purissma Canyon, a remote area near Malibu, where Marlowe is rendered unconscious by a blow to the head from a blackjack. When he wakes up he finds Marriott brutally murdered. He subsequently learns from Anne Riordan, a freelance journalist, that the jade belonged to Mrs. Helen Grayle, the attractive wife of the wealthy, and

The light-hearted tone of RKO's Falcon series with (from left) Edward Gargan as the inept Detective Bates, Amelita Ward as Jane Harris, Cliff Clark as Inspector Timothy Donovan and Tom Conway as Tom Lawrence, the Falcon, in *The Falcon and the Co-Eds* (1943).

elderly, Lewin Grayle. He visits them and after Lewin leaves the room, Helen makes sexual advances to Marlowe who resists her. When Marlowe learns that Marriott has been paying money to Jesse Florian, he realizes that the two cases, Moose's missing lover and Marriott's murder, are linked.

Marlowe visits Jules Amthor, a "psychic consultant," after finding Amthor's business card on Marriott's body. He discovers that Amthor was operating a blackmail racket involving information divulged to him from wealthy women. Marlowe, again, is hit over the head and taken to a private clinic where he is injected with drugs. After waking up he confronts Dr. Sonderborg, the head of the sanatorium. He escapes after suffering from a drug induced nightmare. He discovers Jesse Florian's body and learns that she has been murdered by Moose. Marlowe visits Laird Brunette, a gangster who operates a gambling ship off the coast of Santa Monica. Brunette, after some persuasion, agrees to contact Malloy on Marlowe's behalf.

In the climax to the story, Marlowe realizes that Helen Grayle is Velma Valento and that she was Malloy's partner in the bank robbery eight years ago. When the robbery failed, Velma betrayed Moose to the police and secured a reward for his capture. Nevertheless, Moose still loves her. In the past eight years Velma has transformed herself into a socialite through her marriage to Grayle. Jesse Florian, aware of Helen's past as a burlesque dancer, subsequently blackmailed her. Jules Amthor employed

Marriott as a go-between for his blackmail operation. Helen, afraid that Marriott would expose her sordid past, murdered him at Purissma Canyon. When Moose emerges from hiding Helen shoots him and escapes. She eventually re-surfaces in a Baltimore cafe and when the police catch up with her she commits suicide. The novel ends with Marlowe speculating to Lieutenant Randall that she may have committed suicide to protect her husband, an "old man who had loved not wisely, but too well."[128] When Randall accuses Marlowe of being sentimental, the private detective tells him that it "sounded like that when I said it."[129]

Sales of the novel were solid and RKO, searching for plot material for its Falcon series, purchased the film rights for only $2,000, an agreement that Chandler later claimed was one of "almost unparalleled stupidity on the part of my New York agent."[130] Chandler would have been even less impressed if he was aware that Michael Arlen received $2,200 for nothing other than RKO using the Falcon's name, and that screenwriters Lynn Root and Frank Fenton were paid $7,000 for their script. *Farewell, My Lovely* became *The Falcon Takes Over.*[131]

The Falcon Takes Over

The Falcon Takes Over is a sensational melodrama. It includes some action, mystery, a good deal of comedy and superior hero admired by the ladies. When the reviewer for the *Motion Picture Herald* attended a screening of *The Falcon Takes Over* at the Pantages Theater on May 9, 1942, he reported "a ripple of chuckles sweeping through the audience at regular intervals [which] indicated pleased acceptance."[132] The Falcon (Gay Lawrence), as opposed to Chandler's Philip Marlowe, lives an affluent lifestyle in New York where he maintains an elegant town house, complete with valet. He often wears evening dress and exhibits a "suave air of world-weary Anglophobia."[133] He is assisted by Goldie (Allen Jenkins) who performs the same function as the hero's sidekick, and comedy relief, in the series western. The police, unlike the hard-boiled tradition, are dumb and function as comedic foils. Their inept behavior only reinforces how smart the amateur detective is. The film opens with bright, upbeat music over credits which show a cartoon gentleman with top hat and cane. This lighthearted tone of the opening is in marked contrast to the opening moments in *Murder, My Sweet* three years later (see below). The Falcon moves in affluent circles so Florian's dive in the novel, and the 1944 film, is transformed into Club 13, an upmarket Manhattan night club. The Falcon appears in top hat, tuxedo and walking cane.

Root and Fenton's script retains the bare structure of Chandler's story while removing all vestiges of the novel's presentation of Marlowe as vulnerable and, in Sonderborg's clinic, emotionally fragile. He is always in control, never dependent on others and superior to everybody else. The prolonged drug induced nightmare in the novel is eliminated. Marlowe's confrontation with Jules Amthor in the novel, resulting in the detective being hit over the head, is transformed into a comedy sequence involving Goldy and a benign Jules Amthor (Turhan Bey), a cheap, fake fortune teller in a turban. He is not the sinister psychic as described in the novel:

I looked him over. He was thin, tall and straight as a steel rod. He had the palest finest hair I ever saw. It could have been strained through silk gauze. His skin was as fresh as a rose petal. He might have been thirty-five or sixty-five. He was ageless. His hair was brushed straight back from as good a profile as Barrymore ever had. His eyebrows were coal black, like the walls and ceiling and floor. His eyes were deep, far too deep. They were the depthless drugged eyes of the somnambulist…. And they were also eyes without expression, without soul, eyes that could watch lions tear a man to pieces and never change, that could watch a man impaled and screaming in the hot sun with his eyelids cut off.[134]

Moose Malloy and his obsession with his Velma posed a problem for screenwriters Root and Fenton determined to keep the film light-hearted. Reluctant to abandon the Falcon formula of mystery, laughs and romance, the scenes with Moose appear as if they belong in another film. Moose is pathetic, murderous, sentimental, dangerous. There is nothing similar to him in the other Falcon or Saint films. For a brief period, *The Falcon Takes Over* enters Chandler's world of sexual obsession and pathos. As Anne Riordan explains to Marlowe near the end of the novel:

He was in love with her. … It didn't matter to him she hadn't written to him in six years or ever gone to see him while he was in jail. It didn't matter to him that she had turned him in for a reward. He just bought some fine clothes and started to look for her the first thing when he got out. So she pumped five bullets into him, by way of saying hello. He had killed two people himself, but he was in love with her. What a world.[135]

The two detective traditions are differentiated mainly through the film's use of lighting. While the sets for most of the film are brightly lit, when Moose appears George Robinson's low-key photography highlights his psychological instability. This is most apparent after Diana Kenyon (Helen Grayle in the novel) lures the Falcon away from the Swan Club to a deserted country road. When she pulls out a gun Falcon remains calm and seemingly in control. He tells her that he knows she is Velma and that she is part of a blackmail scheme involving Amthor, Marriott and Burnett. When she orders her chauffeur to pull over so that she can shoot the Falcon, the chauffeur, to Velma's surprise, turns out to be Moose who replaced the real chauffeur. When Malloy approaches her, Diana fires multiple bullets into him despite the fact that he was not trying to harm her. The two traditions—the hard-boiled world of Velma and Moose and the comedic world of the Falcon merge to be replaced by an epilogue which returns the film to the gentleman tradition with the Falcon surrounded by admiring women.

Murder, My Sweet *(1944/1945)/1945)*[136]

Hammett's Spade and Chandler's Marlowe exist in different worlds. Chandler's is a world that endorses an ethical universe, a world of (moral) meaning. Not so Hammett. As the editors of *The Annotated Big Sleep* note, while Chandler readily acknowledged his debt to Hammett ("I give him everything"), the two writers were "profoundly different" with Chandler's fiction presenting a "dose of idealism."[137] His stories assume the world, however corrupt, has meaning. Hammett does not. When Adrian Scott, a newly appointed producer at RKO, discovered that the studio owned the rights to Chandler's *Farewell, My Lovely,* and that Paramount was adapting James M. Cain's *Double Indemnity* with Chandler writing the screenplay with Billy Wilder, Scott realized that RKO could make a more faithful version of the novel without paying additional royalties to the author. Director Edward Dmytryk, keen to move from low budget films, was anxious to be involved. As Chandler was unavailable, Scott selected New York journalist John Paxton to write the screenplay. Where possible Scott and Paxton retained Chandler's first-person narration which gave Dick Powell ample opportunity to exploit Chandler's cynical, witty dialogue. Scott and Paxton decided to tell the story via a flashback. This decision affected the tone of the film as Marlowe is first presented as physically vulnerable, wearing a bandage around his eyes as he recounts his story to Lieutenant Randall (Don Douglas). The setting is a hostile environment, a police room as rendered by cinematographer Harry Wild's high contrast lighting which directs a harsh light on Marlowe's face surrounded by cops in a darkened room.

Marlowe's life on the margins of mainstream society is emphasized by his narration which opens the flashback sequence that occupies almost the entire film. In his office, he watches the evening traffic pass below his window:

> I'm a homing pigeon. I always come back to the stinking coop no matter how late it is. [Marlowe explains that he had been looking for a barber on behalf of the man's wife. As he talks the camera moves past him out through the window until it stops on the city lights] And I never found him. I only found out how big this city is. My feet hurt and my mind felt like a plumber's handkerchief [a montage of shots of the city at night concludes with Marlowe sitting in the empty office lit only by a flashing neon light outside]. There's something about the dead silence of an office building at night. Not quite real. The traffic below was something that didn't have anything to do with me.

Marlowe works in a cheap office located in a broken-down building in the city's business district.[138] By society's (1940s) standards his lack of money meant he was, as Chandler remarked, "a failure and usually he knows it. He is a failure because he hasn't any money. A man who, without physical handicaps, cannot make a decent living is always a failure and usually a moral failure."[139] This is reiterated by Lieutenant Randall in the film when he tells Marlowe that "you're not a detective, you're a slot machine. You'd slit your own throat for six bits plus tax!"

Marlowe, unlike the Falcon, is vulnerable. This is reinforced by Dick Powell's voice-over: "I caught the blackjack right behind my ear. A black pool opened up at my feet. I dived in. It had no bottom. I felt pretty good—like an amputated leg." An extended version of this takes place during Marlowe's drug induced hallucinatory nightmare after he is kidnapped and taken to a bogus clinic:

> "Black pool opened at my feet again and I dived in [Marlowe is shown lying on the floor, out of focus]. The last thing I remember I was going somewhere. It was not my idea" [Marlowe is dragged along the floor]. "The rest of it was a crazy coked up dream. I had never been there before" [a series of expressionistic images beginning with Marlowe falling into a black void, followed by his pursuit through a series of doors unattached to a wall. First, Moose Malloy chases him, followed by a man in a white coat carrying a hypodermic needle. Marlowe begins to fall again until a bright light floods the screen. This is gradually shown to be the ceiling light of Marlowe's dingy sanitarium room]. "The window was open but the smoke didn't move" [a web is superimposed on the screen. Marlowe yells out and then laughs. An attendant and Moose

(From left) Miles Mander as Leuwen Grayle, Anne Shirley as his daughter Ann and Dick Powell as Philip Marlowe in RKO's *Murder, My Sweet* (1945), directed by Edward Dmytryk.

come into the room. When Marlowe tells them the stairs are made of dough, the guard remarks to Moose that this guy is nuts. After they leave the room Marlowe attempts to get off the bed but collapses]. "Okay Marlowe, you're a tough guy, you've been sapped twice, choked, beaten silly with a gun, shot in the arm until you are crazy as a couple of waltzing mice. Now let's see you do something that's really tough, like putting your pants on."

Marlowe eventually escapes but not before confronting Doctor Sonderborg (Ralf Harolde). Marlowe's hysterical voice and faltering physical condition, again, expose his instability: "I'm in a wild mood tonight. I want to go dancing on the foam. I hear the banshees calling. I haven't shot a man in a week."

Marlowe continues to struggle and eventually overcomes all obstacles. Both novel and film end on an upbeat note. In the novel, after Helen shoots Moose, Marlowe explains to Anne that there will be "a nice shakeup here in Bay City. The chief has been canned and half the detectives have been reduced to acting patrolmen."[140] Anne tells him:

"You're so marvellous," she said. "So brave, so determined, and you work for so little money. Everybody bats you over the head and chokes you and smacks your jaw and fills you with morphine, but you just keep right on hitting between tackle and end until they're all worn out. What makes you so wonderful?"

"Go on," I growled. "Spill it."

Anne Riordan said thoughtfully: "I'd like to be kissed, damn you!"[141]

The film ends in the same manner. The epilogue shows Anne (Anne Shirley) escorting Marlowe, still wearing bandages around his eyes, out of the police station onto the street where they embrace.

In 1950 Chandler published an essay titled "The Simple Art of Murder." It expresses his disdain for the classical detective, what he called the "English formula."[142] It was, he wrote, the kind of story "you will find almost every week in the big shiny magazines, handsomely illustrated, and paying due deference to virginal love and the right kind of luxury goods."[143] This kind of detective fiction, he maintained, was "too contrived, and too little aware of what goes on in the world." The "only reality the English detection writers knew was the conversational accent of Surbiton[144] and Bognor Regis."[145] Hammett's fiction, on the other hand, Chandler argued, "had a basis in fact; it was made up out of real things."[146] It was "spare, frugal, hard boiled"[147] and

> Hammett took murder out of the Venetian vase and dropped it into the alley; it doesn't have to stay there forever. …[he] wrote for people with a sharp, aggressive attitude to life. They were not afraid of the seamy side of things; they lived there. Violence did not dismay them; it was right down their street. Hammett gave murder back to the kind people that commit it for reasons, not just to provide a corpse; and with the means at hand, not with handwrought duelling pistols, curare, and tropical fish. He put those people down on paper as they are, and he made them talk and think in the language they customarily used for these purposes.[148]

There are, however, crucial differences between Chandler and Hammett. Differences that Chandler was well aware of when he wrote that "all this (and Hammett too) is for me not quite enough."[149] Chandler, not Hammett, demanded a "quality of redemption,"[150] an ethical dimension in his detective:

> But down these mean streets a man must go who is not himself mean, who is neither tarnished nor afraid. The detective in this kind of story must be such a man. He is the hero, he is everything. He must be a complete man and a common man and yet an unusual man. He must be, to use a rather weathered phrase, a man of honour, by instinct, by inevitability, without thought of it…. He must be the best man in his world and a good enough man for any world.[151]

As Paul Skenazy notes, Chandler's fiction "exemplifies how life might be lived humanely and selflessly—independent of society's hypocrisies, sympathetic to criminal miscreants, but personally free from immoral collusion."[152] This view is supported by crime novelist Ross Macdonald, who pointed out that Chandler's novels are novels of sensibility recording the "wry pain of a sensitive man coping with the roughest elements of a corrupt society."[153] Chandler acknowledges this aspect himself when he notes that his detective is a "lonely man" in "search of a hidden truth."[154] The "hidden truth" is the author's liberal humanistic view of the world.

Hammett shared Chandler's dislike of the classical detective and a rigid formula that was dependent on the detective solving the crime, an attribute he mocked in the final exchange between Spade and Brigid in *The Maltese Falcon*. Similarly, the seemingly romantic quest for the "fabulous" Falcon proves futile and absurd. But the two men shared almost diametrically opposite views of existence. As James Naremore observes, the "world, as Spade explains to Brigid in his parable about the Flitcraft case, is founded on a void."[155] This is even more apparent in *The Glass Key*. As Naremore asks:

What, finally, are we to think of Beaumont and Madvig? How are we to condemn the city without feeling like the "respectable element" whom Beaumont mocks? There is no answer to these questions, because, like nearly all of Hammett's novels, *The Glass Key* ultimately deals with what Stephen [sic] Marcus calls the "ethical unintelligibility of the world." Thus, when Ned Beaumont reveals the identity of the villain, we do not feel that the story has been brought to neat closure. At best, something criminal has been exposed in society's basic institutions; the villain's crime is merely a symptom of a deeper, systemic problem that seems beyond the power of the individual to solve.[156]

The Crime/Suspense Film 1941–1944

Following Huston's *The Maltese Falcon, Stranger on the Third Floor* (1940), *I Wake Up Screaming* (1941), *Street of Chance* (1942), and a few other films, there was a pause in the production of hard-boiled crime films after America's entry into the Second World War on December 7, 1941. Part of this was due to pressure from government agencies, such as the Office of War Information, to produce films that presented a positive image of the United States, films that espoused the "general wartime ideology of commitment and community."[157] "Negative" films, it was claimed, ran counter to the collective ethos of "wartime mobilisation."[158] However, this pause did not last long and late in 1942 the major studios became increasingly concerned that many of the films in production, or pre-production, would not be popular in 1943. They began planning a shift away from war-related stories. On December 16, 1942, *Variety*, under the heading "New War Themes May Veer to 'We're on the Offensive Now,'" reported that the studios were "viewing with considerable alarm the piling up of war stories, feeling being that the box-office appeal of such yarns may reach saturation point long before many of them have been placed into actual work."[159]

There was also a fear in Hollywood that once long casualty lists were widely reported the public would begin to recoil from "too much wartime fare."[160] As a consequence *Variety* reported that "many top officials are considering a wide swing to detective and mystery stories as well as additional escapist films and comedies."[161] On November 10, 1943, *Variety* noted that the studios have been hiring pulp magazine writers such as Steve Fisher and Frank Gruber.[162] This shift was accompanied by institutional changes involving the Office of War Information's regulation of screen stories with regard to the combat front and domestic home front. These changes, along with a liberalization of censorship by the PCA, encouraged hard-boiled film adaptations of novels by authors such as Cornell Woolrich and Dorothy Hughes.

Steve Fisher, just prior to his death in 1980, wrote an essay titled "Pulp Literature: Subculture Revolution in the Late 1930s," where he argued that he, along with Cornell Woolrich, Frank Gruber and a few other writers, transformed the *Black Mask* style of crime story from the "objective, hard-boiled writing promoted by Joseph Shaw and the earlier editors of *Black Mask Magazine* to the subjective, psychologically and emotionally heightened writing favored by Fanny Ellsworth who replaced Shaw in 1936."[163] In his essay Fisher argued that in the late 1930s there was a paradigm shift in *Black Mask Magazine* crime fiction away from the "unemotional" style of Hammett and the first-wave of "Black Mask boys" to a "more subjective, emotional, psychologically driven style of crime story thriller primarily developed by himself and Cornell Woolrich … under the direction of Fanny Ellsworth."[164] During the period, from January 1937 to June 1944 Woolrich contributed 22 stories to *Black Mask* while Fisher had nine stories published in the magazine between August 1937 to April 1939. One of Fisher's stories was "Wait for Me" and it appeared in the May 1938 issue of the magazine. Fisher explained that the plot concerned

> a white Russian whore in Shanghai trying to escape the country, a U.S. sailor tagging along after her everywhere, calling out "Wait for me," but she didn't, and in her devious manipulations to obtain a … passport, was murdered in an upstairs room while the sailor waited for her below. All he wanted to say was that he would marry her, and that she could have a legitimate passport.[165]

Fisher singled out this story as representative of a changing sensibility in crime fiction, one that was encouraged by Fanny Ellsworth. And when the influential *Black Mask* shifted its emphasis, the other magazines, according to Fisher, "began to take notice of this not so subtle style change—the subculture revolution had started."[166] *Black Mask* publisher Keith Alan Deutsch extends Fisher's argument by claiming that

> "The Ellsworth Shift," led to the creation of the film genre we now know as noir through the writings of Steve Fisher, particularly his film scripts, and through the novels and fiction of Cornell Woolrich, whose writings we now call noir, although the term was originally applied only to film. This dark new style and psychology in crime fiction-narration favored by Fisher and Woolrich in their tense crime tales was a perfect match for the dark shadows and frightening, expressive camera angles developed in German and Hollywood horror cinema.[167]

Deutsch concludes that

> Fisher's and Woolrich's best *Black Mask* fiction set the stage for the noir revolution in popular fiction and popular film. Fisher's novel, *I Wake Up Screaming,* created the blueprint, and *Black Mask* under Fanny Ellsworth was the inspiration, for the full emergence of the noir genre that has had an enduring impact on film and fiction in popular American and world entertainment.[168]

While Deutsch's assertions that Steve Fisher's 1941 novel *I Wake Up Screaming*, along with the changed emphasis at *Black Mask* under Fanny Ellsworth, created the blueprint for the full emergence of noir is overstated, Fisher's essay highlights a change in the crime melodrama. This shift, as will be argued more extensively with the impact of Paramount's 1944 production of *Double Indemnity,* revolved around the meaning of virtue in melodrama and the role of the hero. In sensational melodrama poetic justice demanded that virtue be recognized and, in most cases, be rewarded. Following *Double Indemnity* there was a more morally complex presentation. In films such *The Postman Always Rings Twice, Detour, They Won't Believe Me, Raw Deal, So Dark the Night, Pitfall, Criss Cross, The File on Thelma Jordon* and *Crime of Passion* the demarcation between victim and persecutor became less clear. In other films virtue is presented not just as vulnerable but as traumatized. See, for example, *Stranger on the Third Floor, Street of Chance, The Chase, Out of the Past, Fear in the Night, I Wouldn't Be in Your Shoes, Sensation Hunters, Money Madness, Where Danger Lives.*

The Suspense Melodrama: The Traumatized "Hero"

Cornell Woolrich

The "hard-boiled film adaptations" noted by *Variety* did not, in the main, feature hard-boiled detectives as there were relatively few hard-boiled detective films in the 1940s. The most popular pulp writer, at least in terms of film adaptations, was Cornell Woolrich. And Woolrich did not write hard-boiled detective stories. His favored form was what his biographer Frances Nevins calls "paranoid thrillers."[169] Yet many of his stories, with their excessive, often logically incomprehensible plots that relied heavily on chance and last-minute rescues, were variations on sensational melodrama without the controlling influence of savior heroes. His protagonists were always victims, never heroes.

Woolrich never developed a series character like Marlowe or Spade. Woolrich reasoned that if the protagonist is a series character, the audience knows that he/she cannot die. He always wanted to retain the option of deciding the character's fate. Instead of the comforting presence of the tough detective, Woolrich's ordinary protagonists were trapped in an "incomprehensible place where beams happen to fall, and at the same time are predestined to fall, and at the same time are toppled over by malevolent powers; a world ruled interchangeably by chance, fate and (to borrow a phrase from Mark Twain) God the malign thug."[170] They are stories, as Frank Krutnik points out, that contain "tortuously elaborate passages of masochistic delirium."[171]

In his two dozen plus novels and more than 200 short stories and novelettes, Woolrich worked and reworked a number of themes and narrative paradigms. They included, as Francis Nevins explains, the "Noir Cop story" exposing the brutality of a sadistic cop; the "Clock Race story" with the protagonist racing against time to save someone from something dreadful; the "Oscillation story" where trust in a loved one gradually erodes; the "Headlong Through the Night story" which traces the last hours of a haunted man lost in an impersonal city; the "Annihilation story" where chance, or fate or God suddenly removes a loved one; the fatalistic story where the reader is forced to share the final hours of a morally problematic protagonist knowing they will die in a painful way at a particular time; and the "Waking Nightmare story" where the protagonist comes to after some form of blackout caused by amnesia, drugs or hypnosis.[172] Whatever the paradigm, all involve pain and suffering, physical and psychological torment. They represented Woolrich's view where humans were always at the mercy of forces beyond their control. What other writer, Nevins concludes, "created a milieu so worthy of the name *noir*?"[173]

Woolrich was born in New York in 1903 and after his parents separated in 1907 he remained with his father in Mexico until, as a teenager, he joined his mother in New York. His fatalistic view of the world was shaped early. After his death the following fragment was found among his papers: "one night when I was eleven and, huddling over my knees, looked up at the low hanging stars of the Valley of Anahuac, and I knew I would surely die finally, or something worse."[174] This was the beginning of "the sense of personal, private doom" that he felt throughout his mostly unhappy life since "I had that trapped feeling, like some sort of a poor insect that you've put inside a downturned glass, and it tries to climb up the sides, and it can't, and it can't, and it can't."[175]

In 1921 he enrolled at Columbia University but abandoned his studies after the success of his first novel, *Cover Charge* (1926). When the rights to his second novel, *Children of the Ritz* (1927), were purchased by First National Pictures, Woolrich went to Hollywood to work on its adaptation. He remained with First National as a staff writer for a period but never received a screen credit. In 1930 he married Gloria Blackton, the daughter of pioneer film producer J. Stuart Blackton. The marriage, however, was never consummated, and after he left his wife, a diary was found detailing his homosexual affairs during their marriage. Woolrich returned to New York to live with his mother in an occasionally destructive relationship in a series of hotels, mostly the Hotel Marseille, until she died in 1957.

In the early 1930s Woolrich abandoned mainstream fiction following his inability to complete his seventh novel, *I Love You, Paris*. Desperate for money during these Depression years, he turned to pulp magazines. His first crime/suspense story, "Death Sits in the Dentist's Chair," published in *Detective Fiction Weekly* on August 4, 1934, opens with the following:

> There was another patient ahead of me in the waiting room. He was sitting there quietly, humbly, with all the terrible resignation of the very poor. He wasn't all jittery and alert like I was, but just sat there ready to take anything that came, head bowed a little as though he had found life a succession of hard knocks.[176]

This bizarre story of a man who discovers that his brother's fingers have been removed, along with his tongue, by an insane dentist was, like much of Woolrich's fiction, influenced by the economic misery and pain caused by the 1930s Depression. In the next thirty years, mainly between 1934 and 1949, he returned to the same settings—the cheap dance hall, the precinct station backroom, the rundown movie theater and the seedy hotel room. Writing with frenetic haste and reportedly not reading his fiction after the first draft, he allowed many logical flaws and a great reliance on coincidence and chance to resolve his tales. With no interest in the "whodunit," his stories focused on psychologically tormented protagonists who conveyed the author's paranoid view of the world. His protagonists were often lost, emotionally and figuratively, in a bewildering and hostile universe.

In 1938 Columbia paid Woolrich $448.75 for the rights to his short story "Face Work" which was published in *Black Mask* in October 1937. The film was produced under unique circumstances. Columbia, in an attempt to circumvent the 1927 British Cinematograph Films Act which required a quota of "British" films to fulfill the minimum allotment of British screen time, set up a unit at the Willows Park Studios at Victoria on Vancouver Island.[177] For a time these films qualified as "British" films. Hollywood actors Rita Hayworth and Charles Quigley, and others, were stationed at Willows Park and starred in a succession of low budget films. Their final film at Willows Park was Columbia's adaptation of "Face Work," which they re-titled *Convicted*. This was the twelfth and final Columbia film produced at Willows Park before the British parliament closed this loophole. It was also the fifth co-starring role for Hayworth and Quigley. The film was directed by Leon Barsha, an editor and producer at Columbia, and scripted by Edgar Edwards, an English-born writer and actor. The story is a race-against-time, a narrative device frequently used by Woolrich. In this story Jerry Wheeler (Rita Hayworth) desperately tries to save her young brother Chick (Edgar Edwards) from execution after Ruby Rose, the femme fatale, is murdered. To ingratiate herself into the underworld and find the real killer, Wheeler develops a new identity, an exotic dancer named "Angel Face." Her dancing attracts the attention of sadistic nightclub owner Milton Militis (Marc Lawrence), the man who tortured and murdered Ruby Rose. After Wheeler uncovers incriminating evidence linking Militis to Rose's death, she is kidnapped by Militis who plans to physically torture, and then murder her. However, she is rescued in the nick of time by police detective Burns (Charles Quigley).

Convicted was a low budget ($65,000) film with a 15-day shooting schedule. Columbia had minimal expectations for these films as their primary purpose was to fulfill the studio's quota requirements in the United Kingdom so that their A budgeted films would receive a British release without a penalty. Woolrich subsequently recycled aspects of this plot in *Phantom Lady* and *The Black Angel*. Both novels were adapted to the cinema. Woolrich's second suspense novel, published after *The Bride Wore Black,* was *The Black Curtain,* published in 1941. Paramount bought the rights for $2,225 soon after publication and this was the working title until the studio decided to change it to *Street of Chance*. The film was released on October 3, 1942. With a budget of $227,752 and a filming period from January 22 to February 19, 1942, the film starred Burgess Meredith as Frank Thompson, Claire Trevor as Ruth Dillon and Louise Platt as Frank's wife Virginia. The most interesting section, in terms of conveying Woolrich's sense of an endless urban nightmare, is the first half where Garrett Fort's screenplay replicates the novel's gothic overtures involving a bewildered protagonist, Frank Thompson in the film, Frank Townsend in the novel. Both novel and film open in a similar manner to Hammett's Flitcraft parable. A man is walking down a street when material from a construction site nearly kills him:

> First everything was blurred. Then, he could feel hands fumbling around him, lots of hands. They weren't actually touching him; they were touching things that touched him. He got their feel one step removed. Flinging away small, loose objects like chunks of mortar or fragments of brick, which seemed to be strewn all over him. Every minute there was less of these. Then, dimly he heard a voice say: "Here's the ambulance now."[178]

The film opens in the same manner. Frank Thomson, walking along Tillary Street, is nearly killed when scaffolding from a building site collapses and a large cement block narrowly misses his head. This act of pure chance becomes a life changing moment for him. Initially he is unsettled, especially after a boy hands him his hat with the initials DN on the sweatband. This turns to anxiety after he arrives "home" to find out that his wife, Virginia, no longer lives there, and has not for some time (more than three years in the novel, one year in the film). When he goes to her new address, he finds her maiden name on the door and she is visibly shaken when she sees him. After she accepts him back his trauma intensifies:

> In the still of the night, long after they'd put out the lights and lay quiet in the darkened room, he suddenly started upright, cold sweat needling his forehead. "Virginia, I'm scared! Put on the lights, I'm frightened of the dark! Where was I? *Who* was I, all that time?"[179]

Cornell Woolrich's 1943 novel *The Black Angel* reworked his motif of the race against time by a wife or sister to save a loved one from execution. In Universal's 1946 adaptation, alcoholic pianist Martin Blair (Dan Duryea) attempts to reconcile with his wife Mavis Marlowe (Constance Dowling) with the present of a jeweled heart. After Mavis rejects him, she is found dead.

Frank returns to his former job and tries to resume his life as he remembered it. However, a sinister man, "Agate Eyes," begins following him. To escape, Frank runs to a subway and jumps onto a train car just as it pulls out from the station. However, Agate Eyes runs after him and catches up with it. Unable to get at Frank, he pulls out a gun and smashes the glass door panel as the train pulls away (a similar attack takes place in a taxi in the film):

> He didn't know who the man was, nor what he wanted with him, nor even who it was that *he*, the one he wanted, was supposed to be. He only knew that the bottomless black abyss of that anonymous past was not passive, lifeless, after all; it had just emitted a blood-red lick of flame towards him, as if seeking to drag him back into its depths and consume him.[180]

The film condenses the next section in the novel as Frank quits his job and spends days terrified in the park, hoping that Agate Eyes will not find him. However, one night, unable to sleep, he notices men hidden in the shadows outside their apartment. This culminates in a nightmarish attack on his home as he and Virginia flee. He persuades Virginia to move upstate to live with her mother while he retraces his steps to the accident in Tillary Street. At this point the novel and the film diverge. In

Book Two of the novel, "The Curtain Lifts," Woolrich spends considerable time documenting Frank's sad, lonely existence trying to find somebody who recognizes him from his former life. Forty pages later, with only thirty cents in his pocket, he hears a fire siren and wanders down to a street that crosses Tillary Street. He meets a slim and vibrant woman, Ruth Dillon, who recognizes him as her lover. Over the next few weeks he discovers that she works in the upstate village of New Jericho and that he, Frank, was known as Dan Nearing and is wanted for the shotgun murder of his employer, Harry Diedrich. He also learns that the mysterious man chasing him is Detective Joe Marucci.

The film covers this in a few scenes with Frank meeting Ruth (Claire Trevor) soon after returning to Tillary Street. The second half of the film and the last section of the novel are similar as Frank tries to find out who killed Dietrich. Ruth, in both the novel and film, is devoted to Frank/Dan. It is clear in Woolrich's story that they are sleeping together while, under Joseph Breen's tight control, the film is careful to show him distancing himself from her romantic overtures. In a cruel twist, the film suddenly exposes Ruth as the killer. It ends with Frank, coldly, telling her that he is married to Virginia and intends returning to her. Ruth pulls out a gun and dies, accidentally, when Frank struggles with her to get possession of the weapon. He is exonerated by Ruth's dying confession, conveniently heard by Marucci. Frank is now free to return to his wife. The novel, on the other hand, pins the murder on two peripheral characters. Ruth, nevertheless, dies in the process. The novel ends on a wistful note compared to the film as Frank, on a train back to his wife, raises a two finger salute to Ruth's small headstone in the graveyard as the locomotive "gave a long, wailing whistle of unutterable sadness."[181]

Woolrich's third suspense novel, *Black Alibi*, was published in April 1942 and RKO purchased the screen rights for $5,175. Val Lewton produced the film adaptation which was titled *The Leopard Man* (1943). Both novel and film concern the stalking of victims in a small town, New Mexico in the film, South America in the novel, by a rogue leopard (film), jaguar in the novel. The film's set piece, and one of the most chilling moments in the Hollywood cinema, involves a teenage Mexican girl, Teresa Delgado (Margaret Landry), forced by her mother to travel at dusk to a local store to buy corn meal for her father's dinner. Expertly directed by Jacques Tourneur, assisted by cinematographer by Robert de Grasse, this is one of Lewton's seminal moments of horror executed primarily by sound, composition and editing. The young girl's terrifying walk culminates in her unseen death outside her house, which is filmed from inside the house. Only her screams, and a rivulet of blood, mark her demise.

The next film adaptation of a Woolrich novel, under his William Irish pseudonym, was Universal's *Phantom Lady*, directed by Robert Siodmak and produced by Joan Harrison. The novel was published in August 1942 and the film was completed by October 1943 and released on January 28, 1944. The screenplay by Bernard C. Schoenfeld follows the novel to about the halfway point and then it transforms the Woolrich story into a gothic mystery involving an insane killer. The novel is based on "Face Work" which, in turn, was a reworking of his 1935 short story "Murder in Wax." In *Phantom Lady* a young woman, Carol "Kansas" Richman (Ella Raines), enters the underworld in an attempt to save her boss from the gas chamber. The highlight of the film is the "cat-and-mouse" game as Carol follows a suspect through the streets of New York, culminating in his death on the Third Avenue Elevated platform. There is also the notorious "drum" session where Carol seduces a drummer, Cliff Milburn (Elisha Cook, Jr.) in an all-night jam session. The film closes after the killer, sculptor Jack Marlow (Franchot Tone), traps Carol in his apartment. She is saved by the last-minute arrival of the police.

Adaptations of the 1942 novelette "Dormant Account" as part of Columbia's low budget "Whistler" series, *Mark of the Whistler* (1944), were followed by three film adaptations in 1946. RKO's *Deadline at Dawn*, based on the 1944 novel of the same name, preceded Universal's *Black Angel*. In *Black Angel* Catherine Bennett (June Vincent), assisted by alcoholic pianist Martin Blair (Dan Duryea), saves her adulterous husband after he is charged with the murder of his mistress, Mavis Marlowe. The heroine, as in "Face Work," has to ingratiate herself into the world of a sadistic nightclub owner. However, in a twist, the murderer is shown to be Bennett's helper, Martin Blair, who killed his estranged wife, Marlowe, in a drunken stupor.

The Chase

The third film adaptation of a Woolrich novel in 1946 was his 1944 novel *The Black Path of Fear*, the fifth in the Black series, and a reworking of his 1942 novelette "Havana Night." This story takes place between dusk and dawn in Cuba. After Bill Scott, the narrator, leaves the boat in Havana with a woman, the wife of a gangster, she is stabbed to death in a crowded bar. Scott is blamed for the killing and he is forced to flee from the police. Not knowing anyone in this alien environment, his only protection comes from La Media Noche, a prostitute. *The Black Path of Fear* is one of Woolrich's more overt examples of sensational melodrama with its secret passages, last minute escapes, sinister Cubans, hostile police, dope smoking dens, drug smuggling gangsters and a sadistic husband who imprisons his wife. Woolrich's "hero" is impotent as a savior figure. He cannot save himself or the heroine. Instead, he is dependent on a Cuban prostitute to protect him and to devise the plan that will extricate him from the police.

The novel begins *in medias res* with the narrator Bill Scott and Eve, the wife of a gangster, Eddie Roman, arriving in Havana a little before 10:00 p.m. on a boat from Miami. They are taken by horse and carriage to "Sloppy Joe's," a huge, crowded open-air bistro on Zuluetta Street. In the bistro Eve has a premonition that she is about to die. A sidewalk photographer asks if they want their picture taken and as the flashlight powder fizzles, Eve slowly sinks to the floor:

> "I've got to go out alone in the dark," she sighed, "and I've always hated the dark."[182]

As the police take her body out of the bistro, Scott muses:

> So she went out that way, into the black Havana night, without diamonds, without love, without dreams.[183]

The police close in around Scott as he salutes Eve with the daiquiri she left standing on the bar. He is "left alone with my dead"[184] and a hostile policeman. Scott's guilt is confirmed by the jade handled knife embedded in Eve's back as it is similar to the one he purchased at Tio Chin's curio shop after arriving in Havana. When the owner of the shop verifies that it is the actual murder weapon, the police arrest Scott.

Returning with the police through the labyrinth of passages to the mouth of an alley in Chinatown, Scott makes his escape as they approach "sinister-looking door-ways,"[185] and "there weren't many left to pick from"[186]:

> There were two left, one on each side of the way, both unlighted, both alike as afar as looks went. … It was a toss-up. I've often wondered what would have happened if I'd picked the one on the left instead of the one on the right. Two doorways in a darkened alley; one spelled life and one spelled death.
> I picked the one on the right.[187]

This is the stuff of sensational melodrama.[188] In the novel, not the film, La Media Noche and Scott spend considerable time together and he tells her his story which takes the form of a long flashback recounting his time in Miami where he worked for Roman as a chauffeur. Gradually he falls in love with Roman's wife Eve, who likes to be driven to a secluded spot on the beach each evening where she can look at the horizon, dreaming of her escape from her abusive husband. After she persuades Scott to take her away, they arrive at the Miami dock just ahead of Roman and his body-guard, Bruno Jordan. After Eve is murdered in Havana, La Media Noche assists Scott clear himself.

Secret passwords, Asian zombies, opium pipes and a rescue in the nick of time confirm the story's melodramatic basis. After extricating himself from Havana, Scott returns to Miami where Jordan accidentally shoots his boss. Jordan then dies when he falls over a balcony and his throat is ripped out by Wolf, the servant's dog. Scott returns to Havana where he meets La Media Noche and they part in front of Sloppy Joe's:

> "I'd like to ask you in for a drink," I said, "but—"
> "I know. There's someone waiting for you in there. Flowers on the grave."
> She dusted off my sleeve with a comradely flick of her hand, and that was our way of saying good-by, I guess. Two ships that pass in the night; two paths that cross in the dark.[189]

Scott goes into the bistro and salutes Eve with a daiquiri, before snapping it against the bar. The final line in the novel: "It was lonely standing there by myself at the bar like that."[190]

The *Springfield Republican* described the novel as a thrilling "tale of atmo-sphere and mordant character portraiture, laced with desperate action and sus-pense, crowned with vengeance…. Woolrich holds your attention from first to last."[191] Thomas Renzi, on the other hand, argues that "Bill Scott may be the protagonist, but he deserves less recognition than an anti-hero. The traditional anti-hero, because of some redeeming virtue (integrity, perseverance, self-sacrifice), earns our admiration in spite of his moral flaws and social improprieties. However, this particular Wool-richian protagonist lacks any outstanding redeeming trait to set him above his fellow humans. Bill Scott … never does anything to win our admiration or give him the sta-tus of hero."[192]

Film producer Seymour Nebenzal bought the rights to Woolrich's novel and announced in January 1946 that Philip Yordan would write the script. In March

Robert Cummings as Chuck Scott is framed for the murder of Lorna Roman (Michéle Morgan) in *The Chase* (1946), screenwriter Philip Yordan's radical adaptation of Cornell Woolrich's 1944 novel *The Black Path of Fear*.

Robert Cummings was selected for the lead role of Chuck Scott and Joan Leslie as Lorna Roman. However, problems over Leslie's contract with Warners pushed filming back to May and she was replaced by Michèle Morgan when her legal problems could not be resolved. Writer, producer and director Arthur D. Ripley was signed to direct the film and he and Yordan made substantial changes to Woolrich's story which begins with Scott, a penniless, unemployed veteran, finding a wallet in front of a Miami diner. When he returns it to its owner, Eddie Roman (Steve Cochran), the gangster offers him a job as chauffeur. While driving Roman and his bodyguard Gino (Peter Lorre), Scott is amazed to discover that Roman has a second set of controls in the back seat which he uses to override Scott's control of the car as they race a train to a railway crossing, with Roman putting the brakes on at the last minute to avoid a crash.

There is a gothic element in the film, unlike the novel, with Lorna Roman (Michèle Morgan) imprisoned by her sadistic husband. Her only outlet is a nightly drive to the beach with Scott. She offers Scott $1,000 to take her to Havana. Scott agrees and buys tickets on the *Cuba* which sails at 11:00 p.m. He then settles down on his bed to wait for the pick-up time. On board the ship a romance/sexual relationship blossoms. At this point the film follows Woolrich's narrative. Lorna dies in a nightclub, La Habana, Scott is blamed by the police, after the incriminating knife is found embedded in her and a photographer takes her picture just as the murder occurs. Scott is about to be arrested when he flees from the police and, after a chase through a labyrinth of alleys and passages, he finds refuge in the room of an impoverished woman, Midnight (Yolanda Lacca). However, the relationship between Scott and Midnight is, unlike the novel, only fleeting. After Scott locates the photographer, he finds him dead and the incriminating negative missing. Gino suddenly appears and brutally murders Scott.

This represents a major departure from the novel. The film fades out on Scott's dead body and then fades in to show him asleep in his room in Roman's mansion. In other words, the entire narrative, without any formal indication, is a dream from the time Scott fell asleep while waiting to take Lorna to Havana to his "murder." We subsequently learn that Scott suffers from amnesia as a result of malaria he contracted in the Pacific while serving in the navy. Distressed and disoriented, he fails to remember that Lorna is waiting for him to take her to Havana. Instead, he contacts his navy psychologist, Commander Wilson (Jack Holt), who takes him to the Florida Club to discuss his case (diagnosed as "anxiety neurosis"). At the Florida Club Scott discovers the tickets to Havana in his coat pocket. The tickets are booked for the *Cristola* sailing at 11:30—not the *Cuba* 11:00. Scott collects Lorna and they board the ship. After Roman and Gino discover they plan to sail that night, they race to stop them. Roman, in his quest for more speed, deploys his back seat control device, only this time his car hits the train at the crossing. The film ends with Scott and Lorna, with the same driver of a horse-drawn carriage that appeared in his dream, outside the same nightclub.

The Ripley/Yordan film blends a number of elements not found in the novel, including the motif of the unemployed veteran with psychological problems (featured in films such as *The Blue Dahlia, Somewhere in the Night, Crack-up, The High Wall, Crossfire, Ride the Pink Horse* and *The Crooked Way*). The film, unlike the novel, accentuates the gothic aspect, including a scene where Roman hits his wife after discovering an entry in her diary describing her desire to escape from her brutal husband. The major change, however, is the dream sequence which, although not used by Woolrich, is consistent with his fiction which often traverses the liminal space between dream and reality.[193]

The ending of the film is also different from the novel. Woolrich's tale ends on a characteristic moment of loneliness and romantic loss. Lorna is dead and Scott is alone in a Havana bar. Ripley's film, on the other hand, closes on a seemingly sentimental, romantic ending. Scott is reunited with Lorna outside the same Havana bar as in his dream. But there is a sting in the tail as the driver of their horse and carriage watching them kiss is the same sinister driver (Martin Garralaga) that appeared in Scott's dream. And his dream ended with Lorna's murder and Scott's death.

Fear in the Night

Woolrich's "Waking Nightmare story" paradigm provides the basis for the 1947 low budget Paramount film *Fear in the Night* (1947). This film had its origins in

Woolrich's short story "And So to Death," published in *Argosy* on March 1, 1941, was reprinted two years later in a collection of his fiction under the title "Nightmare" and it is known by this title today. The story opens with:

> First, all I could see was this beautiful face, this beautiful girl's face; like a white, slightly luminous mask, swimming detachedly against enfolding darkness. As if a little private spotlight of its own was trained on it from below. It was so beautiful and so false, and I seemed to know it so well, and my heart was wrung.[194]

In a young man's nightmare he "dreams" he is fighting a man when a woman appears and tries to hand his attacker an awl. The young man grabs it and stabs the other man to death. This takes place in an eight-sided room with mirrored walls. After killing the man, the woman runs off and the young man places the body in a closet. Next morning the young man, Vincent Hardy, wakes up believing it was all a nightmare. However, when he goes into his bathroom he finds bruises on his neck, a button and a key in his pocket. Troubled, he seeks help from his brother-in-law, Cliff Dodge, a homicide cop. While Cliff dismisses the "dream," Vince becomes increasingly agitated.

To try and cheer Vince up, Cliff and his wife Lil take the young man for a drive into the country in Cliff's "new second hand Chevy." When thunder is heard, Lil becomes distressed, and they drive from the park. Although Vince claims he has never been in this area before, he directs them to a remote house where they take shelter from the rain. After Vince locates the front door key in a potted plant, and the light switch inside the house, Cliff becomes troubled by Vince's intuitive knowledge of the house. Vince then sneaks upstairs to find the octagonal mirrored room. Cliff walks in and they find blood in the closet after Cliff uses the key to open it. Downstairs, in the kitchen, Cliff accuses Vince of taking advantage of their relationship to cover up a killing. As he is about to hit the young man, a local deputy walks in and takes Cliff and Vince to see Sheriff Waggoner who explains that a murder took place in the house with another killing, Mrs. Fleming, the occupant of the house, found in the driveway. She died after giving the police a detailed description of the man who attacked her and her lover (Dan Ayers) in the mirrored room. Vince fits the description and he faints in the sheriff's office.

Cliff takes Vince back to his apartment and tells him he has thirty minutes to get away. If he is still there after that time he will be arrested and Cliff will resign from the police force. After Cliff leaves, Vince attempts suicide by cutting his wrist with a razor blade. Cliff arrives in time to save him. Cliff and Vince deduce that Cliff was hypnotized into killing Ayers by Joel Fleming, a former hypnotist. Cliff sends Vince back to the Fleming house to trap Fleming into making a confession which will be recorded by the police hiding in the house. Fleming, however, hypnotizes Vince again, taking his gun away and ordering him to commit suicide by jumping into a nearby lake. Cliff saves Vince, the police shoot at Fleming's car, forcing it to crash and burst into flames, and the story ends with Vince facing time in jail until the arraignment. Cliff agrees to support him.

Woolrich's story could have been a detective story with Cliff the hero saving Vince from both the electric chair and from drowning. But it wasn't. Instead Woolrich focuses on the traumatized young man. It is, as Nevins remarks, one of

"Woolrich's most powerful … shorter works, permeated by the existential terror of being out of control of one's life, of being at the mercy of malignant forces inside one's own flesh. Is this how Woolrich viewed his homosexuality?"[195] Certainly the film questions how culpable are we for any wrongdoings we may commit. And how God, or Providence, is complicit in our actions. During Cliff's confrontation with Vince in the kitchen of the Fleming house, after they have discovered the blood in the closet, Cliff throws a punch at Vince:

> He sent another one up at me. I swerved my head, and this time it just grazed me. My recalcitrance—it must have seemed like that—only inflamed his anger. "Are you gonna answer me, Vince? Are you gonna answer me?"
> "I can't. You're asking me things I can't." A sob of misery wrenched from me. "Ask God—or whoever watches over us in the night when we're unconscious."[196]

Paramount's adaptation of the Woolrich story was released as *Fear in the Night* in April 1947.[197] It was, reportedly, shot in 10 days and produced by William H. Pine and William C. Thomas, known as the "Dollar Bills" for their reputation of bringing in low budget films on time and on budget. The film was scripted and directed by Maxwell Shane who had been writing scripts for the Pine-Thomas productions for some time. Shane, an admirer of Woolrich, remained faithful to the short story with the exception of adding a girlfriend, Betty Winters (Kay Scott) and changing Vince's suicide attempt from cutting his wrist to jumping out of the hotel window.

I Wouldn't Be in Your Shoes

Thirteen months after the release of *Fear in the Night* Monogram released *I Wouldn't Be in Your Shoes*, produced by Walter Mirisch and based on Woolrich's novelette of the same name which was published in *Detective Fiction Weekly* on March 12, 1938. In many ways, *I Wouldn't Be In Your Shoes* is as revealing of Woolrich's world view as the Flitcraft parable is in expressing Hammett's attitude to the universe. Woolrich's tale subverts the basis of melodrama as it highlights the destructive role chance can play, to show how humans are at the mercy of a malevolent god. Francis Nevins sums up the internal logic of the story when he writes that "we are given two incompatible but mutually reinforcing accounts of the nature of the universe:

> (1) innocent lives are destroyed by a tightly knit pattern of events so dependent on multiple coincidences that some sadistic power beyond blind chance must be in control;
> (2) innocent lives are destroyed by a situation in which there are only two logical possibilities but neither makes sense or squares with what is known.
> This in a nutshell is Woolrich's metaphysics."[198]

I Wouldn't Be in Your Shoes is a story rooted in the Depression and the impoverished lives of Tom and Ann Quinn, who live in a one room apartment in the tenement district of New York. One August night Tom throws his shoes out of the window at a pair of stray cats that disturb their sleep. As the shoes are expensive orthopedic shoes, Ann reacts angrily, and tells Tom to recover them from the back yard. After a while he returns without the shoes and explains that they must have gone into a neighbor's

(From left) **Elyse Knox, Don Castle, Rory Mallinson and Regis Toomey in Monogram's** *I Wouldn't Be in Your Shoes* **(1948), an adaptation of Cornell Woolrich's 1938 short story.**

window. At the same time Wonter, an elderly recluse living nearby in a waterfront shack, is murdered. The next day Tom returns from work to learn from Ann that his shoes were placed neatly wrapped in newspaper on their doorstep.

The police investigate Wonter's death and conclude it was a robbery as the old man was believed to have money hoarded in his shack. A clear footprint at the scene of the crime enables the police to trace the crime to Tom and they begin a surveillance of the couple. At the same time Tom returns home from work with a wallet containing more than $2000, claiming he found the money on the subway steps. He decides that they should keep the money although Ann has her doubts. After waiting a few days to see if anyone contacts the newspaper's lost and found column, they embark on a shopping spree. The police arrest Tom and he is sentenced to death for the murder of Wonter. However, on Christmas Eve, a few days before Tom's scheduled execution, a young detective, Bob White, decides to investigate and finds Wonter's hidden money in jam-filled tins in his cellar. He concludes that Tom may be innocent and interrogates Ann, who remembers the shoe-throwing incident. This leads White to a young man, Kosloff, who lived in a nearby apartment at the time of Wonter's murder. White travels to see Kosloff in Pittsfield, Massachusetts, as the young man is about to propose to his girlfriend. The policeman discovers that recently Kosloff received a good deal of money. White takes him back to New York where witnesses verify that Kosloff knew of Wonter's wealth. He is arrested and Tom is released.

This, so far, is a fairly conventional melodrama where chance plays a decisive part. Woolrich, however, systematically destroys the melodramatic basis of his tale towards the end of his story. He creates a parallel between Tom and Kosloff. One is innocent and one guilty and the author refuses to make a choice. He constructs a plausible case for Kosloff as he did for Tom. Kosloff moved back to Pittsfield because his mother was ill. His wealth ostensibly came from money secreted in his late mother's house as she did not trust banks. Just as the police did not initially believe Tom, now they don't believe Kosloff. Tom is released and Kosloff replaces him in jail. However, the story's downbeat epilogue shows Ann leaving Tom as she doubts his innocence. The reader is left not knowing if Tom killed Wonter. Or did Kosloff? And the lives of every character in the story, innocent or guilty, are destroyed.

Woolrich's story uses chance and coincidence as a formal device to highlight his view of existence as one ruled by chance. A world the studio was not prepared to replicate in Steve Fisher's screenplay. The film begins in *media res* with Tom Quinn (Don Castle) on death row, just hours before his execution. When the other inmates encourage him to tell his story, he begins to think about the events leading up to his predicament. He and wife Ann (Elyse Knox) are living in a one room New York apartment. He is an unemployed dancer and she works in a local dancing "academy" where she encourages men to "dance" with her. Agitated at her late homecoming, he asks her where has she been. She tells him "around the world in a rowboat," a reference to a persistent admirer who she calls "Santa Claus" as he gives her larger than average tips for the attention he receives. The film follows the outline of Woolrich's story, although it is Ann, not Tom, who wants to keep the $2000. The major difference is that Fisher's screenplay sets up a different ending quite early in the film. When the police arrive to arrest Tom, they include Police Inspector Clint Judd (Regis Toomey), and Ann discovers that he is "Santa Claus."

After Tom is convicted of Wonter's murder Judd offers to help Ann providing she will marry him. Judd sets up John Kosloff (Robert Lowell) as the fall guy but when this scheme falls apart, he still insists that Ann live in an apartment he has purchased. Unwilling to follow Woolrich's unresolved ending, Steve Fisher needed to find a killer for the film. To seek the author's advice, he went to New York and phoned Woolrich, who suggested he use the ending in his (Fisher's) screenplay for the Twentieth Century–Fox film *I Wake Up Screaming* (1941). In this film the villain, not the killer, is an obsessed cop who frames the hero.[199]

Fisher took Woolrich's advice and the film, unlike the short story, establishes "Santa Claus" as the murderer. Obsessed with Ann, he tried to frame her husband for the killing. However, Fisher's screenplay may have been more daring than the release print. Thomas Renzi, in his chapter on the novelette and film, was unable to secure a print and worked from the film's Dialogue Sheets. In this source, the film ends not knowing whether Ann and Inspector Stevens (Charles D. Brown) are able to reach the prison governor in time to stop Tom's execution: "Stevens steps forward and promptly arrests him [Judd]." Then he tells another detective to alert the governor who is standing by on an open line. Ann asks, "Will Tom be…?" However, the story ends before she receives an answer."[200] On the other hand, the release print which I viewed had a more conventional ending—Stevens shoots Judd and the epilogue shows Tom and Ann traveling to California to re-ignite their career as a dancing duo.

Woolrich's creative period was largely over by the late 1940s although he continued to write. His short story "It Had to be Murder," published in *Dime Detective* in February 1942, and reprinted as "Rear Window," was filmed by Alfred Hitchcock in 1954. His last strong novel was *I Married a Dead Man,* published in 1948. The beginning of the story is pure Woolrich—an everyday person trapped in a hostile universe with little hope of salvation. Although the specific nature of the trap varied from story to story, its function was always the same—to dramatize Woolrich's paranoid view of existence whereupon his protagonist is shown to be impotent and unable to understand, let alone control, her/his world. *I Married a Dead Man* is, like *I Wouldn't Be in Your Shoes,* a story where he refuses to identify the killer. Unlike the film adaptation, titled *No Man of Her Own* (1950), the person who killed Helen's husband is not revealed, and the novel ends with Helen's quiet cry, "We've lost. That's all I know. We've lost. And now the game is through."

Paramount bought the rights to the novel and Barbara Stanwyck starred as the hapless heroine. The film, of course, replaced Woolrich's nihilistic ending with an upbeat closure. The end of *No Man of Her Own,* directed by Mitchell Leisen and scripted by Sally Benson and Catherine Turney, brings in a minor character as the killer. While *I Married a Dead Man,* as Francis Nevins notes, "marked the culmination of almost fifteen years of white-hot creativity that permanently shaped the landscape of *noir,*"[201] no Hollywood film in the 1940s was prepared to endorse Woolrich's nihilistic view of existence. No studio was prepared to follow Woolrich's belief that first "you dream, and believe the dream is reality; then you die, or even worse you beg for the release of death and it doesn't come."[202]

"Pseudo Woolrich": Stranger on the Third Floor

While Woolrich had nothing to do with the low budget RKO film *Stranger on the Third Floor* (1940), it has all the hallmarks of a Woolrich story. It prefigures many of the qualities associated with film noir later in the decade.[203] RKO historian Richard Jewell points out that it was "B-unit curiosity … a premature film noir, a picture that should, by all historical rights, have been produced in 1944 or 1945—not 1940."[204] It also disrupts the neat chronology of those imposing a linear development of "film noir" from the "non-noir" crime films of the 1930s to its "full bloom" after 1944. However, Hollywood genres, cycles and trends are never neat, as Wheeler Winston Dixon and others demonstrate with regard to film noir.[205] Sheri Chinen Biesen, for example, describes this and similar films produced before the Japanese attack on Pearl Harbor as "proto-noir film" as an attempt to differentiate between the early, so-called "under-developed" noir films and the appearance of "full-blown noir films."[206]

What is more significant is the shift within the suspense/crime melodrama in the early 1940s. Sensational melodrama, a bipolar world involving characters devoid of "psychological conflict,"[207] Brooks's "pure psychic signs,"[208] who exist purely to participate in the clash between moral absolutes, no longer dominated the crime/suspense melodrama. They were replaced by more complex characters, characters who were often psychologically traumatized. A fascinating example of this is the 1943 RKO production *The Fallen Sparrow* (1943) which is discussed later. However, this film was preceded by the 1940 film from the same studio, *Stranger on the Third Floor*. Both films show the influence of the gothic tradition. Glenn Erickson highlights this when he notes that the "psychological effect" renders *Stranger on the Third Floor* more like an Edgar Allan Poe story such as *The Tell-Tale Heart*.[209]

However, RKO, in 1940, did not know what kind of film it was, describing it as a "crime drama novelty."[210] The *Hollywood Reporter* called it a "heavy psychological drama" while noting that a

STRANGER ON THE THIRD FLOOR

PETER LORRE
JOHN McGUIRE
MARGARET TALLICHET
CHARLES WALDRON

Produced by LEE MARCUS • *Directed by* BORIS INGSTER
Story & Screen play by FRANK PARTOS

Although Peter Lorre is top billed as the serial killer, the film focuses on Michael Ward's (John McGuire) psychological turmoil and his girlfriend Jane's (Margaret Tallichet) attempt to save him after he is accused of murder in RKO's *Stranger on the Third Floor* (1940).

"good third of the picture shows the psychosis of the reporter as he broods over his actions, while his thoughts are spoken aloud."[211] *Variety*, on the other hand, described the film as "too arty for average audiences." The trade publication *Harrison's Reports* described the film as a different type of "melodrama." In its review, the trade paper argued that the film's appeal was "strictly limited" as the story was "too harrowing—at its conclusion, one feels as if one has gone through a nightmare."[212]

Stranger on the Third Floor was not a commercial success. The direct costs were $129,486 with a final costing of $171,192 (just $72 over budget). However, its domestic North American earnings totaled only $112,000 with foreign earnings, affected by the loss of markets in Europe due to the Second World War, reduced to $74,000. This resulted in a $56,000 loss. At the end of the year the head of the B unit at RKO and the producer of *Stranger on the Third Floor,* Lee Marcus, was replaced.[213]

The film begins with the murder trial of Joe Briggs (Elisha Cook, Jr.), a young taxi driver accused of slashing the throat of Nick Nanbajan (Charles Judels), the owner of a neighborhood diner. The prosecution's star witness, reporter Michael Ward (John McGuire), saw Joe with Nick just prior to the murder. Although Ward did not see Briggs kill Nick, his testimony is crucial in convicting the taxi driver. However, Jane (Margaret Tallichet), Ward's fiancée, is not convinced and she becomes upset when the jury delivers a guilty verdict. Michael, initially, is unconcerned about Joe's fate as he is more interested in the bonus he will receive from his newspaper for his exclusive story. This money, he hopes, will enable him to leave his shabby boarding house and marry Jane.

When Michael returns to his boarding house after the trial, he cannot hear his neighbor Meng (Charles Halton) snoring in the next apartment. Ward begins to speculate what might have happened to Meng. His anxieties finally erupt in the film's major sequence, a harrowing nightmare characterized by stylized sets, tilted camera set-ups, exaggerated props and Nicholas Musuraca's chiaroscuro lighting that throws huge diagonal shadows across a set that is extended out of perspective by Van Nest Polglase's abstract art design. This startling sequence, an adaptation of German expressionism, was devised by Russian born director Boris Ingster and Hungarian screenwriter Frank Partos[214] who wanted to visually portray Ward's psychological fragility and destabilization. It represents an extreme example of Brooks's argument that the melodrama's excessive rhetoric constantly strives to break through everything that constitutes the "reality principle," all its censorships, accommodations, tonings-down.[215] The sequence includes what was to become an important motif in the crime film during the 1940s, the arbitrary nature of justice. The judge in the nightmare dissolves into a composite image showing the scales of justice on one hand and a scythe on the other. Ward's nightmare ends with the jury collectively shouting at him that he is "guilty."

Ward's nightmare exposes facets that he himself could not admit to—namely his desire to kill Meng. This desire becomes associated with his sense of guilt that his testimony regarding Briggs was based on self-interest—a combination of money, lust and ambition. And he now faces the same predicament following Meng's murder. The circumstantial evidence that convicted Briggs was going to convict him. The latter part of the film transitions into a conventional crime melodrama as Jane hunts down the killer. Nevertheless *Stranger on the Third Floor,* despite its inability to find an audience in 1940, is a remarkably prescient film.

Michael's latent desire to murder Meng is expressed early in the film when Meng interrupts a discussion between Michael and fellow reporter Martin (Cliff Clark) in Nick's diner:

> MICHAEL: Did you ever want to kill a man?
> MARTIN: My son, there's murder in every intelligent man's heart.
> MICHAEL: He's no man! He's a worm. The kind you ought to jump on with heavy boots.
> MARTIN: You'll have to do an awful lot of jumping. The earth is full of them.
> MICHAEL: It would be a pleasure to cut his throat!

As he delivers this line Michael is shown fondling a knife.

Michael's antipathy towards his neighbor comes to a head one evening when Michael and Jane are forced to take shelter in Mike's room in the boarding house. Normally, their romance is conducted in public places such as the park or movie theaters. As they enter his room, Jane is concerned about the improprieties of the situation, an unmarried young woman in a man's room, while Mike is eager to explore the romantic possibilities. As he tries to kiss her, she pulls away and attempts to deflect his ardor with small talk ("do you talk in your sleep?"). When he notices that her feet and stockings are wet, he begins drying her legs as Meng and the landlady Mrs. Kane (Ethel Griffies) enter his room. While Kane lectures Mike on her rules with regard to women in the room, Meng shows more interest in Jane's bare legs. Frustrated, Mike erupts, grabs Meng by the throat, and calls him an "obscene old fool." He tells Kane to get Meng out of his room "before I kill him!"

The studio emphasized the psychological aspects in promoting the film: "HE DREAMS a killing then has to prove his innocence!" "Haunting nightmare turns into grim reality ... as murder witness almost dreams himself into the electric chair."[216] This film, Frank Krutnik points out, shows "how much of the intensity of the *noir* suspense thriller derives from its introduction of characteristic horror story elements into the crime film."[217]

I Wake Up Screaming *(1942)*

Twentieth Century–Fox's adaptation of Fisher's hard-boiled novel *I Wake Up Screaming* starred Betty Grable, Victor Mature and Carole Landis. The studio was obviously nervous about producing an A budgeted film based on a crime novel with its major musical star Betty Grable. To avoid sounding too provocative, the film's working title was *Hot Spot* and it was previewed under this title on October 31, 1941. However, when the film went into general release on January 16, 1942, it reverted to the title of Fisher's novel. The result was a generic mixture of comedy, hard-boiled crime and romance and Edward Cronjager's cinematography is fully representative of the film's hybrid nature. When Ed Cornell (Laird Cregar) appears he is usually filmed from a low angle to emphasize Cregar's large physique and the physical threat he represents to the hero and heroine. His psychological torment, his "dividedness," is also indicated by lighting half of Cregar's face in shadow and the other half in bright light. Yet when he is not on screen the lighting and compositions become more conventional for the romantic interludes and comedic moments. And Grable, as the heroine Jill Lynch, receives the full Hollywood glamor treatment to highlight her flawless physical features.

The film's formal dichotomy extends to Cyril Mockridge's score. For some of the dark, urban scenes he assimilates Alfred Newman's famous musical cue "Street Scene." However, this is often overpowered by various reworking of Harold Arlen's sentimental tune "Over the Rainbow" which is heard virtually every time Grable appears. And, more jarringly, when Cornell elaborates his dark obsessions to Frankie Christopher (Victor Mature). Carole Landis also gets to sings a song, "The Thing I

Victor Mature (left), Laird Cregar and Betty Grable in 20th Century–Fox's *I Wake Up Screaming* (1942) which was previewed in October 1941 under the title *Hot Spot*.

Love," while Betty Grable's musical number, singing to a record in a musical store, was deleted during the editing of the film.

The casting of Grable and her role as the sweet sister of the murdered woman, Vicky Lynn counterpoints the film's theme of sexual obsession leading to murder. As Glenn Erickson points out: "Putting Grable in a *noir* seems almost a contradiction. She glides through scenes with perfect, I mean *perfect*, hair (count the comb lines on her temples) and remains a pastry bon-bon no matter what happens to her."[218] Similarly, Dwight Taylor's screenplay emasculates some of the hard-edged tone of Fisher's novel. This is evident in the film's opening sequence which resembles the opening moment in *Murder, My Sweet* (1944). Frankie Christopher is being questioned by the police following the murder of Vicky Lynn. The lighting is harsh, the police are threatening, but Christopher is unfazed. The film proceeds into a flashback as Christopher explains how he met Vicky. The novel, on the other hand, is much tougher. After Christopher discovers Vicky's body, he is questioned at the police department:

The light was bright and hot and my eyes burned and there was sweat on my face and my tongue was thick and heavy. They kept smoking cigarettes and talking. They kept talking. I tried to make answers but my lips were parched and stuck together. I was thirsty and they picked up a spittoon and washed my face with the water in it. The water and the tobacco juice. I licked my lips with my dry tongue. I tried to see but I couldn't. The light was like the sun. It was like the desert and the sun. Now they jerked me to my feet and took me out in the hall. The pupils of my eyes were dilating but I still couldn't see anything. Somebody hit me. He smacked me right across the mouth. I felt the blood hot in between my teeth and I tried to suck it out and drink it. They hit me again. It felt like my jaw was broken. They hit me with fists. They took hold of my hair and bounced my head against the wall. They shook me up. They pulled me away from the wall and knocked me down. They picked me up and knocked me down again. I could feel the pain and the rising welts. All of my teeth were aching. That was the worst. All of my teeth kept aching at once. I had a mouth full of ache. My tongue was cut. My eyes were swollen. They knocked me down again and jerked me up. Some guy held me by the front of my shirt. My brown sports shirt. He pushed me backwards into the same room with the light. I choked on the smoke. I was bleeding like hell. They sat me down.

"You're going to hang, mister."[219]

The film was unwilling to risk its large budget and major stars on such a hard-edged presentation of the world. The film's hero, Frankie Christopher, does not capture Fisher's depiction of a vulnerable hero. Instead he is a fast-talking sports promoter who decides, along with a fading film star, Robin Ray (Alan Mowbray), and newspaper columnist Larry Evans (Allyn Joslyn) to promote waitress Vicky Lynn, Pygmalion style, into a celebrity. They succeed only too well, as she has no further use for them and decides to leave New York, and them, for Hollywood. However, just prior to her departure she is murdered. The chief investigating officer, Ed Cornell, seems convinced that Christopher killed Vicky and he begins persecuting the sports promoter.

The film's melodramatic basis is clear with Christopher the victim of an obsessive, powerful villain. He is assisted by the victim's sister Jill and they eventually expose the killer, the timid, pathetic switchboard operator Harry Williams (Elisha Cook, Jr.). Williams, like Cornell,[220] is obsessed with Vicky, and when she rejects him, he kills her. It is Ed Cornell and, to a minor degree, the sad switchboard operator Harry Williams, who go close to fulfilling what Alain Silver describes as an "example of the developing film noir style."[221] However, the film, except for a limited number of scenes, remains resolutely upbeat. An exception is an early morning scene when Christopher wakes up in his bed and notices Cornell sitting in a chair just watching him. Similarly, the film's climax exposes Cornell's sad, psychotic "shrine" to Vicki just prior to his suicide. The film, like the novel, closes on a romantic note with Jill and Frankie, now married, dancing in a night club.

Dorothy Hughes and The Fallen Sparrow (1943)

RKO's 1943 adaption of Dorothy Hughes's 1942 novel The Fallen Sparrow is usually overlooked[222] in studies of film noir.[223] Like Stranger on the Third Floor it does not fit neatly into the historical development of noir. It should have been released three or four years later during the post-war film cycle that focused on veterans returning to mainstream society with psychological problems caused by the war— such as The Blue Dahlia, Somewhere in the Night, Crack-up, The High Wall, Crossfire, Ride the Pink Horse and The Crooked Way. The focus in The Fallen Sparrow is on a war hero suffering from post-traumatic stress at a time when the United States was battling for its survival. The Office of War Information and other government

John Garfield as Kit McKittrick, the psychologically troubled veteran from the Spanish Civil War, combating Nazi agents, including Toni Donne (Maureen O'Hara), in RKO's 1943 adaptation of the Dorothy Hughes novel *The Fallen Sparrow*.

agencies normally frowned on such films that did not dramatize the importance of the war effort—especially films that showed the damaging legacy of war (the Spanish Civil War). *The Fallen Sparrow* is a remarkable film for a 1943 release as screenwriter Warren Duff, in his adaptation of Hughes's novel, does not shy away from concentrating the drama on a traumatized hero battling his doubts and anxieties.

Released in New York on August 19, 1943, *The Fallen Sparrow* was a box-office and critical success. *Variety* listed it as one of the top grossing films in 1943 with $1.5 million in rentals in the United States. RKO purchased the rights to Hughes's novel soon after its publication in 1942 and the studio spent months casting the lead role of John "Kit" McKittrick, an American volunteer in the Spanish Civil War (on the defeated Loyalist side) who is tortured for two years by Nazi agents in Spain. After James Cagney, Cary Grant, Randolph Scott and George Brent refused the role, RKO borrowed John Garfield from Warners as part of an exchange whereby RKO traded the film rights to *Of Human Bondage* and *The Animal Kingdom* for Garfield and Joan Leslie for the Fred Astaire musical *The Sky's the Limit* (1943). The producer of *The Fallen Sparrow*, Robert Fellows, defied opposition from RKO executive William Gordon, who was worried about the political context of the film, specifically the possibility of offending Spain. Fellows ignored suggestions from Gordon to transfer the story to German Occupied France.[224] Joseph Breen also opposed the film on the same grounds.

The novel begins with descriptions of Kit McKittrick's reaction to the torture he suffered in a Spanish prison from Nazi agents acting on the orders from the "little man" in Berchtesgaden (Hitler)[225]:

> It was the Wobblefoot!
> Quivering, he [Kit] scuttled to the far corner, pressed frenziedly against the dirt wall. The deformed steps pounded against his eardrums. He thirsted…. He couldn't endure it. He'd have to tell. But he couldn't tell.
> He didn't want to die. He wanted to live.[226]

The film, unlike the novel, begins in November 1940 with a prologue that warns "in a world at war many sparrows must fall." It shows Kit (John Garfield), after five months convalescing from a nervous breakdown on an Arizona ranch, returning to Manhattan following the death of a close friend, policeman Lieutenant Louie Lepetino. Two years of torture in Spain, which only ended when he escaped from the Fascist prisoner-of-war camp, left him severely traumatized. As he reads a newspaper report of Lepetino's "accidental" death, after "falling" from a New York building, the train enters a tunnel and Kit's anxious face is suddenly reflected in the train's window. As he looks at the image of himself, the image of a divided character, his narration articulates the film's major discourse, Kit's battle with himself: "Hide! Go on! Let's have it! Can you go through with it? Have you got the guts for it? Can you go through with it or have they made you yellow?"

Kit's "double image" encapsulates the twin discourses running through the narrative—the internalized plot involving Kit's psychological battle with himself and the external plot, the melodramatic "surface" plot, concerning Nazi spies infiltrating New York. Kit visits Inspector Tobin (John Miljan), the officer in charge of the investigation into Lepetino's death. He dismisses Kit as a dilettante and tells him to return to his fancy friends in Manhattan. Kit rejects the advice and visits an old friend, Ab Parker (Bruce Edwards), who invites him to share his apartment in Manhattan. Without support from the police, Kit begins the investigation himself and this takes him back into Manhattan society, including his former girlfriend Barby Taviton (Patricia Morison) and singer Whitney ("The Imp") Parker (Martha O'Driscoll).

Warren Duff's screenplay improves Hughes's novel by stripping away some of her convoluted plot digressions, while also changing the names of some of the characters: "Wobblefoot," the chief Nazi villain, becomes a German sadist (Christian Skaas) with a deformed foot and Content Hamilton becomes Whitney Parker. Duff also eliminates Kit's mother and stepfather while making subtle changes to the ending of the film. And, importantly, Duff adds additional scenes to strengthen the battle taking place inside Kit's tortured mind. At his first meeting with Ab in the film, Kit describes his experience in the prison camp:

> It was pretty tough. First you didn't think you could take it. Then you did. It was as if somebody stuffed you in a bottle and put the cork in. It was dark and hot [the low-level camera slowly moves in towards Kit's face as the bright lighting reveals the sweat forming]. You lived mostly by sounds … water dripping in the hall [Roy Webb's score[227] reinforces the actual sound of a dripping tap on the soundtrack] … wait for the boot to come and the drag of that foot [Webb's

score simulates the sound of a boot dragging along the floor]. When that came you knew they would take you upstairs and beat you up and do their little tricks [Webb's score continues to simulate the noise of a scraping boot] … you heard the drag of that foot, you try to hide against the wall or crawl into a hole only there wasn't a hole to crawl into. You try to hide in the corner and feel like a dog that's been whipped and cupped…. I couldn't take it anymore. I have to tell. I [Ab interjects as Kit's torment threatens to get out of control].

This scene, which is not in the novel, is repeated in different ways throughout the film. The longest, and most effective, example of Kit's psychological trauma occurs when he is alone in Ab's apartment at night. He discovers the note he sent to Louie pleading to him to get him out of the Spanish prison along with Louie's badge. They trigger painful memories and a breakdown as the note in his pocket confirms that the Fascists are watching him in Manhattan. The effectiveness of this scene, without dialogue, is conveyed by Garfield's emotional response accompanied by Webb's "psychological" score simulating the sounds Kit experienced in prison. The sounds are reinforced by Nicholas Musuraca's chiaroscuro lighting, with a very bright light on Kit's face against a dark background, Robert Wise's editing and Richard Wallace's direction that keeps the camera low and fluid. The scene begins with Kit's response to the discovery of the note. In an attempt to escape the sounds [in his head] he seeks solace in alcohol. As he reads his note his words are inserted on the screen: "You've got to help me out…. I cannot stand this much longer, sometimes I think I've lost my reason … please help me, Louie, please help me." The film cuts from an insert of the note to Kit's face as sweat begins to form while dripping water and a sliding boot are heard. These sounds intensify as he traces the sound of water to a tap to the kitchen. Kit continues to drink to, unsuccessfully, ease his torment. He then opens a window to let in the sounds of the city in another failed attempt to stifle the noises in his head. The scene ends with Kit pounding on a piano, in a manic fashion, in a futile attempt to achieve peace with himself.

Later, when searching for the sound of the scrapping boot in the apartment of Ab's cousin, singer Whitney Parker (Martha O'Driscoll), he nearly collapses in her clothes closet, an incident he subsequently describes to her:

You don't hear it. It isn't there, it's in your head, like the doc said. All right, suppose it is there, what are you afraid of? You're in New York now. This isn't Spain…. You've got to find out. You've got to get hold of yourself. What did you come back for? To hide because you hear the sound?

He then goes outside the apartment to check the [empty] hallway and looks down at his trembling hand. When he asks Whitney if she also hears the sound [of the boot dragging across the floor] she tells him no and that he will "be back at the ranch [in Arizona] if you keep on like this!"

The film gradually dovetails Kit's inner torment with the source of his anxieties. His psychological fears take a more literal form as he begins to suspect a group of refugees seeking the information he refused to divulge in the Spanish prison—the location of the battle standard [the Babylon Goblets in the novel] of Kit's Loyalist brigade in Spain. Hitler, or the "little man in Berlin," is determined to recover the standard as it belonged to the brigade that killed a general close to Hitler. The Fascist leader subsequently vowed to kill all those responsible for the general's death and

hang the brigade's standard on his wall. Only Kit knows where it is hidden. Kit's paranoia never weakens, especially after he learns from Whitney's pianist Anton (John
Banner), that he never really escaped from his Spanish prison—the Fascists let him
escape so that they could keep him under constant surveillance through Spain, on
the ranch in Arizona and in New York.

The "refugees" include noted "Norwegian" historian Dr. Christian Skaas (Walter Slezak), a crippled academic with a special interest in the history of torture, his
nephew Otto Skaas (Hugh Beaumont) and Toni Donne (Maureen O'Hara), the
granddaughter of Prince Francois de Namur (Sam Goldenburg), another refugee,
along with Whitney's piano-playing accompanist Anton. In fashionable Manhattan society, these "refugees" are sponsored by wealthy patrons such as the Tavitons,
headed by Kit's former girlfriend Barby Taviton. The Nazis also install an agent,
Roman (Erford Gage), in Ab's apartment to monitor Kit.

There are three important scenes involving this group. The first takes place at
the Tavitons's home where Christian Skaas describes, with great relish, the effectiveness of various methods of torture. This has a detrimental effect on Kit, stirring up
memories of his recent torture in Spain which is the exact effect intended by Skaas.
However, it has the opposite effect on Barby, who becomes (sexually) excited by
his descriptions of torture. The second gathering occurs at the palatial residence of
Prince Francois de Namur, the place where Lepetino supposedly committed suicide.
Here the prince shows Kit his family banners and invites him to drink a toast from
a set of goblets bearing the medallion of the Lion of San Rafael. Wary of being poisoned, or drugged, Kit insists that they exchange goblets before drinking. The third
gathering, the climax of the film, also takes place at Prince Francois's residence where
Whitney performs the melodramatic musical number "Tsigane," described in the
novel as "vicious. There's madness in it—and death."[228] It was the song sung by Whitney when Lepetino supposedly committed suicide.

Donne invites Kit to the function where she promises to give him an answer as
to whether she is prepared to renounce her allegiance to the Nazi agents and join
him. However, as Whitney performs the "Tsigane" to the assembled guests, Toni
betrays Kit by setting up a trap where Christian Skaas, having drugged Kit's drink,
threatens him with an injection of a truth serum. Skaas, no longer wheelchair bound,
approaches Kit in a darkened study with a hypodermic needle as Kit struggles to
remain conscious. However, Kit, slumped over a desk, manages to shoot Skaas,
thereby killing his Spanish tormenter. Kit gives Toni one last chance to leave the
Nazis after she tells him that the Germans are holding her young daughter. He tells
her to join him in a Chicago hotel. Toni, again, deceives Kit by boarding a flight to
Lisbon to rejoin the Germans. Kit has her arrested and takes her place on the flight to
recover the battle standard which is hidden in a hotel in Spain. As the police escort
Toni, who he loves, from the plane Kit observes: "another sparrow has fallen."

Nicholas Musuraca's high contrast lighting, Richard Wallace's low angle compositions, Roy Webb's "psychological" score, Kit's torment, Barby Taviton's "decadence,"
and Christian Skaas's sadism shift the film from the external to the internal, from the
realm of action/thrills to the psychological. There is, of course, a melodramatic plot
involving Nazi spies interspersed with an occasional burst of patriotism regarding

the need to defeat Fascism. But this film is not, on the whole, a sensational melodrama. It is not an espionage film. The ending has shades of both *The Maltese Falcon* and *Casablanca*—depending on your interpretation of Toni Donne. Is she a femme fatale or a victim? Or both? Finally, despite her claim that she has a child in Germany and must get back to protect her, Kit is unwilling to take the risk and jeopardize the war effort. So, he has her arrested and they exchange glances in the final sequence of images as the police take her away. The last image is a close-up of Donne's anguished face as she watches Kit leave on the clipper to Lisbon.

The New York Times August 20, 1943, review of the film, merely signed "T.S.," argued that out "of a bizarre idea, RKO has produced a strange and restless melodrama that opened yesterday at the Palace." The film "emerges as one of the uncommon and provocatively handled melodramas of recent months." In complimenting the film, the review congratulated the director, Richard Wallace, for the way he used both soundtrack and camera to suggest stress in Kit's "fear-drenched mind":

> A street lamp shining through a fire escape throws a lattice across a sweating face; in a shadowy room, the remembered footsteps mingle with the tinkle of a bell and become the sound of dripping water from a leaking faucet. And again, when the climax is being quietly prepared at a refugee gathering in a mansion, the strident strains and swirling skirts of a gypsy dancer brush momentarily across the silence between the warring opponents.

Dorothy Hughes and Ride the Pink Horse *(1947)*

Ride the Pink Horse, published in 1946, is arguably Hughes's masterpiece. It shares Hammett's nihilistic view of a world devoid of meaning. Yet Universal's 1947 film adaptation, by Ben Hecht, Charles Lederer and, without screen credit, Joan Harrison, reworks her novel into an ethical melodrama, restoring the moral legibility that the novel denies. While the film retains the bare bones of Hughes's plot, a hard-boiled protagonist seeking revenge against a powerful man, the moral context and characterizations are very different. A comparison between the film and the novel provides a stark example of how Hollywood consistently resisted, and reworked, novels that subverted the tenets of melodrama.

Hughes's novel begins, like the film, with her protagonist, called "Sailor," arriving in a border town, after a long, hot, dusty trip by bus from Chicago. His frustration and anger intensify when he discovers that the town's hotels are full, due to the local Fiesta. The target of his visit, a wealthy senator, has secured accommodation at the only high-class hotel in town, the *La Fonda*. Sailor's rage and sense of alienation escalate as he is virtually powerless in this strange, alien culture. He hates the town ("stupid hick town"), the locals, the Mexicans ("spics") and the indigenous inhabitants, the "Indians," as Hughes, filtering the story through the bigoted eyes of Sailor, piles on the racist epithets. Sailor expresses no interest in the Fiesta (or its origins) as he only wants to collect what he feels is owed to him by the Senator (the "Sen") and get out of town as quickly as possible. With this money he plans to go to Mexico and buy a hotel. Nothing goes to plan. The presence of an American policeman, McIntyre, the head of Homicide in Chicago, only makes life more difficult as

McIntyre ("Mac") has a long history with Sailor. Both grew up in the same impoverished neighborhood. McIntyre's aim is to get Sailor to join him in bringing the Senator to justice for killing his wife.

Despite the wide-open spaces of New Mexico, Hughes's novel presents Sailor
trapped in this small border town. This is effectively conveyed by the repetitive, cir-
cular structure of the novel as Sailor moves back and forth in the same locations
meeting the same people again and again. Amidst the superficial gaiety of the Fiesta,
a dark undercurrent permeates her story involving young girls from bordering villages who paint themselves up to attract young boys, and visitors, for sex on the lawn
in front of the Federal Building at night. The Senator, with his money and influence,
is always just out of reach of Sailor who is forced to keep on the move, covering the
same landscape again and again:

> He rounded the corner and retraced his way up the slight hill. He turned left and continued
> down the street. There must be some place with a room for him. … He walked on in the dark-
> ness, the shops growing meaner, the way more dark…. Murky bars with muted sounds and
> sounds not muted, acrid smell of cheap liquor stanching your nostrils…. Dark little houses,
> country, vacant fields. Beyond that, mountains….
>
> And standing there the unease came upon him again. The unease of an alien land, of dark-
> ness and silence, of strange tongues and stranger people, of unfamiliar smells, even the
> cool-of-night smell unfamiliar. What sucked into his pores for that moment was panic
> although he could not have put a name to it. The panic of loneliness, of himself the stranger
> although he was unchanged, the creeping loss of identity. It sucked into his pores and it oozed
> out again, clammy in the chill of night.[229]

Sailor is trapped in this hostile labyrinth, an "alien wasteland" of revelers, children, young girls, drunks, Mexican assassins, McIntyre, the Senator and his mistress.
They all gather to witness the symbolic death of Zozobra, a forty-foot-tall pup-
pet made of papier-mâché and dirty sheets "with a misshapen head, hollow eyes,
pointed flapping ears, shapeless flapping mouth … [and] giant clawlike hands."[230] To
the locals Zozobra is the personification of evil and its "death" represents the end of
gloom, the cleansing of the society. The burning of Zozobra, however, has the opposite effect on Sailor as he watches the reaction of the crowd while the body of the pup-
pet disintegrates,

> where that hideous groaning face floated above the fire and smoke and noise, above the crowd's
> lust for destruction of evil. In destroying evil, even puppet evil, these merrymakers were
> turned evil. He saw the faces, dark and light, rich and poor, great and small, old and young.
> Fire-shadowed, their eyes glittered with the appetite to destroy. He saw and he was suddenly
> frightened. He wanted to get away.[231]

Sailor's only companions are a Mexican, whom he naturally calls "Pancho," and
Pila, a fourteen-year-old Indian girl. Pancho proudly operates "Tio Vivo," the fes-
tival's merry-go-round for children. While racially demeaning both Pancho and
Pila, Sailor takes a liking to the young girl and offers to buy her a ride on Tio Vivo.
Although the ride is closed, Pancho accepts a dollar from Sailor and encourages Pila
to ride the pink horse:

> He felt like a dope after saying it. What difference did it make to him what wooden horse an
> Indian kid rode? …the pink horse was the colored lights and the tink of music and the sweet,
> cold soda pop.[232]

Sailor is not sure why giving Pila a ride on the pink horse is so important. Was it, he speculates, "placating an old and nameless terror"[233] as Pila's "black stone eyes"[234] remind him of a teen-age experience when his teacher took the class to an Art Institute where one of the exhibits, the granite head of a woman, evoked genuine fear in him:

> He had known fear, real fear, for the first time in his life as he'd stood there. He thought he'd known it before. Fear of the old man's drunken strap, fear of the old woman's whining complaints. Fear of the cop and the clap and the red eyes of the rats that came out of the walls at night. Fear of death and hell. Those were real fears but nothing like the naked fear that paralyzed him before the stone woman. Because with the other things he was himself, he could fight back, he had identity. Before her, his identity was lost, lost in the formless terrors older than time.[235]

While not dismissing the physical threat to Sailor from the Senator and his men, the novel is more concerned with the existential threat to Sailor. When the Senator's men injure Sailor in a knife attack, he is saved by the Mexican. Yet nothing can salvage Sailor's psychological disintegration during the Fiesta. Obsessed by a desire for money, he refuses to assist McIntyre's attempts to bring the Senator to justice. Instead, Sailor kills the Senator. Panic stricken, he searches for Pancho to help him but when McIntyre tracks him down, Sailor pleads with the policeman that it was self-defense. McIntyre agrees but tells him:

> You don't want to go straight. You turned your back on the right way a long time ago. You chose the wrong way, the easy way.... Twice as tough as it would have been if you'd taken the right turn a long time ago. Too tough for you. You couldn't take it.[236]

Once again, McIntyre offers to help Sailor and will testify that Senator Douglass pulled his gun out first and that Sailor was helping to bring him in. Although Sailor's record will probably result in some jail time, McIntyre says he will assist him after he gets out. Sailor, however, rejects McIntyre's offer: "Sailor got to his feet, slowly listening to words, words that were like dream words, like in a bad dream."[237] Again, for the last time, Sailor makes the wrong decision and reasons that beyond "the mountains was freedom,"[238] where he could make it across the border to Mexico, join with his partner and become "big shots in no time."[239] So Sailor shoots Mac and the novel ends with Sailor running blindly into the desert:

> Sailor was weeping as he ran, weeping for Mac. No sound stirred behind him, there was no sound in the night but his running steps, his tears. ... It was too late.
>
> He ran on, into open country this quickly; plunging into the wastes of endless land and sky, stretching forever, for eternity, to the far-off barrier of the mountains. The night was cold, colder than before. All he had to do was keep moving on and on until he reached the mountains. On the the other side was freedom. Escape from this dread dream.
>
> *You can't get away.* It couldn't be Mac he heard pitying, Mac was dead. *You can't get away.* Blindly he stumbled on.[240]

The film adaptation changed Hughes's story into a tale of moral reformation involving the re-assimilation of a disillusioned veteran back into society—the reverse of the novel. It changed Sailor, a gangster, into Gagin, a disillusioned veteran returning to society. He travels to New Mexico, and the border town of San Pablo, to blackmail war profiteer Frank Hugo (Fred Clark) into exchanging an incriminating

Young Pila (Wanda Hendrix) assists the badly wounded veteran Lucky Gagin (Robert Montgomery) in Universal's *Ride the Pink Horse* (1947). The film was based on Dorothy Hughes's 1946 novel and it was directed by Robert Montgomery and produced by Joan Harrison.

cancelled check for money. His motivation is not just money but to avenge the death of a wartime buddy, Shorty Thompson, murdered by Hugo's men. In the novel Sailor avoided military service due to the influence of the Senator who was his benefactor at that time. Gagin, like Sailor, is initially intolerant of Mexicans and the local indigenous people. But, unlike Sailor, he undergoes a transformation and learns the error of his ways and comes to trust "Pancho" (Thomas Gomez) and Pila (Wanda Hendrix), a young indigenous girl. In the film's climax he has to depend on Pila and government agent Bill Retz (Art Smith) to save him from Hugo and his men after he is badly wounded.

A similar transformation involves Pila in the film as she becomes Gagin's moral compass. While she disappears about two-thirds into the novel, the film elevates her into a moral sign of pristine innocence and absolute knowledge.[241] With her assistance, the reformation of Gagin is rendered complete when he rejects the money from Hugo and gives the incriminating check to Retz. Hugo, in berating Gagin for being a "sucker," spells out the film's moral values:

> This guy [Gagin] makes me laugh. His idea of big money! He's got me right where it hurts
> and all he asks for is 30 grand. Guys like you work all their lives breaking their backs trying to
> earn meat and potatoes. You end up borrowing enough money to buy a hole in the ground to

be buried in. Then, when a chance to make some real scratch, what do you do? Mice like you and Shorty. You ask for peanuts. You know what's going to happen when you get out of here. He's [Retz] going to give you a lot of gas about duty and honor. Fill you with fancy words like responsibility, patriotism. That's how he's going to get that check. And what are you going to have? Nothing! … All your life you waste time worrying about small fry things. About a job, about a two buck raise, about getting a pension….

The climax to the novel, unlike the film, makes it clear that Sailor has no intention of living by these values. Instead of cooperating with the policeman (Mac), he dreams of forming a partnership with his friend Ziggy in Mexico where "they'd be big shots in no time, white Palm Beach suits and the best hotel suites and dames hanging around their necks. That was better than stir or grubbing in a factory all your life. Mac was nuts."[242]

The novel exposes the futility of Sailor's dream. Just as Jeff Bailey discovers in *Out of the Past,* there is no escape for Sailor: "you can't get away."

Out of the Past[243]/Build My Gallows High

> INT. GAMBLING ROOM—NIGHT
> This is a small room. There is a dice and roulette table. The players are mostly American….
> At the roulette table, Kathie is playing and Jeff stands beside her, hands in his pockets, hat tilted back a little …He is watching her as she lays a stack of chips on the number thirteen.
> JEFF: That isn't the way to play it.
> KATHIE: Why not?
> JEFF: Because it isn't the way to win.
> KATHIE: Is there a way to win?
> JEFF: There's a way to lose more slowly.
> —Scene 44 from Frank Fenton's screenplay for *Out of the Past*. The Final Script, October 24, 1946

Dore Schary, after he assumed control of production at RKO, never had high expectations for *Out of the Past*. The studio released the film in November 1947 on a double bill with a re-release of the 1936 Fred Astaire–Ginger Rogers musical *Follow the Fleet*.[244] Most of the cast shared Schary's expectations and little money was spent on promoting the film despite the fact that it attracted positive reviews. In essence, it was regarded as just one of 40 films released by the studio that year. Richard Jewell, in the second part of his financial history of RKO, points out that while *Out of the Past* was a film the studio "had almost completely overlooked…. It would eventually be recognized as one of the best RKO movies of them all."[245] Andrew Sarris, in his 1968 book *The American Cinema: Directors and Directions 1929–1968*, lauded Jacques Tourneur and described *Out of the Past* as Tourneur's masterpiece, "a civilized treatment of an annihilating melodrama."[246] *Variety*, in its November 19, 1947, review, described the film as a "hard-boiled melodrama strong on characterization."

Out of the Past was based on Geoffrey Homes's novel *Build My Gallows High*. Homes was the pseudonym for Daniel Mainwaring. After RKO studio reader Bill Koenig read Mainwaring's novel in September 1945 he recommended the studio purchase it while expressing his delight at the story's "intricate tale of love, lust, and deception." He described it as a "worthy addition to the rough, tough school of Chandler, Cain and Burnett."[247] Although Koenig suggested Bogart for the lead role, Warners would not release him. John Garfield was approached and after initially indicating he was interested, dropped out as did Dick Powell. Producer Warren Duff then offered the role to contract player Robert Mitchum. It was Mitchum's first lead role at the studio and it is now hard to imagine the film without him as Jeff Bailey.

RKO paid Mainwaring $20,000 for the rights and he was hired to write the screenplay. Unfortunately Mainwaring's screenplay incorporated some bizarre ideas, including a suggestion that the "Kid," Jeff Bailey's deaf-mute assistant, narrate the film.[248] Mainwaring also suggested that Jeff and Kathie (Mumsie in his script and in his novel) meet when he saves her from a shark attack in the Pacific Ocean.[249] Duff and director Jacques Tourneur rejected these ideas and Duff hired James M. Cain, at a cost of $16,666.67,[250] to rework Mainwaring's draft. Cain ignored Mainwaring's contribution and wrote a new story. He submitted two drafts, one on March 11, 1946, and another on April 3, 1946. He also renamed the femme fatale Maisie Clemmens, a facsimile of Phyllis Dietrichson from *Double Indemnity*.[251] He put forward two options with regard to the ending. The first was a "happy ending that wraps everything up neatly,"[252] with Maisie sent to the electric chair and Jeff about to marry Ann. His second option concludes with Jeff shooting Maisie and the police then killing Jeff.[253] Duff rejected both and Cain did not receive a screen credit. Duff then offered the project to British born novelist, script writer, and script "doctor" Frank Fenton to carry out a major revision of Mainwaring's draft. Fenton was

Jane Greer and Robert Mitchum in Jacques Tourneur's *Out of the Past* (1947). The film was based on the novel *Build My Gallows High* by Geoffrey Homes (aka Daniel Mainwaring).

paid $8,333.33 which was considerably less than Cain and Mainwaring. The latter was paid $11,083.33 for his work on the script.[254] Fenton did not receive a screen credit although much of the film, especially the brittle dialogue, is his work.

Filming took place from October 23, 1946, to January 9, 1947, and included location filming in the small town of Bridgeport in the Sierra Nevada Mountains and surrounding areas such as the Sonora Pass and Lake Tahoe. The Acapulco beach scenes were filmed at the Leo Carrillo Beach in Malibu. Prior to the start of filming director Jacques Tourneur was concerned about the convoluted nature of the plot and feared that audiences would not be able to follow it. He subsequently claimed he "made big changes, with the agreement of the writer."[255] The film's complex plotting, with multiple characters and both shifts in time, due to the extended use of flashbacks, and changes in the settings, also worried reviewers such as *New York Times* critic Bosley Crowther. Even Robert Mitchum became confused and at one point he said to Jane Greer, "I think we lost three pages in mimeo. Don't tell anybody."[256]

The film begins with Whit Sterling's henchman Joe Stefanos (Paul Valentine) pressuring ex-private detective Jeff Bailey (Robert Mitchum), who runs a small gas station in Bridgeport, to visit Sterling (Kirk Douglas) in Lake Tahoe. As he travels to Tahoe, Bailey explains to his girlfriend Ann Miller (Virginia Huston) how he was involved with Sterling and his girlfriend Kathie Moffat (Jane Greer). His flashback focuses on his relationship with Kathie in Acapulco and how he helped her escape from Sterling. The gangster wanted her returned, as she shot him, and, he claimed, stole $40,000. They escaped to San Francisco and lived happily until Jack Fisher, Jeff's former partner in his New York private detective agency, discovered them and tried to blackmail Jeff. During a fight between Jeff and Fisher, Kathie shot Fisher and abandoned Jeff, leaving him to dispose of Fisher's body. He also found Kathie's bank account book which confirmed that she stole $40,000 from Sterling.

The extended flashback ends at Sterling's Lake Tahoe house where Jeff learns that Kathie has returned to the gangster. He also discovers that Kathie testified that he (Bailey) killed Fisher. As a consequence he is blackmailed into accepting Sterling's demand that he obtain incriminating tax records from Leonard Eels (Ken Niles) in San Francisco. Eels' secretary/mistress, Meta Carson (Rhonda Fleming), also working for Sterling, is supposedly helping him. However, Carson and Kathie, with Whit's knowledge, attempt to frame Bailey after Eels is murdered. In an effort to extricate himself from this set-up, Jeff acquires Sterling's incriminating tax records. He returns to Lake Tahoe and tells the gangster to let Kathie take the fall for Fisher's death. For this, plus $50,000 in cash, Jeff agrees to return Sterling's tax documents. Just as Jeff is about to extricate himself his plan goes astray when Kathie murders Sterling. Now in control, she tells Jeff she wants to resume their affair in Mexico. When she leaves the room, Jeff phones the police who set up an ambush. When Kathie realizes that Jeff has betrayed her, she shoots him and the police kill her. In the film's epilogue, Ann returns to a local man, Jim Caldwell (Richard Webb), after the Kid lies and tells her that Jeff was planning to run away with Kathie.

Out of the Past is often grouped with films featuring hard-boiled detectives such as *The Maltese Falcon, Murder, My Sweet* and *The Big Sleep* (1946). *Out of the Past* shares very little with these films. The focus in *Out of the Past* is not exposing the killer and solving the crime but on the inability of the central protagonist to escape from the destructive impact of fate. In this sense the film has more in common with Woolrich's tales of romantic longing and despair. Unlike Sam Spade or Philip Marlowe, Jeff Bailey is never in control. His sense of bewilderment is reinforced by the film's convoluted narrative, multiple locations including rural Bridgeport (California), New York, Mexico City, Acapulco and San Francisco, and a lengthy flashback sequence. Finally he realizes that it is pointless to struggle any further. This occurs after he discovers Whit Sterling's body in his Lake Tahoe house. His plan to return to Ann with $50,000 and recover the affidavit that will exonerate him is no longer a possibility, as described in Fenton's script:

> CLOSE on Jeff. His expression saddens as he realizes that his world has come down around his ears.
>
> Kathie appears:
>
> KATHIE's VOICE (QUIET): You can't make deals with a dead man.
>
> Jeff turns slowly. CAMERA ANGLES PAST him to reveal Kathie standing in the door leading into the library. She is dressed for traveling.
>
> KATHIE: Let's get out of here.
>
> JEFF: Is there some place left to go?
>
> KATHIE: I think so.
>
> JEFF: You're running the show now?
>
> KATHIE: I'm running the show.
>
> He turns and smiles a little and follows her.
>
> EXT. TERRACE—NIGHT
>
> As they come out on the terrace. Kathie stops and looks at the dark mountains.
>
> KATHIE: Remember the mountains, higher than these and always snow on them?
>
> JEFF: I am trying to remember something else.
>
> KATHIE: (puts a hand on his arm) I know it won't be the same at first. But after a while it will be—because I haven't changed.
>
> JEFF: No, you haven't.
>
> KATHIE: I never told you I was anything but what I am. You just wanted to imagine I was, and that's why I left you …Now we're back—to stay.

She tells Jeff that the affidavit is useless, Whit's dead, along with Fisher, Eels and Stefanos.

> KATHIE: Someone has to take the blame. They've nothing on me. But I'll make a fine witness—for the Prosecution. (sweetly) Don't you see? There's only me to make deals with now.
>
> JEFF: Build my gallows high, baby.
>
> KATHIE: No … we're starting all over. I want to go back to Mexico. I want to walk in the sun again and find you waiting. I want to sit in the same moonlight and tell you the things I never told you … until you don't hate me, and until some time you love again.
>
> JEFF: They'll always be looking for us. They'll never stop till we die.
>
> KATHIE: I don't care—just so they find us together.
>
> She puts her arms around him and he stands there, not holding her, his face a mask except for a slight cynical smile of defeat.

After telling him that "we deserve each other," Kathie leaves the room and Jeff phones the police. When she returns Jeff tosses his wine "glass into the fireplace and takes her arm while she watches his face, curiously, half smiling, as they go out." They die on a mountain road.

Why does Jeff die? In a melodrama people normally die because they transgress society's institutional rules or the prevailing moral values. Or they die to sacrifice themselves for the greater good, such as the protagonists in the combat films released after the Japanese attack on Pearl Harbor. Jeff does not fit into these categories. Unlike the novel, he does not kill anyone. He did bury Fisher's body but this was a relatively minor infraction and could have been explained as protecting Kathie. He did not break any marital vows unlike like the male protagonists in films such as *Pitfall, The Chase, The Macomber Affair, The File on Thelma Jordon, The Big Clock, Where Danger Lives* and *Human Desire*—and they survived. And he did not die trying to save someone. Unlike Sam Spade, he did betray his "private eye code" by deceiving Whit Sterling, in part to protect Kathie from his vengeance. In other words, the film's logic repudiates melodrama's central function by denying any sense of poetic justice.

Frank Krutnik argues that Jeff's crime was that he violated "the whole regime of masculine authority"[257] through his inability to control Kathie. Daniel Mainwaring admitted in an interview in 1972 that the characterizations and themes in *Out of the Past* owe much to *The Maltese Falcon*.[258] While Sam Spade lusted after Brigid O'Shaughnessy, he never deceived himself as to her true nature. Not so Jeff Bailey. As Kathie points out to him: "I never told you I was anything but what I am. You just wanted to imagine I was." Krutnik argues that Jeff's fall resides in his "desire to escape his responsibilities and the power of patriarchal law."[259] This is clear when he cedes his masculine "authority" to her on the beach to Acapulco. Knowing that she probably stole the $40,000 from Sterling, he tells her "Baby, I don't care" after she denies stealing the money.

Out of the Past provides a stark moral contrast between the two women: one "good" (Ann), the other "bad" (Kathie). The conventional, almost mandatory outcome was for the "bad" woman to die leaving the virtuous woman for the hero (*Street of Chance, Leave Her to Heaven, Pitfall, Where Danger Lives, Human Desire*). This was one option in James M. Cain's draft screenplay where Jeff is reunited with Ann after the death of the femme fatale. One of the reasons why *Out of the Past* is remembered today is that, unlike most crime melodramas produced in the 1940s, this does not happen. Another reason is the film, unlike *The Stranger on the Third Floor, I Wouldn't Be in Your Shoes, The Chase, Ride the Pink Horse* and *The Woman in the Window*, never deviates from its central premise, the destructive impact of an unalterable fate. This is established in an early scene when Whit's henchman Joe Stefanos explains how he virtually stumbled upon Jeff in remote Bridgeport:

> JOE: Well, I'm driving down this road and who do I see pumping gasoline but my old chum from the old times—of course there's a different name on the sign.

Fate is Jeff Bailey's recurring enemy throughout the film. No matter how hard he tries he cannot extricate himself. After Jeff and Kathie leave Acapulco for San Francisco he resumes his vocation as a private detective and opens an office.

> JEFF: It was a cheap little rathole that suited the work that I did—shabby jobs for whoever'd hire me. It was the bottom of the barrel and I scraped it, but I didn't care. [a grim smile] I had her.

After hiding out in out of the way places like "little movie houses in North Beach," they begin to drift back to "more familiar places … the ball parks and the race tracks. Why not? After all, there wasn't one chance in a million we'd bump into our past." At a race meeting at Bay Meadows, Jeff's narration repeats the ominous warning, "one chance in a million." After he makes a winning bet, he grins at Kathie and heads towards the pay window:

> As Jeff stands in the line formed at the Pay Window. There is a line between his line and the next at the windows and in the far line he sees Jack Fisher [Jeff's former partner in his New York agency] waiting, just as Fisher sees him. Jeff hurriedly cashes in his tickets and leaves, while Fisher still waits behind a fat lady all balled up with her winning ducats.
>
> JEFF'S VOICE: One chance in a million was all that chump ever had in life … and he made it good. He just stood there with our lives in his pocket, because I know if he ever saw her he'd sell us both for a dollar ninety-five. (pause) And so we had to separate….

Alone, Jeff heads towards Los Angeles hoping Fisher would follow him. After a few days, believing he has lost his former partner, he returns to Kathie who is walking towards their little cabin off the highway at Pyramid Creek. He stops the car, takes her into his arms and "holds her long as she presses against him":

> JEFF'S VOICE: It was meeting her somewhere like in the first time … there was still that something about her that got me—a kind of magic or whatever it was. [pause] Well, I held her and we could laugh.

Fisher, however, did not follow Jeff, he followed Kathie. When Fisher tries to blackmail Jeff, a less attractive side of Kathie's personality emerges as she tells Jeff: "Why don't you break his head, Jeff?" Jeff is taken aback as the script notes: "there is a pause—now for the first time we will begin to really know Kathie." The two men fight until "a shot rings out." Jeff "stands there stunned. Slowly his eyes turn to Kathie. The pistol is in her hand. Her eyes are flashing. Excited. … We know from Jeff's manner that Fisher is dead. Kathie stands over him. Her eyes now are hard and cold, without emotion…. Jeff remains motionless. The death of Fisher; the growing realization that what he had always feared in Kathie is really there—has momentarily left him stunned."

Kathie leaves Jeff with Fisher's body and drives away. He picks up her bank book which confirms that she stole $40,000 from Sterling. He completes the flashback by telling Ann:

> JEFF: [quietly]I buried him up there. I wasn't sorry for him or sore at her.
> I wasn't anything.

Damien Love argues that *Out of the Past* was the film that "came close to defining him [Mitchum] and the whole noir style."[260] He writes that his

> dreamily sassy stoicism represented disenchantment raised to the abstract level of music. Action is something that he finds easy to resist. He knows he's turned his back completely on the world; but there's a *frisson*, because he can remember what it was like back there, and is encumbered, slightly, by the guilt and the hope in the memories….
>
> The Mitchum loser-hero always carried himself as though he was in control of events, either because, for all his wit, he was just dumb enough to believe that he was. Or maybe because he was smart enough to realise that it didn't really make any difference what he did, or what happened to him. Not in the long run.[261]

Jeff Bailey is not a melodramatic hero. He can only comment on his actions, never alter them. He is, as Andrew Spicer notes, a "passive" figure "enveloped in a coruscating fatalism."[262] For this reason *Out of the Past* is closer to tragedy than melodrama—not because Jeff dies, but because in the arbitrary world presented in the film he never had a chance. Fates that cannot be altered belong to tragedy, not melodrama.[263] While virtue exists in the film,[264] its moral significance is systematically degraded, its content is "nothingness."[265] As Jeff tells Ann, "I wasn't anything."

Criss Cross *(1949)*

Robert Siodmak's *Criss Cross* is similar to *Out of the Past.* Both films present protagonists doomed by cruel universe. This, in the case of *Criss Cross,* represents a stark change from its source novel by Don Tracy which was published in 1934 as *Criss-Cross.* The novel begins with broken down ex-boxer "Johnny Thompson," real name Benjamin S. Neischtadt, working as an armored guard for the Laird Armored Car Agency. Years of boxing have left Thompson with a facial disfigurement, a badly broken nose, that resulted in crowds calling him "Flat Nose." Thompson is in love with Anna Krebak, a woman who humiliates him on a regular basis. Professionally, he receives a boost after he prevents a hold-up which receives wide coverage in the local newspapers. Soon after, Anna, now married to gangster Slim Dundee, invites Johnny for a meal with her and Slim at their apartment. Anna's sudden interest in Johnny is, perversely, provoked by the fact that Johnny is forbidden fruit, as she is a married woman. He responds with a mixture of guilt and lust.

One night, after nearly catching Johnny with Anna, Slim makes Johnny a proposition to participate in the robbery of Johnny's armored truck. After explaining the details, he warns Johnny that he cannot afford not to participate. Despite some initial hesitation, Johnny agrees although he soon realizes that Slim plans to use the robbery as pretext to murder him. During the robbery Johnny kills Slim and becomes a hero after saving the company's payroll. He subsequently receives a series of promotions while continuing his sexual relationship with Anna. However, his mental condition deteriorates as he constantly hears Slim laughing at him from the grave. One night, arriving home ahead of schedule, after dreaming of becoming president of the company and having an operation to straighten his nose ("Maybe Anna would like me better with a straight nose"),[266] he discovers Slade, his younger brother, in Anna's bedroom. The novel concludes with Johnny's anguished cry, "I could hear Slim's bellowing laugh."[267]

Producer and screenwriter Mark Hellinger bought the rights to Don Tracy's novel with plans to produce the film by his newly formed Valley Studio company. Anthony Veiller wrote a draft screenplay where he changed the setting from an armored car robbery to a racetrack robbery. However, after Hellinger died on December 21, 1947, at the age of 44, the board of directors of his estate sold the property, which included the film rights to Tracy's novel as well as the contracts of director Robert Siodmak and Burt Lancaster, to Universal. Production began in June 1948 with a new script by Daniel Fuchs and, uncredited, William Bowers.

Burt Lancaster as Steve Thompson is obsessed with Yvonne DeCarlo as Anna Dundee in Robert Siodmak's *Criss Cross* (1949).

In the film adaptation "Flat Nose" Johnny Thompson (aka Benjamin S. Neischtadt) becomes tall and handsome Steve Thompson (Burt Lancaster); Anna Krebak, Polish, dark haired and beautiful, becomes Anna Dundee (Yvonne De Carlo), dark haired and beautiful; gangster Slim Dundee, "good looking, … [tall] and straight with wide shoulders and big hands,"[268] becomes shifty Slim Dundee (Dan Duryea); and Johnny's younger brother in the novel, Slade, who stutters and ultimately betrays Johnny, becomes dull, loyal and inconsequential Slade Thompson (Richard Long). The tone of Tracy's cynical, hard-boiled novel is transformed into a romantic tragedy involving Steve Thompson's doomed longing for a woman who puts her own needs above all others.

Siodmak disregarded Hellinger's plans for the film and, borrowing aspects of his 1932 German film *Stürme der Leidenschaft*, focused on the destructive impact of fate. This is conveyed by the film's spectacular opening sequence, a nighttime aerial shot that slowly moves along a busy street until the camera swoops into a parking lot to show Steve holding Anna, who tells him, "After it's over … it'll be just you and me … the way it should have been all along from the start." This theme is overtly articulated by Steve after his return to the family home in the working-class suburb of Bunker Hill in Los Angeles as he searches for his ex-wife, Anna. Eventually he finds her in their old night spot, the Round-Up Club. In one of the film's major set pieces, Siodmak employs

Yvonne DeCarlo as Anna Dundee is married to gangster Slim Dundee (Dan Duryea) in Robert Siodmak's *Criss Cross* (1949).

music, the exciting rhumba sounds of Esy Morales and his band, and clever editing as the images are cut to the music, to expose the depths of Steve's obsession with Anna as he watches her dance with a young man (Tony Curtis). The film cuts between her sensual movements and images of Steve's longing. As he returns to his family home his narration tells it all: "From the start, it went one way. It was in the cards, or it was fate, or a jinx, or whatever you want to call it, but right from the start."

After Steve and Anna, now married to Slim Dundee, are caught together in a comprising situation with Steve in his undershirt, Slim tells his wife: "Baby, it don't look right." To extricate Anna and himself, Steve tells the gangster that he called Anna to his house to discuss his plan to rob the armored car company. While Slim is initially skeptical, he becomes interested after Steve tells him he will be the inside man. With the help of Finchley (Alan Napier), an alcoholic criminal mastermind, they undertake the robbery during Steve's scheduled payroll run. After Dundee kills an elderly guard, Steve wounds the gangster and saves the payroll. Now a public hero, he wakes up in a hospital with his left shoulder immobilized. A friend, Lieutenant Pete Ramirez (Stephen McNally), although deeply suspicious of Steve's involvement in the robbery, warns him that Slim will send a hit man to kill him. This sets up a superbly executed representation of paranoia, an almost silent sequence. Siodmak, in a series of cleverly composed point of view shots that alternate from Steve, helpless

"CRISS X CROSS"

STARRING

BURT LANCASTER

YVONNE DeCARLO

DAN DURYEA

with
STEPHEN McNALLY
RICHARD LONG

Screenplay by
DANIEL FUCHS
Based upon the novel by
DON TRACY
Produced by
MICHEL KRAIKE
Directed by
ROBERT SIODMAK

A UNIVERSAL-INTERNATIONAL RE-RELEASE

Copyright 1958 by Universal Pictures Co., Inc.   Country of Origin U.S.A.   Property of National Screen Service Corp. Licensed for display only in connection with the exhibition of this picture at your theatre. Must be returned immediately thereafter.   R 58 \ 27

"CRISS X CROSS"

STARRING

BURT LANCASTER

YVONNE DeCARLO

DAN DURYEA

with
STEPHEN McNALLY
RICHARD LONG

Screenplay by
DANIEL FUCHS
Based upon the novel by
DON TRACY
Produced by
MICHEL KRAIKE
Directed by
ROBERT SIODMAK

A UNIVERSAL-INTERNATIONAL RE-RELEASE

Copyright 1958 by Universal Pictures Co., Inc.   Country of Origin U.S.A.   Property of National Screen Service Corp. Licensed for display only in connection with the exhibition of this picture at your theatre. Must be returned immediately thereafter.   R 58 27 in his hospital bed, to his view of the hospital corridor and a strange man, "Mr. Nelson" (Robert Osterloh), waiting outside, implicates the viewer in Steve's helplessness.

Steve begins to trust Nelson and asks him to watch his hospital door for intruders. This is just one more double cross in the film. Nelson kidnaps Steve, who bribes him to take him to a remote shack in Palos Verdes where Anna is waiting. As soon as Nelson drops Steve off at the shack, Anna realizes that Nelson will tell Slim where she and the money are located. She begins packing up and plans to abandon Steve after telling him that he has always had an unrealistic fantasy of her, and the world:

> STEVE: You loved me.
> ANNA: Love! Love! You have to watch out for yourself. That's the way it is. I'm sorry. What do you want me to do? Throw away all this money! You always have to do what is best for yourself. That's the trouble with you, it always was from the beginning. You just don't know what kind of world it is.
> STEVE [RUEFULLY]: I'll know better next time.

Dundee arrives before Anna can get away. After telling Steve that he also loved Anna, he shoots both of them just as the police arrive. As Glenn Erickson observes: "the shock of the last image [the body of Anna lying across Steve's body] is its lack of romantic embellishment. I'm surprised that anybody approved such a complete downer of an ending. Of course, it makes **Criss Cross** as fascinatingly morbid as any *film noir* on the books."[269]

The Criminal-Adventurer Melodrama and "Retributive, Purgative Terror"

The concept of virtue, however defined, is crucial to melodrama. A sense of virtue or innocence is integral to melodrama's bipolar clash between "good" and "evil." In sensational melodrama, the realm of moral absolutes, virtue is easily discerned. Not so with some "noir" films as virtue, criminal behavior and the inevitability of retribution are intertwined. These films are not whodunits as they are much closer to the gothic qualities of "retributive, purgative terror."[270] Cain, Cornell Woolrich, and Dorothy Hughes did not write whodunits as they, along with Steve Fisher and a few others, shifted the emphasis in the crime melodrama. It took Hollywood eight years to have the courage to confront Joseph Breen, thanks mainly to Billy Wilder, and bring Cain's sensibility to the screen. The effect on Hollywood and the crime melodrama was profound as the focus shifted from a clear demarcation between good characters and bad characters, between detectives and villains, to ordinary people who commit extraordinary crimes. In the process, Hollywood followed Cain's point of view of forcing audiences to share the criminal journey of these

Opposite, top: **Caught in a compromising situation with Anna Dundee (Yvonne DeCarlo), Steve Thompson (Burt Lancaster) is forced to devise a robbery plan to satisfy Anna's husband Slim (Dan Duryea) in** *Criss Cross* **(1949). Tom Pedi as Vincent, a member of Dundee's gang, is in the background.** *Bottom:* **Criminal mastermind Alan Napier (Finchley) works out the details of the armored car robbery with (from left) George Lynn (Andy), Dan Duryea and Burt Lancaster in** *Criss Cross* **(1949).**

Hollywood's Melodramatic Imagination

Yvonne DeCarlo and Burt Lancaster trapped at the climax in *Criss Cross* (1949).

people who, despite their crimes, were presented less as perpetrators and more as victims.[271]

Cain was never interested in the hard-boiled detective or stories about heroic cops. He did not write whodunits.[272] He removed the comforting presence of the detective-narrator who invariably played a mediating role between the reader and the corrupt world he moved in.[273] Instead he wrote about ordinary people who break society's moral codes for very basic reasons. They are haunted by the consequences of desire following their inability to contain their "aberrant" impulses. And, most importantly, his readers are forced to share their "aberrant" impulses and transgressions knowing that punishment was inevitable. As a consequence, they are inveigled into an alliance with them. The end result, writes Skenazy, is that we "begin to suspect not only the fallibility, but the immorality and inhumanity of 'justice.' A curious kind of order resolves each tale but it has little to do with law and far more with issues of fate and conscience—even with Catholic intonement."[274]

In both his 1936 novella *Double Indemnity* and his 1934 novel *The Postman Always Rings Twice*, Cain's protagonists confront a moral choice early in the story. In *Double Indemnity* insurance salesman Walter Huff (Walter Neff in the 1944 film) of the General Fidelity of California, realizes that Phyllis Nirdlinger (Phyllis Dietrichson in the film) is planning to kill her husband:

I couldn't be mistaken about what she meant, not after fifteen years in the insurance business. I mashed out my cigarette, so I could get up and go. I was going to get out of there, and drop those renewals and everything else like a red-hot poker. But I didn't do it. She looked at me, a little surprised, and her face was about six inches away. What I did do was put my arms around her, pull her face up against mine, and kiss her on the mouth, hard.[275]

Later that night, at home in his bungalow in the Los Feliz hills, he ruminates about his decision:

I lit a fire and sat there, trying to figure out where I was at. I knew where I was at, of course. I was standing right on the deep end, looking over the edge, and I kept telling myself to get out of there, and get quick, and never come back. But that was what I kept telling myself. What I was doing was peeping over that edge, and all that time I was trying to pull away from it, there was something in me that kept edging a little closer, trying to get a better look.

A little before nine the bell rang. I knew who it was as soon as I heard it.[276]

Cain's novella had its roots in the trial of Ruth Snyder and her lover Judd Gray for the murder of Snyder's husband Albert Snyder. In 1925 Ruth began an affair with Gray and encouraged him to kill her husband. With the assistance of insurance agent Leroy Ashfield, Ruth took out three insurance policies on Albert without his knowledge, paying the premiums herself. One policy, a $48,000 life insurance policy, doubled the payout ("double indemnity") if Albert died as a result of either accident or crime. After seven attempts by Ruth to kill Albert, Judd joined her in the early hours of March 19, 1927, when he leapt out of the shadows at the drunken husband who was beaten with a sash window weight, garroted with picture wire and smothered with chloroform-soaked rags.[277] One of the reporters who attended the trial, which began on April 18, 1927, was Cain. After Ruth tried to blame Gray for the murder, he confessed that Ruth was his partner in the killing. Both were convicted and on January 12, 1928, both were executed in the electric chair.

Double Indemnity

Soon after the publication of *Double Indemnity* in Liberty magazine, representatives of MGM, Paramount, 20th Century–Fox, and Columbia expressed interest in buying the story for Cain's asking price of $25,000. However, their interest soon dissipated after Joseph Breen warned them not to consider a film adaptation. Breen objected to the "general low tone and sordid flavor" of the story as it was "unacceptable" to show to "mixed audiences" in the theater.[278] However, by the summer of 1943 Breen's censorship policy was in the process of change. As Leonard Leff and Jerold Simmons point out:

Breen always believed that the Production Code embodied fundamental principles of Christian morality. ... Yet he also recognized that the war had unleashed forces that Hollywood could not ignore.[279]

After *Double Indemnity* was reprinted in a collection entitled *Three of a Kind*, Paramount executive Joseph Sistrom purchased the rights for $15,000. When the studio submitted a treatment to Breen, he again rejected the project. Nevertheless, the studio went ahead and hired Raymond Chandler after Billy Wilder's usual collaborator,

Charles Brackett, withdrew as he thought the material sordid—although he did work on the initial treatment.

In September 1943 when Breen and the PCA were confronted with the screenplay their criticisms were reduced to what Richard Schickel described as of a "piddling nature."[280] This included an obvious warning to make sure Phyllis's bath towel fully covers her when she greets Neff at the start of the film as well as a prohibition against showing too many details in the murder of Phyllis's husband. However, aside from these nitpicking details, the challenge *Double Indemnity* represented to the Code was much more fundamental as the film threatened the Code's basic principle required of all Hollywood films: "correct standards of life, subject only to the requirements of drama and enter-

Edward G. Robinson, Fred MacMurray and Barbara Stanwyck in Billy Wilder's *Double Indemnity* (1944).

tainment, shall be presented" and the "sympathy of the audience should never be thrown to the side of crime, wrongdoing, evil or sin."

The casting of Fred MacMurray in the lead male role was critical to Wilder's desire that the killer be perceived as a ordinary guy. MacMurray, initially, resisted Wilder and the studio was also surprised by Wilder's choice as nobody had a high opinion of him as an actor, including MacMurray himself.[281] Yet Wilder was sure that he could exploit MacMurray's screen persona as he felt that there was a "scuzzball, … who in some part of his soul—that part that shrewd Barton Keyes could discern and hoped to develop—knew better than to be what he was, do what he did. And physically he was perfect for the part, his size and solidity contrasting so ironically with the psychological insubstantiality he projected."[282]

Although Raymond Chandler and Billy Wilder had a troubled relationship, with

Chandler threatening to leave at one point, the film's dialogue and narrative structure are superior to Cain's novella. Chandler's decision to participate was surprising as he detested Cain's fiction:

> James Cain—faugh! Everything he touches smells like a billygoat. He is every kind of writer I detest, a faux naif, a Proust in greasy overalls, a dirty little boy with a piece of chalk and a board fence and nobody looking. Such people are the offal of literature, not because they write about dirty things, but because they do it in a dirty way.[283]

In many ways Chandler's fiction is the antithesis of Cain. Whatever Chandler called his detective, Mallory, Ted Carmady, John Dalmas or Philip Marlowe, he was a moral figure, a modern knight engaged in the quest for justice. Cain, on the other hand, reversed the narrative perspective of the mystery genre. He delved into the minds of adulterers and killers without the safety net of a strong moral voice. In his preface to *Three of a Kind* he argued that crime fiction had traditionally been written from the "least interesting angle, which was whether the police would catch the murderer."[284]

The film's dark opening with Neff confessing into a dictaphone is not found in Cain's story as it was devised by Wilder and Chandler:

> Office Memorandum: "Walter Neff to Barton Keyes, Claims Manager, Los Angeles, July 16, 1938. Dear Keyes: I suppose you'll call this a confession when you hear it. Well, I don't like the word 'confession.' I just want to set you right about something you couldn't see because it was smack up against your nose. … When it came to picking the killer, you picked the wrong guy. You want to know who killed Dietrichson? Hold tight to that cheap cigar of yours. Keyes, I killed Dietrichson—me, Walter Neff, insurance salesman. 35 years old, unmarried, no visible scars [Neff looks down at his shoulder wound]—until a while ago, that is. Yes, I killed him. I killed him for the money and for a woman. I didn't get the money and I didn't get the woman. Pretty isn't it?"

The film follows Cain's novel, in broad terms, until the murder of Phyllis's husband. Thereafter the Wilder/Chandler version eliminates various sub-plots and characterizations. Importantly, they reduce Phyllis's motivation to pure greed by eliminating Cain's depiction of her as an insane mass murderer. The major change in the Chandler/Wilder script concerns the ending as the film jettisons Cain's climax involving a double suicide in shark-infested waters. It replaces this with two sequences. The first is the final confrontation between Walter and Phyllis, where she has a last-minute change of mind which is poorly motivated. Why, after nearly 100 minutes of scheming to get her husband's money, including having sex with two men she doesn't love, Walter and Lola's boyfriend Nino Zachetti (Byron Barr), does Phyllis not fire the second shot and kill Walter? Especially after he makes it easier for her by walking towards her. Richard Schickel disagrees and describes the "final confrontation between Walter and Phyllis [as] masterful—simple, direct, yet rich with overtone."[285] But it can only really be explained by melodramatic contrivance, a desire for melodramatic pathos.

The other major imponderable with regard to the film concerns Neff's execution in the gas chamber with Keyes watching his execution, a scene that Wilder filmed but deleted during the editing process. If this scene had been retained, what effect would it have had? Instead, Wilder, like Huston in *The Maltese Falcon*, opted to end the film with a sentimental, comforting moment. If Wilder had retained the ending as filmed, it would have upset Breen and the PCA, which described the sequence as "unduly gruesome."[286] The sequence was filmed at a cost of $150,000 and Wilder later described it as "one of the best scenes he's ever made."[287] It is described in the Wilder/Chandler shooting script, Production PF-134, dated September 25, 1943, as the final sequence in the film, "Sequence E." It begins in the witness room in San Quentin's "death chamber," where two guards enter the room along with a group of witnesses, including newspapermen, as they

> form a group around the outside of the gas chamber, some looking in through the glass windows, some standing in the background on low platforms against the wall. The camera slowly begins to move in and down, and centers on Keyes, as he enters the room and stands behind the door. His face is seen through the bars of the door, which is then closed, and the camera moves to a closeup. His eyes follow the action of the closing door, then slowly look towards the gas chamber.[288]

The door to the gas chamber opens and Neff comes in between two guards.

> He is wearing a white open-necked shirt, blue denim pants, and walks barefooted on a coconut matting. He moves into the gas chamber, looks through the windows in the direction of Keyes and nods quickly, recognizing him. The guards turn him around and seat him in one of the two metal chairs, with his back to the witnesses. They strap his arms, legs and body to the chair. The guards go out.[289]

The guards leave the gas chamber for an ante-chamber where the "warden, executioner, two doctors, the minister and the acid man"[290] stand. The executioner closes the door, a guard spins the wheel to tighten it and seal the gas chamber, and the witnesses "are intently watching Neff in the gas chamber."[291]

The warden indicates to the acid man that it is time to proceed and he releases the "mixed acid into a pipe connecting with a counter-sunk receptacle under Neff's chair."[292] The warden then nods to the executioner who "pushes a metal lever. (This immerses the pellets of cyanide in the acid under the chair.")[293] The script suggests that this be filmed in a medium shot from a high angle towards the executioner.[294] The next shot in the script indicates that the camera is to shoot above Neff's head towards the spectators outside the gas chamber with Keyes in the center as the gas floats up in the chamber "between the camera and spectators. Keyes, unable to watch, looks away."[295]

The script describes in detail the procedure following Neff's death with two doctors attending. The first doctor listens on a stethoscope connected to the gas chamber until he indicates to the warden that Neff is dead. A guard then tells the spectators, including Keyes:

> "That's all, gentlemen. Vacate the chamber, please."[296] All the witnesses leave, except Keyes who stands, shocked and tragic, beyond the door. The guard goes to him and touches his arm, indicating to him that he must leave. Keyes glances for the last time towards the gas chamber and slowly moves to go out.

The script ends with the devastating impact of the execution on Keyes:

> Camera shooting through the open door at Keyes, who is just turning to leave. Keyes comes slowly out into the dark, narrow corridor. His hat is on his head now, his overcoat is pulled

around him loosely. He walks like an old man. He takes eight or ten steps, then mechanically reaches a cigar out of his vest pocket and puts it into his mouth. His hands, in the now familiar gesture, begin to pat his pockets for matches.

Suddenly he stops, with a look of horror on his face. He stands rigid, pressing a hand against his heart. He takes the cigar out of his mouth and goes slowly on towards the door, camera panning with him. ...slowly [he]walks out into the sunshine, stiffly, his head bent, a forlorn and lonely man.

FADE OUT
THE END [297]

Instead of this lengthy sequence in the gas chamber, Wilder ended the film on the second to last sequence in the script, when Keyes confronts Neff in his office at 4:30 a.m.

KEYES: How are you doing, Walter?
[Neff manages a faint smile]
NEFF: I'm fine. Only somebody moved the elevator a couple of miles away.
KEYES: They're on the way.
NEFF: [slowly and with great difficulty] You know why you didn't figure this one, Keyes? Let me tell you. The guy you were looking for was too close. He was right across the desk from you.
KEYES: Closer than that, Walter.
[The eyes of the two men meet in a moment of silence.]
NEFF: I love you, too.
[Neff fumbles for the handkerchief in Keyes' pocket, pulls it out and clumsily wipes his face with it. Then, clutching the handkerchief against his shoulder, he speaks to Keyes for the last time.]
NEFF: At the end of that ... trolley line ... just as I get off ... you be there ... to say goodbye ... will you, Keyes?
FADE OUT
END OF SEQUENCE "D" [298]

In the release print Wilder eliminates Neff's final comment to Keyes, "At the end of that ... trolley line" as well as his plea to Keyes to attend his execution ("you be there ... to say goodbye, will you Keyes?"). The film ends with Neff telling Keyes "I love you too." As he fumbles for a crumbled cigarette, which he pulls out of his pocket, Keyes completes the task of lighting it after it fails to ignite, a reversal of the repetitive action throughout the film where Neff keeps lighting Keyes's cigars.

Richard Schickel agrees with Wilder's decision to drop the execution chamber sequence: "the idea of having Neff, after dispatching Phyllis, ... find peace by dying in the comforting company of Keyes seems inevitable." [299] It "permits Neff a gentle, almost wistful end after all his desperate exertions. Like the conclusion of a Hitchcock movie it restores order to the disordered universe of the movie, and it does so lightly, rightly." [300] To "Wilder, Neff was a 'victim, not a murderer,' and it seemed wrong to emphasize, as the execution scene did, his criminality." [301]

James Naremore, on the other hand, points out that the elimination of the gas chamber sequence was extremely significant in changing the tone of the film:

One thing, however, is clear: Keyes's lonely walk out of the prison would have thrown a shadow over everything that preceded it. It was not until *Sunset Boulevard* and *Ace in the Hole* that Wilder would produce such a savage critique of modernity. Although the released version of his famous thriller remains an iconoclastic satire that challenges the censors, it is a lighter entertainment than the original and a much easier product for Hollywood to market.[302]

Nevertheless, *Double Indemnity* was a landmark film as producers hailed it as an "emancipation of Hollywood writing."[303] As a result, the PCA was flooded with scripts involving "murder and eros."[304] James Cain, excited by the film's impact, told the press that producers "have got hep to the fact that plenty of real crime takes place every day and that it makes a good movie…. The public is fed up with the old-fashioned melodramatic type of hokum."[305] On the other hand Fred Stanley, writing in *The New York Times* in 1944 after the release of *Double Indemnity,* was more precise in specifying the type of melodrama that emerged from the success of the film. He described this change as initiating a dark, "red meat" cycle involving "certain types of storied sordidness and ultra-sophistication."[306] He also noted how the film was able to bypass Breen's prohibitions and show that "Hollywood is learning to use finesse in dealing with a variety of different plot situations which, if treated … obviously, would be unsuitable."[307]

The Postman Always Rings Twice *(1946)*

The critical and commercial success of *Double Indemnity* encouraged MGM in October 1944 to consider a film version of Cain's *The Postman Always Rings Twice.* The studio had acquired the rights ten years earlier, in March 1934, for $25,000, a month after the publication of the novel. Cain developed the idea for the novel from his experiences driving through California, and one particular encounter with a gas station operated by a "bosomy-looking thing"[308]:

> Commonplace, but sexy, the kind you have ideas about. We always talked while she filled up my tank. One day I read in the paper where a woman who runs a filling station knocked off her husband. Can it be this bosomy thing? I go by and sure enough the place is closed. I inquire. Yes, she's the one—this appetizing but utterly commonplace woman.[309]

After screenwriter and friend Vincent Lawrence told Cain about the Judd Gray–Ruth Snyder murder case he formulated the notion of the self-destructive spiral[310] whereupon lust and greed would lead to murder. After the murder, mistrust, hate and betrayal would supplant the partners' desire for each other. Cain wrote the novel between March and September 1933, the worst year of the Depression. Its initial title was *Bar-B-Q.* Following its publication in February 1934 the book attracted considerable notoriety and strong sales, as well as two unauthorized film versions: Pierre Chenal's French version *Le Dernier Tournant* (1939) was followed by Italian director Luchino Visconte's first film, *Ossessione* (1943). MGM began pre-production of the first authorized version in late 1944 and Breen approved the script in May 1945.

Cain's first novel formed a prototype for many of his stories which Paul Skenazy describes as "extravagant melodramas of violence and passion."[311] The extravagance, however, is in the behavior of his characters, not the style of writing. Frank, the drifter, meets Cora, the unhappily married co-operator of a small diner in Glendale, in chapter 1. By chapter 2 they are lovers. In chapter 4 they attempt to murder Cora's husband Nick. During chapter 8 they continue their intimate relationship while Nick is convalescing in hospital following the botched attempt on his life. After temporarily separating and reuniting, the lovers successfully murder Nick on a lonely country road between Glendale and Santa Monica at night. They have sexual intercourse in the dirt alongside the car with Nick's battered body inside the vehicle. As Skenazy points out, within "forty-six pages of the paperback edition the lover's wish has come true."[312] Retribution follows. Their car suddenly rolls down the mountain and Frank is badly injured.

During the subsequent investigation the lovers turn on each other, as Grey and Snyder did. Unlike the trial of the real-life duo, a cunning lawyer, Katz, devises a scheme involving the insurance companies to gain their release. While Cora is sentenced to six months' probation, she also receives a $10,000 insurance payout. Following the acrimony that developed between them during the trial, their relationship continues to deteriorate. Frank resents his dependence on Cora as she has the ability to incriminate him with Sackett, the district attorney. When she leaves Frank to visit her ailing mother in Iowa, Frank runs off to Ensenada with Madge, an animal trainer. However, he is drawn back to Cora and, after overcoming a blackmail attempt, they reignite their love affair and marry. Cora is subsequently killed in a car accident. Although innocent of Cora's death, Frank is convicted and sentenced to death. The novel ends with his "confession" to a priest. His confession is, in effect, their story.

Under the direction of Tay Garnett and cinematographer Sidney Wagner, the film utilizes, unlike *Double Indemnity,* the MGM "house style" of flat lighting and bright sets. The film's determination to sanitize Cain's earthy novel is reinforced by the mainly white costumes worn by Lana Turner as Cora. Cora, in the novel, is a working-class woman who dresses accordingly. The film also jettisons one of the key aspects of Cain's novel—the sadomasochistic attraction between Frank and Cora. For example, the first meeting between Frank and Cora in the novel provides a stark contrast with Lana Turner's goddess-like entrance in the film.

> *The Novel:* Then I saw her. She had been out back, in the kitchen, but, she came in to gather up my dishes. Except for the shape, she really wasn't any raving beauty, but she had a sulky look to her, and her lips stuck out in a way that made me want to mash them in for her.[313]
>
> *The Film:* Preceding Cora's entrance, an open lipstick container rolls along the floor into the diner from another room. The script reads "Insert lipstick—Pan slowly from lipstick to Cora."[314] The script continues "Standing in the kitchen doorway, almost imperiously, … is Cora … wearing a white playsuit, shorts and a halter, plain white high heeled pumps … looking at Frank impassively."[315] Garnett's camera executes a low angle pan from the lipstick on the floor up Turner's legs, and, if the audience did not get the sexually charged meaning of the scene, the film cuts to hamburger meat sizzling on the cafe's grill.

Paul Skenazy is correct when he points out that there is a "disturbingly antiseptic quality to the whole film; buildings, interiors, and landscapes seem staged and the characters appear to have no relation to the environment. The sexuality is downplayed."[316] Dressing Turner mostly in white was MGM's attempt to eradicate Cain's emphasis on the "sexuality, orality and violence"[317] that attracted the couple in the first place. For example, in chapter 2 of Cain's novel Nick leaves Frank and Cora alone as he travels to Los Angeles to purchase a neon sign.

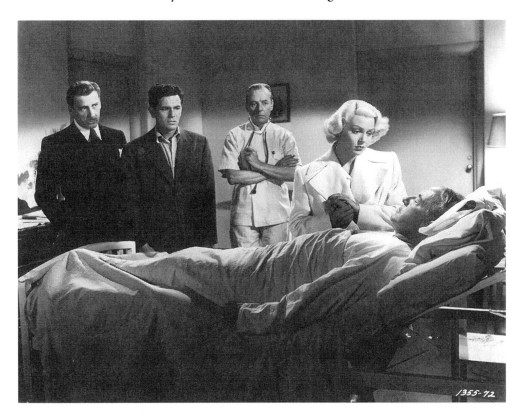

(From left) Leon Ames, John Garfield, Edward Earle, Lana Turner and Cecil Kellaway in MGM's *The Postman Always Rings Twice* (1946).

> FRANK: I took her in my arms and mashed my mouth up against hers … "Bite me! Bite me!" I bit her. I sunk my teeth into her lips so deep I could feel the blood spurt into my mouth. It was running down her neck when I carried her upstairs.[318]

This follows his first night at the diner when his lust for Cora makes him vomit with sexual frustration: "I let everything come up. It was like hell, the lunch, or the potato, or the wine. I wanted that woman so bad I couldn't even keep anything on my stomach."[319] Cora responds to his abusive, animal-like need for her:

> Next day I was alone with her for a minute, and swung my fist up against her leg so hard it nearly knocked her over.
> "How do you get that way?" She was snarling like a cougar. I liked her like that
> "How are you, Cora?"
> "Lousy."
> From then on, I began to smell her again.[320]

The novel's association between violence and sex climaxes with Nick's murder on a lonely road at night. Because of the necessity of making it appear that they were also injured in the car accident, Frank begins "to fool with her blouse, to bust the buttons, so she would look banged up."[321] Cora immediately responds to Frank's treatment:

> She was looking at me, and her eyes didn't look blue, they looked black. I could feel her breath coming fast. Then it stopped, and she leaned real close to me.

"Rip me! Rip me."

I ripped her. I shoved my hand in her blouse and jerked. She was wide open, from her throat to her belly.[322]

Then Frank hits her in the eye as hard as he could and Cora falls down:

She was right down there at my feet, her eyes shining, her breasts trembling, drawn up in tight points, and pointing right up at me. She was down there, and the breath was roaring in the back of my throat like I was some kind of animal, and my tongue was all swelled up in my mouth, and the blood pounding in it.

"Yes! Yes, Frank, yes!"

Next thing I knew, I was down there with her, and we are staring in each other's eyes, and locked in each other's arms, and straining to get closer. Hell could have opened for me then, and it wouldn't have made any difference. I had to have her, if I hung for it.

I had her.[323]

After sexual intercourse, Frank and Cora lie there, listening to "this gurgle from the inside of the car."[324]

At the end of the story, just after they renew their love for each other, fate intervenes. Cora dies in a car accident and Frank is convicted of her murder. Melodrama's poetic justice. Both the novel and the film close with virtually the same dialogue. In the film Frank, in a moment of pathos, accepts his death as poetic justice:

Father, you were right. It all works out. I guess God knows more about these things than we do. Somehow or other, Cora paid for Nick's life with hers. And now, Father, would you send up a prayer for me and Cora, and if you could find it in your heart, make it that we're together, wherever it is? [the priest nods].

The Postman Always Rings Twice was a profitable film for MGM despite its high production costs ($1,683,000) that were exacerbated when director Tay Garnett went on a drinking binge following problems filming the beach scenes at Laguna Beach. The film earned $3,741,000 in North American rentals and another $1,345,000 overseas, giving it a profit of $1,626,000.[325]

The commercial success of both *Double Indemnity* and *The Postman Always Rings Twice* had a substantial impact on the attitude of the major studios towards big budget crime films. Instead of detective and cop films, studio crime stories began to present flawed protagonists trapped in the "fatalistic inevitability of their own destinies, and the intense pressure of determinism one feels ruling their lives."[326] However, there was always a nervousness in the major studios with regard to their expensive productions to deviate far from the ethical world of melodrama. Inevitably, with a few exceptions such as *Out of the Past* and *Criss Cross,* they returned to the comforting world of melodrama and its vision of an ethical universe. Not so their low budget film units and the films produced by marginal studios such as Monogram and Producers Releasing Corporation (PRC).

The Transgressive World of the Low Budget Crime Melodrama: Detour *(1945),* Decoy *(1946) and* Money Madness *(1948)*

Joseph Breen opposed a film adaptation of *The Postman Always Rings Twice* for nearly ten years. In the early 1940s, aware that circumstances had changed, he relaxed his opposition to a film version. By September 1945 he was defending the film to the Federal Council of Churches of Christ in America.[327] However, Breen was "relieved that Metro and [MGM producer] Carey Wilson—not a renegade studio or loose horse like Howard Hughes—would adapt the novel."[328] And, from his point of view, he was correct in anticipating that a major studio, especially MGM, would be hesitant to recreate Cain's "sordid" world and risk losing their audience. The "renegade" studios that Breen feared were studios such as Monogram and PRC as they were less dependent on box-office revenues to fund their productions. Their films were sold on a flat rental basis. As a consequence they were often prepared to take risks that the majors, with their big budgets, expensive stars, and high production costs, were not inclined to undertake. A-budgeted films needed to maximize their audience potential as revenue was distributed as a percentage of the box office revenue.

Robert Lowery, Doris Merrick, Eddie Quillan, Nestor Paiva and Maurice Murphy in Monogram's *Sensation Hunters* (1945). The film was retitled *Club Paradise* in 1950 for television screenings.

Although Monogram was a member of the Motion Picture Producers and Distributors of America (MPPDA), and thereby bound by the Production Code, it released a number of films such as *Sensation Hunters* (1945) and *Decoy* (1946) that would never have been considered by a major studio. It is also possible that their films, which rarely played the prestigious first run urban picture palaces, did not always receive the same intense scrutiny that Breen and the PCA applied to major studio productions. *Sensation Hunters*, for example, includes a scene showing one of the women (Mae) working in a seedy nightclub in desperate need of medical attention after an infection becomes serious. This is a thinly veiled reference to a failed abortion, a sequence that Breen, a devout Catholic,

Hugh Beaumont and Ann Savage in *Apology for Murder* **(1945).**

would normally have censored. Breen's determining principle, the principle of compensating moral values which was discussed in detail in Chapter Three with regard to William Wyler's production of *The Letter*, involved a calculus of retribution to punish evil while rewarding innocence. It was his way of making sure that a "moral voice" is clearly discernible throughout the film. In the 1940s Breen's desire for a pervasive moral voice faltered, especially in low budget crime films where melodrama's mandatory presentation of a "felt sense of justice" dissipated.

This challenge to the fundamentals of melodrama can be seen when PRC's ultra-low budget production of *Apology for Murder* (1945) is compared with Paramount's A budgeted production of *Double Indemnity*. PRC's intention was always to exploit the success of the large budget studio film with a cheap ripoff. For example, the working title of the PRC film was *Single Indemnity*.[329] The fact that the PRC film had a running time of only 67 minutes, compared with 107 minutes for the Paramount film, meant that motivations, events and characterizations had to be severely truncated and this contributed to the film's tough, unsentimental presentation. For example, its femme fatale, Toni Kirkland (Ann Savage), was a good deal more vicious than her counterpart, Phyllis Dietrichson, in *Double Indemnity*. She does not have a sentimental last-minute change-of-heart with regard to the film's male protagonist, reporter Kenny Blake (Hugh Beaumont). Instead, she is consistently heartless and mercenary. PRC's promotion for the film described her as "An Irresistible She Devil."

Similarly Monogram's *Sensation Hunters* (1945) traces the cruel plight of a sympathetic young woman, Julie Rogers (Doris Merrick), who falls in love with an immoral man, Danny Burke (Robert Lowery), who offers her to a gangster to repay a debt owed to him. Although the film was a morality play, the young woman does little to justify the pain inflicted on her. She is a victim of an homme fatale, a hostile family, an unfeeling society, a duplicitous girlfriend and fate. And the ending is left unresolved[330]—she either dies by gunshot or is arrested for murder. None of these outcomes are, by the ethical standards of melodrama, deserved.

Detour

Detour has been described as the "quintessential 'B' feature noir."[331] In October 1944 PRC producer Leon Fromkess bought the film rights to Martin Goldsmith's 1939 novel Detour: An Extraordinary Tale for $15,000. Rumors circulated that John Garfield was eager for Warner Brothers to secure the rights.[332] Warners offered Fromkess $25,000 to sell the rights to them but the producer refused.[333] On October 30, 1944, Martin Mooney, PRC's associate producer, sent a treatment by Martin Goldsmith to Joseph Breen. While Goldsmith received the sole screenplay credit, much of the screenplay was written by Mooney and Ulmer. They discarded many of Goldsmith's characters, including his use of multiple narrators. Mooney and Ulmer decided to focus on the consciousness of Al Roberts (Tom Neal),[334] the film's central character. As Ulmer's biographer Noah Isenberg points out, what remained was a "threadbare quality … with its intermittent reliance on the total suspension of belief, [which] made for a good match with Ulmer's aesthetic."[335] Instead of Goldsmith's sprawling narrative, the film presents a hero who delivers

> half his lines in a pained, edgy voice-over—whose primary task, beyond recounting his life as a cursed nightclub pianist and cursed hitchhiker, is explaining the inexplicable, proving to himself as well as the audience that he is essentially powerless in his losing battle against fate.[336]

There are many myths about the making of Detour. The oft repeated figure of a $30,000 budget and a six-day shooting schedule is incorrect. The film was budgeted at $87,579.75, and it came in at $117,226.80. While this was relatively generous by PRC standards, it was minuscule compared to budgets allocated by the major studios. The myth of the six-day shooting schedule, perpetuated by Ulmer and the film's female star, Ann Savage, was also incorrect. Studio records show that filming in the studio took place between June 14 and June 29, 1945, with an additional four days on location.[337]

Ulmer bypassed or ignored some of Breen's objections to the film, such as his decree that there should be no suggestion of a sexual relationship between Al Roberts (Tom Neal) and Vera (Ann Savage). In the cheap Los Angeles apartment, which occupies much of the latter portion of the film, Vera's sexual advances towards Al are, by 1940s film standards, remarkably frank. As Ann Savage later noted: "That was an overt motion there, not subtle anymore.… When she gets up to go to bed, she's quite drunk and she reaches over to touch his shoulder and he really rejects her. It's a real rebuff and this infuriates her."[338] Specifically, Breen told the producer that Roberts and Vera must live in separate apartments and must not register as Mr. and Mrs. Haskell. This was also ignored.[339]

Breen was also concerned about the depiction of Vera's "profession" and he insisted that there should be no suggestion that she was a prostitute. Instead, he advocated that she should be seen as a crook. While Ulmer does not literally portray Vera as a prostitute, he goes close in her opening sequence when Al discovers her hitchhiking in front of a gas station. After his offer of a lift ("Hey you! Come on, if you want a ride") Ulmer shows her approaching the car with a reverse tracking shot that, as Isenberg describes, "helps to convey her 'sexual knowingness,' as one critic has argued."[340] To this end, the director insisted that her clothes be tightly fitted, which was confirmed by Ann Savage in a 1996 interview: "He [Ulmer] took my sweater and he pulled it real tight and he had the wardrobe woman take this big lap of wool in the back and pin it from the neck down to the bottom of the sweater. And then he said, 'Don't turn around.'"[341]

Ann Savage's portrayal of Vera is unlike any other femme fatale from the period—much less stylish, more overtly sexual and far more vicious. She fulfills Roberts description that she "looked like she'd just been thrown off the crummiest freight train in the world." Ulmer discarded the "saccharine, dolled-up style that the hair and makeup artists had initially confected for her,"[342] and insisted that large dollops of cold cream were rubbed through her hair to give it a greasy look together with the application of a dirty-brown toner to her face.[343] She was drilled by Ulmer to deliver her lines rapidly and with venom. As James Naremore notes, Savage's Vera "makes every femme fatale in the period look genteel by comparison"[344]:

> Al compares her with Camille, but clearly she is no wilting, sacrificial heroine of sentimental melodrama; instead, she taps into a raw nerve of greed and exploitation that lies at the core of the film. Ruthlessly hard and half crazed, she lolls about the Los Angeles hotel rooms in her bathrobe, downing straight whiskey, chain-smoking, and plotting to get rich. She probably knows that she is dying, but she easily dominates Al, first insulting him and then inviting him to bed. A sullen, dangerous, yet sympathetic figure, she leaves an indelible impression, and it is impossible to imagine any A-budget picture that would have been allowed to depict her. When Al sits alone in the Reno diner and recalls her image, he seems to be looking into a void.[345]

Promotion of the film accentuated Vera's sexuality while highlighting Al's passivity. With her tight dress and ankle straps, Vera is shown smoking a cigarette while leaning on a lamp post next to Al: "He went searching for love … but Fate forced a DETOUR to Revelry…. Violence…. Mystery!" The ad claimed that the film was for "Adults Only!" It included three taglines: "I Used My Body for BLACKMAIL!," "Men like me too much … and the police too little," and "I could be a one-man woman … if I could find the right man."[346]

Ulmer decided during pre-production to focus exclusively on the disturbed mind of Al Roberts. This begins in the opening sequence in a Nevada diner when he objects to a customer playing the 1920s Broadway number, by Jimmy McHugh and Clarence Gaskill, "I Can't Believe That You're in Love with Me" on the jukebox. Just prior to filming Ulmer substituted this song for the 1932 Duke Ellington, Irving Mills and Mitchell Parish tune "Sophisticated Lady" which appeared in Ann Savage's copy of the script. The motivation for this substitution was partly budgetary, as it saved the studio $2,000 in royalties, but it also dovetailed with Ulmer's decision to highlight Roberts's melancholy turmoil. The narration resembles a radio drama with many plot details introduced and explained by Roberts's voice-over. At times he even addresses the audience and tells them what they may be thinking of him. At other times he compares the "reality" of his nightmare to "fiction": "If this were fiction," he explains, "I would fall in love with Vera, marry her, and make a respectable woman of her. Or else, she'd make some supreme class-A sacrifice for me and die." Neither happens as the film is not a melodrama. Vera dies but it is only as a result of a bizarre confluence of events which results in the likelihood of Roberts being sent to jail for life or worse.

Ulmer sets the mood from the outset with Roberts wallowing in his self-pity. As the lighting on his face changes, the camera moves to an extreme close-up as Al

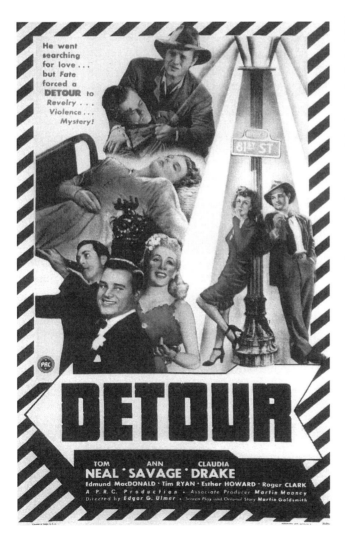

begins his narration. He recalls a happier time in New York at the Break o' Dawn Club where he worked as a piano player with his singer girlfriend Sue (Claudia Drake). While Al grumbles about his lousy luck playing in a third-rate night club, he is content until Sue rejects his offer of marriage so that she can try her luck in Hollywood. Al eventually decides to follow her, but bereft of funds, he is forced to hitchhike across the United States. In Arizona he gets a ride with pill popping bookmaker Charlie Haskell (Edmund Macdonald) who is traveling to Los Angeles. Haskell, after falling asleep, mysteriously dies and in his first major mistake Roberts panics, drags Haskell's body into bushes near the side of the road, and takes his car and money.

His second major mistake, after crossing into California, is to offer

Tom Neal, Edmund MacDonald, Ann Savage, Claudia Drake in Edgar Ulmer's *Detour* (1945).

Vera a ride. After few quiet moments, she turns into a nightmare. She begins by telling him that she knows he killed Haskell as she travelled through Louisiana with him and inflicted the deep scars on his wrist when he made sexual advances. During their journey Vera shifts between tormenting and humiliating Al and, when aroused, expresses a predatory sexual interest in him. Mostly, however, her attitude is one of domination and harassment as she tells him that she knows "a wrong guy when I see one"; "What'd you do, kiss [Haskell] with a wrench"; "You've got all the earmarks of a cheap crook and you killed him. For two cents I'd change my mind and turn you in. I don't like you!" Her abuse is frequent and vicious.

The film's cheap, but effective, production values, show the trip west, mainly, via rear-projection. This ends with Vera and Al confined to a cheap, claustrophobic apartment where he complains "my favorite sport is being kept prisoner." His nightmare does not let up and Vera, drunk and bitter following Al's rejection, grabs an inordinately long telephone cord and runs into the bedroom and locks the door while threatening to report him to the police. In another room, and desperate to stop her, he grabs the cord and tries to pull it back, not knowing that she has wrapped it around her neck.

After Vera's death the film returns to the opening sequence in the Nevada diner where Al realizes he will never see Sue again. He cannot visit Hollywood nor can he work in New York. He gets up and leaves the diner, and in an epilogue added by Ulmer, his narration gives the impression that he might escape capture: "I was in Bakersfield before I read that Vera's body was discovered and that the police were looking for Haskell in connection with his wife's murder. Isn't that a laugh? Haskell got me into this mess, and Haskell was getting me out of it. The police were searching for a dead man." This ending, however, was never going to get past Breen, who insisted on retribution for Al. As he continues to walk along the highway he ruminates about how life might have turned out had he never gotten into Haskell's car:

> "But one thing I don't have to wonder about.... I know" is that "some day a car will stop to pick me up that I never thumbed.... Yes, fate or some mysterious force can put the finger on you or me for no good reason at all."

This change was insisted by Breen long before production of the film began in June 1945. On November 1, 1944, Breen, in response to producer Martin Mooney, declared that it was absolutely essential "that at the end of this story Alex [Al] be in the hands of the police, possibly having been picked up by a highway police-car as he was hitchhiking." To Ulmer's credit, however, he does not acquiesce easily to Breen's demand and there is tension between the visuals and Al's narration—while the voice-over projects his eventual arrest some time in the future, the visuals shows a police car pulling up alongside Al as he walks along the highway.

Decoy

Decoy, another low budget Monogram film, was released in September 1946. It appeared to be a lost film for many years until it was screened at the American

Cinematheque in 2000 where the author of the short story on which the film was based, Stanley Rubin, was in attendance. Glenn Erickson reported that the "movie brought the house down with its odd mix of melodrama, hardboiled gimmicks and unrestrained sadism."[347] Much of this excitement was due to British actor Jean Gillie's performance as the femme fatale, Margot Shelby, one of the screen's more excessive presentations. Gillie, at the time of the film's production, was married to the film's director, Jack Bernhard. She starred in 20 British films before marrying Bernhard in the United Kingdom. After *Decoy* she appeared in one more film, *The Macomber Affair* (1947), which was filmed simultaneously with *Decoy*. Her marriage to Bernhard ended soon after the completion of the film and she returned to London where she died of pneumonia in 1949 at the age of 33.

Stanley Rubin's pulp story involved the life restoring properties of methylene blue. While this chemical compound actually exists, and reportedly has the ability to counteract cyanide poisoning, it does not restore dead people. But this did not stop Rubin. His story was reworked into a screenplay by writer/actor Ned Young and the film begins with disgraced doctor Lloyd Craig (Herbert Rudley) looking at his dazed face in the dirty mirror of a filthy washroom in a roadside gas station 75 miles from San Francisco. Craig hitchhikes to town and finds his way to the apartment of Margot Shelby (Jean Gillie) where shots are heard off-screen. Police Sergeant Joe Portugal (Sheldon Leonard) arrives at the apartment to find Craig dead and Shelby seriously wounded. The film recounts the events leading up to the shooting, as told by Shelby to Portugal, whom she demeaningly calls "Jojo."

Shelby's gangster boyfriend Frankie Olins (Robert Armstrong) is facing execution after stealing $400,000 and killing a guard. Desperate to learn where Olins has hidden the money, Shelby devises a plan with the assistance of another gangster, Jim Vincent (Edward Norris), to steal Olins's body after he is executed by cyanide gas and revive him with methylene blue. To carry out her plan Shelby requires a doctor with access to the prison. To achieve this goal she seduces Doctor Craig. After Vincent's men kill the guard transporting Olins's body from the prison, Craig resurrects Olins and then Olins draws a map showing the location of the money. While trying to kiss Shelby, Vincent shoots Olins and, after recovering the map which is divided between Shelby and Vincent, they begin their road journey to recover the money. To assist them through the police roadblocks, they force the hapless Craig to accompany them. On the way, Shelby murders Vincent by running over his body three times,[348] before gingerly recovering the map from his coat. After locating the money box Shelby, laughing hysterically, shoots Craig.

There is no presentation of virtue in *Decoy*, only evil. The police and the medical profession, normally protected by Breen, are shown in a poor light. Unlike other femme fatales (*Double Indemnity*, *The Postman Always Rings Twice*, *Out of the Past*, *The File on Thelma Jordon*), the film refuses to present Shelby with any redeeming qualities or sentimentalize her. She is in command throughout the film and especially during the epilogue. After Shelby completes telling her story to Portugal she invites him to bring his face down near her face. While this is a film cliché, usually giving the evil woman an opportunity to repent (*Double Indemnity*, *The File on Thelma Jordon* and *The Strange Love of Martha Ivers*), *Decoy* remains resolutely

British-born Jean Gillie in Monogram's *Decoy* (1946).

nihilistic to the end. When Portugal, who, like Craig, Olins and Vincent, is attracted to Shelby, agrees to her request expecting a show of remorse, Shelby merely humiliates him by laughing in his face, as she has done to all of the male characters throughout the film. This moment is followed by the film's ironic epilogue. After Shelby dies, Portugal empties the "money" box which reveals that Olins had the last laugh. The box contains only one dollar and a note: "to you who double-crossed me.... I leave this dollar for your trouble. The rest of the dough, I leave to the worms."

Shelby takes special pleasure in destroying Doctor Craig, who has all of the attributes of a "virtuous" character as he operates a free clinic for the poor people in his local community. Yet the film traces his degradation, his fall from a position of respect while destroying his relationship with his nurse (Marjorie Woodworth). Eventually, he is reduced to the zombie-like figure, disheveled and badly wounded, inspecting his reflection in a dirty mirror in a seedy gas station washroom. Earlier, Craig, disgusted by his actions, smashes a glass over his copy of the medical profession's Hippocratic Oath.

The New York Times review of the film (November 2, 1946) highlights Jean Gillie's performance ("blonde and personable as the femme fatale") while praising the film as a "pretty fair minor divertissement." The review opened with the "double cross which should (but probably won't) end all double-crosses is played out with unrelenting viciousness in 'Decoy,' a melodrama endowed with a driving force which carries the ragged plot along in a manner that is tolerable."

Money Madness

Money Madness (1948) was directed by Peter Stewart (aka Sam Newfield). Newfield was the most prolific director in the history of the American cinema. Based on a story by Al Martin, the film begins at the end of the story when a young woman, Julie Saunders (Frances Rafferty), is sentenced to ten years in jail. This fatalistic overlay opens up twin concerns. Why? And did she deserve it? The answer is no. The flashback begins with Steve Clark (Hugh Beaumont) arriving in Canoga Park by bus where he deposits a large amount of money in a local bank deposit box. However, as he needs to "clean" the money before he can spend it, he insinuates himself into the dull life of a young woman, Julie Saunders, who works at a local cafe and lives with her capricious Aunt Cora (Cecil Weston). Clark, working as a taxi driver, meets Julie when he rescues her from a drunken date.

Steve, without Julie's knowledge, concocts a scheme to gain control of Cora's house. He murders Cora and marries Julie so that she cannot testify against him, and then plants the stolen money in Cora's attic hoping that people will think the money belonged to the old woman. And, as Cora's sole relative, Julie will inherit the money. When Steve admits his crimes to Julie, she tells him that she is going to the police. Steve threatens her life. This situation, a vulnerable, young woman persecuted by an insane, controlling man, is gothic and similar to the dramatic premise in *My Name Is Julia Ross*. Julie, like Julia, executes a series of unsuccessful attempts to escape Steve's control. Eventually, assisted by local lawyer Donald Harper (Harlan Warde), who is in love with her, she makes one final attempt to leave. Steve, aware of Harper's interest in Julie, decides to kill the lawyer. However, the police intervene and shoot Steve. The film's epilogue has the potential to duplicate the sentimental ending to *My Name Is Julia Ross* by ending with Julie and Harper. Not so. The police arrest Julie and the judge sentences her to ten years in jail. Julie's only "crime" is that she cannot escape Steve's control. Instead of marriage to Harper, the last image is the police taking her away. The question is why? What ethical or criminal code has she violated? This film is even more extreme than *Sensation Hunters* in its violation of melodrama's emphasis on poetic justice.

Melodrama's "Leaping Fish"—Horror: The Seventh Victim *(1943);* and Adventure: The Macomber Affair *(1947);* and Gangster: Raw Deal *(1948)*

Linda Williams in *Playing the Race Card* cites Henry James's description of Harriet Beecher Stowe's *Uncle Tom's Cabin* as a "wonderful leaping fish" because of the ability of her story to "effortlessly fly from one medium to another."[349] Williams argues that melodrama executes similar "leaps" from "one spectacular, popular manifestation to another."[350] Its protean abilities enable it to move through, and assimilate, other modes such as comedy, realism and romance. Melodrama provides the aesthetic basis for most Hollywood genres, including the gangster film, the horror film and the adventure film. Each includes a notion of virtue and evil and each strive to end on a sense of poetic justice. But there were exceptions.

The Seventh Victim

The *Philadelphia Inquirer*, in its November 5, 1943, review of RKO's *The Seventh Victim* described the film as a "psychological mystery melodrama." This was a common way in which the trade press indicated that the film was not just a conventional melodrama. This is certainly true as *The Seventh Victim* is not a melodrama. While there are villains in the film, devil worshippers residing in New York, the focus is on the psychological trauma and emotional disturbances of a small group of characters, most notably Jacqueline Gibson (Jean Brooks). Her desire for death, to escape a cruel world, is not something that is countenanced in melodrama. This is encapsulated in the film's prologue and epilogue:

> I run to Death and Death meets me as fast,
> and all my pleasures are like Yesterday.

The film begins with young Mary Gibson (Kim Hunter) leaving Highcliff Academy, a Catholic boarding school, to search for her sister Jacqueline in New York. Before she leaves the school Mary is warned by a female teacher, Miss Gilchrist (Eve March), not to return and take up a teaching position ("Mary, don't come back, no matter if you never find your sister. No matter what happens to you, don't come back!"). The warning is intended to protect Mary from sinister occurrences at the school as Gilchrist explains that she was once in the same position as Mary, about to leave, but she made the mistake of coming back.

Mary's search for her sister takes her to the missing persons bureau where director Mark Robson's camera, assisted by cinematographer Nicholas Musuraca, tracks fluently past a row of desperate people searching for loved ones. Later, in the dark offices of the cosmetic company *La Sagasse*, where Jacqueline worked, Mary witnesses the murder of Irving August (Lou Lubin), a sad little private eye trying to help her. On the subway that night, Mary is threatened by two men carrying August's body. However, in one of the film's most surprising scenes, which prefigured Hitchcock's famous shower scene seventeen years later, Mary is confronted by a middle-aged woman, Mrs. Redi (Mary Newton), while naked in her shower. Redi's visit to Mary is motivated by her desire to stop the investigation of Jacqueline's disappearance. Redi recently purchased *La Sagasse* from Jacqueline on behalf of the Palladists, a group of middle-class devil worshippers in New York.

Mary's journey through New York brings her into contact with a range of characters that are psychologically broken. This includes the failed poet Jason Hoag (Erford Gage) who attempts to help Mary after falling in love with her. When his love is not reciprocated, he tells Mary:

> I am alive yet every hope I had is dead.
> Death can be good. Death can be happy.

Similarly, the disillusioned psychoanalyst Dr. Judd (Tom Conway) who lacks the confidence to treat patients. He tries, unsuccessfully, to protect Jacqueline from the Palladists. Mary also falls in love with Gregory Ward (Hugh Beaumont), Jacqueline's husband. Jacqueline, the most despairing character of all, lives above Dante's Restaurant in a room devoid of furniture, except for a chair and a noose hanging from the ceiling.

The focus of the film is a world without love or meaning. This is made evident at the end. While Gregory and Mary discuss the futility of their love for each other, as Jacqueline is still married to Gregory, Jacqueline prepares to commit suicide. After escaping the Palladists, she returns to her bleak, empty room. Before entering it she meets a neighbor, Mimi (Elizabeth Russell), in the hallway. Mimi is dying from consumption:

> JACQUELINE: Who are you?
> MIMI: Mimi. I'm dying.
> JACQUELINE: No!
> MIMI: I've been quiet, ever so quiet. I hardly move, yet it [death] keeps coming all the time, closer and closer. I rest and rest and yet I am dying.
> JACQUELINE: And you don't want too die. I've always wanted to die. Always.
> MIMI: I'm afraid. I'm afraid of being afraid, of waiting.
> JACQUELINE: Why wait?
> MIMI: I'm not going to wait. I'm going out, laugh, dance, do all the things I used to do.
> JACQUELINE: And then?
> MIMI: I don't know.
> JACQUELINE: You will die!

After two short sequences, one with Mary telling Gregory that although she loves him, she will have to leave New York, and the other with Judd and Hoag confronting the Palladists, *The Seventh Victim* concludes in the hallway outside Jacqueline's room. Mimi, dressed up for her last night on the town, emerges from her room and as she walks past Jacqueline's room there is the sound of a chair toppling over— Jacqueline's suicide as she hangs herself. The film's epilogue shows Mimi walking away down the corridor accompanied by Jacqueline's voice-over: "I run to Death and Death meets me as fast, and all my Pleasures are like Yesterday."

Unsurprisingly, *The Seventh Victim* did not prosper at the box-office and some critics were bewildered by the film. The editing in the final moments even suggests that Mary and Gregory would be better off if Jacqueline were not alive—a suggestion that was reportedly included in an earlier scene between Mary and Gregory that was edited from the release print. On the other hand, evil, in the form of the Palladists, survives and there is no sense of retribution aside from the scorn Judd expresses to them as he leaves their meeting. And Jacqueline, the persecuted victim, finds only release in death in one of the most morbid closures in Hollywood's history. As Glenn Erickson notes:

> Of all of Lewton's films, *The Seventh Victim* seems the most original. It's rather tame for a tale of devil-worshippers but it cuts through to the center of the human dread of loneliness and alienation, the chill that comes when one starts to believe that the effort and strain of trying "to live in the world" just isn't worth it. It's an existential statement about a creeping despair for which we don't have a precise word.[351]

The Macomber Affair

The Macomber Affair (1947), unlike *The Seventh Victim*, is not set in the urban nightmare of New York but on the plains of Kenya, courtesy of extensive location footage filmed by Osmond Borradaile, Freddie Francis and John Wilcox in Africa. This material was edited into footage filmed with the principal cast members at Tecate (Baja California, Mexico) with the interiors shot at the General Service studios in Hollywood. Francis (Robert Preston) and Margot Macomber (Joan Bennett), in a last-ditch attempt to save their marriage, come to Kenya and hire big game hunter Robert Wilson (Gregory Peck) to take them on a safari. On one level, the safari is intended to be the means where Francis can demonstrate his "masculinity" by killing dangerous animals and prove to his wife that he is not a coward. On another level, it becomes the vehicle for the couple to continue their sadomasochistic relationship. Wilson, in the film, but not Hemingway's short story, makes the mistake of falling in love with Margot after having sex with her while Francis is sleeping.

Wilson's sexual liaison with Margot occurs the night of Francis's shame during the hunt. During the day he accompanies Robert into the bushes to put down a

The promotion for *The Macomber Affair* (1947) emphasized the romance between big game hunter Robert Wilson (Gregory Peck) and Margot Macomber (Joan Bennett), the wife of Francis Macomber (Robert Preston): "Gregory Peck makes that Hemingway kind of love to Joan Bennett."

wounded lion. However, when the lion charges the men, Francis panics and runs away—much to the disgust, and pleasure, of Margot. Wilson completes the kill while Francis is mortified by his behavior as it provides Margot with more ammunition to taunt her husband.

The next day Francis redeems himself during the buffalo shoot, and his new-found confidence upsets Margot more than his display of cowardice. She fears she will lose control of their relationship. In a parallel incident to his display of coward-ice involving an injured lion, a wounded buffalo seeks shelter in the bushes. This time Francis insists on accompanying Wilson into the undergrowth and when the buffalo charges the men, Francis stands his ground and fires at the animal. Margot, behind Francis, shoots her husband in the head. Although Wilson is not sure if it is an acci-dent, his report supports Margot's version and the film ends with Margot about to testify at a coroner's jury assembled in Nairobi. The film, intentionally, never con-clusively states whether Francis's death is murder or an accident. The former is most likely.

The film's downbeat, inconclusive ending shows Margot leaving Wilson to face the inquest. There is no presentation of an ethical world as the narrative subverts the conventional melodramatic trajectory as the "hero" (Wilson) and the "coward" (Francis) change places. Instead of celebrating the handsome, brave big-game hunter it traces his fall from grace. He betrays his client, has sex with his wife, loses his hunt-ing license and faces an uncertain future with Margot. Francis, on the other hand, redeems himself just prior to his death. In the film's epilogue, Wilson is left alone to deal with his own doubts and anxieties while Margot's future is equally uncertain as she faces the inquest into her husband's death.

I have only found one source[352] that lists *The Macomber Affair* (1947) as a film noir—E. Ann Kaplan's excellent article, "Hemingway, Hollywood and Female Repre-sentation: The Macomber Affair,"[353] written more than thirty-five years ago. The basic template of the story could easily fit into a noir narrative: a wealthy husband, his beautiful but unfaithful wife, and her lover that ends with the husband's death at the hands of his wife. Yet this tale of violence and passion is not set in the dark city but on the plains of Africa. The film is not interested in the usual spectacle of big-game films, only a perverse triangle with special attention on the battle for control between Francis and Margot. The narrative focus is inward, not outward, psychological, not action. This is brilliantly enhanced by Miklós Rózsa's dark, traumatic score and cine-matographer Karl Struss's bleak imagery.

The script, as written by Casey Robinson and Frank Arnold, was based on Ernest Hemingway's celebrated short story *The Short Happy Life of Francis Macomber* which was first published in the September 1936 issue of *Cosmopolitan* magazine. Bosley Crowther, in his review in *The New York Times* on April 21, 1947, praised the film:

> If you kindly overlook the beginning and the end of "The Macomber Affair," which Benedict Bogeaus and Casey Robinson delivered to the Globe on Saturday, you will find a quite cred-ible screen telling of a short story by Ernest Hemingway, "The Short Happy Life of Francis Macomber," once termed by Mr. Hemingway as one of his best. It is not a romantic story ... and the producers have not improved it by trying to make it so. But without their beginning and ending, which are easy to detect and detach, it makes for a tight and absorbing study of

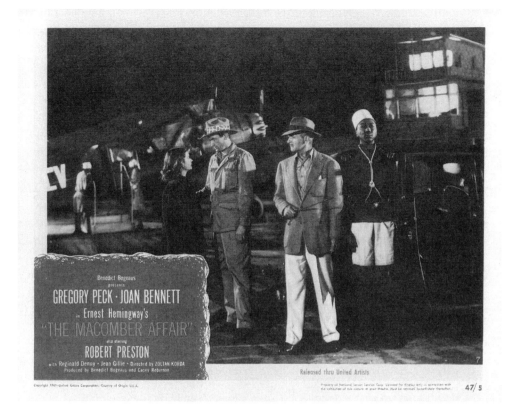

The bleak opening to *The Macomber Affair* (1947) with Margot Macomber (Joan Bennett), Robert Wilson (Gregory Peck) and Captain Smollett (Reginald Denny) on the airport tarmac as the body of Margot's husband Francis is about to be taken from the plane.

character on the screen. Very simply, it is the story of a selfish wife's treachery towards her rich but unmanly husband while on a big-game hunting trip in Africa. When he shamefully shows the white feather in meeting the test of his first lion, she mercilessly taunts and insults him, then cuckolds him with their professional guide. And when he does finally gain his courage and is all set to make a plucky kill, she lets him have it (accidentally?) with a bullet through the back of his head. Obviously, there was no question in Mr. Hemingway's mind of the lady's deliberate intentions. And there is no question in the film, from the way the shooting scene is enacted and with all that goes before. For Mr. Robinson and Seymour Bennett [who did the adaptation, not the screenplay, of Hemingway's story] have followed, in the main part of their script, precisely the details and psychology of Mr. Hemingway's yarn.

As E. Ann Kaplan pointed out many years ago, the film shifts Hemingway's focus on Francis and his "existential plight," to be a "man of the type demanded by the Hemingway code,"[354] to a film noir with Margot coded as a "typical" femme fatale within the "film noir mode."[355] To support her argument, she cites the opening minutes of the film, a scene not found in Hemingway's story. While both utilize a flashback to tell their stories, Hemingway's narrative begins just after the disastrous lion hunt. The film, on the other hand, opens on a more "noirish" moment, the arrival of Margot and Wilson in Nairobi in the grey dawn after Francis's death. Wilson is shown trying to comfort Margot on the plane to Nairobi. On the tarmac, when she asks him "when will I see you," he enigmatically replies: "Later, perhaps." Behind the couple, Francis's body is shown being removed from the plane.

This is followed by Police Commissioner Smollett (Reginald Denny) interviewing Wilson and reminding the hunter of the formalities that have to be addressed, including his detailed report. It also includes Smollett's remark, "I liked the Macombers when I first met them. But sometimes when I looked at them I felt as if I had opened the wrong door in a hotel and seen something shameful." Smollett ends the interview urging the hunter to tell him, "off the record," what really happened on the safari. Wilson declines to comment.

Wilson then visits his usual bar in Nairobi and his usual bartender, Aimee (Jean Gillie), with whom, the film implies, he has had a relationship in the past. This exchange, which is not in Hemingway's story, involves Aimee questioning the big game hunter by using thinly veiled metaphors to imply that something untoward happened on the safari:

> AIMEE: Was it good hunting?
> WILSON: Quite
> AIMEE: Did everyone shoot a full bag?
> WILSON: Everyone
> AIMEE: Mrs. Macomber too?
> [Wilson's reaction indicates that he is aware of what she is implying]
> WILSON: What are you getting at?
> AIMEE: I was afraid you'd get into trouble, Wilson. Are you in trouble?
> WILSON: No!
> AIMEE: Mrs. Macomber?
> WILSON: Not Mrs. Macomber either.
> AIMEE: You don't call killing her husband trouble?
> WILSON: She didn't any more than I did. What makes you think that?
> AIMEE: A woman's intuition, Wilson. A woman would do things that a man wouldn't dream of doing. I'd murder for a man I was crazy about.

After Aimee accuses Wilson of being in love with Margot, the hunter tells her the "thought never entered my mind":

> AIMEE: It does not have to enter your mind.

At the beginning of the film's flashback, the perverse nature of the relationship between husband and wife is detailed. The scene is set in a Nairobi gun shop as Francis and Margot select their rifles for the expedition. Kaplan argues that in this scene, Margot's clothing, a black and white dress with a large hat, along with her handling of the Mannlicher rifle, explicitly codes her as a femme fatale. This coding is reinforced by her seemingly innocent dialogue exchange with Wilson (Gregory Peck) where she refers to the appeal of killing. As she looks down the barrel of the rifle, she tells Wilson, "I am a terrible shot. I never seem to be able to get the target and the gunsight together," a comment that has serious ramifications later in the film. After sending Francis (Robert Preston) away to purchase flowers, Margot continues to flirt with Wilson:

> MARGOT: Tell me, Mr. Wilson, how does it make a person feel killing something?
> WILSON: Oh, I don't know what you mean. Women don't usually like killing.

Robert Wilson (Gregory Peck) ponders Margot Macomber's guilt or innocence in *The Macomber Affair* **(1947).**

> MARGOT: I am not an exception. I'm just desperately curious [she looks directly into Wilson's eyes]. You see, I'm only a woman.

During the scene Margot fondles the gun that will eventually kill her husband.

Hemingway presents Margot differently. Her function in the narrative, as Kaplan points out, is merely an obstacle to Francis's existential fate and his regeneration as a "man." Wilson in the short story is also portrayed differently. While disgusted by Francis's display of cowardice, he grows to like him. But not Margot. Wilson does not respect her or have any romantic interest, beyond opportunistic sexual curiosity. Also, unlike in the film, Wilson is not a romantic figure. He is both older and less physically attractive. He is described as "about middle height with sandy hair, a stubby mustache, a very red face and extremely cold blue eyes with faint wrinkles at the corner."[356] He represents Hemingway's vision of "appropriate" masculinity. While he is a rule breaker, and he whips his "native boys," he has a low opinion of American women—like Margot:

> They are, he thought, the hardest in the world; the hardest, the cruelest, the most predatory and the most attractive and their men have softened or gone to pieces nervously as they have hardened. Or is it that they pick men they can handle? They can't know that much at the age they marry, he thought. He was grateful that he had gone through his education on American women before now because this was a very attractive one.[357]

Benedict Bogeaus
presents

GREGORY PECK · JOAN BENNETT
in Ernest Hemingway's
"THE MACOMBER AFFAIR"
also starring
ROBERT PRESTON
with Reginald Denny · Jean Gillie · Directed by ZOLTAN KORDA
Produced by Benedict Bogeaus and Casey Robinson

Copyright 1947 · United Artists Corporation. Country of Origin U.S.A.

Released thru United Artists

Property of National Screen Service Corp. Licensed for display only in connection with
the exhibition of this picture at your theatre. Must be returned immediately thereafter.

47/5

Eros Films Ltd. presents
GREGORY PECK
"The Macomber Affair" (A)
JOAN BENNETT · ROBERT PRESTON

Wilson, certain that Margot murdered Francis, tells her: "That was a pretty thing to do," he said in a toneless voice. "He *would* have left you too."[358] However, as a pragmatic hunter, unwilling to risk his license,[359] he decides to support her story that it was an accident. His real feelings, however, emerge when he asks Margot: "Why didn't you poison him? That's what they do in England."[360]

The film, on the other hand, is less interested in opportunistic sex between wife and hunter. It is more interested in building a romance between Wilson and Margot. And when, late in the film, he questions her about the killing, she admits that Francis was about to leave her. He asks why she didn't she poison him instead of shooting him? Margot, on the other hand, defends herself by claiming that she thought, early in their marriage, she could change him [Francis] when, in effect, he "changed me and made me what I am." Finally, she admits: "I hated Francis. I wanted him dead. Maybe I killed him. If there is such a thing as murder in your heart, there's your certain answer."

Perhaps the most revealing scene in the film, certainly the most startling, takes place after Francis runs away from the lion. As Margot returns to her cot late at night, after having sex with Wilson, Francis confronts her and asks where has she been? She tells him, with a smile, that she has been out getting a "breath of fresh air." He becomes increasingly agitated, especially after she calls him "a coward":

FRANCIS: You think I'll take anything.
MARGOT: I know you will, sweetie.
FRANCIS: Well, I won't!
MARGOT: O please, let's not talk darling. I'm sleepy.
FRANCIS: There wasn't going to be any nastiness. You said there wouldn't be.
MARGOT: Well, there is now.
FRANCIS: You said there wouldn't.... You promised.
MARGOT: Yes darling, that is the way I meant it to be. The trip was spoiled yesterday. We don't have to talk about it, do we?
FRANCIS: You don't wait long when you have an advantage, do you?

The Macomber Affair refuses to identify clearly who is the victim and who is the perpetrator. The three major protagonists, including Francis, who brutally attacks the support staff after his public display of cowardice, are all morally flawed. Margot is, most likely, a murderer and Wilson has destroyed his reputation and lost his hunting license. He also betrayed his client by sleeping with his wife. The film's moral legibility remains very unclear.

Raw Deal

The homme fatal, the male counterpart to the femme fatale, was a familiar figure in suspense melodramas such as *Sensation Hunters, Money Madness* and *Gaslight*

Opposite, top: Margot Macomber (Joan Bennett) humiliates her husband Francis (Robert Preston, left) in front of Robert Wilson (Gregory Peck) after his display of cowardice in *The Macomber Affair* (1947). *Bottom:* Margot Macomber (Joan Bennett) is attracted to hunter/guide Robert Wilson (Gregory Peck) in *The Macomber Affair* (1947).

Did Margot Macomber (Joan Bennett) murder her husband Francis (Robert Preston)? Captain Smollett (Reginald Denny, right) comes to take Margot Macomber (Joan Bennett) to the coroner's jury leaving Robert Wilson (Gregory Peck) behind.

(1944), *Experiment Perilous* (1944) and *Born to Kill* (1947). His victims were mostly young, vulnerable women imprisoned literally or psychologically in a gothic nightmare. *Raw Deal* reworks this archetype through its presentation of an emotionally traumatized gangster's girlfriend, Pat Regan (Claire Trevor). While appearing to be a gangster film involving its male protagonist Joe Sullivan (Dennis O'Keefe) who is seeking revenge against his corrupt boss, the film focuses more on Pat Regan's psychological trauma.

After the "golden period" of "classic" gangster films in the early 1930s such as *Little Caesar* (1931), *The Public Enemy* (1931) and *Scarface* (1932), which were characterized by gangsters' brash optimism, the gangster film went into decline until 1941. It was briefly resurrected by Humphrey Bogart's disillusioned portrayal of Roy Earle, a gangster out of his time and heading for a lonely death on a remote mountain in *High Sierra*. While there were relatively few gangster films produced in the 1940s, the once energetic gangster was replaced by characters such as Barry Sullivan's emotionally crippled Shubunka in *The Gangster* (1947) or James Cagney as the mother fixated psychopath Cody Jarrett in *White Heat* (1949). While Joe Sullivan in *Raw Deal* is not psychotic or emotionally crippled, he is on a downward trajectory, a victim of fate, a cruel society and poor choices.

Raw Deal began production in late 1947 under the title *Corkscrew Alley* following Eagle-Lion's December 1946 purchase for $1250 of a 62-page treatment by Arnold B. Armstrong and Audrey Ashley under that title. However, producer Edward Small discarded virtually everything in the treatment. In spring 1947 Don Stafford delivered a new screenplay which was reworked by John C. Higgins and Leopold Atlas. In October 1947 Anthony Mann, who worked with Higgins on *T-Men* (1947), was selected to direct. Filming began in mid–November 1947 and continued for 23 days with an additional 3 days for retakes in March 1948. The final budget cost was $522,039. However, prior to production Joseph Breen objected strongly to the film and urged Eagle-Lion to abandon it. He argued that the screenplay "had a low moral tone. It's a sordid story of crime, immorality, brutality, gruesomeness, illicit sex and sex perversion without the slightest suggestion of any compensating moral values whatsoever."[361] This response necessitated some changes to the script, notably eliminating a night scene where Joe Sullivan (Dennis O'Keefe) watches Ann Martin (Marsha Hunt) swimming in a "white scantily cut suit" revealing her "wet, glistening body" whose skin "is aglow with health."[362] More significantly, to address Breen's demand for a "voice of morality," additional dialogue was written for Ann, the "good" girl. This included a weakening of the film's initial thesis regarding Joe as the victim of a deprived childhood. To this end, a speech was written for Ann where she explains to him that her father was a school teacher:

> He died in the war of Depression—only he didn't get any medals or any bands or any bonus. He left three children. And you think you had to fight! Why, the only way you know how to fight is that stupid way with a gun! Well, there's another way you probably never even hard of. It's the daily fight that everyone has—to get food and an education. To land a job and keep it! And some self respect. Safe! I never asked for anything safe! All I want is just a little decency, that's all.

Ann's status as "innocence" is systematically challenged as the film progresses. Late in the film she is forced to shoot a villain to save Joe. She then spends a night alone with him on the beach. By the end of the film she is presented as confused and distraught. Importantly, the narration of the film is reserved for the "bad girl," Pat Regan (Claire Trevor). This unlikely choice enables her to convey her pain and torment to the audience.

Joe Sullivan, with the help of Pat, escapes from prison because he wants "to breathe." To facilitate his escape he kidnaps Ann Martin, a young woman who assisted his lawyer at his trial. However, during their road trip Pat's voice-over, used eleven times throughout the film, records her panic and pain as she realizes that Joe is falling in love with Ann:

> We've made it all right. We've gotten out of town, but for some strange reason I feel worse than before, like a two-time loser. Maybe it's the letdown or the rest of the roadblocks ahead. Or maybe it's because of her sitting next to Joe, where I should be. Where I would be if she weren't there. If she weren't....

Her narration is accompanied by the haunting sound of the theremin, an important attribute to composer Paul Sawtell's atmospheric score. Created by Léon Theremin, the theremin was an electronic musical instrument incorporating two glass oscillators and two antennae, to produce an eerie, almost supernatural sound. In films in the 1940s, such as *Spellbound* (1945), *The Lost Weekend* (1945), *The Spiral Staircase* (1946) and *The Red House* (1947), it was used to convey internal division, emotional vulnerability and/or psychological torment.

The plot concerns Joe's determination to collect $50,000 from gangster Rick Coyle (Raymond Burr) who owes the money to Joe from a recent robbery. Joe arranges to collect the money at Grimshaw's Tackle Store from Fantail (John Ireland), one of Coyle's gunmen. The rendezvous is a trap and in the ensuing fight Ann is forced to shoot, and wound, Fantail. Distressed, she runs out of the store and along the beach, where Joe catches her, and they spend the night together. The next day Joe, realizing that he will only cause problems for Ann, sends her away while seemingly committing himself to Pat. As Ann leaves Joe and Pat rejoins him, the two women pass each other on a lonely road. However, Pat, who should feel elated, is sympathetic to Ann's torment:

> I suppose I should feel some kind of victory, but I don't. I even feel sorry for her.... She too is a dame in love with Joe. And she's lost. I've been behind that eight ball too often myself not to know how she feels....

In the film's climax Fantail kidnaps Ann and takes her back to Rick to be tortured for information. Her situation is perilous as Rick is a sadist. Earlier in the film, when annoyed by his girlfriend Marcy (Chili Williams), he throws a flaming chafing dish into her face. Joseph Breen objected to this scene and only the intervention of his son, Joseph Breen, Jr., who was employed by Eagle-Lion, allowed the filming to proceed. However, the news that Ann has been captured by Coyle is passed on to Pat, not Joe, and she decides not to tell him. In the film's emotional climax, in the cabin of the ship about to take Pat and Joe to South America, Pat's torment is expertly captured by cinematographer John Alton's stylized lighting and Anthony Mann's compositions. Joe, after proposing marriage to Pat, turns off the cabin light as the camera frames her in silhouette on the left side of the screen opposite the cabin clock. The clock is highlighted in the frame to remind Pat (and the audience) that Ann is about to be molested if Joe does not save her. The scene is enhanced by the sound of the ticking clock and the despairing tone of Pat's narration:

> The lyrics were his [Joe's] all right, but the music ... Ann's. Suddenly I saw that every time he kissed me, he'd be kissing Ann.

Her narration ends with her shouting Ann's name. This alerts Joe to Ann's predicament and, in his confrontation with Coyle, he sends Rick to a fiery death after the gangster shoots him. The film's downbeat epilogue shows Joe dying in Ann's arms in a street named Corkscrew Alley as Pat, handcuffed to a policeman, records her response:

> There's my Joe in her arms. A kind of happiness on his face. In my heart, I know this is right for Joe. This is what he wanted.

As Andrew Spicer points out, "Pat is that film noir rarity, a genuinely tragic working-class antiheroine, and *Raw Deal* is a moving elegy to her blighted hopes."[363]

The Melodrama of Ethical Choice: "Domestic Noir"[364]

Glenn Erickson in his review of Robert Siodmak's 1950 film *The File on Thelma Jordon* points out that "not all noir films deal with detectives, cops and professional criminals. One particularly interesting specialty is Domestic Noir, in which seemingly ordinary people, often in a family setting, allow themselves to be sucked into morally compromising straits."[365] This sub-genre includes *They Won't Believe Me* (1947), *Pitfall* (1948) and *Crime of Passion* (1956). The common element in these films, as Erickson points out, "is the precariousness of relationships and the lengths people will go to preserve their social standing. Any violation of unwritten rules can lead to disaster."[366] A familiar theme in each film is the antithesis of the American Dream whereby a loving family and a good job does not guarantee happiness.[367]

This sub-genre approximates the characteristics described by Peter Brooks in his discussion of Henry James. Brooks argues that James's fiction does not belong to the world of sensational melodrama, or, to use Brooks's term, the "world of primary melodrama," because in this type of melodrama "we no longer know how to choose because of our epistemological doubt: we no longer can or need to identify persons as innocence or evil; we must respond instead to the ratios of choice themselves."[368] In the RKO film *They Won't Believe Me* (1947) the film opens with the central character,

The final moment in Anthony Mann's *Raw Deal* (1948) with Dennis O'Keefe as Joe Sullivan and Marsha Hunt as Ann Martin.

Larry Ballentine (Robert Young, left) with his lawyer Cahill (Frank Ferguson) in *They Won't Believe Me* (1947).

Larry Ballentine (Robert Young), on trial for the murder of his mistress Verna Carlson (Susan Hayward). There is little doubt that Ballentine is a morally flawed character as his defense lawyer tells the jury that his client is "heartless, shameful, sordid, cruel" and that "he has been a bad husband and a bad citizen. He's violated half a dozen moral laws. Lied, cheated and betrayed those who have loved him." He is also lecherous, lazy and self-indulgent. Yet the audience is invited to, if not condone, follow his actions through the film's lengthy flashback sequence. Ballentine is associated with three women, including his wife Greta (Rita Johnson). Although two of the women die, their deaths are not directly attributable to Ballentine. While he is attractive to women, he lacks substance. As Frank Krutnik points out, he is "markedly pre-adult, denying responsibility for his own actions."[369] At one point Verna, in frustration, tells him that "you're about as dependable as a four-year-old child."

The film ends with Larry about to commit suicide by jumping from the courtroom window. However, to appease the PCA, a bailiff in the court shoots him before he jumps and he falls out of the window.[370] The film's irony is contained in the epilogue as the foreman of the jury announces the verdict, "not guilty," and the film fades to black. Larry's crime is moral not criminal. As he tells his other mistress Janice (Jane Greer), when she visits him in jail while awaiting the verdict: "The jury doesn't matter—or the judge. I brought in my own verdict."

Married man Larry Ballentine (Robert Young) with one of his girlfriends, Janice Bell (Jane Greer), in *They Won't Believe Me* (1947).

Paramount's *The File on Thelma Jordon* begins and ends with the male protagonist, Cleve Marshall (Wendell Corey), walking disconsolately in the dark street outside his government office. Marshall, an unhappily married assistant district attorney, falls for femme fatale Thelma Jordon (Barbara Stanwyck). In an attempt to extricate her from a murder charge he, as the prosecuting attorney, compromises the trial. Thelma dies at the end of the film leaving Cleve with no job, a problematic marriage and no real future. This inconclusive ending prompted *The New York Times'* 1950 review of the film to describe it as a "strangely halting and confusing work." *Variety* called it an "interesting, femme-slanted melodrama, told with a lot of restrained excitement." Glenn Erickson summed the film up by pointing out that Cleve is almost "begging for an excuse to give up on his home life. It's one thing when a private eye decides something's rotten in the big city, but when an ordinary husband goes bad, Domestic Noirs indicate some kind of failure of the American Dream."[371]

Crime of Passion, an independent production, was released by United Artists on January 9, 1957. It cleverly reworks the figure of the femme fatale within a feminist context to illustrate how marriage and life in suburbia can have a devastating impact on an ambitious and talented woman. Erickson described the film as a *"noir domestique* like Andre de Toth's superb *Pitfall*, dealing with the roots of despair in suburbia."[372] The links to *Double Indemnity* and other noir films of the 1940s are evident,

Joan Tetzel (left) as Pamela Blackwell Marshall who is married to Cleve Marshall (Wendell Corey) who is in love with Thelma Jordon (Barbara Stanwyck) in Robert Siodmak's *The File on Thelma Jordon* (1950).

mainly through the casting of Barbara Stanwyck as Kathy Ferguson. However, unlike her Phyllis Dietrichson thirteen years earlier, it is not greed that motivates Kathy to commit murder but her sense of entrapment in what is presented as a suburban hell, a world characterized by complacency and conformity. In this manner *Crime of Passion* shares a similar discourse to other 1950s films such as *There's Always Tomorrow, All That Heaven Allows* and *Bigger Than Life*.

Crime of Passion is based on a screenplay and original story by Jo Eisinger, who also wrote the screenplay for *Night and the City* as well as the story adaptation for *Gilda*. It is a clever screenplay as Eisinger reworks elements of 1940s melodrama to show how a tough, intelligent newspaper advice columnist is trapped by society's standards and values and has nowhere to go to except marriage and a life of conformity in the suburbs. As a result she directs her energies into promoting the career of her husband, Bill Doyle (Sterling Hayden). However, Doyle, a capable and affable detective, lacks ambition and is comfortable with his position in the police hierarchy and his suburban lifestyle. Initially, Kathy rejects Doyle's dream of a comfortable existence in the suburbs as she tells him on their first date: "For marriage, I read life sentence. Home life, I read TV nights, beer in the fridge, second mortgage." However, her romantic/sexual desire for Doyle overcomes, for a period, her reservations

Sterling Hayden and Barbara Stanwyck in *Crime of Passion* (1957).

concerning married life. Forced to compete with the wives of other policemen, she has sexual intercourse with Doyle's superior officer, on the promise that he will promote her husband. When this fails to eventuate she commits murder and the film ends with Doyle arresting her.

Eight years earlier *Pitfall* dramatized the same scenario from a male point of view. The film was based on author/screenwriter Jay Dratler's 1947 novel *The Pitfall*. Columbia producer Samuel Biscoff submitted Dratler's initial draft for his novel, then titled *Husbands Die First*, to the PCA in 1945 but they rejected it. After Biscoff left Columbia to form an independent film company, Regal Films, he decided to produce a film adaptation of the novel. Dick Powell, who was on the Regal Films Board of Directors, wanted the lead male role of the disenchanted married man, John Forbes, who becomes involved with a model, Mona Stevens (Lizabeth Scott). While the film's screenplay credit went to Karl Kamb, most of the writing was done by William Bowers. As Bowers was under contract to Universal at that time he did not receive a screen credit.

While both film and novel are superficially similar, there are a number of significant differences between them. The main ideological difference was that the film, unlike the novel, ultimately endorses the institution of marriage and in the process, sacrifices the "other" woman, Mona Stevens. Not so the novel, which ends in despair as a corrupt cop (Macdonald) succeeds in destroying the novel's "hero" and assuming

Lizabeth Scott and Dick Powell in André De Toth's *Pitfall* (1948).

control of the "heroine" (Mona), a victim of domestic abuse. The story concludes with a jury announcing that Forbes is guilty of murder:

> I was finished. And only I saw the evil behind that bland face, an evil that came out of him like a throttling gas. Like the throttling gas of the execution chamber.
> That's when I broke down and began to scream. I remember that. It broke up the session. Because I didn't say a word. I just screamed like a madman.
> I knew now that I'd never had a chance since that February sixteenth when I picked up the phone and spoke to him.
> Mac was going to get Mona.[373]

Dratler's novel was never going to make it into a film without radical changes. The screenwriters transformed a nihilistic story into a morality tale about the pitfalls of straying from the "American Dream." This is outlined in the film's opening scene, a scene not found in the novel. At the daily breakfast in the suburbs John Forbes (Dick Powell) complains to his wife and young son about the lack of adventure in his life and the banal, routine nature of married life. Sue (Jane Wyatt), his wife, is not sympathetic. He has a secure job as an insurance investigator, a wonderful family, friends and all that society deems to be (in 1948) integral to the American Dream. Yet he is deeply unhappy. His expressions of dissatisfaction continue during his drive from the suburbs to his office in the Olympic Mutual Insurance Company in downtown Los Angeles. He tells Sue that he "feels like a wheel within a wheel within a wheel":

SUE: You and fifty-million others.

JOHN: I don't want to be like fifty-million others.

SUE: Oh, you're John Forbes. Average American. The backbone of the country.

JOHN: I don't want to be an average American, backbone of the county. I want somebody else to be the backbone and hold me up.

His sour disposition continues after arriving at work, especially after his boss, Ed Brawley (Selmer Jackson), reminds him that they are expected for their weekly card game that night. Forbes's chance for a little excitement comes with the arrival of Macdonald (Raymond Burr), a private investigator, who freelances for the insurance company. Mac has traced items purchased by an embezzler (Smiley) to his girlfriend Mona Stevens (Lizabeth Scott) while telling Forbes of his prurient interest in Mona.

Forbes, businesslike, visits Mona to reclaim the stolen goods. However, while waiting for her he takes out a photo album showing her as a model for the May Department store. Forbes is impressed. After she reminds him that he is a "little man with a briefcase" who is "strictly business" and does only what the company demands of him, Forbes invites her out for a drink. A boat ride near the Santa Monica pier follows. His first transgression is to not list Mona's speed boat among the items bought with stolen money. This changes after Mac, who watched Forbes leave Mona's house after their boat ride, asks why the boat is not on the list of recovered items. This requires Forbes to visit Mona again to explain that he will have to recover the boat, and they begin a sexual affair with Mona initiating their first kiss. When Forbes returns home late that night Mac beats him up outside the family garage.

At this stage Forbes has not revealed to Mona that he is married with a young son. She discovers this when visiting his home. At their next meeting, unlike in the novel, Mona tells Forbes that she does not want to continue their affair. Instead she urges him to return to his family. Forbes agrees and, at this point, the film's narrative divides between Forbes and Mona as they each try to deal with Mac's pursuit of Mona. After Forbes retaliates for the early beating and hits Mac, the private detective visits Mona's husband, Smiley (Byron Barr), in jail and informs him of his wife's affair with Forbes. Following Smiley's release, Mac continues to pressure Smiley. He plies him with alcohol and gives him a gun. The insurance agent shoots Smiley when he attempts to enter his house late at night. Forbes confesses to Sue about his affair with Mona and she tells him that he must keep this from the police to protect their son. Macdonald, pleased that Smiley is dead and that Forbes might be in trouble over the killing, visits Mona and tells her of his plan to take her to Reno. Distressed by the news of Smiley's death, worried about Forbes's future and disgusted with Mac's attempts to coerce her into a relationship, she shoots him.

The final scenes, and the epilogue, reverse the moral basis of Dratler's novel. The film punishes Mona while the novel punishes both of them. However evil, in the form of Mac, is eradicated in the film—not the novel. The only punishment inflicted on Forbes is a guilty conscience. He roams the streets of the city in a zombie-like fashion, wracked with guilt, before confessing the whole sordid tale to the District Attorney (John Litel). Nevertheless, unlike Mona, he escapes with a reprimand and the anger of the district attorney, who tells him that he believes that he has the wrong person (Mona) in the cell upstairs. Forbes rejoins Sue, who is waiting for him outside the Hall of Justice, and the film ends in a bleak, urban setting, a grey morning, and Sue's tentative reconciliation with her husband as she suggests they move to another town to try and rebuild their lives.

The ending is anything but upbeat and hopeful. The grey morning, the disconsolate body language of the two principals and their dialogue suggests that there is no certainty that the marriage will survive. Mona becomes the sacrificial victim—she is never condemned in the film, always acts "morally," she is never manipulative or destructive. In the epilogue she is consigned to jail or worse, while Forbes's "punishment" is to forget his dreams of adventure and excitement and accept the daily routine of a boring job and middle-class domestic life. As Frank Krutnik concludes:

> The institution of the family, which in the latter stages of the film they [Forbes and Mona] both, ironically, seek to consolidate, emerges as a staunchly defended fortress, protected not with military might, and not just through the sanctioning armoury of legal and cultural institutions, but with a far less tangible and more powerfully internally generated force, of guilt and prohibition.[374]

Andrew Spicer describes Joseph Losey's *The Prowler* (1951) as a "powerful allegory about the 'false values' that capitalism induced, the desire for '100,000 bucks, a Cadillac and a blonde,' which corrupt the personable young police officer Webb Garwood (Van Heflin)."[375] Responding to a call from Susan Gilvray (Evelyn Keyes) about

Evelyn Keyes and Van Heflin in Joseph Losey's *The Prowler* (1951).

Webb Garwood (Van Heflin) murders Susan Gilvray's (Evelyn Keyes) husband in *The Prowler* (1951).

a possible peeping tom, Garwood seduces the vulnerable woman. After learning that her husband's will lists $62,000 in cash, he concocts a plan to murder him, take the money and Susan and buy a motor lodge. Which he does. Susan reluctantly lies to protect him at the inquest into her husband's death and then marries Garwood. Soon afterwards she tells him she is pregnant. However, when Garwood realizes that her pregnancy will confirm that they were having an affair before the murder, he pressures her to have an abortion. When she refuses, they hide out in a desert ghost town while awaiting the birth of their child. Complications arise and retribution is achieved when the police shoot Garwood as he tries to escape.

The Prowler was directed by Joseph Losey from Dalton Trumbo's screenplay. Trumbo, however, did not receive a screen credit as he was blacklisted at that time, so Hugo Butler fronted for him. The film was an independent production by Horizon Pictures, a company set up by the film's producer Sam Spiegel, under the name S.P. Eagle, and John Huston. Huston wanted the film made so that his wife Evelyn Keyes, who had been laboring for some years in undistinguished roles at Columbia, would finally get a decent role. Filming took place in April/May 1950 under the title of the original story, *The Cost of Living*. Trumbo was paid $35 to voice the radio broadcasts by Susan's husband which always ended with the slightly ominous "I'll be seeing you Susan."

Webb Garwood (Van Heflin) prepares to murder the doctor who has just delivered Susan Gilvray's (Evelyn Keyes) baby in *The Prowler* (1951).

The Prowler, an early example of Losey's interest in conflicts arising out of sexual power and class differences, themes he would refine in his 1960s British films such as *Eve* (1962) and *The Servant* (1963), was filmed while Losey was under pressure from the HUAC hearings. It is, for 1950, a remarkably explicit challenge to Breen's long-standing principle of morally compensating values. While Breen objected to the film's low moral tone and insisted that the details of the adulterous affair between Webb and Susan, and her pregnancy, be kept to a minimum,[376] he accepted the script on April 10, 1950. This was surprising as the film explicitly acknowledges an illicit sexual affair. The July 2, 1951, review of *The Prowler* in *The New York Times* highlighted the film's aberrant qualities under the heading "Unusual Drama Opens at Criterion." The reviewer noted that the

> people of "The Prowler" are decidedly off the norm.... Neither Van Heflin nor Evelyn Keyes as the strangely mated pair, are not people who fit in or are condoned by formal society. But credit must be given to Van Heflin in essaying an unsympathetic assignment. He is obviously a gambler willing to risk his life to attain those ends he deems best. And he is not a pat villain but a dastard who is human in his final breakdown when he says: "I did it for the $62,000 but I love you, you gotta give me credit for that." Miss Keyes' unvarnished characterization is also one of many shades.

Susan is virtue in the film. But her presentation of virtue illustrates how cultural change had refigured this integral figure in melodrama. Ultimately, she takes an ethical stand while trapped in the remote shack. She defies Garwood when she realizes that he is about to murder the elderly doctor, Doctor James (Wheaton Chambers), who delivered her baby. She warns the doctor to escape with the baby and then hides the keys to Garwood's car. After James departs, she accuses Garwood of murdering her husband and planning to murder the doctor to protect his identity. Garwood, desperately searching for the spare keys, tells Susan:

> So what! I'm no good. But I'm no worse than anybody else. You work in a store you knock down on the cash register. The big boss the income tax. The ward healer you sell votes. The lawyer you take bribes. I was a cop, I used a gun.

Webb's desire for middle-class respectability via marriage to Susan, children and financial security were values shared by the audience for the film in the early 1950s. Yet Losey and Trumbo show how easily this desire can result in obsession, moral corruption and murder. Surprisingly, for such a tough, bleak film, *The Prowler* was a hit at the box-office.

"The Ethical Unintelligibility of the World"[377]: Where Danger Lives *(1950) and* Angel Face *(1953)*

In an April 25, 1953, review of *Angel Face,* the reviewer for *The New York Times* claimed:

> "Angel Face," yesterday's new melodrama at the Mayfair, is an exasperating blend of genuine talent, occasional perceptiveness and turgid psychological claptrap that enhances neither R.K.O., which should know better, nor the participants. A capable cast, headed by Jean Simmons and Robert Mitchum, and a nice, taut story idea have been set adrift in a pretentious Freudian mist that wafts through the handsomely mounted proceedings with disastrous results … fuzzy character motivations, deliberately confusing incidents…. And the absurdly dismal finale.

It concludes with a question as to "why the film itself commits hari-kari, only the Sphinx knows." The reviewer was impressed by the film's basic premise as it promised a melodrama: "a nice, taut story," the production values, "pungent dialogue and a few thoughtful scenes," especially the "early scenes of simmering byplay between this mysterious young lady, her fanatically adored father, Herbert Marshall, and hated stepmother, Barbara O'Neill, with the chauffeur as pawn, promise some tingling, civilized intrigue." When these expectations for a melodrama were not fulfilled, the review turned hostile. Especially when the villain, Diane Tremayne (Jean Simmons), is ultimately transformed into a victim. As Glenn Erickson writes, "Diane is fascinatingly complex…. Unlike a standard femme fatale, Diane derives no pleasure from her crimes, only misery and solitude." She is, he argues, "like a heroine in a horror story, sick with the knowledge that she's doomed herself to isolation." This is consistent with the film's determination to deny the presentation of an ethical universe in its epilogue. As Erickson points out, the film's "shock ending [which] is bleak in the extreme, a violent coda that comes out of nowhere."[378]

Three years earlier Mitchum starred in a superficially similar film, *Where Danger Lives*, in a similar role, a man tormented by a murderous femme fatale. Both films

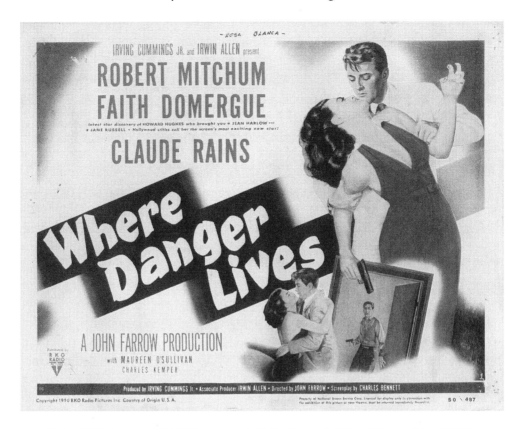

Robert Mitchum and Faith Domergue in John Farrow's *Where Danger Lives* (1950).

are considered "noir" and most commentators point to their similarities. Robert Porfirio and Alain Silver in *Film Noir, An Encyclopedic Reference to the American Style,* for example, argue that "*Where Danger Lives* is in many respects quite similar to Preminger's film, *Angel Face*, particularly the role played by Robert Mitchum as Jeff."[379] Silver and James Ursini reiterate this view in their chapter on John Farrow, the director of *Where Danger Lives,* when they write that Farrow created a "femme fatale unusual even for noir"[380]:

> Margo, the deadly woman of *Where Danger Lives,* is an out-of-control schizophrenic, who seems to truly believe in the fantasies she has concocted to ensnare her hapless lover, Dr. Jeff Cameron. In this she is unlike such classic femme fatales as the cold and cunning Phyllis Dietrichson of *Double Indemnity* but anticipates a later, more conflicted heroine such as Diane Tremayne of Otto Preminger's 1953 *Angel Face.*

Both films share a similar opening. In *Where Danger Lives* Dr. Jeff Cameron (Robert Mitchum) is prevented from going out with his girlfriend Julie Dorn (Maureen O'Sullivan) when he has to attend to a young woman, Margo Lannington (Faith Domergue), who has just attempted suicide. When Margo wakes up she notices a white rose in her hospital room, a rose that Jeff purchased for Julie. However, Margo assumes it is for her. Jeff is immediately attracted to Margo's beauty—and her naked shoulder peeking out from her hospital sheet. His interest intensifies after she asks him, "Why should I live?" Cameron begins seeing Margo, while ignoring Julie. He is attracted not only by her beauty but her vulnerability, especially after she explains that she attempted suicide following the death of her mother and the absence of her "father" in Canada.

Angel Face begins with ambulance driver Frank Jessup (Robert Mitchum) and his partner Bill Crompton (Kenneth Tobey) called to the hillside estate of Catherine Tremayne (Barbara O'Neill) where she is being treated for gas inhalation. While the police maintain that it was accidental, Catherine believes somebody was trying to kill her. As Frank is about to leave the house he notices Diane (Jean Simmons), Catherine's stepdaughter, playing a soft, romantic piece on the piano. Intrigued, he assures her that her stepmother will recover. When Diane becomes hysterical, Frank slaps her face to calm her down. Angry, she slaps him right back. This sadomasochistic foreplay excites and intrigues Diane and she begins to stalk Jessup while simultaneously destroying his relationship with his longtime girlfriend Mary Wilton (Mona Freeman).

Both Jeff Cameron (*Where Danger Lives*) and Frank Jessup (*Angel Face*) deceive their long-standing girlfriends. This breach in an ethical code is followed by a crucial moment in the narrative in each film. Each "hero" is confronted with a profound option and each responds differently. In *Where Danger Lives* Cameron continues to romance Margo until he discovers that Frederick Lannington is not her father but her husband. This revelation occurs in the Lannington mansion when Frederick exposes Margo's true (moral) identity while pointing out that he is not her first lover. With sadistic relish he tells the young doctor that "Margo married me for my money. I married her for her … youth. We both got what we wanted after a fashion." Cameron, disgusted by Lannington's revelation and Margo's deceit, is about to leave the house when he hears Margo's scream for help. When he rushes back to the living room she tells him that her husband ripped an earring from her ear. As Jeff is about to take Margo with him, Lannington hits him over the head with a poker. Jeff knocks Lannington down and goes to the bathroom to attend to his head injury. Dazed, he returns to the living room to find Lannington dead and Margo claiming that Lannington hit his head on the fireplace. Although Jeff's first impulse is to call the police, Margo convinces the dazed doctor that no one will believe him and that they must flee. After failing to catch an overseas flight, they hit the road, driving from San Francisco to the border town of Nogales in Arizona.

Throughout the long drive Jeff, badly weakened by concussion, is under Margo's control. The film reverses a familiar gothic narrative trope involving the persecution of a vulnerable female by a sadistic male. As Jeff's strength diminishes, Margo's power increases. As Silver and Ursini note: "Like a dominatrix or an emotional vampire the femme fatale feeds off the weakness of the victim."[381] The trip down the West Coast is a continuous gothic nightmare. This includes a crooked car salesman, "Honest Hal," who cheats them in a car transaction and a bizarre sojourn in the small town of Pottsville during "Whiskers Week" where, to avoid capture, Jeff is forced to marry Margo by the Justice of the Peace, Mr. Bogardus (Billy House). The newlyweds are then serenaded in their bleak "honeymoon suite" by drunken Pottsville revelers beneath their window.

Nogales, a seedy, corrupt border town, becomes the apotheosis of Jeff's

Psychologically unstable Margo Lannington (Faith Domergue) with Jeff Cameron (Robert Mitchum) on the road trip to hell in *Where Danger Lives* (1950).

nightmare road trip. Desperate to cross the border, they pawn Margo's jewelry, worth at least $9,000, for $750 to bribe their way into Mexico. As they wait in a squalid hotel room behind a theater until 4:00 a.m. for the "coyote" to take them across the border, a flashing neon sign across the alley gives cinematographer Nicholas Musuraca the visual pretext to depict their predicament as a descent into hell. Director John Farrow undertakes a dazzling, bravura seven-minute unbroken sequence in the seedy room which begins with a close-up of Margo looking at her reflection in a dirty mirror before pacing the floor of the hotel room. Farrow and Musuraca continually reframe the different compositions within the room to capture the full emergence of Margo's psychosis. Jeff, paralyzed on the left side of his body, is rendered immobile and sits passively on the bed. Margo, impatient with his helplessness, paces and taunts him with a series of revelations, including the fact that she was under psychiatric care, that she has been hiding Lannington's money in a bank account for some time and that she, not Jeff, murdered her husband. Jeff, despite his impaired physical condition, finally understands the full extent of her damaged mental condition. After he tells her that he pities her, Margo reacts by smothering him with a pillow in the same manner she murdered her husband.

Believing that she has killed Jeff, Margo leaves the room and heads for the truck that will take her safely across the border. However, as Damien Love describes, the "camera waits, resting on the bed and regarding the emptied room until, like a vampire's talon in the crack of a coffin, Mitchum's hand appears, grabbing weakly the worn bedding, and he somehow drags himself after her, the rotted wood of the hotel bannister coming apart in his hands as he stumbles down the stairs."[382] Jeff, in severe pain, refuses to give up his pursuit of Margo as he staggers along a line of porch posts, desperately clinging to them to hold him up, while a low angle composition of Margo shows her emerging from the getaway truck to fire bullets into the body of the masochistic doctor. Again, he survives, against the odds, as the police arrive and shoot Margo. In her dying confession she exonerates Cameron while defiantly telling both Cameron and the police that "nobody pities me." In the film's epilogue, with Cameron recovering in hospital, he is about to send a white rose to Julie when she appears at his bedside.

There is an identical ethical moment in *Angel Face* with a different result. After taking a job as the family chauffeur in the Tremayne household, Frank's lust for Diane's child-like beauty dissipates when he understands that she is planning another attempt on her stepmother's life. Instead of warning Catherine he ignores her murderous intentions. His decision is not based on morality but self-interest. This becomes apparent when Diane comes to his room at 2:40 a.m. and fabricates a tale about her stepmother trying to murder her by turning on the gas. Frank listens, with a sense of disbelief, and then tells her:

> FRANK: If I was a cop, and not a very bright cop at that, I'd say your story is as phony as a three-dollar bill!
> DIANE: How can you say that to me?
> FRANK [SARCASTICALLY]: Oh, you mean "after all we've been to each other"?

He then tells her, "I'm not getting involved—how stupid do you think I am? You hate that woman and someday you're going to hate her enough to kill her. It's been in the back of your mind all along."

Frank remains in the house in the hope that Diane will obtain funding for his planned auto-business from Catherine. When he realizes that this is impossible he tries to reunite with his former girlfriend, Mary (Mona Freeman). Diane, anticipating his move, pleads with him to take her with him, even bringing her suitcase to his room. Rejected, she murders her stepmother the next day by tampering with the family car so that it plummets over the cliff behind the house. However, when Diane learns that her father was also in the car she has a nervous breakdown.

Diane and Frank are arrested for murder. With the aid of a clever defense lawyer, Fred Barrett (Leon Ames), they are acquitted after Barrett forces them to marry to explain the presence of Diane's suitcase in Frank's room prior to the killings. Diane, in an attempt to salvage her conscience following her father's death, goes to Barrett after the trial and confesses to the double murder. Barrett, unconcerned about the morality of the killings, tells Diane that she cannot be tried again under the principle of double jeopardy. After Frank insists on leaving she kills both of them in the same manner—by putting her car in reverse and driving off the cliff at the side of the Tremayne mansion.

Damien Love argues, correctly, that Frank lacks any semblance of morality:

In Preminger's film, playing Frank Jessup, the malcontent low-class ambulance driver who dreams only delinquent dreams of tinkering with girls and hot-rods and maybe spinning those dangerous little cars along fast blank racetracks, Mitchum essayed the most extreme manifestation of his RKO loser-antihero protagonist. Here is a man who exudes an utterly monumental sense of detachment, exhibits an unhealthy willingness to drift whichever way takes least effort and seems likeliest to lead to a warm bed.[383]

As the film progresses it is clear that director Otto Preminger is transforming Diane into the victim. In a bravura sequence, which invokes the emotional power of nineteenth-century theatrical melodrama, Preminger through the use of composition, editing, body language (Jean Simmons) and music shows Diane walking through the empty halls and rooms of the Tremayne household. It begins with Diane walking over to a piano where there is a photo of her dead father, taken when he was much younger, which reminds her of happier days with her beloved father. As she continues through the house she stops at her father's chess board, accompanied by Dimitri Tiomkin's lush, darkly romantic score that rises and falls with her movements. The sequence concludes when she walks outside to the place where she tampered with the family car before walking into Frank's apartment over the garage. As she moves through his two rooms, she picks up his sports coat and hugs it to herself. A time transition from late night to early morning shows Diane spending the night in a chair in Frank's room wrapped in his coat. This long, haunting sequence evokes a mixture of pathos, sadness and madness. Dimitri Tiomkin's score is integral in presenting Diane as a woman with no future.

Unlike the upbeat epilogue in *Where Danger Lives*, *Angel Face* closes on a nihilistic depiction of a world lacking moral meaning, an arbitrary world. After Diane kills them both by driving her car backwards over the cliff, the epilogue shows a taxi arriving at the front door of the mansion. The driver gets out and when nobody appears he sounds his horn. Everybody is dead.

There are few crime/suspense films produced in Hollywood that deviated far from Hollywood's melodramatic imagination. This was particularly true of major films from the major studios. This is not to deny that there was a significant, hard-edged shift in emphasis in the crime melodrama in the 1940s as the comforting world of the amateur detective was relegated to the margins of the industry. However, to replicate the nihilism inherent in Hammett's Flitcraft parable was a step too far for most films as it would have, in all probability, damaged them at the box-office. Huston realized this by not filming the final scene in his screenplay for *The Maltese Falcon*. Similarly, Billy Wilder in jettisoning the gas chamber sequence from *Double Indemnity*. Also Virginia Van Upp, with her upbeat epilogue to *Gilda*, belatedly tried to return the film to the ethical values of postwar America. There were a few studio films, however, that deviated from the tenets of melodrama (*Out of the Past*, *Criss Cross* and *Angel Face*) along with independent productions such as *The Macomber Affair* and *The Prowler*. As a rule it was low budget films such as *The Seventh Victim*, *Detour*, *Sensation Hunters*, *Decoy* and *Money Madness* that took the most risks.

Steve Fisher's insistence that there was a greater emphasis on psychology and emotional instability in the crime melodrama from the late 1930s was also noticeable. This extended to seemingly patriotic war melodramas such as *The Fallen Sparrow*.

Jean Simmons, Robert Mitchum and Mona Freeman in Otto Preminger's *Angel Face* (1952).

The impact of James M. Cain was also significant—not as a screenwriter but through the adaptations of his two major novels, *The Postman Always Rings Twice* and *Double Indemnity*. These films, and the many imitators, transformed the key melodramatic concepts, victims and perpetrators. Victims became perpetrators while virtue, in the more extreme films, was drained of its ethical meaning. Some films even cast doubts as to the existence of a moral universe. As Steve tells Anna at the close of *Criss Cross* as she prepares to abandon him:

> I am different. I never wanted the money. I just wanted you. After we split up I used to walk around the streets in strange cities at night. I use to think about you. I just wanted to hold you in my arms, to take care of you. It could've been wonderful. But it didn't work out. What a pity it didn't work out.

As Miklos Rozsá's score builds, Robert Siodmak's composition of the doomed pair forms a "tragic tableau."[384] The last image is their bodies draped across each other in front of a moonlit ocean. Even more extreme was Jacqueline Gibson's narration that closes *The Seventh Victim*: "I run to Death and Death meets me as fast, and all my Pleasures are like Yesterday." And Jeff Bailey, resigned to the fact that it is useless to struggle further against the destructive impact of fate, tells Kathie Moffat at the end of *Out of the Past*: "Build my gallows high, baby."

Chapter Notes

Introduction

1. Instead of the term "classical" melodrama I will describe films based on action, thrills, spectacle, comedy and romance as sensational melodramas, the most elemental form of melodrama. Others, such as Linda Williams, use the term blood and thunder melodramas. *See* Linda Williams, "'Tales of Sound and Fury…'; or, the Elephant of Melodrama," in Christine Gledhill and Linda Williams, eds., *Melodrama Unbound: Across History, Media, and National Cultures* (New York, Columbia University Press, 2018), 215.

2. Steve Neale, "Melo Talk: On the Meaning and Use of the Term 'Melodrama' in the American Trade Press," *The Velvet Light Trap,* Number 32, Fall 1993, 81, note 76.

3. Linda Williams, *Playing the Race Card: Melodramas of Black and White from Uncle Tom to O.J. Simpson* (Princeton, Princeton University Press, 2001), 15.

4. Peter Brooks, *The Melodramatic Imagination: Balzac, Henry James, Melodrama, and the Mode of Excess* (New Haven, Yale University Press, 1995).

5. Linda Williams, "Melodrama Revised," in Nick Browne, ed., *Refiguring American Film Genre: Theory and History* (Berkeley, University of California Press, 1998), 51.

6. Brooks cites the D. W. Griffith film *Orphans of the Storm* in the preface to his 1995 edition.

7. *Ibid.,* 198.

8. *Ibid.,* 200.

9. See *Ibid.,* 42.

10. *Ibid.*

11. Robert. B. Parker, "Introduction Robert," in Dashiell Hammett, *Woman in the Dark* (New York, Vintage Books, 1989), xii.

12. See Christine Gledhill, "Prologue," in Christine Gledhill and Linda Williams, eds., *Melodrama Unbound: Across History, Media, and National Cultures* (New York, Columbia University Press, 2018).

13. *Ibid.*

14. See Brooks, 24–26. See also Linda Williams, "Melodrama Revised," in Nick Browne, ed., *Refiguring American Film Genre: Theory and History* (Berkeley, University of California Press, 1998), 52.

15. Peter Stanfield, *Horse Opera: The Strange History of the 1930s Singing Cowboy* (Urbana, University of Illinois Press, 2002), 145.

16. *Ibid.*

17. *Ibid.,* 146. Republic paid Johnny Marvin and Autry $50 for the right to use their song in the film. See Holly George-Warren, *Public Cowboy No. 1: The Life and Times of Gene Autry* (New York, Oxford University Press, 2007), 319, note 10.

18. Gene Autry, who recorded the song before the film went into production, did not include the "Home on the Range" motif. Instead he repeated a verse and it was a major hit for him. Roger's version, which has a slower tempo than Autry's, is as good or even better. See Stanfield, *Horse Opera*, 146.

19. Brooks, 25.

20. Williams, "'Tales of Sound and Fury," 214.

21. See Williams, "Melodrama Revised," 52.

22. *Come On Danger!* (1932) was remade three times by RKO. The original story was developed by Bennett Cohen and it was remade as *The Renegade Ranger* in 1938 starring George O'Brien, Tim Holt and Rita Hayworth and in 1942 as *Come On Danger* starring Tim Holt. Cohen's story was also, unofficially, reworked by Betty Burbridge for the Tex Ritter and Jennifer Holt film *Oklahoma Raiders* at Universal in 1944.

23. With a budget of only $31,000 *Come On Danger!* returned a creditable gross of $106,000. The talent working on the film was impressive. Aside from cinematographer Nicholas Musuraca, the music director was Max Steiner and the (uncredited) executive producer was David O. Selznick.

24. See Christine Gledhill, "Rethinking Genre," in Christine Gledhill and Linda Williams, eds., *Reinventing Film Studies* (London, Arnold, 2000), 234.

25. See Jeffrey Richards, *Visions of Yesterday* (London, Routledge & Kegan Paul, 1973), 231.

26. Quoted in Carl Becker, "What Is Still Living in the Political Philosophy of Thomas Jefferson," in S. Fine and G.S. Brown, eds., *The American Past,* Volume 1 (New York, The Macmillan Company, 1965), 90.

27. *Ibid.,* 91.

28. See Yehoshua Arieli, *Individualism and Nationalism in American Ideology* (Cambridge, Harvard University Press, 1964), 161.

29. See George McKenna, *American Populism* (New York, G.P. Putnam and Sons, 1974), xx.

30. See Richards, chapters 15, 16 and 17.
31. *Ibid.*, 234.
32. *Ibid.*
33. *Ibid.*
34. *Ibid.*, 235.
35. *Ibid.*
36. Scott Simmon, *The Invention of the Western Film* (Cambridge, Cambridge University Press, 2003), 215.
37. Bert Linley appeared as Wyatt Earp, a minor figure, in the 1923 film *Wild Bill Hickok* starring William S. Hart.
38. I am discounting Universal's 1937 serial *Wild West Days* as it has absolutely nothing to do with Earp and the shootout at the O.K. Corral, despite the fact that author W.R. Burnett gets a screen credit for the story.
39. *Six Guns and Society: A Structural Study of the Western* (Berkeley, University of California Press, 1977), 32.
40. *Ibid.*, 33.
41. *Ibid.*, 40.
42. Zaresh Haman, "'Get to Fighting or Get Away': The Gunfight at the O.K. Corral," *StMU History Media*, November 3, 2017.
43. See Brooks, 36.
44. See *Ibid.*, 36.
45. See *Ibid.*, 35.
46. *Ibid.*
47. *Ibid.*, 36.
48. *Ibid.*
49. W.R. Burnett, *Saint Johnson* (New York, A.L. Burt Company, 1930).
50. Burnett, 11.
51. *Ibid.*, 9.
52. *Ibid.*, 31.
53. *Ibid.*, 32.
54. *Ibid.*, 51.
55. *Ibid.*, 52.
56. *Ibid.*, 58.
57. *Ibid.*
58. *Ibid.*, 60.
59. *Ibid.*, 66.
60. In pointing to the importance of the Holmesburg stage robbery in the lead-up to the gunfight at the O.K. Corral, Burnett was drawing upon the real-life attempted robbery of the Benson Stage on March 15, 1881, seven months before the O.K. Corral gunfight. The Sandy Bob stage out from Tombstone on its way to Benson was attacked by one man, leading to the death of the driver, Bud Philpot, and a passenger, Peter Roerig. When the horses bolted, the robber took off, thereby missing out on the Wells Fargo haul of $26,000 in silver. The main suspect was Doc Holliday, especially after his common-law wife Kate Elder signed a complaint against Holliday—which she withdrew after she was arrested by Virgil Earp for drunk and disorderly conduct. She also refused to testify against Holliday in court and the case against him was dismissed. There was, however, one other incriminating matter. Immediately after the failed robbery Holliday searched for Billy Clanton, a man he never met before. There was

some speculation that Billy could identify Holliday as the stagecoach bandit and Doc wanted him out of the way. Billy was one of the first killed at the O.K. Corral. See Joyce Aros, "The Benson Stage Debacle," *Tombstone Times*, http://www.tombstonetimes.com/stories/benson.html.
61. Burnett, 96.
62. *Ibid.*, 101.
63. *Ibid.*, 113.
64. *Ibid.*, 129.
65. *Ibid.*, 130.
66. *Ibid.*, 157.
67. *Ibid.*, 188.
68. *Ibid.*, 189–190.
69. *Ibid.*, 191–192.
70. *Ibid.*, 216.
71. *Ibid.*, 225.
72. *Ibid.*, 228.
73. *Ibid.*, 235.
74. *Ibid.*, 236.
75. *Ibid.*, 270.
76. *Ibid.*, 275.
77. *Ibid.*, 276.
78. *Ibid.*, 297.
79. *Ibid.*, 305.
80. Scott Simmon points out that "historically Arizona's Native Americans had no votes to cast, let alone sell, until more than a half a century after the 1880s." Simmon, 212.
81. See *Ibid.*, 213.
82. See Wright, 74–75. Scott Simmon, on the other hand, argues that visually, *Law and Order* "would not look out of place twenty years later in the noir era." Simmons, 213.
83. Gledhill, "Rethinking Genre," 227.
84. Simmon, 213.
85. *Ibid.*
86. *Ibid.*
87. *Ibid.*
88. *Ibid.*
89. *Ibid.*
90. http://www.tcm.com/tcmdb/title/68263/Beast-of-the-City/notes.html.
91. *Ibid.*
92. There are a number of scenes in *Beast of the City*, including Daisy Stevens/Jean Harlow's seduction of Ed, that are similar to blatantly sexual sequences found in many "Pre-Code" films. This includes Daisy telling Ed: "I don't mind taking orders [from Belmonte], but there's one decision that's always up to me." Also, their erotic sparring includes Harlow's suggestive movements on a couch. This follows her gyrating dance for Ed. He responds by grabbing her arm:

DAISY: Say, that hurts a little bit.
ED: And you don't like to be hurt, do you?
DAISY: Oh, I don't know. Kinda fun sometimes if it's done in the right spirit.
Later, when Daisy is trying to get information, she lies on a bed with the drunken Ed.
93. Jack Lait, *The Beast of the City* (New York, Grosset & Dunlap, 1932).
94. *Ibid.*, 199–200.

95. *Ibid.*, 200.

96. http://www.tcm.com/tcmdb/title/68263/Beast-of-the-City/articles.html.

97. See chapter two for a rare exception, *Wyoming Outlaw* (1939).

98. Williams, *Playing the Race Card,* 20.

99. Brooks., 18.

100. *Ibid.*, 20.

101. *Ibid.*, 19–20.

102. Gledhill, "Prologue."

103. *Ibid.*

104. *Ibid.*

105. *Ibid.*

106. See Williams, "Tales of Sound and Fury," 205.

107. Brooks, 18.

108. Simmon, 213.

109. Other gothic westerns include *Haunted Gold* (1932), *The Star Packer* (1934), both starring John Wayne, *Ghost Valley* (1932) starring Tom Keene and *Tombstone Canyon* (1932), starring Ken Maynard and Cecilia Parker. In this film Maynard eventually discovers that the "Phantom" is his long-lost father. Of the films listed by Simmon (page 213) only *Mystery Ranch* can truly be described as a "gothic western." In both *Haunted Gold* and *Ghost Valley* the hero assists the heroine in regaining a ghost town/gold mine from a crooked judge/outlaw. These films have more to do with dispossession, a common theme in the 1930s series westerns. While the mine/ghost town is, seemingly, "haunted" by a hooded figure, a rational explanation is eventually offered and there are no "ghosts."

110. The novella was first serialized in *Red Book Magazine* prior to its publication by Doubleday in 1920.

111. The first film version of White's novel was produced by an independent company and released by Pathé. It starred Jack Conway, a major film director at MGM from 1925 to 1948, as White's hero, William Sanborn. Claire Adams appeared as the heroine, Ruth Emory, and Frank Campeau as the sadistic Henry Hooper. The film, now considered lost, did not have a major impact on the box-office despite favorable reviews. See Ed Hulse, "'Mystery Ranch" (1932). "The Brief Vogue for 'Western Gothic,'" in Ed Hulse, ed., *The Wild West of Fiction and Film* (Morris Plains, NJ: Murania Press, 2018), 228.

112. Stewart Edward White, "The Killer." In Hulse, 236.

113. George O'Brien's series of westerns at Fox often had budgets well in excess of other series and B westerns. Yet their relatively short running times (*Mystery Ranch* is only 56 minutes, for example) meant that his films at Fox, and later RKO, were regarded as B or series westerns.

114. See Andrew Spicer, *Film Noir* (London, Pearson Education Limited, 2002), 45.

115. The sinister, softly spoken performance by Charles Middleton as the depraved villain is similar to his most famous role four years later as Ming "the Merciless," the sadistic emperor of Mongo, who lusts after Dale Arden (Jean Rogers) in *Flash Gordon* (1936).

116. Scott Simmon describes the B western of the 1930s as characterized by its "surrealism." See Simmon, 152.

117. Hulse, 232.

118. *Ibid.*

119. Quoted in Hulse, 231–232.

120. See Stanfield, *Horse Opera*, 6.

Chapter One

1. Williams, "Melodrama Revised," 42.

2. Thomas Elsaesser, "Tales of Sound and Fury: Observations on the Family Melodrama," *Monogram* 4 (1972).

3. John Fell, *Film and the Narrative Tradition* (Norman, University of Oklahoma Press, 1974), 14. See also John Fell, ed., *Film Before Griffith* (Berkeley, University of California Press, 1983). See also Sergei Eisenstein, *Film Form* (New York, Harcourt, Brace & World, 1949) 195–225; Nicholas Vardac, *From Stage to Screen: Theatrical Origins of Early Film: David Garrick to D.W. Griffith* (Cambridge, Harvard University Press, 1949) and Michael Walker, "Melodrama and the American Cinema," *Movie* 29/30, Summer 1982.

4. *Ibid.*

5. *Ibid.*, 17.

6. *Ibid.*

7. See *Ibid.*, 35.

8. Michael R. Booth, *English Melodrama* (London, Herbert Jenkins, 1965), Michael R. Booth, *Hiss the Villain: Six English and American Melodramas* (London, Eyre and Spottiswoode, 1964), Michael R. Booth, *English Plays of the Nineteenth Century: Dramas 1800–1850* (Oxford, Clarendon Press, 1969), David Grimsted, *Melodrama Unveiled: American Theater and Culture 1800–1850* (Chicago, University of Chicago Press, 1968), James L. Smith, *Melodrama* (London, Methuen, 1973), Frank Rahill, *The World of Melodrama* (University Park, Pennsylvania State University Press, 1967), Eric Bentley, *The Life of the Drama* (New York, Atheneum, 1964), Robert W. Corrigan, *Laurel British Drama: The Nineteenth Century* (New York, Dell Publishing Co., 1967), Robert B. Heilman, *Tragedy and Melodrama* (Seattle, University of Washington Press, 1968), Robert B. Heilman, *The Iceman, the Arsonist, and the Troubled Agent* (Seattle, University of Washington Press, 1973).

9. Booth, *English Plays of the Nineteenth Century,* 25.

10. Heilman, *Tragedy and Melodrama,* 88–90. See also Heilman *The Iceman, the Arsonist, and the Troubled Agent,* 22–23.

11. Heilman, *The Iceman, the Arsonist, and the Troubled Agent,* 22.

12. Heilman, *Tragedy and Melodrama,* 89. Linda Williams is critical of Heilman's "overly simplistic notion of the 'monopathy,' based on the idea that each character in melodrama sounds a single emotional note that is in turn simply mimicked by the viewer." See Williams, "Melodrama Revised," 49.

13. Heilman, *The Iceman, the Arsonist, and the Troubled Agent*, 22.

14. *Ibid.*

15. Elsaesser, 5.

16. *Ibid.*, 6.

17. *Ibid.*

18. See Christine Gledhill and Linda Williams, "Introduction," in Gledhill and Williams, eds., *Melodrama Unbound*, 5.

19. For an overview of this association see Steve Neale, *Genre and Hollywood* (London, Routledge, 2000), 186–196.

20. See Steve Neale, "Melo Talk: On the Meaning and Use of the Term 'Melodrama' in the American Trade Press," *The Velvet Light Trap* 32, Fall 1993, 72–75.

21. *Ibid.*, 76.

22. Gledhill and Williams, "Introduction," in *Melodrama Unbound*, 4.

23. *Ibid.*

24. See Williams, "'Tales of Sound and Fury,'" 214.

25. Gledhill and Williams, "Introduction," in *Melodrama Unbound*, 3–4.

26. *Ibid.*

27. *Ibid.*

28. Williams, "Melodrama Revised," 51.

29. Brooks, 14–15.

30. Matthew Buckley, "Unbinding Melodrama," in Gledhill and Williams, eds., *Melodrama Unbound*, 20–21.

31. See *Ibid.*, 21–22.

32. *Ibid.*, 20.

33. *Ibid.*

34. Brooks, 15.

35. *Ibid.*, 42.

36. *Ibid.*, 35.

37. Peter Brooks, "The Melodramatic Imagination: The Example of Blazac and James," in David Thorburn and Geoffrey Hartman, eds., *Romanticism, Vistas, Instances* (Ithaca, Cornell University Press, 1973), 216.

38. Williams, *Playing the Race Card*, 27.

39. *Ibid.*

40. *Ibid.*, 28.

41. See Brooks, 29.

42. *Ibid.*

43. *Ibid.*

44. *Ibid.*

45. *Ibid.*

46. *Ibid.*, 30.

47. Williams, *Playing the Race Card*, 29.

48. *See Ibid.*, note 17, 315.

49. Brooks, 27.

50. Buckley, 25.

51. See *Ibid.*, 24.

52. *Ibid.*, 25.

53. *Ibid.*, 26.

54. *Ibid.*, 27.

55. See *Ibid.*, 23.

56. *Ibid.*, 26.

57. *Ibid.*

58. Christine Gledhill, "Prologue," in *Melodrama Unbound*.

59. Williams, *Playing the Race Card*, 29.

60. *Ibid.*

61. Brooks, 43.

62. Williams, *Playing the Race Card*, 30.

63. *Ibid.*, 38.

64. *Ibid.*, 40.

65. Brooks, xiii.

66. Gledhill and Williams, "Introduction," in Gledhill and Williams, eds., *Melodrama Unbound*, 4.

67. Gledhill, "Prologue," *Melodrama Unbound*.

68. *Ibid.*

69. Gledhill and Williams, "Introduction," in *Melodrama Unbound*, 4.

70. See Brooks 25–27.

71. Brooks, 24.

72. *Ibid.*, 25.

73. *Ibid.*

74. *Ibid.*

75. *Ibid.*, 26.

76. *Ibid.*, 48.

77. *Ibid.*

78. *Ibid.*, 28.

79. *Ibid.*

80. *Ibid.*, 31.

81. See *Ibid.*, 35.

82. Marlisa Santos, "'People Can think Themselves Into Anything': The Domestic Nightmare in My Name is Julia Ross," in Gary D. Rhodes, ed., *The Films of Joseph H. Lewis* (Detroit, Wayne State University Press, 2012), 144.

83. Myron Meisel, "JOSEPH H. LEWIS: Tourist in the Asylum," in Todd McCarthy and Charles Flynn, *Kings of the Bs: Working Within the Hollywood System* (New York, E.P. Dutton & Co., 1975), 86.

84. See https://www.dvdtalk.com/dvdsavant/s4421noir4.html.

85. Ben Singer, *Melodrama and Modernity: Early Sensational Cinema and its Contexts* (New York, Columbia University Press, 2001), 198.

86. *Ibid.*

87. *Ibid.*, 53.

88. *Ibid.*, 39.

89. *Ibid.*

90. *Ibid.*, 40.

91. *Ibid.*

92. E. Deidre Pribram, "Melodrama and the Aesthetics of Emotion," in Gledhill and Williams, *Melodrama Unbound*, 241.

93. *Ibid.*, 242.

94. See *Ibid.*

95. See *Ibid.*, chapter 4.

96. *Ibid.*, 292–293.

97. *Ibid.*, 91. See Singer for an extensive list of "mechanical daredevil exhibitions" that included "The Whirlwind of Death" and "The Globe of Death."

98. *Ibid.*

99. *Ibid.*

100. *Ibid.*, 93.

101. *Ibid.*

102. *Ibid.*, 11.

103. *Ibid.*, 294.

104. *Ibid.*

105. *Ibid.*, 151.

106. *Ibid.*

107. *Ibid.*, 164.

108. *Ibid.*, 165.

109. Quoted in *Ibid.*, 12.

110. *Ibid.*, 167.

111. *Ibid.*, 192.

112. Quoted in *Ibid.*, 200–202.

113. *Quoted in Ibid.*, 198.

114. See *Ibid.*, 202.

115. See Singer 216. See also Geoff Mayer, *Encyclopedia of American Film Serials* (Jefferson, NC, McFarland, 2017), 288.

116. *Ibid.*,198.

117. *Ibid.*

118. *Singer,* 211–212.

119. *Ibid.*, 212.

120. Quoted in *Ibid.*, 210.

121. *Ibid.*, 265.

122. See *Ibid.*, 253–256.

123. *Ibid.*, 213.

124. Ed Hulse, *Distressed Damsels and Masked Marauders* (Morris Plains, NJ, Murania Press, 2014), 145.

125. See Gledhill, "Prologue," in Gledhill and Williams, eds., *Melodrama Unbound.*

126. See Jon Tuska, *The Vanishing Legion: A History of Mascot Pictures 1927–1935* (Jefferson, NC, McFarland & Company, 1982), 3.

127. Singer, 209.

128. *Ibid.*, 240.

129. Steve Neale, "Propaganda," *Screen,* Volume 18, Issue 3, October 1977.

130. *Ibid.*, 25.

131. *Ibid.*, 27.

132. *Ibid.*, 31.

133. *Ibid.*

134. *Ibid.*, 36.

135. See *Ibid.*

136. *Ibid.*, 35.

137. David Stewart Hull, *Film in the Third Reich: A Study of the German Cinema, 1933–1945* (Los Angeles, University of California Press, 1969), 170.

138. See Neale, "Propaganda," 39–40. The same argument applies to William Randolph Hearst's 1917 serial *Patria.*

139. Poor lighting, however, forced the filming of this chapter to move from the Montmartre Club in Times Square to the rooftop nightclub area of the New Amsterdam Theatre. Rudolph Valentino appears as an extra in the nightclub.

140. Ed Hulse, "Patria," *Blood 'N' Thunder,* Number 28, Winter 2011, 50.

141. Quoted in *Ibid.*, 49.

142. Phil Baker and Antony Clayton, eds., *Lord of Strange Deaths: The Fiendish World of Sax Rohmer* (London, Strange Attractor Press, 2015), vii.

143. Julian Symons, *Bloody Murder: From the Detective Story to the Crime Novel: A History* (London, Penguin Books, 1974), 229.

144. Christopher Frayling, *The Yellow Peril: Dr Fu Manchu & The Rise of Chinaphobia* (London, Thames & Hudson, 2014).

145. Frayling writes of his early childhood memories in a Sussex boarding school where "Sax Rohmer's Fu Manchu stories were a popular feature." *Ibid.,* 12.

146. *Ibid.*

147. See Gledhill, "Prologue."

148. Williams, "Tales of Sound and Fury," 215.

149. See Nathan Vernon Madison, *Anti-Foreign Imagery in American Pulps and Comic Books* (Jefferson, NC, McFarland & Company, 2013), online version, 18.

150. *Ibid.*, 82.

151. *Ibid.*

152. *Ibid.*, 30.

153. *Ibid.*

154. See Frayling, 259.

155. *Ibid.* Shiel followed with *The Yellow Danger* in 1905 and *The Dragon* in 1913.

156. Leslie S. Klinger, "Appreciating Dr. Fu-Manchu," in Sax Rohmer, *The Mystery of Dr. Fu-Manchu* (London, Titan Books, 2012), 287.

157. Sax Rohmer, *The Return of Dr. Fu-Manchu* (London, Titan Books, 2012).

158. *Ibid.*, 64.

159. Frayling, 247.

160. Ruth Mayer cites Gina Marchetti's thesis that the myths of the Yellow Peril were rooted in medieval fears of Genghis Khan and Mongolian invasions of Europe. It combines racist terrors of alien cultures, sexual anxieties and a fear that the West will eventually be enveloped by dark, occult forces of the East. See Ruth Mayer, *Serial Fu Manchu: The Chinese Supervillain and the Spread of Yellow Peril Ideology* (Philadelphia, Temple University Press, 2014), loc. 337.

161. Quoted in Frayling, 252.

162. *Ibid.*, 134.

163. See *Ibid.*, 59.

164. Sax Rohmer, *The Mystery of Dr. Fu-Manchu* (London, Titan Books, 2012), 25–26.

165. *Ibid.*, 93.

166. Sax Rohmer, *The Return of Dr. Fu-Manchu* (London, Titan Books, 2012), 237. The book was published in Britain as *The Devil Doctor.*

167. See Ruth Mayer, chapter 1.

168. Judith R. Walkowitz, *City of Dreadful Delight: Narratives of Sexual Danger in Late-Victorian London* (Chicago, University of Chicago Press, 1992), 86.

169. In a 1947 article in the *New Yorker*, Ward described the origin of his "Sax Rohmer" name as emanating from "roaming blade" or "blade runner" whereby he adopted the ancient Saxon term for blade ("Sax") and then substituted a "h" for the "a" in "roamer." See Frayling, 60.

170. Frayling, 275.

171. See Brooks, 5.

172. Sax Rohmer, *The Trail of Fu-Manchu* (London, Titan Books, 2013), 140.

173. *Ibid.*, 141.

174. Brooks, xiii.

175. *Ibid.*, 212.

176. *Ibid.*, 64.

177. *Ibid.*, 65.

178. Frayling, 282.

179. *Ibid.*, 283.

180. *Ibid.*, 282.

181. Rohmer, *The Return of Dr. Fu-Manchu,* 165.

182. *Ibid.*, 166.

183. *Ibid.*

184. *Ibid.*

185. *Ibid.*, 167.

186. *Ibid.*

187. *Ibid.*, 168.

188. *Ibid.*

189. *Ibid.*

190. *Ibid.*, 169.

191. *Ibid.*, 170.

192. William Patrick Maynard, *Blogging the Insidious Dr. Fu-Manchu by Sax Rohmer, Part Four—"Redmoat,"* http://setisays.blogspot.com/2010/04/.

193. Rohmer, *The Mystery of Dr. Fu-Manchu*, 22.

194. *Ibid.*, 23.

195. *Ibid.*, 21.

196. *Ibid.*, 39.

197. *Ibid.*, 40.

198. *Ibid.*

199. *Ibid.*, 40–41.

200. *Ibid.*

201. *Ibid.*, 42.

202. *Ibid.*, 44.

203. William Patrick Maynard, *The Insidious Dr. Fu-Manchu by Sax Rohmer—Part Three—"The Clue of the Pigtail,"* http://setisays.blogspot.com/2010/03/.

204. Brooks, 34.

205. Scott Loren and Jörg Metelmann, "Interview with *Christine* Gledhill," in *Melodrama After the Tears: New Perspectives on the Politics of Victimhood* (Amsterdam, Amsterdam University Press, 2016), 302.

206. Sax Rohmer, *The Trail of Fu-Manchu* (London, Titan Books, 1934), 36.

207. Rohmer, *The Mystery of Dr. Fu-Manchu*, 239.

208. *Ibid.*, 239–240.

209. *Ibid.*, 127.

210. William Patrick Maynard, "Sax Rohmer's Daughter of Fu Manchu," http://setisays.blogspot.com/2012/08/blogging-sax-rohmers-daughter-of-fu.html.

211. *Ibid.*

212. Only the British film production company Stoll Picture Production retained Kára-manèh, although played by white British actress Joan Clarkson in their 1923 serial *The Mystery of Dr. Fu-Manchu,* as the love interest for Dr. Petrie.

213. Frayling, 293.

214. See *Ibid.*, 296.

215. *Ibid.*, 308.

216. *Ibid.*

217. *Ibid.*

218. Jack Mathis, *Republic Confidential: Volume 1. The Studio* (Barrington, IL, Jack Mathis Advertising, 1999), 297.

219. Brooks, 35.

220. See *Ibid.*, 26.

221. Heilman, 129–130.

222. See Gordon Prange, *At Dawn We Slept: The Untold Story of Pearl Harbor* (London, Michael Joseph, 1981); Herbert Feis, *The Road to Pearl Harbor* (Princeton, Princeton University Press, 1950); Roberta Wohlstetter, *Pearl Harbor: Warning and Decision* (Stanford, Stanford University Press, 1962); Albert Russell Buchanan, "Pearl Harbor: Day of Infamy," *History of the 20th Century*, Volume 5, No. 66.

223. Prange, 539–540.

224. Buchanan, 1830–1833.

225. Prange, 580.

226. *Ibid.*

227. *Ibid.*, 582.

228. *Ibid.*

229. *Ibid.*, 582–583.

230. *Samuel Irving* Rosenman, *The Public Papers and Addresses of Franklin D. Roosevelt, Volume 10: The Call to Battle Stations* (New York, Russell and Russell, 1969), 54. The Japanese responded in a similar manner to justify their actions. An Imperial proclamation, broadcast the day after the attack, described the attack as "inevitable" due to the American "ambition to dominate eastern Asia." Consequently Japan had no other "recourse but a call to arms ... so that the source of evil will be speedily eradicated." Quoted in Robert Guillian, *I Saw Tokyo Burning: An Eyewitness Narrative from Pearl Harbor to Hiroshima* (London, John Murray, 1981), 8.

231. *Ibid.*

232. *Ibid.*, 529.

233. *Ibid.*, 550.

234. *Ibid.*, 551.

235. *Ibid.*, 550–551.

236. *Ibid.*, 552.

237. *Ibid.*, 523.

238. Brooks, 34.

239. *Ibid.*, 35.

240. The Roberts Commission was set up by Roosevelt soon after the attack. The Commission needed scapegoats and reasons for the disaster, other than Japanese treachery, and General Short and Admiral Kimmel were nominated to take the blame. However, at a later date and in a different historical and political context, Gordon Prange concluded that culpability for the disaster went a lot deeper than the initial findings of the Roberts Commission: "Kimmel and Short were no more blameless than they were solely blameworthy. The stain of error permeates the entire American fabric of Pearl Harbor from the President down to the Fourteenth Naval District and the Hawaiian Department. There are no Pearl Harbor scapegoats." See Prange, 734.

241. Prange, 171.

242. *Ibid.*, 169.

243. Rosenman, 528.

244. *Ibid.*, 530.

245. *Ibid.*, 515.

246. Prange, 738.

247. *Ibid.*, 583.

248. Quoted in *Ibid.*, 554–555.

249. Quoted in *Ibid.*, 583.

250. *Salute to the Marines* (1943) employs a similar approach with the face of a Japanese villain ("so sorry") imposed over footage of the destruction at Pearl Harbor. See also *Man from Frisco* (1944) and *Betrayal from the East* (1945).

251. See Dan Ford, *The Unquiet Man: The Life of John Ford* (London, William Kimber, 1982), 167.

252. *Ibid.*

253. See Brooks, *The Melodramatic Imagination,* 29.

254. *Ibid.*

255. *Ibid.*, 43.

256. *Ibid.*, 34.

257. Dr. Wassell was also the subject of a Paramount film, *The Story of Dr. Wassell*, released in April 1944.

258. Rosenman, 235.

259. *Ibid.*

260. *Ibid.*

261. *Ibid.*, 237.

262. *Ibid.*

263. *Ibid.*, 229.

264. Ernie Pyle, *Here Is Your War* (New York, Lancer Books, 1943), 272.

265. *Ibid.*

266. See Brooks, 157.

267. *Ibid.*

268. Pyle, 271.

269. Northrop Frye, *Anatomy of Criticism: Four Essays* (Princeton, Princeton University Press, 1973), 41.

270. *Ibid.*

271. http://www.tcm.com/tcmdb/title/91522/ The-Story-of-G-I-Joe/notes.html.

272. See *Ibid.*

273. Duane Schultz, "'The Story of G.I. Joe': Poignant Death of an American Soldier," http:// warfarehistorynetwork.com/daily/wwii/the-story- of-g-i-joe-poignant-death-of-an-american-soldier/.

274. Quoted in Damien Love, *Robert Mitchum: Solid, Dad, Crazy* (London, B.T. Batsford, 2002), 113.

275. *Ibid.*

276. James Agee, *Agee on Film: Volume One* (New York, The Universal Library, 1969), 174.

277. *Ibid.*

Chapter Two

1. Simmon, 158.

2. *See* Garth Jowett, *Film: The Democratic Art* (Boston, Little, Brown, 1976), 200

3. *Ibid.*

4. *Ibid.*

5. *Ibid.*

6. *Ibid.*, 199.

7. Gregory Waller, *Main Street Amusements: Movies and Commercial Entertainment in a Southern City, 1896–1930* (Washington, D.C., Smithsonian Institution Press, 1995), 196.

8. *Ibid.*, 254.

9. *Ibid.*, 197.

10. *Ibid.*

11. *Ibid.*, 255.

12. *Ibid.*

13. *Ibid.* However, when Paramount was forced into receivership in 1933 it had to relinquish the two theaters. In 1936 the Schine Corporation added the Kentucky, Strand, Ben Ali and State to its chain of sixty-five theaters in New York and twenty-five in Ohio. See Waller, note 14, 324.

14. *Ibid.*, 140.

15. *Ibid.*, 142.

16. *Ibid.*, 142–143.

17. Lea Jacobs, *The Wages of Sin: Censorship and the Fallen Woman Film 1928–1942* (Madison, University of Wisconsin Press, 1991), 31.

18. Waller, 234.

19. *Ibid.*, 235.

20. Six years later Dorothy Mackail starred in *Safe in Hell*, a "fallen woman" film.

21. Waller, 235.

22. *Ibid.*

23. *Ibid.*

24. Jane Tompkins, *West of Everything: The Inner Life of Westerns* (Oxford, Oxford University Press, 1992).

25. Lee Clark Mitchell, *Westerns: Making the Man in Fiction and Film* (Chicago, University of Chicago Press, 1997).

26. *Robert Murray Davis, Playing Cowboys: Low Culture and High Art in the Western* (Norman, University of Oklahoma Press, 1992).

27. Richard Koszarski, *An Evening's Entertainment: The Age of the Silent Feature Picture 1915– 1928* (Berkeley, University of California Press, 1990), 181.

28. *Ibid.*, 182.

29. *Ibid.*

30. *Ibid.*, 183.

31. Stanfield, *Horse Opera,* 40.

32. *Ibid.*, 41.

33. *Ibid.*

34. *Ibid.*, 27.

35. See *Ibid.,* 154.

36. Quoted in Hulse, 232.

37. See Stanfield, *Horse Opera,* 6.

38. *Ibid.*

39. See Williams, "Melodrama Revised," 57.

40. Stanfield, *Horse Opera,* 41.

41. *Ibid.*

42. *Ibid.*

43. See Simmon, chapter 15.

44. *Ibid.*

45. *Ibid.*, 151.

46. Stanfield, *Horse Opera,*129.

47. *Ibid.*, 147.

48. See Peter Stanfield, *Hollywood, Westerns and the 1930s: The Lost Trail* (Exeter, University of Exeter Press, 2001), 115.

49. Stanfield, *Horse Opera,* 6–7.

50. *Ibid.*, 129.

51. Singer, 134.

52. *Ibid.*, 294.

53. *Ibid.*

54. Brooks, 205.

55. See Stanfield, *Hollywood, Westerns and the 1930s*, 119–120.

56. Richard B. Jewell, "RKO Film Grosses, 1929–1951: The C.J. Tevlin Ledger," *Historical Journal of Film, Radio and Television,* Vol. 14, No. 1, 1994, 39.

57. See Stanfield, *Horse Opera*, 129–130.

58. *Ibid.,* 130.

59. *Ibid.*

60. *Ibid.*,141.

61. Stanfield, *Hollywood, Westerns and the 1930s,* 110.

62. See, for example, *Hollywood Cowboy* (1937) starring George O'Brien as well as the Gene Autry films *The Big Show* (1936) and *The Old Corral* (1936).

63. On the other hand, as will be explored in Chapter Three, rural and small-town audiences disliked the "sophisticated" metropolitan melodramas favored by the major studios. See Stanfield, *Hollywood, Westerns and the 1930s*, 115.

64. Stanfield, *Horse Opera, 100.*

65. *Ibid.*

66. *Ibid.*

67. *Ibid.*, 89.

68. *Ibid.*

69. *Motion Picture Herald*, June 15, 1935, 59. Quoted in *Ibid.,* 86.

70. Quoted in Boyd Magers, *Gene Autry Westerns: America's Favorite Cowboy* (Madison, NC, Empire Publishing, 2007), 18.

71. *Ibid.*

72. Stanfield, *Hollywood, Westerns and the 1930s*, 57.

73. Jewell, "RKO Film Grosses, 1929–1951," *39.*

74. See Stanfield, *Hollywood, Westerns and the 1930s, 54.*

75. See Geoff Mayer, *Encyclopedia of American Film Serials* (Jefferson, NC, McFarland, 2017), 156–157.

76. Stanfield, *Hollywood, Westerns and the 1930s,* 54.

77. Edward Buscombe, ed., *The BFI Companion to the Western* (London, Andre Deutsch, 1988), 428.

78. *Ibid.,* 427.

79. See Mayer, 15–17.

80. Stanfield, *Horse Opera,* 5–6.

81. See *Ibid.*, 4.

82. *Ibid.*, 1.

83. *Ibid.*, 2.

84. *Ibid.*, 137.

85. Stanfield, *Hollywood, Westerns and the 1930s,* 91.

86. *Ibid.*

87. Mark Roth, "Some Warner Musicals and the Spirit of the New Deal," *The Velvet Light Trap* 17 (Winter 1977), 1.

88. *Ibid.*, 7.

89. *Ibid.*

90. *Ibid.,* 1.

91. Maynard was a volatile actor and a great horseman. After supporting roles at Fox and starring roles at the small independent company Davis Distribution Division, in 1926 First National signed him for a series of relatively high budget westerns. However, when Warner Brothers purchased First National in 1928 the studio did not want to produce series westerns, and its engineers feared that westerns filmed on location would be difficult and expensive, so Maynard's contract was not renewed in 1930. He worked for the low budget company Tiffany Productions before returning to Universal where the studio offered him his own unit under the banner of "Ken Maynard Productions." However, in a familiar career pattern, Maynard soon self-destructed at Universal and was replaced by Buck Jones in 1934.

92. Jim Kitses, *Horizon West* (London, British Film Institute, 2004).

93. Peter Wollen, *Signs and Meaning in the Cinema* (Bloomington, Indiana University Press, 1972).

94. John G. Cawelti, *The Six Gun Mystique* (Bowling Green, OH, Bowling Green University, 1971).

95. Richard Slotkin, *Gunfighter Nation: The Myth of the Frontier in Twentieth Century America* (New York, Harper Perennial, 1993).

96. Henry Nash Smith, *Virgin Land: The American West as Symbol and Myth* (New York, Vintage Books, 1950).

97. Stanfield, *Hollywood, Westerns and the 1930s,* 8.

98. Kitses, 13.

99. Peter Stanfield, *Horse Opera,* 13.

100. Quoted in *Ibid.*, 15.

101. Slotkin, 169.

102. In the novel Wister presented the shootout in just a few lines and not at the end of his book. This traditional shootout to close a western film emerged from the theatrical version.

103. Owen Wister, *The Virginian, a Horseman of the Plains,* https://www.gutenbereg.org/files/1298-h/1298-h.htm, 6.

104. *Ibid.,* 61.

105. Stanfield, *Horse Opera,* 3.

106. Tuska, 189.

107. Paradoxically, director King Vidor filmed *The Texas Rangers* in New Mexico.

108. The term "New Frontiers" was popularized by Henry Wallace, President Franklin Roosevelt's secretary of agriculture. See Simmon, 102.

109. Simmon, 160.

110. Stanfield, *Horse Opera,* 144.

111. Quoted in *Ibid.,* 138.

112. Stanfield, *Hollywood, Westerns and the 1930s,* 113.

113. Better known in Hollywood as Pamela Blake after a name change in 1942.

114. Stanfield, *Hollywood, Westerns and the 1930s,* 114.

115. The film was loosely inspired by real events. Earl Durand escaped from the jail in Cody, Wyoming, after his arrest for poaching elk. Armed with a knife and a rifle, Durand evaded the law for 90 days in the rugged terrain of Yellowstone National Park. However, Durand, unlike Will Parker, was a murderer who killed five members of the posse. He

died, along with a hostage, while attempting a bank hold-up in Powell, Wyoming, and his story was reported in *The New York Times*.

116. Simmon, 163.
117. *Ibid.*
118. Stanfield, *Horse Opera,* 136.

Chapter Three

1. Gloria Swanson, *Swanson on Swanson: The Making of a Hollywood Legend* (Middlesex, Hamlyn Paperbacks, 1982), 324.
2. *Ibid.*, 324–325.
3. See Mark A. Vieira, *Forbidden Hollywood: The Pre-Code Era (1930–1934): When Sin Ruled the Movies* (New York, Running Press, 2019), 133.
4. *Ibid.*
5. Quoted in *Ibid.*
6. Quoted in Vieira, 133.
7. See Stanfield, *Hollywood, Westerns and the 1930s,* 115.
8. Stanfield, *Horse Opera,* 78.
9. *Ibid.*
10. Frank Rahill, *The World of Melodrama* (Philadelphia, University of Pennsylvania Press, 1967), xv.
11. Brooks, *The Melodramatic Imagination*, xvi, Singer, 165.
12. Michael Walker, "Melodrama and the American Cinema," *Movie,* Issue 29–30, Summer 1982, 16–17.
13. *Ibid.*, 17.
14. Rahill, xv.
15. Singer, 165.
16. Williams, "Tales of Sound and Fury," 213–214.
17. Brooks, 5.
18. Guy Savage, *The Letter* (1940), www.noiroftheweek.com/2012/07/the-letter-1940.html.
19. W. Somerset Maugham, "The Letter," *in Short Stories* (London, Vintage Books, 1998), 183.
20. *Ibid.*, 184–185.
21. *Ibid.*, 189.
22. *Ibid.*
23. *Ibid.*, 191.
24. *Ibid.*, 200.
25. *Ibid.*, 193.
26. *Ibid.*, 194.
27. *Ibid.*, 202.
28. *Ibid.*, 207.
29. *Ibid.*, 212.
30. *Ibid.*, 215.
31. *Ibid.*
32. *Ibid.*
33. W. Somerset Maugham, *The Letter with Two Other Plays* (London, Pan Books, 1952), 11.
34. *Ibid.*, 15.
35. *Ibid.*
36. *Ibid.*, 34.
37. *Ibid.*
38. *Ibid.*, 45.
39. *Ibid.*, 46.
40. *Ibid.*, 58.
41. *Ibid.*, 64.

42. *Ibid.*, 66.
43. *Ibid.*, 69.
44. *Ibid.*, 70.
45. *Ibid.*
46. *Ibid.*, 74.
47. *Ibid.*, 75.
48. Jowett, 466.
49. See Jacobs, *The Wages of Sin,* 34.
50. *Ibid.*, 28.
51. See Jowett, 239.
52. The film also inserts a fight between a hooded cobra and a mongoose, taken from the UFA short film *Killing the Killer,* as a heavy-handed prelude to the upcoming confrontation between Li-Ti and Leslie. Just as the death of the cobra is predictable, the film suggests that in this seedy environment, Leslie is no match for Li-Ti. However, the dramatic ramifications of this sequence may have been counter-productive as the review in *Variety* (March 13, 1929) noted: the "crowd at the film's premiere identified it instantly and the effect on the spectators was distinctly bad, introducing as it did a brutal jolt to the whole illusion."
53. Maugham, *The Letter with Two Other Plays,* 69.
54. Glenn Erickson, *The Letter* (1929), https://www.dvdtalk.com/dvdsavant/s3611lett.html.
55. *Ibid.*
56. The emotional impact of the film's final scene between Robert and Leslie is enhanced by the casting of Jeanne Eagels as Leslie. Eagels was a Broadway star throughout the 1920's, especially after her performance as Sadie Thompson in *Rain* which opened in 1922. However, her addiction to drugs caused problems on and off the stage. It came to a head during the stage production of *Her Cardboard Lover* opposite Leslie Howard who objected to her absences and unprofessional behavior. Eagels was suspended by Actors Equity in 1928 for 18 months and, as a consequence, accepted a three-picture contract with Paramount to be filmed at their Astoria studio in New York. *The Letter* was followed by *Jealousy.* However, she was dismissed from her third film, *The Laughing Lady,* after the studio refused to wait until an eye infection cleared up. Eagels was nominated for an Academy Award for her performance in *The Letter.* She did not, however, live to enjoy the critical acclaim as she died, aged 39, from a combination of alcohol, chloral hydrate and heroin on October 3, 1929, seven months after the New York release of *The Letter.*
57. Maugham, *Short Stories*, 215.
58. *Ibid.*
59. Quoted in Andrea Passafiume, *The Letter: The Essentials,* http://www.tcm.com/this-month/article/220540%7CO/The-Essentials-TheLetter.html.
60. Savage.
61. Jacobs, *The Wages of Sin,* 40.
62. Jacobs "Industry Self Regulation and the Problem of Textual Determination," *The Velvet Light Trap,* Number 23, Spring 1989, 12.
63. *Ibid.*

64. *Ibid.*
65. Vieira, 241.
66. Jacobs, *The Wages of Sin,* 115.
67. *Ibid.*
68. *Ibid.*
69. Quoted in *Ibid.,* 114–115.
70. See Jacobs, "Industry Self Regulation and the Problem of Textual Determination," 9.
71. See *Ibid.,* 13.
72. *Ibid.,* 12.
73. See *Ibid.,* 12–13.
74. *Ibid.,* 13.
75. See Jacobs, *The Wages of Sin,* 122.
76. When Bette Davis was honored at the American Film Institute in 1977 Wyler confirmed that Davis vehemently disagreed with the way he filmed this scene as she considered it much too cruel.
77. Quoted in Gabriel Miller, *William Wyler: The Life and Films of Hollywood's Most Celebrated Director* (Lexington, University Press of Kentucky, 2013), 183.
78. *Ibid.,* 186.
79. Maugham, *The Letter with Two Other Plays,* 17.
80. See Richard Maltby, "The Production Code and The Hays Office," *Encyclopedia.com,* https://www.encyclopedia.com/arts/culture-magazines/production-code-and-hays-office.
81. Swanson, 297.
82. *Ibid.,* 299.
83. *Ibid.,* 297.
84. Selina Hastings, *The Secret Lives of Somerset Maugham: A Biography* (New York, Random House, 2010), 199.
85. *Ibid.*
86. *Ibid.,* 200.
87. Quoted in Hastings, 207.
88. Quoted in *Ibid.,* 203.
89. *Ibid.*
90. *Ibid.,* 207.
91. Quoted in *Ibid.*
92. Quoted in *Ibid.,* 203.
93. Maugham, "Rain," in *Short Stories,* 74.
94. *Ibid.,* 75.
95. *Ibid.,* 83.
96. *Ibid.*
97. *Ibid.*
98. *Ibid.,* 78.
99. *Ibid.*
100. *Ibid.,* 81.
101. *Ibid.,* 89.
102. *Ibid.,* 94.
103. *Ibid.,* 107.
104. *Ibid.,* 109.
105. *Ibid.*
106. *Ibid.,* 110.
107. *Ibid.*
108. *Ibid.,* 111.
109. *Ibid.,* 113.
110. *Ibid.,* 115.
111. *Ibid.*
112. *Ibid.*
113. *Ibid.*
114. *Ibid.,* 110.
115. *Ibid.,* 111.
116. *Ibid.,* 109.
117. During his 1920 visit to Hollywood Maugham hoped to receive $15,000 to $20,000 for future screenplays. However, he was disappointed when his offers consisted only of the rights to his 1918 play *Love in a Cottage* and a $15,000 commission for a script that was never used. See Hastings, 254.
118. *Ibid.*
119. *Ibid.,* 256.
120. *Ibid.*
121. Swanson, 295.
122. *Ibid.,* 301.
123. *Ibid.,* 302.
124. *Ibid.,* 304.
125. *Ibid.,* 305.
126. *Ibid.*
127. *Ibid.*
128. *Ibid.,* 308.
129. Swanson learned that Fox had secretly made an offer to Maugham to write a sequel to *Rain.* When the studio discovered that Swanson had bought the film rights to the original story they abandoned their plans.
130. Swanson, 309.
131. *Ibid.,* 310.
132. *Ibid.*
133. *Ibid.,* 311.
134. *Ibid.,* 320.
135. *Ibid.*
136. *Ibid.,* 322.
137. Maugham, "Rain," in *Short Stories,*115.
138. *Ibid.,* 80–81.
139. See www.silentfilm.org/archive/sadie-thompson.
140. *Sadie Thompson* was considered a lost film for many years until, after Swanson's death in 1983, a surviving print was discovered by her estate that had been stored in Mary Pickford's personal collection. The rights were purchased by Kino International and, as a portion of the final reel was damaged, Kino employed Dennis Doros to reconstruct the damaged portions with a montage of stills. A new score by Joseph Turrin was also commissioned.
141. Swanson, 354.
142. *Ibid.*
143. *Ibid.,* 355.
144. Richard Maltby, "More Sinned Against than Sinning: The Fabrications of Pre-Code Cinema," *Senses of Cinema,* December 2003.
145. Maxwell Anderson had a first-hand experience of missionary life as he travelled in many areas of the United States with his father, a minister, until his late teenage years.
146. Davidson: "I'm not going to have this house turned into—into …" Maugham, "Rain," in *Short Stories,* 91.
147. *Rain* was an unhappy film for Crawford in many ways. She claimed she felt alienated from fellow cast members and while making the film she was estranged from husband Douglas Fairbanks, Jr.

This was accompanied by her miscarriage following a fall on the deck of a ship.

148. Quoted in Frank Miller, *Rain, TCM Film Article,* http://www.tcm.com/this-month/article/161058%7C161060/Rain.html.

149. In the early 1950s Spencer Williams starred as Andy Brown in the popular, but controversial, television sitcom *Amos 'n Andy*.

150. Hastings, 104.

151. Quoted in *Ibid.,* 105.

Chapter Four

1. Steve Neale, *Genre and Hollywood* (London, Routledge, 2000), 173–174.

2. Alain Silver and James Ursini, eds., *Film Noir Reader* (New York, Limelight Edition, 1996), 11.

3. See Paul Skenazy, *James M. Cain* (New York, Continuum, 1989), 160.

4. Robert Porfirio, "NO WAY OUT: Existential Motifs in the Film Noir," *Sight and Sound,* Volume 45, Number 4, Autumn 1976.

5. See Robert Porfirio, "No Way Out: Existential Motifs in the Film Noir," in Alain Silver and James Ursini, *Film Noir Reader* (New York, Limelight Press, 1996), 81.

6. *Ibid.*

7. *Ibid.*

8. *Ibid.*

9. Skenazy, 159.

10. *Ibid.,* 159–160.

11. *Ibid.,* 30.

12. James Lee Burke, "A word on James M. Cain," in James M. Cain, *Double Indemnity* (London, Orion Books, 2004), vi.

13. Geoffrey O'Brien, *Hard-Boiled America: Lurid Paperbacks and the Masters of Noir* (New York, Da Capo Press, 1997), 69.

14. The opening line in James M. Cain, *The Postman Always Rings Twice* (London, Panther Crime, 1970), 7.

15. O'Brien, 69.

16. See Steven Marcus, "Introduction," in Dashiell Hammett, *The Continental Op* (London, Pan Books, 1975), 14.

17. Quoted in Richard Layman, *Discovering The Maltese Falcon and Sam Spade* (San Francisco, Vince Emery Productions, 2005), 119.

18. *Ibid.*

19. *Ibid.*

20. *Ibid.*

21. *Ibid.*

22. *Ibid.*

23. *Ibid.*

24. Gledhill, "Prologue."

25. Marcus, 12.

26. Gledhill and Williams, "Introduction," *Melodrama Unbound,* 4.

27. *Ibid.*

28. *Ibid.*

29. *Ibid.*

30. David Bordwell, "Happily Ever After, Part Two," *The Velvet Light Trap,* Number 19, 1982, 2.

31. *Ibid.*

32. *Ibid.*

33. Quoted in *Ibid.*

34. *Ibid.,* 4.

35. *Ibid.*

36. Quoted in *Ibid.*

37. *Ibid.*

38. *Ibid.*

39. See https://theeveningclass.blogspot.com/2007/01/noir-city-5eddie-muller-remarks-on.html.

40. Alain Silver and Elizabeth Ward, eds., *Film Noir: An Encyclopedic Reference to the American Style* (Woodstock, The Overlook Press, 1992), 106.

41. See http://tinyurl.com/y34fcwob.

42. See https://www.allmovie.com/movie/framed-v76046/review.

43. See https://unobtainium13.com/2018/11/23/30-days-of-noir-23-framed-dir-by-richard-wallace/.

44. See http://www.noiroftheweek.com/2011/05/framed-1947.html.

45. See Duncan Gray, "No Other Kind: Close-Up on Fritz Lang's 'Human Desire,'" http://mubi.com/notebook/posts/no-other-kind-close-up-on-fritz-lang-s-human-desire.

46. See *Ibid.*

47. *Ibid.*

48. *Ibid.*

49. *Ibid.*

50. *Ibid.*

51. *Ibid.*

52. *Ibid.*

53. *Ibid.*

54. The film retained, against Breen's wishes, lines such as Gilda's comment to Farrell that if "I were a ranch, they would call me the Bar Nothing." See Sheri Chinen Biesen, *Blackout: World War II and the Origins of Film Noir* (Baltimore, Johns Hopkins University Press, 2005), 148.

55. *Ibid.*

56. Nino Frank, "A New Kind of Police Drama: The Criminal Adventure," in Alain Silver and James Ursini, eds., *Film Noir Reader 2* (New York, Limelight Editions, 1999).

57. Jean-Pierre Chartier, "Americans Also Make Noir Films," in Alain Silver and James Ursini, eds., *Film Noir Reader 2* (New York, Limelight Editions, 1999).

58. *Ibid.,* 21.

59. A key film in this cycle was Warner's 1947 film *Pursued* starring Robert Mitchum as a young man haunted by a childhood trauma. This somber film, influenced by Hollywood's fascination with psychoanalysis in the 1940s, transformed familiar western settings into a nightmarish landscape by cinematographer James Wong Howe. Also *Ramrod* (1947), directed by Andre de Toth, starred Joel McCrea as a cowboy caught up in the destructive machinations of a female landowner, played by Veronica Lake. There was also *Blood on the Moon* (1948), starring Robert Mitchum. In this film a brooding psychological dimension is grafted onto

a traditional western plot involving a gunman who changes his allegiance to defend a female rancher.

60. Frank, 15.

61. *Ibid.*

62. Francis M. Nevins, *Cornell Woolrich: First You Dream, Then You Die* (New York, Mysterious Press, 1988), 113.

63. See Owen Hill, Pamela Jackson, and Anthony Dean Rizzuto, "Introduction," in Raymond Chandler, *The Annotated Big Sleep* (New York, Vintage Crime, 2018), xxiii.

64. Film historian William Everson selected *The Kennel Murder Case,* along with the 1941 version of *The Maltese Falcon* and the 1947 British crime film *Green for Danger,* starring Alastair Sim as Christianna Brand's Inspector Cockrill, as representing the "highest traditions of the movie detective film." See William K. Everson, *The Detective in Film* (Secaucus, NJ, Citadel Press, 1972), 38.

65. http://www.tcm.com/tcmdb/title/80141/The-Kennel-Murder-Case/articles.html.

66. Brooks, 35.

67. See https://en.wikipedia.org/wiki/Philo_Vance.

68. *Ibid.*

69. *Ibid.*

70. See J. Randolph Cox, "Dime Novel," in Rosemary Herbert, ed., *The Oxford Companion to Crime and Mystery Writing* (Oxford, Oxford University Press, 1999), 120.

71. See William L. DeAndrea, *Encyclopedia Mysteriosa: A Comprehensive Guide to the Art of Detection in Print, Film, Radio, and Television* (New York, Prentice Hall General Reference, 1994), 52.

72. See Gary Dobbs, "Introduction," in *Street Wolf: The Black Mask* (Boston, Altus, 2014).

73. One of the exceptions was Paramount's 1935 adaptation of Dashiell Hammett's novel *The Glass Key.*

74. Quoted in Rob Preston, "Introduction," in *Street Wolf,* xiv.

75. *Ibid.*

76. Krutnik, 93.

77. *Ibid.*

78. Quoted in Layman's "There's Only One Maltese Falcon," *January magazine.com.*

79. Hammett claimed that the inspiration for *The Maltese Falcon* was Henry James's novel *Wings of the Dove.*

80. Dashiell Hammett, "Who Killed Bob Teal," reprinted in Richard Layman and Julie M. Rivett, eds., *Dashiell Hammett: The Big Book of the Continental Op* (New York, Vintage Crime/Black Lizard, 2017), 202.

81. *Ibid.,* 205.

82. Dashiell Hammett, *The Maltese Falcon* (London, Pan Books, 1975), 14.

83. *Ibid.,* 15.

84. *Ibid.*

85. *Ibid.*

86. *Ibid.,* 16.

87. "The Girl with the Silver Eyes" (*Black Mask,* June 1924) followed "The House on Turk Street"

(*Black Mask,* April 1924) and together they comprised a 25,000-word novelette. Jeanne Delano, the female protagonist in the Op story, first appeared as Elvira in "The House on Turk Street," a convoluted story that ends with her escaping and, as a consequence of her greed, three men are killed and another goes to the gallows.

88. Layman and Rivett, 151.

89. *Ibid.,* 158–159.

90. *Ibid.,* 158.

91. *Ibid.*

92. I am not including *Satan Met a Lady* (1936) as it virtually has nothing to do with Hammett's novel.

93. A.M. Sperber and Eric Lax, *Bogart* (New York, William Morrow and Company, 1997), 161.

94. *Ibid.*

95. *Ibid.,* 162.

96. *Ibid.*

97. Hammett, *The Maltese Falcon,* 196.

98. Krutnik, 93.

99. *Ibid.*

100. *Ibid.,* 95.

101. *Ibid.*

102. Quoted in Sperber and Lax, 162.

103. Hammett, *The Maltese Falcon,* 201.

104. *Ibid.*

105. Memo from the unit manager announcing completion of shooting for *The Maltese Falcon.* Reprinted in Layman, *Discovering The Maltese Falcon and Sam Spade,* 299.

106. A.M. Sperber and Eric Lax, 163.

107. *Ibid.*

108. Layman, ed., *Discovering The Maltese Falcon and Sam Spade,* 291.

109. *Ibid.,* 291–293.

110. Quoted in A.M. Sperber and Eric Lax, 171.

111. Griffith's review is cited in its entirety in Layman, ed., *Discovering The Maltese Falcon and Sam Spade,* 305.

112. Scheuer's review is cited in its entirety in *Ibid.,* 306.

113. H. Mark Glancy, "Warner Bros financial information in The William Shaefer Ledger," *Historical Journal of Film, Radio and Television,* Volume 15, Issue 1, 1995, 1–31.

114. Symons, 144.

115. Dashiell Hammett, *The Glass Key* (London, Pan Books, 1975), 94.

116. *Ibid.,* 155.

117. *Ibid.,* 9.

118. *Ibid.,* 95.

119. *Ibid.*

120. *Ibid.,* 97.

121. *Ibid.,* 191.

122. *Ibid.,* 183.

123. *Ibid.*

124. *Ibid.,* 184.

125. *Ibid.*

126. *Ibid.,* 217.

127. *Ibid.,* 220.

128. Raymond Chandler, *Farewell, My Lovely* (Middlesex, Harmondsworth, 1975), 253.

129. *Ibid.*

130. Quoted in Al Clark, *Raymond Chandler in Hollywood* (Los Angeles, Silman-James Press, 1996), 22.

131. Gene D. Phillips, *Creatures of Darkness: Raymond Chandler, Detective Fiction, and Film Noir* (Lexington, University of Kentucky Press, 2000), 30.

132. Quoted in Clark, 27.

133. *Ibid.*, 24.

134. Chandler, 130–131.

135. *Ibid.*, 248.

136. The film retained Chandler's title *Farewell, My Lovely* for its first screenings which took place in Minnesota and New England in December 1944. When audiences failed to show, the studio hired Audience Research Incorporated to undertake market analysis and they concluded that the problem was the title. Audiences, the research revealed, expected a Dick Powell musical. *Farewell, My Lovely* was recalled, re-titled *Murder, My Sweet* and after it was re-released with its new title in March 1945 it became a box-office and critical success. The cost of the film was $479,000 and it went on to earn $1,150,000 in the United States and $565,000 overseas—with an overall profit of $597,000 for RKO.

137. Hill, Jackson and Rizzuto, xxvii.

138. See Cawelti, 144.

139. A letter written by Chandler and quoted in Dorothy Katherine Sorley Walker, eds., *Raymond Chandler Speaking* (London, Hamish Hamilton, 1962), 232.

140. Chandler, *Farewell, My Lovely*, 250.

141. *Ibid.*

142. Raymond Chandler, "The Simple Art of Murder," in *Pearls Are a Nuisance* (Harmondsworth, Penguin Books, 1973), 182.

143. *Ibid.*, 190.

144. A southwest suburb of London.

145. *Ibid.*, 194. Bognor Regis is a seaside resort in West Sussex.

146. *Ibid.*

147. *Ibid.*, 195.

148. *Ibid.*, 194–195.

149. *Ibid.*, 197.

150. *Ibid.*, 198.

151. *Ibid.*

152. Skenazy, 157.

153. Quoted in *Ibid.*

154. Chandler, "The Simple Art of Murder," 198.

155. James Naremore, *More Than Night: Film Noir in Its Contexts* (Berkeley, University of California, 1998), 52.

156. *Ibid.*, 54.

157. Krutnik, 136.

158. See *Ibid.*

159. *Variety*, December 16, 1942, 1, 45.

160. *Ibid.*, 45.

161. *Ibid.* See also Krutnik, 37.

162. *Variety*, November 10, 1943, 2.

163. Keith Allan Deutsch, "Steve Fisher, Black Mask, and the Noir Revolution," https://blackmaskmagazine.com/blog/steve-fisher-black-mask-and-the-noir-revolution/.

164. *Ibid.*

165. Quoted in *Ibid.*

166. *Ibid.*

167. Keith Alan Deutsch, "Black Mask Magazine, Steve Fisher, and The Noir Revolution," https://somethingisgoingtohappen.net/2012/08/29/black-mask-magazine-steve-fisher-and-the-noir-revolution-by-keith-alan-deutsch/.

168. *Ibid.*

169. See Nevins, *Cornell Woolrich: First You Dream*, 117.

170. *Ibid.*, 116.

171. Krutnik, 41.

172. See Nevins, 116–117.

173. *Ibid.*, 118.

174. Quoted in Francis M. Nevins, "Introduction," in Cornell Woolrich, *Tonight, Somewhere in New York: The Last Stories and an Unfinished Novel by Cornell Woolrich* (New York, Carroll & Graf Publishers, 2005), 4.

175. *Ibid.*

176. Cornell Woolrich, *Darkness at Dawn: Early Suspense Classics by Cornell Woolrich* (New York, Peter Bedrick Books, 1988), 1.

177. See Geoff Mayer, "Film Noir and Studio Production Practices," in Andrew Spicer and Helen Hanson, *A Companion to Film Noir* (West Sussex, Wiley Blackwell, 2013), 213–214.

178. Cornell Woolrich, *The Black Curtain* (New York, Ballantine Books, 1982), 3.

179. *Ibid.*, 11.

180. *Ibid.*, 17.

181. *Ibid.* 148.

182. Cornell Woolrich, *The Black Path of Fear* (New York, Ballantine Books, 1982), 5.

183. *Ibid.*, 16.

184. *Ibid.*, 7.

185. *Ibid.*, 28.

186. *Ibid.*

187. *Ibid.*, 29.

188. Francis M. Nevins describes the novel as a pulp story. See Nevins, *Cornell Woolrich: First You Dream*, 299.

189. Woolrich, *The Black Path of Fear*, 159–160.

190. *Ibid.*, 160.

191. Quoted in Nevins, *Cornell Woolrich: First You Dream*, 299.

192. Thomas C. Renzi, *Cornell Woolrich from Pulp Noir to Film Noir* (Jefferson, NC, McFarland, 2006), 247–248.

193. See Spicer, *Historical Dictionary of Film Noir*, 332.

194. Cornell Woolrich, "Nightmare," in Bill Pronzini and Martin H. Greenberg, *13 Short Mystery Novels* (New York, Greenwich House, 1984), 91.

195. Nevins, *Cornell Woolrich: First You Dream*, 235. Thomas Renzi is even more adamant that the subtext of this short story is one of Woolrich's more overt representations of his "guilt" from "suppressed homosexual desires." A motif that is also duplicated, according to Renzi, in *Fear in the Night*. See Renzi, 110–119.

196. Woolrich, "Nightmare," 114.

197. In 1956 Maxwell Shane remade his 1947 film as *Nightmare*, starring Edward G. Robinson as René Bressard and Kevin McCarthy as Stan Grayson, the equivalent of Cliff Herlihy and Vince Grayson in the 1947 film. It followed the plot of the earlier film while adding a musical dimension, Cliff is a writer and musician, and it was filmed on location in New Orleans.

198. Nevins, *Cornell Woolrich: First You Dream*, 117.

199. See *Ibid.*, 337.

200. See Renzi, 53.

201. Nevins, 359.

202. *Ibid.*

203. Tom Flinn argues that while *Stranger on the Third Floor* was not entirely successful, it was "particularly impressive in view of the way in which it predicts the conventions of the *film noir*." Tom Flinn, "Three Faces of Film Noir: Stranger on the Third Floor, Phantom Lady, and Criss Cross," in Todd McCarthy and Charles Flynn, *Kings of the Bs. Working Within the Hollywood System* (New York, E.P. Dutton & Co., 1975), 136.

204. Richard B. Jewell with Vernon Harbin, *The RKO Story* (London, Octobus Books, 1982), 150.

205. Wheeler Winston Dixon, "Precursors to Film Noir," in Andrew Spicer and Helen Hanson, eds., *A Companion to Film Noir* (West Sussex, Wiley Blackwell, 2013), chapter 5.

206. See Biesen, 24.

207. See Brooks, 35–36.

208. *Ibid.*, 35.

209. https://www.dvdtalk.com/dvdsavant/s3340floo.html.

210. Quoted in Biesen, 31.

211. *Ibid.*

212. *Ibid.*

213. See *Ibid.*, 33–34.

214. Frank Partos co-wrote a similar film, *Night Without Sleep* (1952) told in flashback and involving composer Richard Morton (Gary Merrill) who discovers at the end of the film that he killed his wife Emily (June Vincent) while drunk.

215. Brooks, 1995, 41.

216. Quoted in Biesen, 29.

217. Krutnik, 49.

218. Glenn Erickson, https://www.dvdtalk.com/dvdsavant/s2026wake.html.

219. Steve Fisher, *I Wake Up Screaming* (New York, Vintage Crime, 1991), 35–36.

220. Fisher modelled Cornell, physically at least, on his friend Cornell Woolrich. See Fisher, *I Wake Up Screaming*, 37, for his description of Cornell which also describes Woolrich.

221. See Silver and Ward, 141.

222. Krutnik (page 189) includes *The Fallen Sparrow* in his "espionage thrillers" category along with Hitchcock's *Foreign Correspondent* (1940) and *Journey Into Fear* (1943). This is strange as *Fallen Sparrow*, with its strong psychological focus, has little in common with these films.

223. It is not included in the comprehensive *Film Noir: An Encyclopedic Reference to the American Style*, edited by Alain Silver and Elizabeth Ward, nor Andrew Spicer's *Historical Dictionary of Film Noir* or even Sheri Chinen Biesen's *Blackout* which focuses specifically on noir films produced during the Second World War.

224. See Andrea Passafiume, "The Fallen Sparrow," http://www.tcm.com/this-month/article/502|0/The-Fallen-Sparrow.html.

225. Dorothy B. Hughes, *The Fallen Sparrow* (New York, Bantam Books, 1979), 3.

226. *Ibid.*, 4.

227. Composer Roy Web's score was nominated for an Academy Award.

228. Hughes, *The Fallen Sparrow*, 35.

229. Dorothy B. Hughes, *Ride the Pink Horse* (London, Penguin Books, 1988), 42.

230. *Ibid.*, 13.

231. *Ibid.*, 14.

232. *Ibid.*, 32.

233. *Ibid.*

234. *Ibid.*, 28.

235. *Ibid.*, 29.

236. *Ibid.*, 186.

237. *Ibid.*

238. *Ibid.*, 187.

239. *Ibid.*

240. *Ibid.*, 187–188.

241. Glenn Erickson, in his review of the Blu-ray release of the film, notes: "As good as Hendricks is in the role, her Pila is still the magical 'dusky savage,' a barefoot peasant version. She's too young and virtuous to fully understand what her two girlfriends are up to when they 'go' with men. She's given the intuition that Gagin has a dramatic destiny, and that she must play a part in it. The film isn't racist because to shows Gagin and Marjorie ignoring Pila or condescending to her, but because it idealizes her as a non-white 'princess,' who is magical but cannot end up with the hero. For the Production Code bigots, a romantic finale is unthinkable… The final scene is touching, and rather novel when Pila 'converts' her experience with Gagin into a legend with herself as the heroine. Her reaction is the reaction of a small child, when our expectation throughout has been that she could be Gagin's lover, if only he'd look at her differently." https://www.dvdtalk.com/dvdsavant/s4742pink.html. On the other hand, *The New York Times* reviewer Bosley Crowther, writing at the time of the film's release, praised Wanda Hendrix as a "little Mexican moon-child who shadows the bruiser through the night and finally is able to assist him in his last violent race with fate and death."

242. Hughes, *Ride the Pink Horse*, 187.

243. Throughout pre-production, including Mainwaring's screenplay, Cain's two drafts and Fenton's final screenplay, the film was titled *Build My Gallows High*. However, after filming was completed, and just prior to its release, the studio commissioned a Gallup poll. Respondents to the poll considered the original title too morbid and the title was changed to *Out of the Past*.

244. See Mary Beth Haralovich, "Selling Noir.

Stars, Gender and Genre in Film Noir Posters and Publicity," in Andrew Spicer and Helen Hanson, eds., *A Companion to Film Noir* (West Sussex, Wiley Blackwell, 2013), 261.

245. Richard B. Jewell, *Slow Fade to Black: The Decline of RKO Radio Pictures* (Oakland, University of California Press, 2016), 72.

246. Andrew Sarris, *The American Cinema: Directors and Directions 1929–168* (New York, E.P. Dutton & Co., 1968), 142.

247. Jewell, *Slow Fade to Black,* 72. Val Lewton, an RKO producer at that time, also recommended that the studio purchase the rights to Mainwaring's novel. See Jewell, 73.

248. See Jeff Schwager, "The Past Rewritten," *Film Comment,* Volume 27, Number 1, January-February 1991, 13.

249. *Ibid.*

250. Cain was almost proud of the fact that he was one of the most unsuccessful screen writers in Hollywood with only two screen credits for screenplays despite regular employment by the major studios, and despite being very well paid for his failed attempts.

251. See Schwager, 15.

252. *Ibid.*

253. *Ibid.*

254. *Ibid.,* 16.

255. See Chris Fujiwara, *Jacques Tourneur: The Cinema of Nightfall* (Baltimore, Johns Hopkins University Press, 1998), 138.

256. Quoted in Eddie Muller, *Dark City Dames: The Wicked Women of Film Noir* (New York, Regan Books, 2001), 20.

257. Krutnik, 106.

258. Mainwaring admitted in an interview in 1972, that the characterizations and themes in *Out of the Past* owe much to *The Maltese Falcon.* See "Screenwriter Daniel Mainwaring Discusses OUT OF THE PAST," *The Velvet Light Trap,* Fall, 1973, 45.

259. Krutnik, 106.

260. Damien Love*, Robert Mitchum* (London, Batsford, 202), 57.

261. *Ibid.*

262. Spicer, *Historical Dictionary of Film Noir,* 227.

263. See Heilman, *Tragedy and Melodrama,* 97.

264. See *Ibid.*

265. See Brooks, 206.

266. Don Tracy, *Criss-Cross* (New York, Triangle Books, 1948), 228.

267. *Ibid.,* 241.

268. *Ibid.,* 13.

269. See https://www.dvdtalk.com/dvdsavant/s1310cris.html.

270. Brooks, 18.

271. See Skenazy, 160.

272. Cain said in a 1978 interview that he was not interested in stories where the cops get the killer. See Skenazy, 158.

273. *Ibid.*

274. *Ibid.,* 159.

275. Cain, *Double Indemnity,* 13.

276. *Ibid.,* 14–15.

277. See https://murder-mayhem.com/double-indemnity-the-real-life-murder-that-inspired-a-crime-noir-classic.

278. See Richard Schickel, *Double Indemnity* (London, BFI Publishing. 1992). See also https://en.wikipedia.org/wiki/Double_Indemnity_(film).

279. Leonard Leff and Jerrold Simmons, *The Dame in the Kimono: Hollywood, Censorship, and the Production Code from the 1920s to the 1960s* (London, Weidenfeld and Nicolson, 1990), 126.

280. Schickel, 56.

281. *Ibid.,* 59.

282. *Ibid.*

283. O'Brien, 73.

284. Skenazy, 157.

285. Schickel, 49.

286. *Ibid.,* 56.

287. *Ibid.,* 63.

288. Screenplay by Billy Wilder, Raymond Chandler, *Double Indemnity,* D-135.

289. *Ibid.*

290. *Ibid.*

291. *Ibid.,* E-136.

292. *Ibid.*

293. *Ibid.*

294. *Ibid.*

295. *Ibid.*

296. *Ibid.,* E-137.

297. *Ibid.*

298. *Ibid.,* D-133-D-134.

299. Schickel, 50.

300. *Ibid.*

301. *Ibid.,* 63.

302. Naremore, 93–95.

303. Leff and Simmons, 127.

304. *Ibid.*

305. Cited in *Ibid.*

306. Quoted in Biesen, 97.

307. *Ibid.*

308. Skenazy, 21.

309. *Ibid.*

310. See *Ibid.,* 22.

311. *Ibid.,* 159.

312. *Ibid.,* 22.

313. Cain, *The Postman Always Rings Twice,* 8.

314. Biesen, 121.

315. *Ibid.*

316. Skenazy, 131.

317. *Ibid.*

318. Cain, *The Postman Always Rings Twice,* 15.

319. *Ibid.,* 13.

320. *Ibid.,*16–17.

321. *Ibid.,* 51.

322. *Ibid.*

323. *Ibid.*

324. *Ibid.,* 52.

325. Biesen, 123.

326. Skenzy,158.

327. Biesen, 120.

328. Leff and Simmons, 131.

329. Paramount realized quite soon that PRC was copying its film and they got an injunction to stop exhibition of it soon after its release.

330. This is unclear in the only print of the film I can find.

331. Spicer, *Historical Dictionary of Film Noir*, 73.

332. Noah Isenberg, *Edgar G. Ulmer* (Berkeley, University of California Press, 2014), 172.

333. *Ibid.*

334. *Ibid.*

335. *Ibid.* With experience as a set designer and director in Germany before moving to Hollywood in 1926 to work with Murnau as art director on *Sunrise*, his breakthrough Hollywood film was the perverse horror film *The Black Cat* (1934). However, he lost his studio contract after falling out with the head of the studio Carl Laemmle over his relationship with Shirley Beatrice Kassler who was married to Max Alexander, Laemmle's nephew, at the time. For the next thirty years Ulmer worked on low budget productions produced on the fringe of mainstream Hollywood.

336. *Ibid.*

337. The contribution of veteran B director Lew Landers, who received $3,000 compared with $750 for Ulmer, which was half of what Goldsmith earned for the screenplay, is also a mystery. In the late 1990s Ann Savage produced her copy of the script, dated May 24, 1945, and only one man was listed as director, Lew Landers. Yet, Savage said that Ulmer supervised her screen test, conducted all of the rehearsals and directed every scene she was in. Although she was friends with Landers, she never saw him anywhere near the film.

338. Quoted in Isenberg, 184.

339. *Ibid.* 183.

340. *Ibid.*, 182.

341. Quoted in *Ibid.*, 182.

342. *Ibid.*, 183.

343. *Ibid.*

344. Naremore, 149.

345. *Ibid.*

346. See Biesen, 166.

347. See https://www.dvdtalk.com/dvdsavant/s2362deco.html.

348. Some prints, including the commercially available DVD copy, show Shelby only running over Vincent once as the scene was censored when the film was edited for television.

349. Williams, *Playing the Race Card*, 12.

350. *Ibid.*, 13.

351. See https://www.dvdtalk.com/dvdsavant/s1765val.html.

352. Steve Neale also noticed the omission of this film when he wrote that it was a "mix of triangle drama and adventure which has never appeared on anyone's list of *noirs*." Neale, *Genre and Hollywood*, 163.

353. E. Ann Kaplan, "Hemingway, Hollywood and Female Representation: The Macomber Affair," *Literature/Film Quarterly*, Volume 13, No. 1, 1985.

354. *Ibid.*, 24.

355. *Ibid.*, 25.

356. Ernest Hemingway, "The Short Happy Life of Francis Macomber," http://faculty.washington. edu/jdb/303/Hemingway/The%20Short%20 Happy%20Life%20of%20Francis%20Macomber. pdf, 4.

357. *Ibid.*, 8.

358. *Ibid.*

359. In an earlier incident Wilson chases the buffalo from the car. Margot, always alert for an advantage, asked him what would happen if they heard about it in Nairobi. He admits to her that it was illegal and if reported he would lose his license. Francis interjects and tells the hunter: "Now she has something on you.'"

360. Hemingway, "The Short Happy Life of Francis Macomber," 37.

361. See Max Alvarez, "Where Love Goes to Die: The Shattering Impact of Anthony Mann's *Raw Deal*," notes to accompany the Blu-Ray release of *Raw Deal*.

362. Quoted *Ibid.*, 20.

363. Spicer, *Historical Dictionary of Film Noir*, 253.

364. This term has been adapted from literary crime fiction. It is also the term used by Glenn Erickson to describe *The File on Thelma Jordon*. See https://www.dvdtalk.com/dvdsavant/s4208jord.html.

365. *Ibid.*

366. *Ibid.*

367. *Ibid.*

368. Brooks uses the term "primary melodrama" whereas I use the term sensational melodrama. See Brooks, 168.

369. See Krutnik, 252, note 15.

370. Jonathan Latimer's script intended Larry's suicide to end the film but Breen opposed suicide as an ending. Yet there is enough left in the film to suggest that Larry wants to die.

371. See https://www.dvdtalk.com/dvdsavant/s4208jord.html.

372. See Glenn Erickson, *DVD Savant Review*, https://www.dvdtalk.com/dvdsavant/s1046pass.html.

373. Jay Dratler, *The Pitfall* (New York, Bantam Books, 1949), 181–182.

374. Krutnik, 153.

375. Spicer, *Film Noir*, 73.

376. See https://catalog.afi.com/Catalog/moviedetails/50254.

377. Marcus, 14.

378. https://www.dvdtalk.com/dvdsavant/s2207face.html.

379. Alain Silver and Elizabeth Ward, *Film Noir: An Encyclopedic Reference to the American Style*, 308.

380. Alain Silver and James Ursini, "John Farrow," in Alain Silver and James Ursini, eds., *Film Noir: The Directors* (Milwaukee, Limelight Editions, 2012), 79.

381. *Ibid.*, 81.

382. Love, 66.

383. *Ibid.*, 78.

384. See Michael Walker, "Robert Siodmak," in Ian Cameron, ed., *The Movie Book of Film Noir* (London, Studio Vista, 1992), 145.

Bibliography

Agee, James, *Agee on Film: Volume One* (New York, The Universal Library, 1969).

Alvarez, Max, "Where Love Goes to Die: The Shattering Impact of Anthony Mann's *Raw Deal*," Notes to accompany the Blu-Ray release of *Raw Deal*.

Arieli, Yehoshua Arieli, *Individualism and Nationalism in American Ideology* (Cambridge, Harvard University Press, 1964).

Aros, Joyce, "The Benson Stage Debacle," *Tombstone Times,* http://www.tombstonetimes.com/stories/benson.html "The Benson Stage Debacle," *Tombstone Times,* http://www.tombstonetimes.com/stories/benson.html.

Baker, Phil, and Antony C. Clayton, eds., *Lord of Strange Deaths: The Fiendish World of Sax Rohmer* (London, Strange Attractor Press, 2015).

Becker, Carl Becker, "What Is Still Living in the Political Philosophy of Thomas Jefferson," in S. Fine and G.S. Brown, eds., *The American Past,* Volume 1 (New York, The Macmillan Company, 1965).

Bentley, Eric, *The Life of the Drama* (New York, Atheneum, 1964).

Biesen, Sheri Chinen, *Blackout: World War II and the Origins of Film Noir* (Baltimore, Johns Hopkins University Press, 2005).

Black, Gregory D., *Hollywood Censored: Morality Codes, Catholics and the Movies* (Cambridge, Cambridge University Press, 1994).

Booth, Michael R., *English Melodrama* (London, Herbert Jenkins, 1965).

Booth, Michael R., *English Plays of the Nineteenth Century: Dramas 1800–1850* (Oxford, Clarendon Press, 1969).

Booth, Michael R., *Hiss the Villain: Six English and American Melodramas* (London, Eyre and Spottiswoode, 1964).

Bordwell, David, "Happily Ever After, Part Two," *The Velvet Light Trap,* Number 19, 1982.

Brooks, Peter, *The Melodramatic Imagination: Balzac, Henry James, Melodrama, and the Mode of Excess* (New Haven, Yale University Press, 1995).

Brooks, Peter, "The Melodramatic Imagination: The Example of Blazac and James," in David Thorburn and Geoffrey Hartman, eds., *Romanticism, Vistas, Instances* (Ithaca, Cornell University Press, 1973).

Buchanan, Albert Russell, "Pearl Harbor: Day of Infamy," *History of the 20th Century,* Vol. 5, No. 66.

Buckley, Matthew, "Unbinding Melodrama," in Christine Gledhill and Linda Williams, eds., *Melodrama Unbound: Across History, Media, and National Cultures* (New York, Columbia University Press, 2018).

Burke, James Lee, "A Word on James M. Cain," in James M. Cain, *Double Indemnity* (London, Orion Books, 2004).

Burnett, W.R., *Saint Johnson* (New York, A.L. Burt Company, 1930).

Buscombe, Edward, ed., *The BFI Companion to the Western* (London, Andre Deutsch, 1988).

Cain, James M., *Double Indemnity* (London, Orion Books, 2004).

Cain, James M., *The Postman Always Rings Twice* (London, Panther Crime, 1970).

Carswell, Sean, "A Lure for the Devil: On James Gunn's 'Deadlier then the Male' and Giles Deleuze's 'The Philosophy of Crime Novels,'" *Los Angeles Review of Books,* November 17, 2019.

Cawelti, John G., *The Six Gun Mystique* (Bowling Green, OH, Bowling Green University, 1971).

Chandler, Raymond, *Farewell, My Lovely* (Middlesex, Harmondsworth, Penguin Books, 1975).

Chandler, Raymond, "The Simple Art of Murder," in Raymond Chandler, *Pearls Are a Nuisance* (Middlesex, Harmondsworth, Penguin Books, 1973).

Clark, Al, *Raymond Chandler in Hollywood* (Los Angeles, Silman-James Press, 1996).

Corrigan, Robert W., *Laurel British Drama: The Nineteenth Century* (New York, Dell Publishing Co., 1967).

Cox, J. Randolph, "Dime Novel," in Rosemary Herbert, ed., *The Oxford Companion to Crime and Mystery Writing* (Oxford, Oxford University Press, 1999).

Dixon, Wheeler Winston, "Robert Wise," in Alain Silver and James Ursini, ed., *Film Noir: The Directors* (Milwaukee, Limelight Editions, 2012).

Dobbs, Gary, "Introduction," in *Street Wolf: The Black Mask* (Boston, Altus, 2014).

Doherty, Thomas, *Pre-Code Hollywood: Sex, Immorality, and Insurrection in American Cinema, 1930–1934* (New York, Columbia University Press, 1999).

Dratler, Jay, *Pitfall* (New York, Bantam Books, 1949).

Eisenstein, Sergei, *Film Form* (New York, Harcourt, Brace & World, 1949).

Elsaesser, Thomas, "Tales of Sound and Fury: Observations on the Family Melodrama," *Monogram 4* (1972).

Erickson, Glenn, *The Letter* (1929), https://www.dvdtalk.com/dvdsavant/s3611lett.html.

Everson, William K., *The Detective in Film* (Secaucus, NJ, Citadel Press, 1972).

Feis, Herbert, *The Road to Pearl Harbor* (Princeton, Princeton University Press, 1950).

Fell, John, *Film and the Narrative Tradition* (Norman, University of Oklahoma Press, 1974).

Fell, John, ed., *Film Before Griffith* (Berkeley, University of California Press, 1983).

Feuer, Jane, "Melodrama, Serial Form and Television Today." *Screen*, Vol. 25, no. 1, January/February 1984.

Fisher, Steve, *I Wake Up Screaming* (New York, Vintage Crime, 1991).

Ford, Dan *The Unquiet Man: The Life of John Ford* (London, William Kimber, 1982).

Frank, Nino, "A New Kind of Police Drama: the Criminal Adventure," in Alain Silver and James Ursini, eds., *Film Noir Reader 2* (New York, Limelight Editions, 1999).

Frayling, Christopher, *The Yellow Peril: Dr Fu Manchu & The Rise of Chinaphobia* (London, Thames & Hudson, 2014).

Frye, Northrop, *Anatomy of Criticism: Four Essays* (Princeton, Princeton University Press, 1973).

Fujiwara, Chris, *Jacques Tourneur: The Cinema of Nightfall* (Baltimore, Johns Hopkins University Press, 1998).

George-Warren, Holly, *Public Cowboy No. 1: The Life and Times of Gene Autry* (New York, Oxford University Press, 2007).

Glancy, H. Mark, "Warner Bros financial information in The William Shaefer Ledger," *Historical Journal of Film, Radio and Television*, Volume 15, Issue 1, 1995.

Gledhill, Christine, "Prologue: The Reach of Melodrama," in Christine Gledhill and Linda Williams, eds., *Melodrama Unbound: Across History, Media, and National Cultures* (New York, Columbia University Press, 2018).

Gledhill, Christine, "Rethinking Genre," in Christine Gledhill and Linda Williams, *Reinventing Film Studies* (London, Arnold, 2000).

Gledhill, Christine, and Linda Williams, eds., *Melodrama Unbound: Across History, Media, and National Cultures* (New York, Columbia University Press, 2018).

Gray, Duncan, "No Other Kind: Close-Up on Fritz Lang's 'Human Desire,'" http://mubi.com/notebook/posts/no-other-kind-close-up-on-fritz-lang-s-human-desire.

Grimsted, David, *Melodrama Unveiled: American Theater and Culture 1800–1850* (Chicago, University of Chicago Press, 1968).

Guillian, Robert, *I Saw Tokyo Burning: An Eyewitness Narrative from Pearl Harbor to Hiroshima* (London, John Murray, 1981).

Gunn, James, *Deadlier Than the Male* (New York, Signet Book, 1942).

Haman, Zaresh, "'Get to Fighting or Get Away': The Gunfight at the O.K. Corral,' *StMU History Media*, November 3.

Hammett, Dashiell, *The Glass Key* (London, Pan Books, 1975).

Hammett, Dashiell, *The Maltese Falcon* (London, Pan Books, 1975).

Haralovich, Mary Beth, "Selling Noir. Stars, Gender and Genre in Film Noir Posters and Publicity," in Andrew Spicer and Helen Hanson, eds., *A Companion to Film Noir* (West Sussex, Wiley Blackwell, 2013).

Hastings, Selina, *The Secret Lives of Somerset Maugham: A Biography* (New York, Random House, 2010).

Heilman, Robert B., *The Iceman, the Arsonist, and the Troubled Agent* (Seattle, University of Washington Press, 1973).

Heilman, Robert B., *Tragedy and Melodrama* (Seattle, University of Washington Press, 1968).

Hill, Owen, Pamela Jackson, and Anthony Dean Rizzuto, "Introduction," in Raymond Chandler, *The Annotated Big Sleep* (New York, Vintage Crime, 2018).

Homes, Geoffrey [Daniel Mainwaring], *Build My Gallows High* (London, Prion Books, 2001).

Hughes, Dorothy B., *The Fallen Sparrow* (New York, Bantam Books, 1979).

Hughes, Dorothy B., *Ride the Pink Horse* (London, Penguin Books, 1988).

Hull, David Stewart, *Film in the Third Reich: A Study of the German Cinema, 1933–1945* (Los Angeles, University of California Press, 1969).

Hulse, Ed, *Distressed Damsels and Masked Marauders* (Morris Plains, NJ, Murania Press, 2014).

Hulse, Ed, "Mystery Ranch" (1932), "The Brief Vogue for 'Western Gothic,'" in Ed Hulse, ed.) *The Wild West of Fiction and Film* (Morris Plains, NJ, Murania Press, 2018).

Jacobs, Lea, "Industry Self-Regulation and the Problem of Textual Determination," *The Velvet Light Trap*, Volume 23, Number 4, Spring 1989.

Jacobs, Lea, *The Wages of Sin: Censorship and the Fallen Woman Film 1928–1942* (Madison, University of Wisconsin Press, 1991).

Jewell, Richard B., "RKO Film Grosses, 1929–1951: The C.J. Tevlin Ledger," *Historical Journal of Film, Radio and Television*, Vol. 14, No. 1, 1994.

Jewell, Richard B., *Slow Fade to Black: The Decline of RKO Radio Pictures* (Oakland, University of California Press, 2016).

Jewell, Richard B., with Vernon Harbin, *The RKO Story* (London, Octopus Books, 1982).

Jowett, Garth, *Film: The Democratic Art* (Boston, Little, Brown, 1976).

Kaplan, E. Ann, "Hemingway, Hollywood and Female Representation: The Macomber Affair," *Literature/Film Quarterly*, Volume 13, No. 1, 1985.

Kitses, Jim, *Horizon West* (London, British Film Institute, 2004).

Klinger, Leslie S., "Appreciating Dr. Fu-Manchu," in Sax Rohmer, *The Mystery of Dr. Fu-Manchu* (London, Titan Books, 2012).

Koszarski, Richard, *An Evening's Entertainment: The*

Age of the Silent Feature Picture 1915–1928 (Berkeley, University of California Press, 1990).

Krutnik, Frank, *In a Lonely Street: Film Noir, Genre, Masculinity* (London, Routledge, 1991).

Lait, Jack, *The Beast of the City* (New York, Grosset & Dunlap, 1932).

Layman, Richard, *Discovering The Maltese Falcon and Sam Spade* (San Francisco, Vince Emery Productions, 2005).

Layman, Richard, "There's Only One Maltese Falcon," *Januarymagazine.com.*

Layman, Richard, and Julie M. Rivett, eds., *Dashiell Hammett: The Big Book of the Continental Op* (New York, Vintage Crime/Black Lizard, 2017).

Leff, Leonard, and Jerrold Simmons, *The Dame in the Kimono: Hollywood, Censorship, and the Production Code from the 1920s to the 1960s* (London, Weidenfeld and Nicolson, 1990).

Lehman, Peter "Editorial," *Wide Angle,* Vol. 4, no. 2.

Loren, Scott, and Jörge Metelmann, eds., *Melodrama After the Tears: New Perspectives on the Politics of Victimhood* (Amsterdam, Amsterdam University Press, 2016).

Love, Damien, *Robert Mitchum: Solid, Dad, Crazy* (London, B.T. Batsford, 2002).

Madison, Nathan Vernon, *Anti-Foreign Imagery in American Pulps and Comic Books* (Jefferson, NC, McFarland, 2013).

Magers, Boyd, *Gene Autry Westerns: America's Favorite Cowboy* (Madison, NC, Empire Publishing, 2007).

Mainwaring, Daniel, "Discusses OUT OF THE PAST," *The Velvet Light Trap,* Fall 1973.

Maltby, Richard, "More Sinned Against than Sinning: 'The Fabrications of Pre-Code Cinema,'" *Senses of Cinema,* December 2003.

Maltby, Richard, "The Production Code and the Hays Office," in *Encyclopedia.com,* https://www.encyclopedia.com/arts/culture-magazines/production-code-and-hays-office.

Marcus, Steven, "Introduction," in Dashiell Hammett, *The Continental Op* (London, Pan Books, 1975).

Mathis, Jack, *Republic Confidential: Volume I. The Studio* (Barrington, IL, Jack Mathis Advertising, 1999).

Maugham, W. Somerset, "The Letter," *Short Stories* (London, Vintage Books, 1998).

Maugham, W. Somerset, *The Letter with Two Other Plays* (London, Pan Books, 1952).

Maugham, W. Somerset, *Of Human Bondage* (London, Vintage Books, 2000).

Mayer, Geoff, *Encyclopedia of American Film Serials* (Jefferson, NC, McFarland, 2017).

Mayer, Geoff, "Film Noir and Studio Production Practices," in Andrew Spicer and Helen Hanson, *A Companion to Film Noir* (West Sussex, Wiley Blackwell, 2013)

Mayer, Ruth, *Serial Fu Manchu: The Chinese Supervillain and the Spread of Yellow Peril Ideology* (Philadelphia, Temple University Press, 2014).

Maynard, William Patrick, *The Insidious Dr. Fu-Manchu by Sax Rohmer—Part Three—"The Clue of the Pigtail"* in http://setisays.blogspot.com/2010/03/.

Maynard, William Patrick, *The Insidious Dr. Fu-Manchu by Sax Rohmer, Part Four—"Redmoat"* in http://setisays.blogspot.com/2010/04/.

Maynard, William Patrick, *Sax Rohmer's Daughter of Fu Manchu,* in http://setisays.blogspot.com/2012/08/blogging-sax-rohmers-daughter-of-fu.html.

McKenna, George, *American Populism* (New York, G.P. Putnam and Sons, 1974).

Meisel, Myron, "JOSEPH H. LEWIS: Tourist in the Asylum," in Todd McCarthy and Charles Flynn, *Kings of the Bs: Working Within the Hollywood System* (New York, E.P. Dutton & Co., 1975).

Menefee, David W., *George O'Brien: A Man's Man in Hollywood* (Albany, GA, BearManor Media, 2009).

Miller, Frank, *Rain, TCM Film Article,* http://www.tcm.com/this-month/article/161058%7C161060/Rain.html.

Miller, Gabriel, *William Wyler: The Life and Films of Hollywood's Most Celebrated Director* (Lexington, University Press of Kentucky, 2013).

Muller, Eddie, *Dark City Dames: The Wicked Women of Film Noir* (New York, Regan Books, 2001).

Naremore, James, *More Than Night: Film Noir in its Contexts* (Berkeley, University of California, 1998).

Neale, Steve, *Genre and Hollywood* (London, Routledge, 2000).

Neale, Steve, "Melo Talk: On the Meaning and Use of the Term 'Melodrama' in the American Trade Press," *The Velvet Light Trap,* Number 32, Fall 1993.

Neale, Steve, "Propaganda," *Screen,* Volume 18, Issue 3, October 1977.

Nowell-Smith, Geoffrey, "Minnelli and Melodrama," *Screen,* Vol. 18, no. 2.

O'Brien, Geoffrey, *Hard-Boiled America: Lurid Paperbacks and the Masters of Noir* (New York Da Capo Press, 1997).

Orr, Christopher, "Closure and Containment. Marylee Hadley in Written on the Wind," *Wide Angle,* Vol. 4, No. 2.

Parker, Robert. B., "Introduction," in Dashiell Hammett, *Woman in the Dark* (New York, Vintage Books, 1989).

Passafiume, Andrea, "The Fallen Sparrow," in http://www.tcm.com/this-month/article/502|0/The-Fallen-Sparrow.html.

Passafiume, Andrea, *The Letter: The Essentials,* in http://www.tcm.com/this-month/article/220540%7CO/The-Essentials-The Letter.htm.

Phillips, Gene D., *Creatures of Darkness: Raymond Chandler, Detective Fiction, and Film Noir* (Lexington, University of Kentucky Press, 2000).

Porfirio, Robert, "NO WAY OUT: Existential Motifs in the Film Noir," *Sight and Sound,* Volume 45, Number 4, Autumn 1976.

Prange, Gordon, *At Dawn We Slept: The Untold Story of Pearl Harbor* (London, Michael Joseph, 1981).

Pribram, E. Deidre, "Melodrama and the Aesthetics of Emotion," in Christine Gledhill and Linda Williams, eds., *Melodrama Unbound: Across History, Media, and National Cultures* (New York, Columbia University Press, 2018).

Pyle, Ernie, *Here Is Your War* (New York, Lancer Books, 1943).

Rahill, Frank, *The World of Melodrama* (University Park, Pennsylvania State University Press, 1967).

Renov, Michael, "From Fetish to Subject: The Containment of Sexual Difference in Hollywood's Wartime Cinema," *Wide Angle*, Vol. 5, no. 1.

Richards, Jeffrey Richards, *Visions of Yesterday* (London, Routledge & Kegan Paul, 1973).

Rohmer, Sax, *The Mystery of Dr. Fu-Manchu* (London, Titan Books, 2012).

Rohmer, Sax, *The Return of Dr. Fu-Manchu* (London, Titan Books, 2012).

Rohmer, Sax, *The Trail of Fu-Manchu* (London, Titan Books, 2013).

Rosenman, Samuel Irving, *The Public Papers and Addresses of Franklin D. Roosevelt, Volume 10: The Call to Battle Stations* (New York, Russell and Russell, 1969).

Roth, Mark, "Some Warner Musicals and the Spirit of the New Deal," *The Velvet Light Trap* 17 (Winter 1977).

Ruhm, Herbert, "Raymond Chandler," in David Madden, ed., *Tough Guys Writers of the Thirties* (Carbondale, Southern Illinois University Press, 1968).

Santos, Marlisa, "'People Can think Themselves Into Anything': The Domestic Nightmare in *My Name is Julia Ross*," in Gary D. Rhodes, ed., *The Films of Joseph H. Lewis* (Detroit, Wayne State University Press, 2012).

Sarris, Andrew, *The American Cinema: Directors and Directions 1929–168* (New York, E.P. Dutton & Co., 1968).

Savage, Guy, *The Letter* (1940), www.noiroftheweek.com/2012/07/the-letter-1940.html.

Schickel, Richard, *Double Indemnity* (London, BFI Publishing 1992).

Schwager, Jeff, "The Past Rewritten," *Film Comment,* Volume 27, Number 1, January-February 1991.

Silver, Alain, and Elizabeth Ward, eds., *Film Noir: An Encyclopedic Reference to the American Style* (Woodstock, The Overlook Press, 1992).

Silver, Alain, and James Ursini, eds., *Film Noir Reader* (New York, Limelight Edition, 1996).

Simmon, Scott, *The Invention of the Western Film* (Cambridge, Cambridge University Press, 2003).

Singer, Ben, *Melodrama and Modernity. Early Sensational Cinema and Its Contexts* (New York, Columbia University Press, 2001).

Skenazy, Paul, *James M. Cain* (New York, Continuum, 1989).

Slotkin, Richard, *Gunfighter Nation: The Myth of the Frontier in Twentieth Century America* (New York, Harper Perennial, 1993).

Smith, Henry Nash, *Virgin Land: The American West as Symbol and Myth* (New York, Vintage Books, 1950).

Smith, James L., *Melodrama* (London, Methuen, 1973).

Sperber, A.M., and Eric Lax, *Bogart* (New York, William Morrow and Company, 1997).

Spicer, Andrew, *Film Noir* (Harlow, Longman, 2002).

Spicer, Andrew, *Historical Dictionary of Film Noir* (Lanham, Scarecrow Press, 2010).

Stanfield, Peter, *Hollywood, Westerns and the 1930s: The Lost Trail* (Exeter, University of Exeter Press, 2001).

Stanfield, Peter, *Horse Opera: The Strange History of the 1930s Singing Cowboy* (Urbana, University of Illinois Press, 2002).

Stewart, Edward White, "The Killer," in Ed Hulse, ed., *The Wild West of Fiction and Film* (Morris Plains, NJ, Murania Press, 2018).

Swanson, Gloria *Swanson on Swanson: The Making of a Hollywood Legend* (Middlesex, Hamlyn Paperbacks, 1982).

Symons, Julian, *Bloody Murder: From the Detective Story to the Crime Novel: A History* (London, Penguin Books, 1974).

Tuska, Jon, *The Vanishing Legion: A History of Mascot Pictures 1927–1935* (Jefferson, NC, McFarland, 1982).

Vardac, Nicholas, *From Stage to Screen: Theatrical Origins of Early Film: David Garrick to D.W. Griffith* (Cambridge, Harvard University Press, 1949).

Viera, Mark A., *Forbidden Hollywood: The Pre-Code Era (1930–1934), When Sin Ruled the Movies* (New York, Running Press, 2019).

Walker, Dorothy, and Katherine Sorley, eds., *Raymond Chandler Speaking* (London, Hamish Hamilton, 1962).

Walker, Michael, "Melodrama and the American Cinema." *Movie* 29/30, Summer 1982.

Walker, Michael, "Robert Siodmak," in Ian Cameron, ed., *The Movie Book of Film Noir* (London, Studio Vista, 1992).

Walkowitz, Judith R., *City of Dreadful Delight: Narratives of Sexual Danger in Late-Victorian London* (Chicago, University of Chicago Press, 1992).

Waller, Gregory, *Main Street Amusements: Movies and Commercial Entertainment in a Southern City, 1896–1930* (Washington, D.C., Smithsonian Institution Press, 1995).

Williams, Linda, "Melodrama Revised," in Nick Browne, ed., *Refiguring American Film Genre: Theory and History* (Berkeley, University of California Press, 1998).

Williams, Linda, *Playing the Race Card: Melodramas of Black and White from Uncle Tom to O.J. Simpson* (Princeton, Princeton University Press, 2001).

Williams, Linda, "'Tales of Sound and Fury …' or, The Elephant of Melodrama," in Christine Gledhill and Linda Williams, eds., *Melodrama Unbound. Across History, Media, and National Cultures* (New York, Columbia University Press, 2018).

Wister, Owen, *The Virginian: A Horseman of the Plains* (New York, Macmillan, 1902).

Wohlstetter, Roberta, *Pearl Harbor: Warning and Decision* (Stanford, Stanford University Press, 1962).

Wollen, Peter, *Signs and Meaning in the Cinema* (Bloomington, Indiana University Press, 1972).

Wright, Will, *Six Guns and Society: A Structural Study of the Western* (Berkeley, University of California Press, 1977).

Index

Numbers in **bold italics** indicate pages with illustrations